THE COMPA...
Nort...

CW00447901

THE COMPANION GUIDES

GENERAL EDITOR: VINCENT CRONIN

*It is the aim of these Guides to provide a Companion,
in the person of the author, who knows intimately
the places and people of whom he writes, and is able to
communicate this knowledge and affection to his readers.
It is hoped that the text and pictures will aid them
in their preparations and in their travels, and will
help them to remember on their return.*

Already published

THE GREEK ISLANDS · SOUTHERN GREECE
PARIS · THE SOUTH OF FRANCE
ROME · VENICE · LONDON
FLORENCE · JUGOSLAVIA
THE WEST HIGHLANDS OF SCOTLAND · UMBRIA
THE COAST OF NORTH EAST ENGLAND
SOUTHERN ITALY · TUSCANY · EAST ANGLIA
THE SOUTH OF SPAIN
IRELAND · KENT AND SUSSEX
NORTH WALES · DEVON AND CORNWALL
MADRID AND CENTRAL SPAIN · BURGUNDY
THE COAST OF SOUTH EAST ENGLAND
THE COAST OF SOUTH WEST ENGLAND

In preparation

SOUTH WEST FRANCE · MAINLAND GREECE · THE ILE DE FRANCE
EDINBURGH AND THE BORDER COUNTRY · SOUTH WALES
TURKEY · THE WELSH MARCHES

The Guides to Rome, Venice, Florence and London are available in
paperback in the Fontana edition

Available in limp back

DEVON AND CORNWALL · NORTHUMBRIA
SOUTH WEST FRANCE

THE COMPANION GUIDE TO

NORTHUMBRIA

Edward Grierson

COLLINS
ST JAMES'S PLACE, LONDON
1976

William Collins Sons & Co Ltd
London · Glasgow · Sydney · Auckland
Toronto · Johannesburg

First published in 1976

© Helen Grierson 1976

Hardback ISBN 0 00 211198 5
Limpback ISBN 0 00 211574 3

Maps by G. Hartfield
Set in Monotype Times
Made and printed in Great Britain by
William Collins Sons & Co Ltd Glasgow

*To my wife, Helen, who worked on
this Guide with me for three years*

Numbers refer to chapters that describe the area

SCOTLAND

Berwick
12,13
11
14
10
Alnwick
14
NORTHUMBERLAND
9
16
15
Morpeth
8
16, 17, 18
Newcastle
South Shields
Hexham
19
6,7
Gateshead
21
5
Sunderland
20
4
CUMBERLAND
Durham
2
DURHAM
CUMBRIA
22
1
3
WESTMORLAND
Darlington
Middlesbrough
CLEVELAND

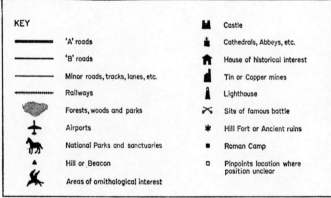

KEY

—— 'A' roads	Castle
—— 'B' roads	Cathedrals, Abbeys, etc.
—— Minor roads, tracks, lanes, etc.	House of historical interest
++++++ Railways	Tin or Copper mines
Forests, woods and parks	Lighthouse
Airports	Site of famous battle
National Parks and sanctuaries	Hill Fort or Ancient ruins
Hill or Beacon	Roman Camp
Areas of ornithological interest	Pinpoints location where position unclear

Contents

Contents

Illustrations

ILLUSTRATIONS

Maps and Plans

❧

Acknowledgements

The writing of this guide was finished just before my husband died. Preparation for the publication of the book remained to be done. I am therefore especially appreciative of the help given to me by so many people.

I am extremely grateful to Mrs B. Archibald and Judge Lyall Wilkes for reading the typescript and for their suggestions, and to the former for her help with the maps and for preparing the index; to Lady Page and Mr Antony Brett-James for reading the proofs; to Mr W. Butler, Director of the Northumbria Tourist Board, who also read the typescript, for much up-to-the-minute information so essential to a book of this nature, and to his staff for their willing assistance to me; to Mrs J. Brown, Tynedale Area Librarian, who went to infinite trouble to get books and pictorial material for us, and to her very co-operative staff.

I owe a great debt to Mr P. W. B. Semmens, Assistant Keeper, National Railway Museum, York, who has produced the Railway Appendix and Bibliography for the guide. Help with the general bibliography was given to me by Professor D. Boulter of the Department of Botany, University of Durham, Mr A. A. H. Douglas and Mr Frank Graham.

I would also like to thank the Dean and Chapter of Durham, the custodians of museums and the many rectors, vicars and vergers who have put their knowledge at our disposal.

I know my husband would have wished to thank Mr Martin Sumner, who acted as his guide over many a bog when visiting ancient camps, and Mrs Barbara Denness and Mr Hylton Edgar who both very generously allowed us to use their photographs. Lord Lambton has been particularly kind in allowing us to publish for the first time a photograph of the statue of his ancestor, Sir John Lambton, struggling with the legendary Lambton Worm, which stands in the grounds of his home at Biddick Hall, Lambton Park.

Finally, I want to thank our daughter, Anne, for choosing the photographs.

Introduction

✿

The Saxon kingdom of Northumbria, stretching at its peak from the Humber to the Forth, embraced a much larger area than is covered in this Guide. But in today's terms Northumbria has come to mean what the Tourist Board brochures enticingly call 'The Holiday Kingdom', that is to say the counties of Durham and Northumberland, the metropolitan county of Tyne/Wear, and the northern half of the Teesside conurbation. There is this justification: that though there are many differences in speech and background between a Durham pitman, a Geordie petrol-pump attendant from industrial Tyneside and a Redesdale shepherd, all tend to think of themselves as brothers. The North-East is a thing apart; the triumphs and tribulations of Sunderland's football team are as deeply felt along the Tyne and the Coquet as those of Newcastle United are hailed or bemoaned on Wearside. To some extent the same is also true of Middlesbrough to the south of the Tees in the new county of Cleveland, which the Northumbria Tourist Board has taken under its wing. However, I regard these areas still as Yorkshire (as I am sure their inhabitants do) and therefore outside the orbit of this Guide.

Until recently our area was largely neglected by the tourist. A few migrants came to see Durham and Hadrian's Wall, but for most Southerners it was remote and backward country on the way to Scotland. All that has changed, and voices are now being raised to protest that this part of England has been oversold to the point when, in summer, its unique quality is in danger of being submerged under the flood of visitors.

I have said 'quality' in the singular, yet physically its component parts are very different. The conurbations at the mouths of the three rivers contain many remarkable sites – St Hilda's Abbey at Hartlepool, Saxon churches at Jarrow and Monkwearmouth, the ruins of Tynemouth Priory standing high on the cliff above the estuary, Vanbrugh's Seaton Delaval Hall, and the planned centre of Newcastle which dates from the middle of the last century and is a masterpiece of Victorian neo-classical – but except for the specialist

13

this is hardly tourist country. Nor, to be honest, is much of County Durham east of the Scotch Corner–Gateshead motorway. This is not to dismiss it, for there is fine agricultural land on either side of the A177, the Stockton–Sedgefield road, and even at its most built-up the scenery has none of the implacable ugliness found in some industrial parts of Britain; the sea is never far away and the whole area is busily refurbishing its image. What is more, it contains some places of the greatest interest: the old church at Pittington, Houghton le Spring, Washington Old Hall, Lumley Castle, the Lambton big game park, and relics of the birth of railways at Darlington and Monkwearmouth. West of the A1(M) lies almost another country in the fine upper valleys of the Tees and Wear, also a wealth of architectural treasures extending right up to the Tyne – Gibside Chapel, Raby Castle, Chester le Street spire, the tiny Saxon church at Escomb, the Cosin woodwork at Brancepeth, the Bowes Museum, the open-air industrial museum at Beamish, and Durham itself, one of the marvels of Europe. The motorist who wants to reach them must merely remember that here and there he will have to pass through a work-a-day landscape overlying the coal mines that long provided the county with its living.

The coalfield stretches beyond the Tyne into coastal Northumberland as far north as Blyth. All this area is industrialised, but it covers only a fraction of one of the largest of English counties, and outside of it Northumberland is an almost wholly unspoilt countryside of hills and rivers, farms and forests and small market towns, with forty miles of grand coastal scenery and the nature reserve of the Farne Islands to round things off. In summer at the height of the tourist season some of these favoured areas attract crowds in large numbers, but even in August you can drive along the roads of inland Northumberland in comparative peace, and for most of the year the visitor from the South or the Midlands will find an astonishing freedom from traffic. The sense of space, of uncluttered countryside, is exhilarating. The views are wide, the air is clear. Only the weather is below par; for though statistically Northumberland is only a few degrees colder and wetter than Kent it would be dishonest to pretend that its spring and summer do not *feel* a great deal less warm and sunny – April indeed in these parts is still a winter month, as May can be also. Autumns, on the other hand, are usually fine, October being a particularly good month.

In planning a guide to an area so scenically diverse and rich in tourist sites I have had to accept the facts of geography and have avoided imposing too rigorous and artificial a framework. Since most visitors probably come from the South, my general plan has been to follow a route from Scotch Corner to Durham City and then up the eastern side of the counties as far north as Berwick, returning through the west and centre by Wooler, the Cheviots, Rothbury, Bellingham, Hexham and the Roman Wall, then over the watersheds into Weardale and Teesdale to Barnard Castle on the Yorkshire border.

As a general plan this has advantages. It is coherent; it follows the main lines of communication; and in Northumberland it happens that most of the big tourist attractions are conveniently placed near to the line of march. However, in County Durham the plan largely breaks down. Here the jewels are not strung on a necklace but are widely scattered. The old County Palatine, indeed, can only be covered in a series of loops, which can best be mounted from a base in the city of Durham itself. May I indicate certain preferences? No railway enthusiast should miss Darlington or the old station at Monkwearmouth, no American Washington Old Hall. Gibside Chapel is classical perfection; it lies on the northern edge of its county and can be visited equally well from Newcastle or Hexham, though I have chosen to include it in a tour from Durham. Upper Teesdale is beautiful country and High Force a most elegant waterfall. So is Cauldron Snout. The Bowes Museum is the quaintest, as it is certainly the grandest thing of its kind outside London. The visitor to County Durham, in other words, must pick and choose.

Once one is across the Tyne the schematic shape of the Guide asserts itself (apart from some wobbling between Newcastle and Morpeth) and continues all the way up to Berwick and down the flank of the Cheviots to Rothbury. Here, however, the Durham problem recurs, for in the area watered by the rivers Coquet, Rede, North and South Tyne and East and West Allen there is so much to visit that there has to be a return to the circular tour before the southward journey is resumed to its end at Barnard Castle.

The visitor will find his interest and convenience greatly increased if he takes with him a good road map and sheets 64, 70, 71, 76, 77, 78, 84 and 85 of the One-Inch series of the Ordnance Survey. If he intends to do any serious walking he should certainly consult some of the excellent guides to the Cheviots, the Border Forests, the Simonside Hills and the Pennine Way recommended by the Ramblers' Association and the Forestry Commission.

The Roman Wall has spawned a prodigious literature, and guide books to it are readily available at the various sites and in every bookshop. Pre-history is less well served, though for every Imperial camp there are thirty or forty remains of stone circles, Iron Age forts and Romano/British hut settlements scattered on the hillsides and above the streams, most of them in the smallish triangle between the Cheviots and the rivers Breamish and Tweed. This is less familiar ground, and those interested should most certainly get George Jobey's *Field Guide to Prehistoric Northumberland* (Frank Graham, 6 Queen's Terrace, Newcastle upon Tyne, NE2 2PL). At the time of writing Part Two of this invaluable work is on offer, but not apparently Part One, which is still to be published!

Our Guide has fortunately not been affected by the recent changes in county boundaries: the planners have hived off large industrial complexes to make metropolitan counties of them, yet culturally and emotionally Tyneside remains Northumbrian and north Teesside part of Durham, whatever may be shown on tomorrow's maps.

A few words in general. To get the best out of the area beyond the big towns a car is highly desirable and in many cases necessary, for the charming branch lines that served remote districts have been axed by British Rail and rural bus services are not always frequent. Particularly in County Durham churches are normally kept locked for fear of vandals, but keys are always available, and I have included details of where to get them in the body of the text – this kind of treasure hunt can be fun in itself for a visitor who likes meeting people and getting the local angle on life. A list of hotels is included among the appendices; also details of the opening hours of houses, parks and museums; and for railway enthusiasts there is classified information about the many interesting sites that survive in the land of *Locomotion*'s birth just a century and a half ago.

This is the second Collins Guide to deal with Northumbria, for John Seymour's *Companion Guide to the Coast of North-East England* covers the whole length of it from the Scottish border to the Tees. I hope the reader will find that the two books are complementary in the areas where they cross each other's tracks: a sailor's and a landsman's view, if you like, of this beautiful and historic part of Britain.

EDWARD GRIERSON

Tarset, Hexham
April 1975

Chapter 1

From Scotch Corner to Durham City

❦

Entry into County Durham from the south is across the Tees, the longest and most beautiful of its rivers – yet, at its mouth, the most polluted. For many centuries it was a true frontier, dividing a Yorkshire subject to the King's writ from a palatinate under the semi-independent sway of a bishop. Certain cultural differences still linger, but geologically, as to the eye of the visitor, South Durham is now a projection of the old North Riding along the whole length of the stream. In the west the charming market town of Barnard Castle mirrors Yorkshire's Richmond. Durham's sleek and sleepy Sockburn peninsula is as Yorkshire as Wensleydale cheese. And at the industrialised mouth of the river, where Middlesbrough faces Stockton, Billingham and the Hartlepools, no stranger dumped down unexpectedly could guess from his surroundings on which bank he stood.

This first impression is misleading, for County Durham as a whole is not in the least like its more rural southern neighbour. It differs equally markedly from Northumberland. It is the odd man out in the northern counties. Man as a social being came there later than in the surrounding areas and left far fewer traces of his occupancy. This was due to the inhospitable nature of its soil. In the west the limestone uplands, with their strata of sandstone and shale, differ very little from similar areas in North Yorkshire and Cumbria – it is fine fell country, seen at its best in the upper valleys of the Tees and Wear. But as one moves eastward across the county the picture changes. For long periods it lay under the sea. The deep sandstones and shales of the central sector contain the coal seams and veins of crystallised limestone packed tight with the bones of marine organisms – the Frosterley marbles used in many Durham buildings. Nearer the sea the coal lies deeper, under successive layers of sand and magnesium limestone, and in the south-east red sandstone, containing the raw material for yet another of the region's industries, the extraction of commercial salt. During the Ice Age masses of Boulder Clay were laid down as a top dressing. For many centuries

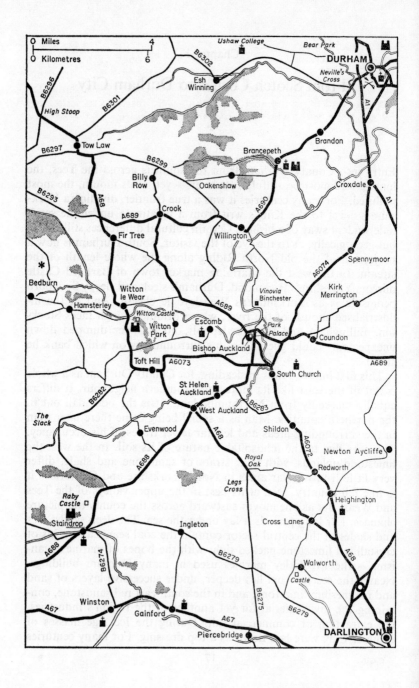

in the central sector the ice lingered, melting into the brackish waters of a lake which eventually forced their way through to the sea along the lines of least resistance, now marked by the 'denes', those deep-cut clefts in the ground that are such a feature of East Durham. Till the land had dried out such conditions were resistant to settlement by primitive man, who preferred the drier hill-tops of the country beyond the Tees and the Tyne. North Yorkshire and Northumberland are dotted with Iron Age camps; there are few in Durham, though one important Bronze Age find has been made in upper Weardale. Only with the coming of the Romans does the archaeological evidence support the presence of large-scale settlement.

Historically, therefore, Durham was a late developer. It owed its medieval fame to a Northumbrian saint and a line of militant Norman bishops. But it owes its present prosperity to something indigenous to it: to the great coalfield underlying the eastern half of the county which has created its modern culture and image. At Nationalisation, in 1946, Durham and Northumberland, forming the Coal Board's North-East Region, operated one hundred and eighty-eight pits employing one hundred and forty-eight thousand men: today there are forty-two pits and a labour force of forty thousand. Far more than any other single factor, coal *made* County Durham; provided its bread and butter and shaped its landscape and even the men (and once upon a time the women and children too) who worked it – a heritage at once tragic and splendid. In no other part of England does the underlying structure of a landscape dominate it so completely and so visibly in everything one sees around one, from the pit heaps, the rows of miners' cottages climbing the hillsides, to the great Victorian viaducts spanning the valleys. For of course it was the growing demand for coal that turned inventive minds to the development of horse-drawn transport from the pit-head along rails, and then by a natural progression to the use of the steam engine as a source of locomotive power, and eventually to George Stephenson's triumphant exploitation of the colliery railway to serve the passenger public.

In a very special sense, therefore, Chaplin's *Modern Times* began in County Durham. Stephenson's *Locomotion Number One* at Darlington's North Road station is the visible symbol; and so is the ravaged landscape which Victorian developers left behind them. In the subsequent rat-race to affluence Durham did not do well. During the Depression of the 1930s it fared worse than any other part of industrial Britain, apart perhaps from Wales and the Clyde. Lately it has been making a comeback, with the booming prosperity of

19

Teesside and the new understanding of the importance of coal to the economy. All its faults are on the surface; its virtues tend to be hidden away. It is not an easy landscape to absorb nor one of immediate attraction, but for the discriminating it remains one of the most interesting of English counties, a synthesis of the old and the new which can be sampled – to take just one instance – in the presence, within a few miles of one another, of buildings as diverse as Durham's great Norman cathedral, the huge Consett Iron Works, the ruins of Finchale Priory, the Catholic seminary of Ushaw College with its links with medieval Douai, and the pit village of Pity Me.

The visitor from the south normally enters the county along the A1, off which the A68 diverges a few miles after Scotch Corner. To the east of this junction, and reached by taking a fork off the A1 Motorway, some four miles further on, lies **Darlington**. It has a beautiful Early English church, and should certainly be on the itinerary of everyone interested in the birth of railways. I have included it in a circular tour of Durham City which also takes in industrial Teesside. The visitor can, if he chooses, go this way from the start and still end up comfortably in Durham for the night. But to do so would be to miss the much more attractive entry by Escomb, Staindrop, Raby Castle, Bishop Auckland and Brancepeth, which together represent that older *persona* of the county that existed from Saxon times till the coming of the Industrial Revolution.

One mile beyond Scotch Corner, therefore, fork left at the entrance to the motorway on to the B6275 which enters the palatinate at the Tees crossing at **Piercebridge**, a pretty village under whose green lies a third-century Roman camp covering eleven acres, one of the largest in Britain. Recent excavation has uncovered traces of a Roman villa (*circa* 275) near the present church. Another trace of the Roman presence stands on a hill on the west side of the A68, the Piercebridge–West Auckland road, about a mile south of the village of Royal Oak – a stone known locally as 'Legs' Cross' since it carries an inscription which seems to be to *Leg X*, the Tenth Legion. But this is somewhat off our route and hardly worth the detour. Piercebridge's hotel, *The George*, is on the Yorkshire bank of the river and therefore strictly outside my brief, but it is one of the better stopping places on the road and the clock in its coffee room is said to have inspired the famous ballad *My Grandfather's Clock*, written in the 1880s by a visiting American, Henry Clay Work.

At the T-junction at the northern end of the village turn left on to the A67 towards Barnard Castle for **Gainford**, which hides itself rather coyly from the traveller. It has a wide green ringed with trees and attractive houses, and on a bluff above the river a thirteenth-century church with fine fourteenth-century lancets and ogee-topped windows. Much of the stone is from the Roman fort at Piercebridge. In medieval times Gainford stood at the centre of the vast manor of the Baliol family, and the terraced houses leading west from the green to the gabled Jacobean **Hall** (completed 1605) with its circular seventeenth-century dovecote and stack of eleven chimneys still give it a patrician air, though the village's prosperity in Georgian times was largely due to the number of Darlington shopkeepers who settled here on their retirement. Their houses line the elegantly curved **High Row**. Notice the **Mansion House** (*circa* 1760) with its Adam porch, and on the Upper Green above South Terrace the beautiful three-storey **West House** next to the Co-op.

At the next crossroads turn right on to the B6274 for **Staindrop**, the old estate village of Raby Castle, in medieval times the home of the powerful Neville family. A long straggling village with inter-connecting greens, it shows at its best from the east, where church and bridge and the Raby park combine in a setting that has hardly changed for centuries.

Staindrop, Brancepeth and Durham Cathedral itself all hold their share of Neville bones, liberally risked in the service of their country on a dozen battlefields. Staindrop was the Nevilles' home church. But its first foundation pre-dated the family's arrival with the Conqueror – it was Saxon, and traces of its blocked windows and roof line can still be made out on the north wall at the east end of the present nave. In Norman times the tower was added, but not as we see it today, for its upper stage is of the fifteenth century.

The twelfth century saw the addition of a chancel and aisles whose arches on the south side bear the characteristic nutmeg motif. The eastwards extension of the church and the building of the vestry came towards the end of the thirteenth century, together with the north transept and its three fine lancet windows. Vestries are not usually interesting, but here at Staindrop there is an unusual double decker, the lower floor of which was intended for the priest, the upper for a hermit, who could see the high altar through a squint. The unrestored sedilia is a particularly fine one.

In 1343 Ralph, Lord Neville, was granted permission from Durham Priory to found and endow three chantry chapels, each with a priest in charge. It was a deeply pious age, and when seventy years later the church attained collegiate status it was further beautified by oak stalls and an oak screen – somewhat shorn now without its rood loft, but the only pre-Reformation work of its kind in the county. Most striking of all are the **Neville Tombs** immediately to the left on entering the church. Nearest to the door lies Ralph Neville, first Earl of Westmorland, with effigies of his two wives on either side of him – Margaret, daughter of Hugh, Earl of Stafford (d 1370), and Joan Plantagenet, daughter of John of Gaunt. Ralph was therefore a brother-in-law of Henry IV and worthy of his splendid alabaster tomb. His wives are not actually buried here, however, for Margaret lies at Brancepeth in another Neville church, and Joan far away at Lincoln beside her mother, Catharine Swynford. Close by is another altar tomb of blackened Elizabethan oak, once gay with many colours. On it lies the effigy of Henry Neville, fifth Earl, also supported by two wives. The table below them is divided into compartments containing figures of their children, whose names are written above. Three further niches are filled with heraldic shields displaying the arms of Neville and Plantagenet together with those of Manners and Cholmondley, the families of his wives.

Beyond the bridge in a park in which graze herds of red and fallow deer stands the old Neville stronghold of **Raby Castle**, the largest and most resplendent in the county.

The family name was Norman, 'Neuville', and they came over with the Conqueror, but within a few generations they had become largely Saxon by blood through a series of marriages into the pre-Conquest nobility, acquiring in the process enormous estates in Durham and North Yorkshire. The defence of the county palatine came increasingly to depend on them, and it was the head of their house, Ralph, Lord Neville, who in 1346 played the leading part in defeating the invading Scots at the Battle of Neville's Cross. His son John, who had fought in the battle as a boy, was the builder of Raby, and *his* son took the next step up the slippery feudal ladder by marrying Joan Beaufort, daughter of John of Gaunt. This was real preferment: the Nevilles were nearing the steps of the throne itself. Soon they had reached it. They had enough strings to their bow. Joan Beaufort had twenty-one children, the youngest being Cecily, known in the north as 'the Rose of Raby', who married Richard, Duke of York, her father's ward. Born a Lancastrian, she had become a Yorkist and central to the dynastic political struggle of the time. It was her husband who raised the Yorkist claim to the throne. His death in the defeat at Wakefield prevented her from becoming Queen, but she was the mother of two kings, Edward IV and Richard

III, and aunt of a king-maker, the famous Warwick, the most powerful man of his time. The Princes in the Tower were her grandsons, and her eldest grand-daughter, Elizabeth of York, became the wife of Henry VII and the first queen of the new Tudor dynasty. Well might the Nevilles, now Earls of Westmorland, boast of their vital importance on the national stage. But in 1569 they were unwise enough to join in the Catholic rebellion (known as The Rising of the Northern Earls) against the government of Queen Elizabeth. In the third canto of *The White Doe of Rylston* Wordsworth sets the scene:

> Now was the North in arms: they shine
> In warlike trim from Tweed to Tyne,
> At Percy's voice: and Neville sees
> His followers gathering in from Tees,
> From Wear, and all the little rills
> Concealed among the forkéd hills –
> Seven hundred knights, Retainers all
> Of Neville, at their master's call
> Had sate together in Raby hall!

The Old Religion was still a great popular force, and wild scenes of rejoicing greeted the rebels' entry into Durham and the singing of Mass once more in its cathedral. The whole North could have fallen. There was no one to halt the southward march to Wetherby, for the Queen's Lord President of the Council, the Earl of Sussex, lay immobilised at York, starved of men and money by a parsimonious government.

Yet it all came to nothing. The earls had hoped to rescue the imprisoned Mary, Queen of Scots from Tutbury and proclaim her, but hearing that she had been moved to Coventry they could think of nothing better to do than go home and besiege a neighbour's castle. Then at the first whisper of the approach of Sussex's army they told their followers to disperse – a truly ignominious end; but then unlike their wives, who had been hot for action, they themselves had not really wanted to rebel. Northumberland died on the scaffold; Lord Neville abroad as a pensioner of Spain; his countess as a pensioner of Queen Elizabeth, who showed this amount of compassion. But the Nevilles' hold on their lands was broken for ever: the family disappeared from history.

In 1626 Raby, along with neighbouring Barnard Castle, was bought from the crown for £18,000 by Sir Henry Vane, principal secretary to Charles I. Here he entertained his master in the days before the Civil Wars. His son Henry Vane the Younger was a still more remarkable and forceful man. Governor of the colony of Massachusetts at the age of twenty-three, he returned home to become a Member of Parliament, a friend of Pym and Hampden, and one of the foremost of those who hounded Laud and Strafford to the block. When war broke out he chose the Parliamentary side; but his individualism and love of freedom ran deeper than any political loyalty, and during the Protectorate he became so sickened by Roundhead tyranny, against which he protested in a widely circulated pamphlet, that Cromwell had him arrested and imprisoned. This did not save Vane at the Restoration from Royalist vengeance and execution on Tower Hill – the only Parliamentary leader not a regicide to suffer in this way. Even on the scaffold the character and reputation of the man came out. The authorities feared the effect this skilled propagandist might exercise over the people, and drowned his last words in a fanfare of trumpets. 'It is an ill cause that dare not hear the words of a dying man,' he remarked to those around him. Strangely enough, the grandson of this victim of Charles II was a century later to marry the Merry Monarch's grand-daughter and reach high favour at the Hanoverian court as Earl of Darlington. No preferment could blunt the radical streak inherent in the Vanes, however, for the third Earl was to become one of the principal sponsors of the Great Reform Bill of 1832, spending a quarter of a million pounds buying up rotten boroughs – he controlled no fewer than six – to build up the Whig vote. For these exertions a grateful government created him a Duke (of Cleveland). It proved to be the summit of the Vane fortunes and this branch of the family was soon to die out. However, another branch still holds Raby, in the person of Lord Barnard.

From the outside Raby appears like some film-maker's dream of a feudal castle, with its nine towers planted solidly down in the middle of its wooded deer park. Apart from some eighteenth- and nineteenth-century additions to the south front, most of the fabric is fourteenth-century or, in the case of Bulmer's Tower, earlier; but if John, Lord Neville, were to come back to earth he would find himself sadly puzzled to know where the curtain wall of his castle had gone and what had become of his moat, now converted into two elegant lakes in the grounds.

The public entrance is through a fortified gateway – all that is left of the original outer wall – crowned by stone effigies of warriors looking north along the old invasion route. We shall see similar effects at Alnwick, the stronghold of the Percy earls. Inside this gateway is the square-arrowheaded bastion of Clifford's Tower, the largest and strongest of Raby's fortifications. Going, then, anti-clockwise, beyond a watchtower (at the centre of the west facade) is the splendid gateway of Neville's Tower, once the only entrance to the inner courtyard, with its long vaulted passage and heraldic arms. The south front faces a lake and has three towers along its length. The octagonal tower at the centre is part of the nineteenth-century restoration, but the oddly shaped pentagon of Bulmer's Tower at the south-eastern angle is the oldest part of the castle and may incorporate in its lower stages part of a manor house of King Canute which is supposed to have stood on this site. Its windows, as else-where in the castle, are disconcertingly modern.

The impression given by the **Interior** of Raby is one of grandeur, a little too self-conscious and here and there a little run to seed where the silks and damask of wallpapers and furniture have begun to fray.

Outstanding, because so evocative of the past, are the fourteenth-century **Kitchen** and the **Servants' Hall**, whose enormously thick walls suggest that it was once a guard-room. Tree trunks are used as beams across the angles of the kitchen ceiling.

The castle **Entrance Hall** (1325) is equally remarkable in its own idiom: an ancient room largely transformed in the eighteenth century in the 'Gothick' style by the Second Earl's architect, John Carr of York, a man of profoundly original and inventive mind, who provided here a variation on the *porte cochère* by making room for visiting coaches to drop their passengers actually *inside the hall*. Equally grandiose is the **Baron's Hall** above it on the first floor. Even in medieval times it was big enough to accommodate all seven hundred of the knights of Raby, but in the 1840s another fifty feet and three three-light windows were added to it and it was given a massive hammer-beam roof by another architect of inventive daring – William Burn. Of the old stonework only the minstrels' gallery survived. Most of the original furniture had already been sold in the 1740s, and their present replacements can hardly be said to look at ease in their environment. Perhaps nothing could.

Burn's transforming hand can be seen again to even more re-markable effect in the **Chapel**, for here he virtually replaced one building with another placed inside it like a nut in a shell – a piece of sheer fantasy, where the stoothing and plaster of the walls are lined so as to resemble stone and the vaulting of the ceiling and other details hint at themes used in Arab mosques.

What, then, shall we say of the third of the creations of this versatile architect – the **Octagonal Drawing Room**, in which everything, from the gorgeously gilded ceiling to the matching mirror over the fireplace, the chandelier, the gilt and white door, the French marquetry table and cabinets, the Aubusson carpet and the yellow silk wallpaper was planned as a unity? It is superbly successful of its kind, but like the Barons' Hall hardly a place in which to linger and relax. The room in fact suffers in comparison with the Small Drawing Room, whose plaster ceiling and array of sporting prints recall the more masculine and down-to-earth world of the Regency. Burn himself is more relaxed in the handsome Dining Room, where his ceiling of squares within squares is beautifully attuned to a room only marred by an appallingly coloured carpet. From this, even the portraits on the walls seem to be trying to look the other way.

The portraits are among the great attractions of Raby. Some of the finest hang in this dining room: Sir Godfrey Kneller's *Alexander Pope*, a Van Dyck of the First Duke of Hamilton, Sir Joshua Reynolds's charming study of Lady Katharine Pawlett as a child, and Lely's of Sir Henry Vane the Younger, which brings out the un-yielding integrity of the man. A portrait of the elder Sir Henry also hangs in the room and they make an interesting contrast in life-style: the renegade Cavalier and the renegade Roundhead. The sporting pictures in the Small Drawing Room include two delightful studies of eighteenth-century rural life: *The Raby Kennels*, 1820, showing the First Duke of Cleveland being adored by hounds, and J. F. Herring's *Ponies in Raby Stableyard*. In the Library, which also houses some fine pieces of Sèvres, and the Raby Hunt glass, is *Nell Gwynne* by Sir Peter Lely, and in the Ante-Library adjoining it some pictures by Pieter de Hoogh and David Teniers the younger.

The gardens make a pleasant contrast: ten acres of lawns and flowerbeds, with yew hedges on the verge of the park. The coach house has a collection of carriages on view. Parts of the old stables with their stalls still in place have been converted into a tea room, creating an original but rather twee effect. The castle's opening hours are also a little eccentric.

Moving east from Staindrop we leave behind the elegant eighteenth-century landscape and have the normal pattern of east Durham: sizeable farms and pockets of the old culture surviving among the pit heaps and the housing estates. Compared with the Black Country it is still reasonably unspoilt – there are fields surrounding even the most ravaged pit villages, and the moors and the sea are never far away – but from Raby Deer Park to Shildon Colliery is much further in spirit than the seven miles that divide them on the ground.

West Auckland, where the A688 from Staindrop to Durham crosses the north–south axis of the A68, is typical. Until the beginning of the 1960s it was a run-down but mellow and gracious village grouped around one of the large greens so common in the county.* Restoration was needed. Destruction was applied – and what has been lost can be seen in the eighteenth-century housing that has managed to survive. As some recompense West Auckland Hall has been preserved and recently restored.

The direct route to Durham is through Bishop Auckland. There is, however, a short and very rewarding detour to the west. From the green, therefore, follow the A68 (signposted to Corbridge) some five miles nearly to the outskirts of Witton le Wear, then turn off to the right for **Witton Castle,** a genuine (though restored) medieval stronghold which has entered the modern age in style with a huge camping and caravan site, car park, café, bar, and open-air swimming and paddling pools for the children. Not a place for the retiring or the ultra-sensitive, perhaps, but the gardens, with their formal yew hedges, the grey battlements of the castle among the woods and the general sense of relaxation and happiness are irresistible, and fabulous value at the price.

Witton Castle is now very much a product of our time. Just off our route is a home of a very different kind. It stands on private ground; special permission has to be got to visit it; and only those interested in archaeology or pre-history would be advised to try to find it. For those so inclined, cross the A68 to the village of **Hamsterley** (not to be confused with the place of the same name near Ebchester in the Derwent valley), take the first to the right just beyond the pub along the road signposted to Bedburn, and after a quarter of a mile turn sharp right again at the Knitsley Quarry sign. Follow this for a mile to the farm at the top of the hill, where permission should be asked to cross the fields downhill into the woods to **The Castles,** a large stone-walled enclosure with protective mounds and ditches which seems to have been built by Romanised Britons in the dark ages after the departure of their mentors. By Roman standards it is a clumsy, primitive work, not even well sited, for it is commanded on one side by higher ground. Lying tumbled in ruins by the banks of a burn and smothered by trees, it creates a poignant impression, the forlorn survivor of an empire that has deserted it. Virtually no traces have come to light of burials within its walls or even of the usual bric-à-brac of pottery, and it may be that the place was no sooner built than it

*The greens are the survivors of the compounds inside medieval villages, into which the cattle were driven at night to protect them from raiders.

was abandoned, as the tribes fled further west from the encroaching Saxons. One word of warning to the visitor who, with an Ordnance map in his hand, might think of taking a short cut and entering without permission: there is liable to be a bull in the field. 'He's quite quiet and good-natured, really,' the farmer assured me as he most generously and kindly waved me on to his land. An occasional bellow in the distance was all I heard, but it usually pays to be careful as well as polite on such occasions.

All this large area in the quadrilateral bounded by the A68, B6293, B6278 and B6282 roads is fine, unspoilt country, particularly in **Hamsterley Forest** where there is a Nature Trail. At **Wolsingham**, which has the oldest Agricultural Show in England, the road comes down again into the Wear valley, to run westward toward Stanhope (see p. 305).

To return, however, to Witton Castle and the eastern side of the county. From here, lovers of church architecture should make their way the short distance across country by minor roads to **Escomb**, where standing trimly among flats and bungalows at the bottom of a steep hill is one of the two oldest and most complete Saxon churches in England, hardly changed at all in the thirteen hundred years since its foundation. Its only rival is at Bradford-on-Avon. It is kept locked as a precaution against vandals, but the key can be had at the corner bungalow almost exactly on the diagonal between the church and an excellent pub, *The Saxon*, which has a terrace overlooking the square. You will in any case always find someone to direct you.

County Durham is well endowed with Saxon work, and at Monk-wearmouth and Jarrow we shall be visiting two famous churches of that period associated with the life of Bede. But there has been much rebuilding and restoration at both of them. All the more helpful, therefore, to see at Escomb how they must have looked in the middle of the eighth century in the great historian's time.

The ground plan is simple and austere: a long, narrow, high-walled nave, forty-three and a half feet by fourteen and a half feet, with a chancel of ten feet by ten feet. There are no transepts, no aisles, no tower – a plan derived from Roman Gaul which reached its full development in Northumbria and nowhere else. From the out-side you can see that all but the upper courses of the walls consist of large squared stones, many of them showing the diamond broaching, the chiselled criss-cross pattern, typical of Roman stonemasons. There can be no doubt that most of these stones came from the Roman camp at *Vinovia* (Binchester) two miles away. One of them in particular – inscribed *Leg VI*, commemorating the Legion which came over with Hadrian and is believed to have built *Vinovia* – has one of the finest hypocausts in Britain.

The outside of the church is interesting throughout for what it tells you about the date and the methods of its builders. At the corners of the nave and chancel can be seen the 'megalithic coigning', the setting of large stones alternately to north, south and west, so often used in Saxon walling. Two of the original round-headed windows remain: one above the twelfth-century porch, the other further to the east on the same side. Between them is a sun-dial, thought to be the oldest in Britain – there is another but less venerable one over the porch. The two lancets in the south wall are of the thirteenth century, but all the larger windows are much later additions – the only intrusive elements in the fabric of this marvellous church. High on the west wall are grooves indicating the presence of another structure, whose foundations, excavated in 1968, seem to have been almost exactly the same size as the chancel. There are traces of yet another vanished building outside the now blocked doorway in the north wall.

The interior gives the same impression of austere and moving simplicity. Its builders were poor men who borrowed wherever and whenever they could. They quarried the stone for their walls from Roman *Vinovia*, and when they wanted a chancel arch they seem to have found that too in the same camp and simply re-erected it entire. There is a similar case of self-help at Corbridge in Northumberland. Under the Escomb arch are traces of painting, probably twelfth-century. Further use of Roman stone can be seen on a jamb of the most easterly window of the north wall of the nave, inscribed *Bono/Rei/Publicae/Nato*, 'to the Man born for the good of the State'. It may once have formed the base for the statue of an Emperor. Behind the altar is a stone with sculptured cross probably earlier than the church itself.

Return to the A6073 and turn left for **Bishop Auckland,** now a small industrial town on the edge of the coalfield, but originally a settlement that sprang up during the reign of William Rufus around the country home of the bishops of Durham.

The town has an ancient bridge of the Wear and a pleasant market place leading directly into the palace grounds that stand on a steep wooded bluff above the river. They are open to the public: the palace itself is not. The gateway at the entrance with its clock tower is a Gothic Revival fantasy designed by Richard Bentley, a member of Horace Walpole's Strawberry Hill circle. Paradoxically this charming erection makes it easier to see Auckland in terms of its Norman builders, who created it as a mixture of baronial hall and rest house – it was never a fortified dwelling, for in really troubled times the bishops would take refuge in their impregnable castle in the loop of the Wear at Durham. Most of their work has perished, but the Great Hall built by Bishop de Puiset (Anglicised as Pudsey) *circa* 1190 still stands and is a deeply impressive building. The addition of a clerestory in the seventeenth century has ruined the interior effect, but externally adds to its attractions.

The palace is the bishop's private home, but permission to go over the great hall is sometimes given on application to the chaplain, advisedly well in advance. The building has had a chequered history. Originally in Pudsey's day it had a steeply pitched roof with louvre openings to take the smoke from a central brazier. It was altered in the fourteenth century by another compulsive builder, Bishop Anthony Bek, who added two free-standing chapels, one on top of the other. A baronial hall it remained, however, till the troubled times of the Civil Wars. Charles I was held here as a prisoner in 1646. After the Cavalier defeat the whole complex was bought by the Parliamentarian Sir Arthur Hazelrigg for £6,102 8s 11½d. During the Commonwealth most of it was pulled down, including Bek's chapels, and the stone was used to build a new house on the site; but by some miracle the great hall itself survived. With the Restoration came the backlash. Hazelrigg's ungodly house was pulled down and the great hall was converted into a chapel. The moving spirit of the new regime was Bishop Cosin, who had been forced into exile with the collapse of the Royalist cause but now returned to refurnish many Durham churches stripped by the iconoclasts. He was a man of vision and taste. Here at Auckland, however, his conversion of an old and famous building lacked humility. His raising of the side walls and the insertion of clerestory windows have spoilt the internal proportions and produce a chilling effect which not even the beautiful woodwork of his screen and stalls, the painted ceiling, the heraldic shields, the tapestries and the angels mounted on the corbel shafts can wholly rectify. It looks and feels a shell of something which once had life. The emptiness and sense of desolation are emphasised by the bat droppings that lie everywhere on the tiled floor and on the carved stalls. Only these eerie little night creatures seem to find Bishop Auckland chapel an acceptable home. Cosin himself lies in the midst of this grandiose but sad mausoleum.

A couple of miles back along the Barnard Castle Road, the A688, is the church of **St Helen Auckland**: for the specialist only, since it is hemmed in by industrial development and one has to look hard for the 'oasis' of pleasant houses surrounding it of which Pevsner wrote in 1953. They are still there, but the village group effect has gone. Yet for those who take the trouble St Helen's is a gem of a small church, an almost completely unspoilt building of the late twelfth and early thirteenth century. Like so many Durham churches it is almost certain to be locked, but the key can be had from the verger, Mrs Graham, 16 Melrose Avenue in the new housing estate, or from Mrs Walls of Old Hall, which is down the farm track diagonally across from the church on the opposite side of the main road. St Helen's has no tower; it squats low, as though hiding from the traffic. There is a proliferation of Early English windows and some Perpendicular ones. Of the two chapels one was probably founded as a chantry around 1233. Seen looking west from the altar the white-washed walls and dark grey stone of columns and arches of the nave give a soberly beautiful and harmonious effect, though the arcading on the south side is actually later and plainer than to the north and a closer look reveals a number of intriguing variations in the décor of arches and capitals. The chancel stalls have poppy-heads in two sizes – Pevsner says the carvings on the back of the stalls are original seventeenth-century work. The porch is unusual, being one of the only two in County Durham that have an upper chamber.

This other and still more elaborate two-decker can be seen at **St Andrew Auckland**, also called **South Church**, which is Bishop Auckland's ancient parish church, a mile out of the town – if coming from St Helen's, turn right at the traffic lights, from which point the tower appears beyond the long dip in the road. Like all collegiate churches housing a body of canons it was larger and richer than the norm. Pevsner says it is one of the biggest parish churches in the county, but at St Andrew's there is no doubt expressed about it – it is *the* biggest, all one hundred and fifty-seven feet of it, and this fact is proudly proclaimed on framed notices on the wall. Very handsomely indeed it stands on its mound under its tall buttressed tower at the junction of two busy roads: not, like St Helen's, cowed by its environment, but dominating it.

Inside it is very spacious, perhaps too spacious for its own comfort; it lacks intimacy. Most of the fabric is of the fourteenth century, though the clerestory was a later Perpendicular addition and during the nineteenth century there were further alterations to the south transept and the east end of the church. The very dark chancel stalls with their misericords were made for Bishop Langley, *circa* 1417. At

31

the west end, on the north side, are two recumbent figures: a lady of the fourteenth century and an unknown knight *circa* 1340, his head covered in a basinet, his legs elegantly crossed below the knee and his feet resting on what is evidently from its mane meant to be a lion, though it looks more like a pig. All the paint has gone from the knight's fine long surtout covering the chain mail, and the oak from which he is carved is black with age: it makes him the more impressive, a remote and mysterious warrior who must have lived through the humiliating times of Edward II and died just before the triumphs of Crécy and Poitiers.

However, the chief treasure of this impressive church is a **cross** which Pevsner dates to about 800, fragments of which came to light in the foundations of the south transept during rebuilding in 1881. Here the bird and scroll decoration of earlier Saxon crosses has been transformed into what one expert, Sir T. D. Kendrick, has called 'a hard and ruthless barbarism'. Everyone must judge for himself, but some of the minor figures of dogs trying to bite their tails seem to have almost a playful air. Syrian influence (how on earth did it reach Auckland?) has been detected in the figure of Christ bound to the cross with cords.

Like its sister church at St Helen's, St Andrew's is always kept locked, but keys are available. Ring the Parish Office (mornings only) Tel. Bishop Auckland 4671, or write to it in advance at Lightfoot Institute, Kingsway, Bishop Auckland, DL14 7JN. The cross alone is worth the trouble for anyone interested in Saxon workmanship.

Railway enthusiasts might like to know that two miles south of the Aucklands lies **Shildon**, where Timothy Hackwood, superintendent for the Stockton and Darlington line and builder of the famous engine the *Royal George*, once lived. His home is now a museum. The mile-long railway tunnel near by was the spot where George Stephenson's *Locomotion Number One* was placed on the rails for its historic run.

From Bishop Auckland market place the direct route to Durham is by the A6074. Much the more attractive approach however is along the A689 in the direction of Crook, turning right off it on to the minor road to Willington and right again on to the A690 for **Brancepeth**, where it is claimed Tennyson wrote 'Come into the garden, Maud'.

Here you feel as if you were walking into the past. The rich man in his castle ... the poor man at his gate ... the church tower among

32

Durham Cathedral from across the river

Durham Cathedral nave, looking east

the trees. The illusion is complete even down to the row of eighteenth-century cottages; and only from the far side of the graveyard does the visitor become aware of the fairways and bunkers of Brancepeth's excellent golf club laid out in what was once a park where deer and wild white cattle roamed.

The estate was for four hundred years in the possession of the Nevilles of Raby, and it was here in the winter of 1569 that it became the meeting place with the Percys where the Rising of the Northern Earls was planned. After the failure of the rebellion it was forfeited to the crown and subsequently given by James I to his Scottish favourite, Robert Carr. It eventually passed to a Sunderland banker whose grand-daughter married Viscount Boyne, in whose family it has remained.

Seen from the park the vast chessmen turrets of the castle look impressively baronial. However, only sections of the early fifteenth-century walls built by the First Earl, brother-in-law of Henry IV, survive. These are the Neville and Bulmer towers on the south-west front; most of the rest is the work of an Edinburgh architect, John Patterson, who was called in to restore the ruined fabric in 1817. Sad to say, it is no longer occupied except by Alsatian guard dogs, whose furious barking accompanies your stroll under the walls and at dusk can sound sinister indeed. It is not on public view.

Passing the entrance to the castle you come to one of the most gorgeously furnished churches in the North, dedicated to an Irishman, St Brandon, one of the only two such dedications in the country. It is liable to be locked against vandals, but the key can be obtained in the village from the rector.

The oldest parts of the structure, the tower and the west bays of the nave, date from the twelfth century; the east bays, transepts and the chancel arch from the thirteenth. Pevsner dates the present re-built chancel to the fifteenth century, and it certainly looks of this time, to judge from the beautiful five-light east window, but there is also authority for thinking that it may be considerably earlier, built to the order of Ralph Neville, Lord of Raby. This Ralph in his roisterous youth once paid his annual rental of a stag, which he owed to the Prior of Durham, by presenting the animal in person with a flourish of hunting horns during High Mass in the cathedral, only to be set upon by the indignant monks. Of his two sons one was the victor of Neville's Cross over the Scots and reposes in glory in Durham nave; the other, Robert Neville, known as 'the Peacock of the North', lies here in Brancepeth chancel, in an enormous stone effigy, seven feet nine inches long. A famous warrior, he slew Richard

Fitz Marmaduke on Durham's Framwellgate Bridge and was himself killed in battle, at Berwick – an ill man to cross, and grimly impressive even on his tomb. On the other side of the chancel are wooden effigies of the Second Earl of Westmorland (d. 1484) and his countess. Their collars are interesting. His is of white roses with a pendant boar: hers is of suns and roses. The chancel has two side chapels, one taken up with an organ, the other, on the north side, honouring the man who did more than any other to beautify the church by commissioning the wonderful wood carving all around.

John Cosin, whom we have met already in Auckland Palace, was made Vicar of Brancepeth in 1625 but was ejected during the Commonwealth to make way for a Puritan divine, coldly listed among the register of rectors hanging on the wall as 'Henry Leaver, an Intruder'. At the Restoration Cosin was made Bishop of Durham and at once set to work to collect a band of skilled craftsmen to repair the damage done by the Puritans in his diocese. His superb woodwork can be seen in Durham Cathedral, in Bishop Auckland Palace, at Easington (where his son-in-law became Rector in 1662), at Haughton le Skerne and Sedgefield, but nowhere to better effect than here at Brancepeth. All the woodwork is his with the exception of the nave roof (which is fifteenth-century Neville work) and the high altar screen; and he personally designed the Jacobean porch which makes so splendidly fitting an entrance to the church. Two periods of Cosin woodwork can be distinguished: the earlier, plainer work, including the nave pews, the pulpit and the chancel roof, probably dating from the 1620s when he first came to Brancepeth, and the more ornate later work seen in the choir stalls, the high family pews in the transepts, the font cover and the rood screen, so Gothic in style that it is often mistaken for a product of the medieval mind. The whole church is exquisite; even the gratings covering the heating pipes are elegant. Cosin obviously expected to be buried within its walls, for he provided himself with a memorial tablet commemorating his own death which may be seen on the north wall of the nave. However, when the time came he was Bishop of Durham and was therefore laid among his sumptuous furnishings in Bishop Auckland chapel. His church seating plan for his Brancepeth parishioners, segregating the females from the males, can also be seen – a work of unenlightenment worthy of Henry Leaver the Intruder.

Five miles further along the A690 is the city of Durham.

Chapter 2

The City of Durham

☙

Durham is, unquestionably, one of the most impressive sights in Europe. Yet the motorist travelling on the A1 within a mile and a half of its centre can easily fail to notice the place at all, for it lies in a bowl of hills and is screened from the road by modern ribbon development. Perversely enough it is from the railway, which has ruined so many English cities – from the windows of the *Flying Scotsman* and the *Talisman* gliding by over the viaduct – that the best grandstand view is to be had of the complex of Norman castle and cathedral lining the promontory above the river and the small grey town below. Pevsner, who devotes fifty-nine pages to it, sees its only rivals in Prague and Avignon.

The temptation to see Durham as a relic preserved in amber, an ornate jewel set in the heart of an industrialised hinterland of pit villages and Bingo halls, is hard to resist. St Cuthbert's pectoral cross in its glass case in the Monks' Dormitory of the cathedral might be its symbol. What saves the city from preciousness is something that Cuthbert himself (posthumously) provided: its prestige as a place of pilgrimage, and as a capital – once the home of the Lord Bishops who ruled the county palatine as quasi-independent sovereigns and now the seat of the third oldest English university and the scene of the annual Miners' Gala which fills its streets with marching bands and processions and has drawn every Socialist leader of note to its rostrum over the years. Durham may look old-fashioned, but it is ageless: an amalgam of bishops in mitres and pitmen out with their whippets, for this most picturesque and splendid of small English towns is also the world of Andy Capp.

St Cuthbert, now lying under his slightly repellent slab behind the high altar of the cathedral, was the real creator of Durham's fortunes, through the agency of the faithful monks who, in flight from Viking raids, carried off his body from Lindisfarne and finally deposited it here, after a century-long halt on the way at Chester le Street and a shorter period at Ripon. Such was his prestige during the Middle Ages, Camden, the Elizabethan chronicler, tells us, that the keys of

Durham Castle were hung for safe keeping on his shrine whenever the bishopric fell vacant, and remained there till a new appointment was made. His alleged antipathy to women kept that suffering sex for years from even entering the cathedral nave. Attempts to build a Lady Chapel close to his tomb had to be abandoned and the works re-sited at the opposite end of the church when cracks in the fabric signified his extreme displeasure at such an intrusion; and even a Queen of England, Philippa, wife of Edward III, was later to find herself evicted from the Prior's lodgings in the middle of the night for fear of incurring the old curmudgeon's wrath. Actually there seems to be no good evidence that in life he objected to women at all.

Cuthbert apart, the sheer strength of the Durham peninsula in the loop of the river on which cathedral and castle now stand also powerfully contributed to the importance of the site in the eyes of Saxon and later English monarchs in search of a bastion against the Scots. It was the Normans who first made use of these natural advantages. The Conqueror had been prepared to leave the Saxon occupants of the place alone, but when they were unwise enough to join in a rebellion against him he came north, savagely crushed them, and imposed on them a Norman bishop, Walcher, and erected a stone castle next door to the church to hold them down.

Bishop Walcher was full of plans for reform, including the provision of new accommodation for the monks. It was he who probably also built the beautiful chapel in the castle. He was given little time, however, for the hatred felt for the invaders led to his murder and the second harrying of the North.

It was easy enough for the Normans to carry out reprisals against this rebellious country, but quite another matter to administer it. The traditional rulers were the earls of Northumberland who had inherited the powers of the ancient kings of Northumbria. The Saxon earl, Waltheof, had been married to the Conqueror's niece, but that did not prevent him in his turn from rebelling against the crown; whereupon William Rufus hit on the ingenious solution of linking the political powers of the earldom with the sanctity and prestige of the bishopric in the person of one militant Norman ecclesiastic. Thus the County Palatine of Durham was born.

The new bishop's powers were to be those of a king within his realm. The law was his law. He had his own judges and seal and his own council; therefore Durham sent no Members of Parliament to Westminster but was represented there by the bishop alone. He had the right to create his own barons. He had his own army which he often led in person. He coined his own money. He enjoyed rights of forfeiture for treason – the lands of Bruce and Baliol came to the bishopric in this way. He alone had the right to grant permission for crenellation of castles, the right to create new boroughs, the right of Admiralty of the shores, the right of pardon. This addition of political supremacy to the already great powers of the bishopric was a risk, but a calculated one. To have given such a position to a lay baron would have meant perpetual danger from an over-mighty subject. But the royal trust in the bishops was justified: their great prerogatives were not abused and there was never an armed rebellion against the crown by the counts palatine, however overbearing and quarrelsome they might sometimes have proved to be.

The first incumbent, William de Carileph, was a choice very much in keeping with that wonderfully energetic Norman race which had torn Saxon society apart and was busily remaking England in its own image. Carileph, returning to Durham in 1091 from a period of exile, pulled down the Saxon church. On 11 August 1093 the first three stones of the new cathedral were ceremoniously laid, one by Malcolm, King of Scotland, one by Carileph, and one by the Prior, Turgot. When, three years later, Carileph died, the east bays of the choir aisles with their stone vaulting were complete, the earliest known example of this type of roof. Ranulf Flambard, who succeeded to the see, pressed on with the building, and by 1104 both transepts and the choir were finished. Flambard was now able to bring Cuthbert's body from the monastic buildings to the feretory behind the high altar of his church. He was an enthusiastic planner. It is to him that we owe Palace Green, cleared of its out-buildings as a precaution against fire, Framwellgate Bridge, the church of St Giles, the Kepier Hospital, and far away by the banks of the Tweed, Norham Castle, the northern fortress guarding the border with Scotland.

The building of the cathedral's nave and aisles with the stone vaulting over them was carried on by the monks in the five years interregnum that followed Flambard's death. By the time the next bishop, Geoffrey Rufus died, the cathedral was more or less complete, and it only remained for later generations to add the three towers, the chapels at the east and west ends, the cloisters and some of the conventual buildings. Rufus had been responsible for the north and south doorways of the nave and the chapter house, generally acknowledged to be the most beautiful in England – later to be wantonly destroyed in 1796 as being too draughty for Hanoverian canons. It had taken just thirty years for Carileph's plans to be translated into stone, and the bulk of his work can still be seen today, seemingly untouched by time.

In 1153 another outstanding man took over the see and ruled it for forty-two years. This was Hugh de Puiset, called Pudsey. He was reputed to be the great-grandson of William the Conqueror, and he certainly acted like it. He quarrelled with the Archbishop of York, who refused to recognise his election by the monks; he quarrelled with the monks, who objected to his attempts to discipline them; and finally he quarrelled with the king, Henry II, with whose rebellious sons he sided, only escaping punishment because a repetition of the Becket affair would have been politically too embarrassing. He proposed himself as a Crusader to Richard Coeur de Lion and even went to the lengths of building a galley so lavishly furnished that even the pots and pans were made of silver. Richard, however, preferred his money to his company and bribed him to stay at home by making him Earl of Northumberland. Evidently a turbulent spirit, but an artistic one. We should be grateful to him, for we owe him some of the most beautiful things in Durham: the splendid Norman doorway at the entrance to the hall in the castle, part of his Constable's Hall above, and the delicate Lady Chapel, now called the 'Galilee', at the cathedral's west end.

The equally fine but very differently-styled Chapel of the Nine Altars, in the form of an East Transept, was added in the middle of the thirteenth century to the plans of Bishop Richard le Poore, with funds raised by the sale of indulgences throughout the country. The west towers went up between 1217 and 1262 (their battlements were added in 1773); the one hundred and fifty-five-foot-high bell tower above the crossing was begun in 1465 – and the silhouette of Durham was complete: in Sir Walter Scott's well-known lines,

> Half house of God,
> Half castle 'gainst the Scot.

The county palatine had been created as a buffer against these northern enemies of the English crown, and its bishops continued to play their part in its wars. Two men destined to be Scottish kings, Baliol and Bruce, were vassals of Bishop Anthony Bek, another in the line of militant priests who served the Plantagenets on the frontier. Bek fought in Edward I's army at Falkirk, and the sword he used that day hangs in Auckland Palace. One of his successors, Bishop Hatfield, seems to have been at Edward III's siege of Calais. In his absence, the Scots, at French urging, came south to ravage the palatinate, only to be defeated outside the city at the battle of Neville's Cross by an army led by the Archbishop of York, Lord

Percy, and Ralph, Lord Neville, who commanded the Durham contingent and who lies in effigy in the cathedral nave. St Cuthbert also seems to have had some part in the victory, for his corporal cloth was carried into battle by the 'haliwerfolk', the 'holy man people', and was later incorporated into a banner of red velvet used in similar crises as late as Flodden in 1513. Inspired perhaps by Ralph Neville's tomb, Bishop Hatfield had one built for himself under his bishop's throne, the highest in Christendom. On a less exalted level he also built an octagonal kitchen for the use of the prior and the monks which remains one of the most fascinating parts of the conventual buildings of Durham.

The end of the fourteenth and the beginning of the fifteenth century saw a spate of new building: the cloisters and the Monks' Dormitory (now the cathedral museum) date from this time. In early Tudor days was added the Castle Kitchen, which still provides meals for the students of the university. It was commissioned by Bishop Fox, the godfather of Henry VIII and patron of Cardinal Wolsey. Incidentally, Wolsey himself was for a while Bishop of Durham, if by accident. In his great office of Chancellor he had called on Bishop Ruthall to provide a full account of the royal estates in the county palatine. Through a clerical error Ruthall' secretaries provided instead a full account of the revenues *of the bishopric*, so enormously wealthy that poor Ruthall, justly fearing the King's reaction to the discovery, lay down and died on the spot. Wolsey, who as an experienced pluralist naturally succeeded him, remained an absentee bishop; but, in anticipation of his coming, quantities of his favourite cinnamon-scented rushes were planted in the park at Auckland Palace, where their successors grow to this day.

It was Wolsey's successor, the pious Bishop Tunstall, who had to face the consequences of Henry's break with Rome. Tunstall was a scholar, a friend of Erasmus, but like Cranmer for much of his life sadly irresolute. In 1535 Henry suspended him, as he did all the bishops, then reinstated him to emphasise his new authority as Head of the English Church. Tunstall accepted this. During the Catholic rebellion of the north, the 'Pilgrimage of Grace', he fled from his diocese to avoid being implicated. He then meekly agreed to head the Council of the North (set up as a result of the rising) which created a royal court in the palatinate and deprived him and his successors of any independent jurisdiction. In 1536 all the smaller monasteries were forfeited to the King, and Durham lost her cells at Finchale, Wearmouth, Jarrow, Lindisfarne, Lytham, Stamford and Durham College in Oxford, later to be re-endowed as Trinity College. The

39

King's greed and appetite were insatiable. In 1538 his commissioners perpetrated the ultimate by rifling Cuthbert's tomb, and on 31 December 1540 the great monastery itself was handed over to 'The Illustrious and Invincible Prince, our Lord Henry VIII'. The suffering but durable Tunstall continued on the see-saw of royal favour and disfavour for the next three reigns. Disgraced under the ultra-Protestant Edward VI he was reinstated by Mary. Asked to change his coat again under Elizabeth he at last screwed himself up to a refusal, had most of his revenues confiscated, and died in London as the unwilling 'guest' of the Archbishop of Canterbury, whom in a final burst of courageous defiance he had refused to consecrate.

Durham was fortunate, for it was refounded in 1541 as a secular cathedral, no longer boasting a prior, but at least a dean and twelve canons. Generous allowances were made to all those who did not secure a prebend, and most of the forty resident monks seem to have managed to stay on, in one capacity or another. This toleration of the past was shortlived, however, for under Dean Horne Cuthbert's original tomb in the cloister was destroyed and most of the images were smashed. Fortunately the books in the library survived. The following dean, Whittingham, was a rabid reformer, intent on stripping the cathedral to the bare walls, being ably assisted by his wife, who used gravestones to tile her wash-house and burnt the sacred banner of St Cuthbert.

Sanity returned at last with a realisation of what had been lost. Early in the seventeenth century the fight to restore the beauty of both cathedral and castle began under Bishop Neile, who had two devoted assistants in Laud and Cosin. It was a hard struggle, for the Reformers were still powerful, led by Canon Peter Smart, who fired impassioned broadsides from the pulpit at his enemies. He had a particular abhorrence of the altar which had been set up at the east end of the cathedral. 'They court spiritual fornication who bow their bodies before that idol,' he declared. Though silenced by a gaol sentence, he was to rise again when the sectarian struggle became merged in the Civil Wars. The bishopric, with the exception of the town of Sunderland, was solidly Royalist. It was overrun by the Scots in 1640 and 1644, and after the defeat at Marston Moor fell completely under the Puritan yoke. The Prayer Book was abolished; bishoprics were abolished; and the eighty-year-old Bishop of Durham was reduced to tutoring in a private family for the last ten years of his life. All the houses and lands belonging to the see were sold, Durham Castle being bought, for some inscrutable purpose, by the Lord Mayor of London. All episcopal powers ceased, and

Durham, no longer represented by a bishop in the House of Lords, sent Members of Parliament to Westminster for the first time. The dean was imprisoned for many years and most of the clergy went into exile. As for any argument as to where altars should or should not be placed, this soon became quite academic, for in 1650, after Cromwell's victory at Dunbar, three thousand of his Scottish prisoners were lodged in the cathedral, where they burnt every piece of woodwork they could lay their hands on to keep themselves warm.

That Durham survived even these attentions will surprise no one who stands today under those huge pillars and those immense vaults of stone. It was not a very combustible building. It might even have stood some pounding from the Lord Protector's cannon. But Cromwell was no particular enemy of Durham, where he planned to set up a university: a bright idea only taken up one hundred and seventy years after his death. With the Restoration the pendulum swung back again under Bishop Cosin, the 'young Apollo' against whom Peter Smart had thundered from the pulpit. The cathedral was given new furniture: choir stalls, a carved oak screen, and the superb font cover; and the castle its staircase, one of the grandest in England.

Yet if Durham in Good King Charles's Golden Days and through to the pudding times of the Georges was a world of plenty, all too much of it rubbed off on the friends and relations of the bishops, often worthy men, but careless about finances, and nepotists on a grand scale. Not always under his successors were the high artistic standards of Cosin maintained. During the 1780s, instead of re-placing worn parts of the fabric of the outer walls, the cathedral architects pared off a thousand tons of stone, destroying many of the Norman mouldings in the process. This vandalism is sometimes wrongly attributed to James Wyatt, who has enough to answer for. It was he in 1796 who removed the glass from the windows in the Nine Altars chapel because he thought it made the church too dark; and it was only at the last moment that he was prevented from pulling down the Galilee Chapel to make way for a grand ceremonial entrance. Perhaps it was a mercy when, in 1836, on the death of Bishop Van Mildert, the last remaining powers of the bishops were taken from them and the King became the Count Palatine. Seven centuries after Carileph the see of Durham became as other sees.

Entrance to the cathedral is by the north doorway, a very late addition dating from 1780 when Wyatt destroyed the original entrance and the two chambers above it. The famous twelfth-century **Bronze Knocker** – a ring hanging from the jaws of a grotesque beast – was fortunately retained from the days when it had been used by criminals seeking 'the liberty of St Cuthbert'. The rights of sanctuary had attached to most churches from the seventh century, and here at Durham under the protection of its powerful monastery the system was highly developed. Monks in the rooms above kept watch day and night to admit the fugitive, who would then ring the great bell of the cathedral. He had to make a formal statement of his crime and was given a black gown with the yellow cross of St Cuthbert on the shoulder. Fed by the monks, he was allotted a place to sleep in the south aisle, where he could remain for thirty-seven days, during which time he had either to come to terms with those who were in search of him or 'abjure the kingdom', in which case he was conducted from parish to parish by local constables until he reached a port. The register of those who found sanctuary at Durham between 1464 and 1524 is still in existence. This licence to flout the Common Law was not finally abolished till 1624.

Beyond Wyatt's doorway is the most splendid of all early Norman churches. The first impression, looking along the nave towards the high altar, is of immense size and solidity. Yet Durham is not larger than most Norman churches; it is considerably shorter, for instance, than Ely. Part of the impression of depth is created by the alternation of round and compound pillars with their varying decoration which hold up the eye, so that the altar beyond the Neville Screen seems infinitely far away: the fine proportions of arcades, triforium and clerestory also draw attention upwards into vistas of soaring height. A sense of powerful unity and order imposes itself at once on the imagination. Vast though it is, it seems the work of one man's mind and vision translated on the instant into stone – and this is not far from the reality, for apart from the Galilee Chapel, behind you as you stand facing the high altar, and the Chapel of the Nine Altars at the far east end, hardly visible from this point, you are looking at the interior of the Norman church almost exactly as it was planned by Carileph and as it stood on the day of its completion forty years later, in 1133. No other medieval English cathedral, save possibly Salisbury, has such a unity of time and space.

Strength is the keynote of the building; but it is not brute strength. The huge cylindrical piers of the nave – twenty-seven feet high and seven feet wide – have the solidity of an Egyptian temple, but any tedium in the design is countered by the way they are grouped into couples with the compound pillars, and by the decoration they carry:

spiral patterns, the first erected; zigzags, introduced about 1110; and later lozenges and close vertical flutings. The same coupling of bays is repeated in the triforium; and above it in the clerestory the windows are flanked by pairs of arches. In Durham, as with the animals into the Ark, everything goes by twos. Drawing it all together is the wonderful stone ribbed vaulting, the earliest surviving example in European architecture of this improvement on the old tunnel or groined vault which enabled much wider spaces to be roofed. The aisle vaults in the choir were the first to be built and were probably completed by 1096. We know that the original high vault over the choir was completed in 1104, the year in which Cuthbert's shrine was removed from the cloister to its place of honour in the feretory. On the night before the great ceremony the masons working to clear away the scaffolding high above the site of the new tomb met with difficulties and went to bed with the job unfinished, but during the night it collapsed, injuring nothing – one of the Saint's most practical and thoughtful miracles. By the thirteenth century this vaulting was in an unsafe state and was rebuilt in the later style of the vaulting of the Chapel of the Nine Altars, but marks of the original can still be traced in the clerestory wall facing the chancel. The north transept was vaulted by 1110, but the south transept had at first a wooden roof and was not stone-vaulted until 1133, when the nave roof was also completed.

The height of the nave and choir from the floor to the crown of the vault is seventy-five feet. As usual in Norman churches, there are three storeys: the main arcade, the triforium (which is about half the height of the arcade), and the clerestory, both galleried. The tremendous weight of the vault is carried on transverse arches which rise from the compound pillars, that is to say from every second bay. In between, in the nave, a ribbed arch rests at triforium level on corbels; and in the choir and transepts, on short pilasters. The transverse arches are not rounded, as one would have expected for this period, but pointed, so enabling them to bear much greater strain. Durham is one of the earliest buildings to use this form of arch, the precursor and herald of Gothic. The triforium gallery is as wide as the aisle below. On the inside the containing arch embracing the two small arches has chevron ornamentation, introduced into this country between 1110 and 1120. The arches thrown across the triforium between every bay to take the stress of the ribbed vaulting are in effect the earliest form of the flying buttress, still in the chrysalis stage and hidden from the eye.

The crossing is supported by four great composite piers, one shaft of which reaches far up into the one hundred and fifty-five-foot-high tower which was raised in 1465 above the original ceiling. Here in the tower we get the recurring theme of two arches above the gallery, and, higher still, twin two-light windows.

Forty years after the completion of Carileph's Norman church Bishop Pudsey made the first addition to it: a Lady Chapel, known at least from 1186 as the 'Galilee', because it was here that the city's pageant of Christ's return to Galilee was staged. A marble line in the floor of the nave immediately to the east of the north door still marks the point beyond which women could not pass. Pudsey's attempts to build a chapel for them at the east end were frustrated by St Cuthbert's evident wish to keep them well away from his tomb; and the work had therefore to be transferred to the west end of the church, where the ground was eminently unsuitable, being poised above the steep cliff which descends to the river. This lack of space accounts for the great width of the chapel as opposed to its length. However, Pudsey had excellent precedents from Cluny and Ely for a work of this kind at the west end of a church, and the result is a masterpiece.

The Chapel has five aisles divided by arcades, each of five arches. The arches are round-headed, and they and the capitals were originally painted in spiral and zigzag patterns. The columns, two to each pier, were of Purbeck marble, giving a very slender line, but in the fifteenth century Bishop Langley added sandstone shafts to them, probably for appearance's sake and in imitation of similar work at Auckland Palace, since they bear no part of the weight. The general effect of the chapel is distinctly Moorish and in great contrast to the solidity of the rest of the cathedral. It is of one storey only and has a wooden ceiling. The central west doorway was kept until Bishop Langley's time, but he filled it in to provide a main altar and a burial place for himself, replacing it with two side doorways from the north and south aisles. Traces of twelfth-century wall painting can be seen in the arched recess to the north of the altar. Special privileges were given to this chapel by the Pope in the fourteenth century, allowing babies of the excommunicated to be baptised and the excommunicated themselves to worship here. The remains of Bede were brought from Cuthbert's tomb in the feretory to the chapel in 1370 and given their own gold and silver shrine. This was destroyed during the Reformation, but at least the King's commissioners had the decency to rebury the great historian's bones in the tomb where they still lie.

When in the thirteenth century it became clear that the three eastern apses of the cathedral and its choir were in a dangerous condition appeals for help were made beyond the see, and from as far afield as Glasgow and Norwich money from the sale of indulgences came pouring in to finance the rebuilding of the east end of St Cuthbert's church. The work began in 1235 and took almost as long to complete as the whole of the original church. The architect was Master Richard de Farinham. The plan adopted, to build another transept, was an unusual one, though similar work was being done at Fountains Abbey in Yorkshire, and at the same time (1220–1237). The chapel is distinguished by its great height – it is set five feet nine inches below the level of the choir – and by the light that fills it. There are no fewer than nine lancets on the east wall corresponding to the nine altars, and above them a central rose window (whose original Perpendicular tracery was, regrettably, removed by Wyatt in 1795) with three lancets on each side of it. On the north is the wonderful six-light window with geometrical tracery known as 'The Joseph Window', probably put in about 1280. The tremendous thickness of the walls enabled an inner and an outer layer of tracery to be made, with brilliant effect. On the south side this depth led to an inner and an outer mullion on the two coupled lancets which are divided by a vaulting pier. The construction of this chapel went on without any disturbance to the three apses and the choir of the original east end until the new building was nearly finished, rather on the lines of a celebrated feat of construction on the island of Gozo, where a completely new church has been built over the body of a predecessor in which services never ceased. When at Durham the time came to demolish the unwanted buildings the choir was extended eastward by an additional bay which was wider than the others and pointed instead of rounded. The junction of the old and new walls was masked by arcading and by slim columns on corbels above it. The vaulting of the north and south bay extensions of the chapel is quadripartite; the centre vault has two ribs rising from each of four piers, but so arranged that when they near the centre they merge into the circle containing the beautiful carving of the Four Evangelists, which well repays study through binoculars. The vaulting in the sections facing the aisles is sexpartite with a transverse rib askew – the fascinating answer the builders gave to the problem which arose because the aisles were narrower than the section of the chapel to which they had to be joined.

If we turn from the fabric to the **Monuments, Glass and Furnishings**, it has to be admitted that with one or two shining exceptions Durham is poorly represented when compared with other cathedrals of similar wealth and size – the result of the havoc wrought during the Reformation and the Civil Wars. Before 1538 the church was full of colour – painted pillars, side chapels, tombs – seen by light filtered through the medieval glass, of which only a few fragments remain. Modern attempts to show samples *in situ* of how the stonework must have looked in its prime are highly misleading, because the colours now seem crude as seen by the all-too-revealing light shining through plain or modern glass.

The cathedral's greatest treasure was of course St Cuthbert's shrine, described in the *Rites of Durham* as being 'exalted with most curious workmanship, of fine and costly green marble, all limmed and builded with gold', and so 'richly invested' by the pilgrims who flocked there to offer 'fervent prayers to God and holy St Cuthbert for his miraculous reliefe and succour', that it was judged to be 'one of the most sumptuous monuments in all England'. The jewels and ornaments which covered the shrine were thought too tempting to be exposed except during festivals, in particular on Durham's great day of the year, 30 March, the anniversary of the Saint's death; but even the cover normally kept lowered over them was a thing of beauty, richly decorated with paintings and images of the Holy Family. This cover worked on pulleys with bells attached, so that when it was being raised by the attendant monks everyone inside the church would hear it and hurry to the shrine. However, centuries of tradition and devotion were nothing to Henry VIII's commissioners, who arrived in 1538 and wasted little time in stripping it. Some years passed before even the Saint's bones were given sanctuary inside the cathedral. The slab that now lies over them behind the high altar is distinctly spartan.

Cuthbert's shrine had been separated from the nave by two great stone screens: the Rood Screen and the Pulpitum, which latter had a central entrance to the choir and was decorated with the figures of thirty-two kings and queens of England, and, touchingly enough, of Scotland, in spite of border raids and wars. After all, had not Malcolm laid one of the cathedral's foundation stones? Both these screens were destroyed. The stone reredos, known as the **Neville Screen**, survived, though stripped of its one hundred and seven sculptured figures. Built, some say, of stone from Caen, others, of Dorset clunch, it was made in London and shipped north in sections to be assembled by Durham masons working for Lord Neville, who paid most of the bills. The donor's father, Ralph, had been one of the victorious commanders at the Battle of Neville's Cross; and in gratitude for this and for the munificence the family had always shown towards the see both these magnates were allowed to have their tombs placed inside the cathedral, where before them even some bishops had thought themselves unworthy of burial. Both tombs (1367 and 1388) survive, if in a somewhat mutilated state. In the choir is the chantry chapel containing the tomb and alabaster effigy of Bishop Hatfield under his vainglorious episcopal throne.

Of the ancient furnishings that have survived the most colourful is the early sixteenth-century **Clock**. This somehow escaped the activities of the Scottish prisoners after Dunbar and now stands, gaily painted in blue, red and gold, in the south transept, close to the stairway leading to the central **Tower**. The medieval choir stalls were not so lucky and were broken up for firewood. Their splendid replacements look Gothic but were actually carved by John Clements for Bishop Cosin, who also ordered the most superb of Durham's ornaments, the wooden **Font Cover**, a marvellous forty-foot-high octagon rising in tier upon tier of Gothic gables and tracery. Cosin also built a new carved rood screen, unfortunately replaced in Victorian times by a marble one by Sir Giles Gilbert Scott.

The **Monastic Buildings** stood at the south side of the church, and their cloisters can be entered directly from the south aisle. Both the doorways are more ornate on the cloister side. The one to the east was built by Bishop Pudsey and is similar to one in the castle; the west door is remarkable for its fine twelfth-century ironwork.

The present **Cloisters**, replacing earlier work, date from the same period as the nave, but their arcading was renewed in the fifteenth century and new tracery was put in around 1773, altering their appearance for the worse. The fifteenth-century wooden ceiling was restored in 1878. Now the most serene and tranquil spot in the whole of Durham, they were in the time of the monastery's greatness a workshop humming with activity. The open sides of the complex were glassed in: on the east by windows depicting the life and miracles of St Cuthbert, on the north by plain glass, which allowed the daylight to penetrate into the monks' cubicles or 'carrells', three to a window, each containing a reading desk. The novices were taught in a 'fair stall of wainscot' in the north-west corner, near the present entrance to the museum; and near by was a washing place with latticed cupboards to allow air to dry the towels.

The earliest buildings are on the east side. Entering from the cathedral by Pudsey's doorway, we pass the tunnel-vaulted parlour, above which is the choir school, once a library. The **Chapter House** next to it has had an unhappy history. Built originally in 1130, its east end was destroyed in a particularly wanton fashion in 1796, reputedly to enlarge the dean's garden. The architect, James Wyatt, simply let the roof fall in, causing the maximum amount of damage. In 1895 it was restored to its Norman proportions, but only the west end is original. Original, too, and well worth seeing, is the monks' short-term **Prison**, which is connected to it. A small chapel for prayer, a smaller gaolers' room and a tiny black hole in the wall for the prisoner, this was for the less heinous offenders and well-calculated to bring anyone to heel and avoid the much grimmer main gaol. Special permission from the Dean and Chapter (The College, Durham. Tel. 64266) is needed to view all these monastic buildings except the Monks' Dormitory. The south side of the cloister used to be the scene of a Maundy Day ceremony at which the monks would wash children's feet and give them food and money. The refectory, on the left, the vaulting of which dates from 1071 and resembles work in the Norman chapel at the castle, is now known as Dean Sudbury's Library. A very beautiful room ... but special permission, I fear, alas! Just to the south-west is the fascinating **Kitchen** built by John Lewyn in 1366: a square converted into an octagon by four immense corner fireplaces. Its vaulting is composed of eight intersecting semi-circular ribs with a central louvre for light and ventilation. The cloister's west side is taken up by the thirteenth-century undercroft to the dormitory which was used as a common-room, the only place where the monks (as opposed to their Prior and other high officials) could sport a fire. Behind it was a garden and bowling alley.

Further round the cloister at the head of a staircase is one of the finest things in all Durham, the **Monks' Dormitory** (1398/1404): one hundred and ninety-four feet long and thirty-nine feet wide, with its superb original roof, one of the most remarkable in Britain. It shows to better advantage to us than it did to the monks who once inhabited it, for in their day it was divided up into little 'chambers of wainscot' like a honeycomb. The unfortunate novices were herded together at the south end where not a glimmer of daylight could reach them, but the monks in the cubicles had their share of a window as in the carrells below. You can still see the hollows in the stonework where the dividing screens were fixed.

The **Museum** inside the dormitory is a large receptacle for illustrated books and manuscripts, rings, seals and coins, richly worked copes of bishops and priors, and a formidable array of Saxon crosses, some original, some plaster, grouped together in such a way as to suggest the yard of a monumental mason and funeral director. It is a collection which some find hard to enthuse over, and it sadly de-

Durham from the railway viaduct

Raby Castle

St Lawrence's Church, Pittington, showing the magnificent north arcade, with its alternating piers based on those in Durham's nave

Gibside Chapel, near Rowland's Gill; a fine example of the work of James Paine. It was built in 1760 as a mausoleum for the Bowes family

tracts from the appearance of the nobly proportioned room that houses it.

However, near the entrance are gathered some of the most moving survivals of Saxon worship to be found in England: St Cuthbert's **Coffin**, his pectoral **Cross**, his portable **Altar**, and a **Maniple and Stole** presented to the shrine by King Aethelstan well over a century before the Conquest.

The coffin itself is central to the history of Durham, and a rare old mystery it is.

St Cuthbert died in 687 and was buried in the church on Lindisfarne. Eleven years later the monks dug him up and found the body 'incorrupt'. So at least they said. It was then placed in a black oak coffin carved with the likenesses of 'divers beasts, flowers and images, which seemed to be inserted, engraved or furrowed out of wood'. This coffin was kept above ground, carefully guarded by the monks, and was carried with them on their wanderings after they had left Lindisfarne to escape from Viking raids – fragments of it are those we now see pieced together in the main showcase of the museum. These fragments, found inside two other coffins, one dating from 1104, the other from 1540, came to light in 1827 when the tomb at Durham was dug up by the Rev. James Raine, a stern Protestant divine, in search of evidence to confute Catholic belief in the miraculous properties of Saints. By then St Cuthbert's body was no longer incorrupt. A reconstruction of the coffin was made and put on show, using the fragments of the original oak. What is now in the museum, however, is the fruit of another reconstruction undertaken during the Second World War by the Harvard scholar, Dr Ernst Kissinger.

Unlike Mr Raine, Dr Kissinger was seeking the truth; but the result of his research is to raise more questions than it solves – one of which will occur to everyone at a glance. How can it be that the body of a man – a tall man according to tradition – could have been placed inside a box of the shape and size of a small Victorian cabin trunk? Evidence – if anything about this topic can be dignified as evidence – points to the fact that the Saint was found lying on his side, stretched out, not doubled up like a child in the womb. Is Dr Kissinger's reconstruction therefore wrong? Or – as the Rev. James Raine would certainly have said – is the case simply that the monks lied about the miraculous preservation of their saint and only a broken skeleton lay inside the coffin they carried around with them for so many years?

A counter-objection arises here. If the coffin was as small as that, how could anyone suppose that a man's incorrupt body lay within it? The monks were not fools: they must have known there were limits to lay credulity. And the coffin was openly carried around by men whose prestige and livelihood depended on popular acceptance of their story. Later, admittedly, the coffin was buried where it could not normally be seen. But sometime it *was* seen, for in 1104 they opened it up themselves to have a look at it and declared the body still incorrupt; and opened it again for the second time in the same year to satisfy a jealous abbot from a rival house who had scoffed at their tale.

Detailed descriptions of what was found on these occasions survive, as to the placing of the Saint's body, of its clothing and of other relics that had found their way inside: the bones of a number of lesser persons, which were removed as unworthy, and those of Bede in a linen bag and the skull of St Oswald, which were allowed to remain. Many of the objects described in these reports may be seen in the museum. There is the **Maniple** and **Stole** which were presented to the shrine by King Aethelstan about 933. They were made between 909 and 931 by order of Queen Aelflaed, daughter-in-law of Alfred the Great, and are the earliest known pieces of English embroidery. Their delicate beauty is striking proof of the cultural standards of the times, and many of the designs were used when about 930 the lost art of book illumination was resumed in the Saxon kingdoms. There is the ivory **Comb** mentioned in 1104 as being slightly reddened with age. This was probably a ceremonial comb used at a bishop's consecration, perhaps at Cuthbert's own. His personal '**Altar** of silver' was described by the chronicler. This was originally of wood, later covered by his followers with silver, then again stripped, so that we see it as it was in the Saint's lifetime. All the articles of great value catalogued as being in the coffin in 1104 were missing by 1827. The tomb had been rifled by the King's commissioners in 1538. Cuthbert's gold and sapphire ring was taken and sold, eventually to find its way to the Roman Catholic seminary at Ushaw College, where it still is. One trophy the vandals failed to find was the Saint's **Pectoral Cross**, which was not listed as being in the coffin in 1104 but was discovered by Mr Raine hidden under the vestiges of robes. It is of gold studded with garnets, the central boss, now empty, no doubt originally holding a small relic. The workmanship is interesting. It was at one time thought to have been made in Cuthbert's lifetime, but it has recently been suggested by Dr T. D. Kendrick that it may be still earlier work from the Britons of fifth-century Strathclyde. Certainly it shows signs of having been twice repaired, which would suggest that it was already old when Cuthbert wore it. Was it perhaps St Aidan's?

The very number and variety of the articles found in the coffin or at some stage removed from it add to the mystery of its size. Was it just a receptacle, and did the Saint himself lie elsewhere? There is a story that after the destruction of the tomb by Henry VIII's commissioners the body was reburied in a place known only to three Benedictines, who handed on the secret on their deathbeds – a variation of the story of the ingredients of Green Chartreuse. Perhaps it is safest to conclude that legends and marvels have always accompanied St Cuthbert, and to leave it at that.

The bishops, who were also abbots of this great ecclesiastical complex as well as counts palatine, had naturally many residences – a palace at Auckland, a huge fortress at Norham on the Tweed, and several country houses and hunting lodges – but their main headquarters were in Durham **Castle**, which still faces the cathedral across the lawns of Palace Green: a place so strong that even the Scots in centuries of marauding never managed to take it, and yet spacious and grand enough for the most worldly and luxury-loving cleric.

The Saxon monks who in 995 chose this high ground in the loop of the river for their home saw to the protection of its open side by the building of earthworks crowned by a palisade, replaced by stone after the Conqueror's visit in 1072. A Durham monk, one Lawrence, who became prior in 1149, has left a fine description of the castle as it existed just before Bishop Pudsey's huge rebuilding programme. 'The unyielding city,' he wrote, 'is defended . . . by a solidly built house . . . which stands out all radiant with eminent beauty. Each wall is girded with a beautiful wing, and every wing dies into a threatening wall.' This is a reference to the keep, probably on the site of the present kitchen. Other 'beautiful structures' existing in his time were the predecessor of the great hall and the eleventh-century Norman chapel which still stands. Most of the surviving building we now see is of the twelfth century, with additions of the fourteenth and sixteenth and an octagonal keep built in the year of Queen Victoria's accession on the site of a much earlier one of Bishop Hatfield's (Bishop of Durham 1318/33).

The approach from Palace Green is across a filled-in moat to the twelfth-century gateway, which still shows its Norman origins in the arch and the vaulting. The crenellations at the top and sides are due to Wyatt, who did many worse things elsewhere. The castle is still very much in use as one of the colleges of Durham University, but parties are taken round by official guide at fairly frequent intervals throughout the day. Before going in it pays to stand for a moment in the courtyard to get one's bearings. To the left, on the west side, are the kitchens and dining wing. Ahead, on the first and second floors, are Bishop Pudsey's two halls, one masked by a gallery added at the time of the Reformation. Where the two wings meet is the tower containing Cosin's famous **Black Staircase**. At the north end is Bishop Tunstall's chapel and his clock tower and beyond them on its mound the nineteenth-century keep, which is still in use and is not open to the public.

The castle proper is entered through Cosin's portico (1663) and the original doorway put in by Bishop Bek. Beyond a wooden door, once part of Cosin's choir screen, is the **Buttery**, with Tudor-timbered walls and huge serving hatches worthy of the mountains of food that must have passed through them. Records survive from a somewhat earlier time of a visit to the castle by Edward III and his queen, Philippa of Hainault, when the fare included two thousand three hundred fresh herring, thirty-three geese, one hundred and ninety-two chickens, one thousand one hundred eggs, with half a porpoise and fifteen piglets thrown in for good measure. Over the hatches can be seen Bishop Fox's arms of a pelican feeding her young. The **Kitchen** beyond, once a guardroom, is a Fox conversion, with Tudor brickwork and roof and three gargantuan fireplaces. It is still in business as a kitchen for the college students, and some of the tables in it have been serving food for hundreds of years.

This same sense of continuity is met with on the other side of the Buttery in the **Great Hall**, now the college dining hall. It is one of the largest medieval rooms in Britain, comparable with those at Christ Church, Oxford, and Trinity, Cambridge, and surpassed only by Westminster Hall. The wooden musicians' gallery is nineteenth-century, but the two stone galleries on either side of it, intended for trumpeters, date back to Fox. The windows have been greatly altered and only two on the west side bear any traces of original work.

Beyond the north end of the hall is Bishop Cosin's remarkable **Black Staircase** of 1665. When built it was simply bonded into the wall, and Tuscan columns had to be added much later when the whole structure began to sag. It still does. This beautiful staircase forms the link with the north wing and the two Norman halls built by Pudsey. The lower one was quite early divided up into smaller rooms, and Bishop Tunstall built a gallery in front of its exterior wall in order to give a direct approach to his new chapel at the east end. On the left can be seen this once exterior wall and its magnificent and very elaborate entrance doorway. The upper mouldings, always protected by a roof, still show up sharply, but the jamb mouldings are weathered, probably because the flight of stone steps leading from the courtyard to this main entrance to the castle had open arcades. Tunstall's chapel itself is interesting chiefly because of the carved stalls, many of which he brought from his other palace at Auckland. One of the seats has a carving of a man pushing a woman in a wheelbarrow. The organ was once part of the cathedral's instrument built by the celebrated Father Smith.

Up a second flight of stairs is the **Constable's Hall**, now known as the Norman Gallery – and 'gallery' is the right description now that all the northern section has been partitioned off into offices. The arcading, particularly on the south side, shows what a magnificent place it must once have been: a superb pattern of tall arches over each window, flanked by pairs of smaller ones, all with rich zigzag decoration.

The **Norman Chapel** comes as the climax of the guided tour: now restored after the severe damage it suffered in 1840 when the keep was under construction. 'Not too spacious but sufficiently handsome,' noted Lawrence the monk. They were not over-given to praise in those days. A small building, with a nave and two aisles and six circular piers, its honey-coloured stonework glows gloriously in the dimmest light; its capitals are adorned with figures of plants and animals and grotesques. It was probably built between 1070 and 1080 and is one of the most moving and beautiful sights in Durham.

Yet the joys of the city by no means depend only on its cathedral and castle; they are only part of its ambience; and the visitor who drives away after seeing them without making one of Sir Nikolaus Pevsner's 'perambulations' is depriving himself of a unique experience, for I know of no other British town except Edinburgh where buildings of great distinction in a wide variety of styles from medieval to modern rub shoulders so harmoniously and in such a compact space. The whole of Durham can be seen on foot in a matter of a few hours: a visit which can be happily enlarged into days without tedium.

If you have toured medieval Durham, the best plan is to take a look at its Stuart and Georgian face and leave Victorian and modern additions till last. By a fortunate chance the city is so arranged that the progression comes naturally and a car is needed only for the final lap.

Start, then, from the castle and walk towards the cathedral along

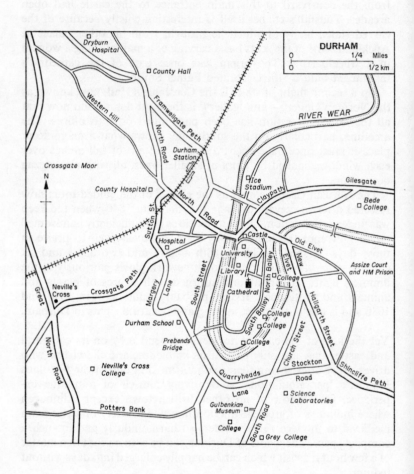

the left-hand side of **Palace Green** past Bishop Cosin's Hall, not actually built by Cosin but a century later when it was the arch-deacon's house. Its doorway is one of the most decorative creations in Durham. Next to it is the old Bishop's Hospital which actually *was* built by Cosin, in 1666, as an almshouse – it is now used by the university for lecture rooms. Across the green is the Union Building of 1820 and the Salvin Library (1858), the north part of which is another Cosin creation of 1669. These are flanked by the Exchequer built by Bishop Neville in the fifteenth century and by the seventeenth-century fabric of the Grammar School, founded in 1541.

Palace Green is superb by any standards, but living constantly in the limelight, on the processional route to the doors of the cathedral, it has a self-conscious air and lacks the cosy charm of its neighbouring streets and College Green to the south. Near the Chapel of the Nine Altars, Dun Cow Lane leads into the **North Bailey**, facing the representation on the north-east end of the cathedral of the dun cow and the two milkmaids who traditionally directed St Cuthbert's monks to the site of 'Dunholm', the place the Saint had posthumously chosen for his final resting place and which he had recommended to these faithful bearers of his coffin in a dream. Till the milkmaids stepped in they had been sorely puzzled to know where Dunholm was.

North Bailey, with its extension of South Bailey, once enclosed within the curtain wall of the castle and shut off by the Watergate leading to the river, must be among the most unspoilt and charming streets in Britain: a straggling curve of Stuart and Georgian housing, most of it in university ownership. It is an enclosed street, with buildings pressing closely on either side, and the occasional gaps that allow glimpses of the cathedral and the outside world add immeasurably to its charm: a decorous place with a strong flavour of Jane Austen. Opposite the entrance from Dun Cow Lane is the church of **St Mary Le Bow**, a name recalling the arch or 'bow' in the steeple of the old church through which the road once ran. The steeple fell in 1637 and the church was so seriously damaged that it was not rebuilt for twenty years. A tower was added in 1702 and a grand restoration took place in 1875. Inside it has Cosin-style woodwork and a rood screen, stalls and font cover of Queen Anne's time. It is normally kept locked and permission to view has to be got from St Chad's College next door. Alongside it is Bow Lane, from the bottom of which there is a view of the old town walls, most of which have now been pulled down.

Walk southward along North Bailey and there is a fine view of the

Chapel of the Nine Altars, seen head on, and then of the sixteenth-century gatehouse leading into **College Green**. As the name implies, this became the home of the cathedral canons after the dissolution of the monasteries when the old premises were put to new use. It is still very much the churchman's home from home. Less formal than Palace Green, it is nearly as rich in fine buildings, some might say richer: the medieval Exchequer with early eighteenth-century font; the Deanery; and the monastery's octagonal Kitchen with its rose garden. Opposite, across the green, is a terrace of Georgian houses, displaying at the west end a blocked arcade which probably formed part of the medieval granary. The choir school on the west side has a facade of 1800 but parts of it are obviously much older. The free-standing octagon near by is an early Gothic Revival conduit house of 1751 and looks particularly charming among its trees. Was it put up to match the octagonal kitchen? Behind it is a nineteenth-century imitation Tudor building, the Registry, to add a final bizarre touch to the scene. In the north-west corner close to the Galilee Chapel are the stables. The north wall with tiny windows in the loft was probably part of the monks' latrines, with a window to each seat. Far below, down the cliff that falls steeply to the river, in Stygian gloom, is the Norman prison, once reserved for long-term offenders. Special permission is needed to visit this grim dungeon.

Opposite the gate at the entrance to College Green, North Bailey merges into **South Bailey**, the more attractive of the two. On its right-hand side, tucked into a natural break in the street line, is the tiny church of **St Mary the Less**. A church has stood here since the twelfth century, but it was in ruins by Victorian times and was rebuilt in 1846/7 by Pickering without much attempt to retain the spirit of the original. The pseudo-Norman chancel arch is, however, a spirited piece of derring-do, and we should be grateful to Pickering for preserving the beautiful early thirteenth-century sculpture of Christ in Benediction which now stands over the entrance to the vestry. South Bailey ends with the archway of the **Watergate** (1778), beyond which lie woods and the river crossed by the elegant **Prebends' Bridge** (1772) by George Nicholson, with three high semi-circular arches. From its parapet there is a view upstream to the far older **Framwellgate Bridge** of Bishop Flambard, rebuilt towards the end of the fourteenth century, widened in 1760 and substantially remodelled in 1892.

From Prebends' Bridge there is almost an embarrassment of good walks along the river banks and through the woods. If time is limited cross to the west bank and walk towards Framwellgate for the most famous of all Durham views: of the towers of the cathedral rising in splendour above the trees and the mill house and weir. It is a reminder of the great part the river played in the foundation of Durham – and still plays, as a stage for university regattas and for family outings in a boat. Here as elsewhere in Durham the town and gown atmosphere is unmistakable: an echo of what Oxford must have been before the arrival of the motor car.

An alternative walk is to turn right below the Watergate without crossing Prebends' Bridge, along a track that passes the old mill house (now the School of Archaeology) and up a lane realistically called 'Windy Gap', close under the walls of the Galilee Chapel, to emerge in Palace Green. Or again, without crossing Prebends' Bridge, one can turn left through the woods past the little nineteenth-century folly/temple known as the Count's House. Near by in the early 1800s lived the remarkable three-feet-three-inches-high Polish dwarf, Count Joseph Boruwlaski, a great favourite in Durham society. 'Tom Thumb's uniform', preserved in the Town Hall, belonged to him. The walk ends at **Elvet Bridge**, like Framwellgate a very ancient structure, many times widened and rebuilt since Bishop Pudsey created it in 1160.

Across Elvet Bridge is the 'new town' (like Edinburgh's a splendidly Georgian affair) that grew up outside the city walls. Of its streets **Old Elvet** is the most attractive: a very gracious assemblage of eighteenth-century houses that have to keep company with the screaming red brick of the Shire Hall (1897/8). The two best Durham hotels are in this area, one of them, the *Royal County Hotel*, with memories of Cromwell and allegedly of Charles II, whose names it has boastfully seen fit to blazon in capital letters on the walls of its gruesomely trendy bar. At the top of the hill are the Assize Courts, now the Crown Court, 1809/11 by Francis Sandys, completed by Ignatius Bonomi, a very sympathetic building and well placed – next to the gaol. Off New Elvet is **St Oswald's Church**, associated with the hymnologist John Bacchus Dykes who wrote *Holy, Holy, Holy, Our Blest Redeemer*, and *Nearer my God to Thee*, sung as the *Titanic* went down. From here there is a fine view of the cathedral towering above the town. St Oswald's itself does not give an impression of age but actually dates from the twelfth century, though the east end was rebuilt in 1864. It has some fifteenth-century choir stalls and an unusual sedilia, but perhaps its most attractive feature is the west window of Ford Madox Brown glass made in 1864 by Morris and Company. Near by in Hallgarth Street is Hallgarth House (1700), and up an alley opposite it traces of the medieval monastery's tithe barn.

Back over Elvet Bridge is the city centre, at its heart the market place, all revolving nowadays around the whims of the traffic police-man in his wood and glass cubicle, a real god in the machine who could in a moment snarl the whole city up in an inextricable traffic jam. Tentative attempts to 'pedestrianise' the area are under way, and in time it may be completely banned to the motor-car. Here the atmosphere is predominantly Victorian, and none the worse for that. The city church of **St Nicholas**, the National Westminster Bank Building (1876) and the equestrian **Statue** of the third Marquess of Londonderry by R. Monti (1861) vie with Philip Hardwick's **Town Hall** (1851), which has a most striking and beautiful hammer-beam roof in imitation of Westminster Hall.

Out of mercy to the overworked visitor one should end one's con-ducted walk around Durham at this point – near the car parks in Claypath. Really determined sightseers who care to continue east up Gilesgate will find at the top of the hill opposite St Giles's Church a path leading to a fourteenth-century gatehouse, all that is left of the **Kepier Hospital** founded by Bishop Flambard and moved to this site by Pudsey. After the Dissolution of the Monasteries it passed into the hands of John Heath, a Londoner, whose wooden effigy in Elizabethan dress can be seen in **St Giles'**.

For the final visit in Durham take the car and make for the southern ring road. From the market place cross Elvet Bridge, fork right into New Elvet, right again into Church Street, cross the traffic lights into South Road, take the first road right and then smartly left into the congerie of university buildings for the **Gulbenkian Museum**, the only museum in Britain wholly devoted to oriental art. It is a treasure house for the specialist but also has great appeal for any lover of rare and beautiful things. The building itself is modern and purpose-designed. It has an unusual slatted iron roof, a high gallery round two sides, and three tiers of galleries below, approached by a wide descending staircase at one end and a circular iron staircase at the other. The museum has an Egyptian Room, but perhaps the most appealing exhibits are Malcolm MacDonald's collection of Chinese pottery, the Dragon Robes of the Chinese court, the Japanese paint-ings and jade, and the mysterious 'Tankas', which look like banners of embroidered silk but are really paintings representing the divine principles, used at Buddhist ceremonies to assist meditation.

Colourful events in Durham include the **Miners' Gala** on the last Saturday in July; the University Regatta in mid-June; the Festival of Twentieth-Century Music held in the great hall of the castle in

October; and Oak Apple Day, 29 May, when the cathedral choir sing from the top of the tower, fulfilling a promise given by the monks who from this same perch watched the English victory at Neville's Cross in 1346. The Tourist Information Office is next to the Town Hall.

Before leaving Durham I should mention three remarkable places in its vicinity: Finchale Priory, the old church at Pittington, and Ushaw College.

First, then, **Finchale** (pronounced 'Finkle'), for many years a holiday home for the monks of Durham.

Take the Consett road out of the city, turning off it for Framwellgate Moor. At the first set of traffic lights in the village turn right for Newton Grange, after which the Priory is signposted.

The approach through housing estates and through waste land used as a wartime dump is an odd preparation for the Arcadian scene where the track ends: grey ruined walls, a farmhouse, the curving river running placid and deep above the weir between meadows and a wooded bluff. There is a caravan camp near by, but it is hidden by the rise of the ground and a belt of trees.

Here in 1115 at the age of fifty came a hermit called Godric, a seafaring man who had been to the Mediterranean and the market-places of the Levant, and here he stayed for another half century till at last he died and they could canonise him. After retiring from the sea he had spent eleven years searching for a suitable retreat, until told by St Cuthbert in a dream that Finchale was the place to go. As will be remembered from the legend of Dunholm and the milkmaids, Cuthbert was never very strong on directions, and it was only during a chance visit to Durham monastery that Godric actually discovered where Finchale was.

After that his progress was rapid. Tales were told of his asceticism and of his habit of spending a whole night standing in the river with water up to his neck. Such credentials were irresistible and the pilgrims began to arrive, building him first a rough shelter and a wooden church and then in 1150 a rectangular stone one, dedicated to St John the Baptist. After his death at the age of one hundred and five the hermitage was occupied by a pair of curator monks till in 1196 it became a daughter cell of the Durham monastery. Extensive rebuilding was begun in 1237 and has left a most interesting and unusual legacy. Many religious houses made a practice of putting up temporary structures while their new chapels and cloisters were being built, but it is very rare to come across extensive and well-preserved traces of them, as here at Finchale. They lie to the east of the church near the river and include a hall which would have been used for dining, a solar at the north end, and a large room beyond it which was probably the warming house.

The church, rebuilt in 1296, incorporated much of the earlier work. It had north and south aisles to both nave and choir, a low vaulted crossing tower carrying a spire, a south transept containing an altar to the Virgin and a north transept and chapel dedicated to St Godric himself. This proved altogether too massive a building for the needs of the handful of monks who used it, and in 1364 it was scaled down by the removal of the aisles and the founder's chapel. The evidence for this can still be seen in the blocked arches and the new tracery windows that were substituted. At the same time the south aisle of the nave was incorporated into the cloister to form a north walk, and the whole cloister was rebuilt.

Far more of this cloister survives than the low crumbling walls and foundations in the grass usually met with at such sites, and this makes it easier to visualise Finchale as it was in the days of its prosperity. In the chapter house the original stone benches still line the walls, and there is a fine vaulted cellar to the refectory. However, most of the monastic buildings seem soon to have fallen into disuse, once the custom grew for the monks on their annual holiday to be allowed into their prior's hall to dine and amuse themselves. This building – in form a medieval manor house – is now being excavated. Its most interesting feature is an oriel window in the cellar which was said to have the mystic property of removing sterility and guaranteeing pregnancy to any woman who (after appropriate ceremonies) sat on the seat beneath it. The historian Grose remarks cynically: 'It may perhaps be needless to observe that since the removal of the monks it has entirely lost its efficacy.' That may or may not be, but certainly there must have been some hearty laughter in the neighbourhood when immediately after the dissolution of the house under Henry VIII the Prior married. Some verse commemorates this union:

> The Prior of Finkel hath got a fair wife
> And every monk will have one.

A far cry from the ascetic St Godric. A cross in the grass of the choir marks the spot where his coffin once stood.

At about the same distance from Durham, almost due east of the city, is a unique architectural gem, the old church at **Pittington**.

However, only the dedicated enthusiast would be urged to seek it out, for it is hidden away behind crooked roads at Hallgarth, a mile outside the village, and even when found it is certain to be shut. But when the keys are finally unearthed (they can be had from Miss M. Reed, 6 Front Street, Low Pittington) an eye-opening surprise awaits the visitor to this remote and ancient church in its belt of trees, a place the world has passed by.

The richness of the arcading inside is due to the priors of Durham who for centuries had a country retreat in the neighbourhood and liked to worship in style. They wanted, too, a style that reminded them of their own cathedral church, for the extraordinary **North Arcade** of Pittington, built in Bishop Pudsey's time, has the same pattern of alternating cylindrical and octagonal pillars as Durham's nave and the arches above them resemble those in the Galilee Chapel. The effect, especially of the writhing decoration of the cylindrical piers, as though a vast python has wound itself around them, is remarkable but almost too overwhelming for so small a church. The south arcade has less bravura: it is Early English, as are the upper stages of the otherwise Norman tower. The tiny windows above the north arcade are part of a Saxon church which stood on the site. The grave cover under the tower carries an inscription, 'One bearing the name of Christ is buried in this grave' – apparently a reference to a man named Christian, one of Pudsey's masons. In the jambs of the most westerly of the Saxon north windows are two of the very few wall paintings that survive in the county: on one side the consecration of St Cuthbert by St Theodore; on the other St Cuthbert's vision of the death of a holy man falling out of a tree.

Ushaw College, the great Roman Catholic seminary, stands four miles west of the city, reached by a minor road off the A1. The College's origins lie with the Reformation and the flight of many persecuted Catholics to the Netherlands, where in 1568 William Allen (created a Cardinal in 1587) founded the English College at Douai for the training of missionary priests to win back England to the Old Religion. During Queen Elizabeth's reign four hundred and fifty priests came back secretly to their homeland, of whom a third were captured and killed – martyrs to set beside the Protestant victims of Mary Tudor.

The repression of English Catholics did not end with Elizabeth's death. In one way or another, if in less violent forms, it persisted well into the middle of the nineteenth century, Catholics being long barred from all important offices under the crown. However, in

1792/3 a group of refugees from Douai, driven out by a fresh perse-
cution at the hands of French revolutionaries, came back across the
Channel and, after living in a variety of houses near Durham, in
1808 eventually settled at Ushaw.

Their first buildings were modest in size and Georgian in spirit,
but this changed during the nineteenth-century religious revival and
its reflection in stone in the shape of Victorian Gothic, whose high
exemplar was Augustus Welby Pugin. In 1842 he began work on St
Cuthbert's chapel at Ushaw. His work was carried on by his son,
E. W. Pugin, and by Dunn and the brothers Joseph and Charles
Hansom. The spiritual drive of the foundation itself through all the
years since Allen's work at Douai has never altered and can be
sensed by any visitor, whatever his religion, who steps inside the
place. It is a missionary spirit. The Douai martyrs, still lovingly remembered, are near the heart of it, as are the names of the six
cardinals, fifty archbishops and bishops and the many thousands of
priests who have been trained here. And in a sense the buildings
declare it too, in the sumptuous decoration of chapels and in the
long, bare corridors and the austere classrooms and studies that
surround them.

The College is open to visitors, but as this is a busy workaday
institution it is best to write or telephone well in advance, either to
the President or to the Procurator. In plan the buildings recall
monastic foundations that would have been familiar to William Allen
and also the colleges at Oxford and Cambridge that were arising
about this time – a complex of quadrangles, courts, lecture rooms,
halls and refectories, a library, an infirmary, a cemetery, and several
chapels, of which that named for **St Cuthbert** is by far the grandest,
just as the ring, taken from his coffin, is among the most celebrated
of Ushaw's relics and is still used by the Roman Catholic bishops of
Hexham and Newcastle at ordinations of priests. The chapel's
original builder was the elder Pugin, but it was much altered and
enlarged in the 1880s by Dunn and Hansom. It consists of a sanctuary
and choir separated by a rood screen from an ante-chapel. The total
length is one hundred and sixty feet (the choir alone being ninety
feet) and the height to the apex of the roof is fifty-six feet. The effect
is certainly superb to any lover of high Gothic Revival; the colours
are very striking, a spectacular kaleidoscope, with every tint thought
out down to the tiling of the floor. Particularly effective is the view
from the ante-chapel through the arch of the rood screen to the reds
of carpets and roof at the high altar, or from the altar towards the
great west window, which is Pugin's east window translated. Much

of the glass in St Cuthbert's is of Pugin's design, as are the choir stalls: fairly prosaic work, to be honest, and not a patch on Cosin's at Brancepeth. Pugin's again is the **Paschal Candle** opposite the arch of the rood screen – a gloriously Gothic work that was exhibited at the Great Exhibition of 1851. Also in the ante-chapel is Karl Hoffman's statue 'Our Lady of Help', carved from a single block of white Italian marble. Near by in the Sacred Heart Chapel is A. W. Pugin's original altarpiece for the main church: a subdued but appealing work.

Grouped close to St Cuthbert's and the cloisters are a number of smaller chapels, all Gothic in spirit but individual in colour scheme: the faded blue and green **Lady Chapel** (1882/5) with a most attractive ceiling and the altar of Our Lady of the Rosary; E. W. Pugin's **Mortuary Chapel**, sometimes called 'St Michael's' or 'Purgatory'; the Chapel of **St Charles Borromeo** (completed 1859), containing a stone screen behind the altar; and opposite it, across the narrow passage of the cloister, the Oratory of **The Holy Family** (1852), with a fine Adoration of the Magi by Von Roden. All these are the work of the younger Pugin. Much larger is the chapel of **St Bede**, containing Hansom's original ceiling but otherwise very much in the modern idiom, and the Chapel of **St Joseph the Worker** by A. W. Pugin, completed by his son. It has some interesting small wood carvings of the Stations of the Cross and Karl Hoffman's statue of the Saint.

A still larger room that began life as a chapel is now the **Exhibition Hall**, often called 'The Music Room' and in fact a theatre and concert hall. The refectory behind the central quadrangle is an enormous though graceless room. The **Library** at the east end of the south front is even larger – one hundred and twenty feet long and thirty feet high – by the Hansom brothers. It contains a fabulous collection of books and medieval MSS. Perhaps the most unexpected discovery is the fine modern swimming bath at the centre of the labyrinth: rather like coming on a squash court in the Vatican. But it is a timely reminder to the visitor that for all its long memories and traditions Ushaw is essentially a place for the young. Incidentally, there has been a swimming pool of a kind on this same spot for a century, which must surely make it one of the earliest built in England – another small instance of planning and the missionary spirit.

Chapter 3

Durham Circular – to Teesside

From Durham take the A177, the Stockton road, to Coxhoe. A left turn here at the traffic lights and then a right turn shortly afterwards leads a mile through the industrial village of Kelloe to **St Helen's, Church Kelloe** in a rural setting. It is normally locked but the rectory is near by and it is worth going in search of the key to see the church's remarkable late Norman **Cross** against the north wall of the Chancel. There are three tiers of decoration featuring St Helena, the discoverer of the traditional 'true Cross'. Above, an angel is seen handing her a scroll, presumably the general directions or else a command from the Almighty. In the middle sector the Saint is seen again with another female figure, probably her mother. In the bottom panel, now armed with a sword, she threatens Judas to make him reveal the resting place of the cross, which is seen rising between them. He carries a spade.

The church itself has been much restored but contains interesting features, including an unusual mix of lancet, Perpendicular and Decorated windows. The squat tower is Norman and the whole building is heavily buttressed. Church Kelloe has long been a well-endowed living, and past incumbents have made great efforts to embellish it – hence the handsome choir stalls and, a more recent addition, the woodwork of the altar by the 'mouse man'. There is a memorial tablet to Elizabeth Barrett Browning, who was born at the now demolished Coxhoe Hall.

Return to the A177 for **Sedgefield**, a small market town grouped around a green, and rich in unpretentious Georgian houses, survivors from the days when it was a staging post on the main route between Yorkshire and the North. The motor car restored it to prosperity and it is now a lively, bustling place with a popular National Hunt racecourse. Its Shrove Tuesday football game has been played for well over nine hundred years. The best lay building is the Queen Anne manor house, now the Council Offices, with a sundial dated 1707. Across the green from it is the imposing late Georgian rectory and a church with one of the richest interiors in the county.

Locomotion Number One, Darlington North Road Station Railway Museum. A replica of the train is on view at Beamish Open Air Museum, near Stanley

The Nineteenth Century: Iron and Coal (AD 1861), one of eight mural paintings by William Bell Scott at Wallington Hall

Killhope Wheel, Upper Weardale. The 34-foot-high overshot water wheel, an impressive relic from the former Park Level Lead Crushing Mill

There was a Norman foundation on this site, but apart from the tower of 1490 the present fabric is thirteenth century. The pillars of the nave date from 1246/56 and are so reminiscent of the Chapel of the Nine Altars at Durham that it seems certain that the same masons were engaged on both. The transepts appear to be of a slightly later time. A clue to the date of the chancel is given by a stone (no longer visible) inscribed 'Sir Andrew de Stanelae, Master of Greatham, lies here.' It is in the traditional position of a founder's stone and would suggest *circa* 1280. If Sir Andrew had known that this memorial to himself would be completely hidden by a night storage heater he might have repented of his generosity. Incidentally the Greatham Hospital at the mouth of the Tees of which he was Master is still in being and still after seven hundred years devoted to its charitable purpose of providing a home for 'poor brethren' (see page 75).

The real charm of Sedgefield lies in the interior furnishings: in particular, the beautiful carved woodwork of the screen, with its lozenge patterns – a direct quotation from the nave pillars of Durham Cathedral – and the panelling of the chancel and choir stalls. The resemblance here to Cosin's furnishings at Brancepeth and Bishop Auckland is no accident, for Denis Granville, who came to Sedgefield as rector in 1667 and was the inspiration behind most of the work, was Cosin's son-in-law. Sadly, this distinguished churchman and man of taste was driven from England during the Glorious Revolution of 1688. Regarding rebellion against his lawful sovereign, James II, as 'a hellish crime', he was naturally a target for the Whigs who came in with William and Mary: a devoted Protestant at the papist court in exile at St Germain, he was anathema to the Jacobites, who let him die in poverty. 'My religion and loyalty are not of the new cutt but of the old royall stamp,' he wrote. He was no Vicar of Bray.

Apart from his furnishings, Sedgefield church has three other points of special interest: the magnificent beams of the fifteenth-century roof revealed during restoration work in 1915; the big octagonal font, probably donated about 1450 by a wealthy Newcastle merchant, Roger Thornton; and, at the east end of the north aisle of the nave, a pair of brasses that may be of the Hoton family of about the same time, showing a man and a woman as skeletons inside their shrouds.

Near Sedgefield is **Hardwick Hall**, built by John Paine for a Stockton merchant, John Burdon. Modernised and pebble-dashed it is now a

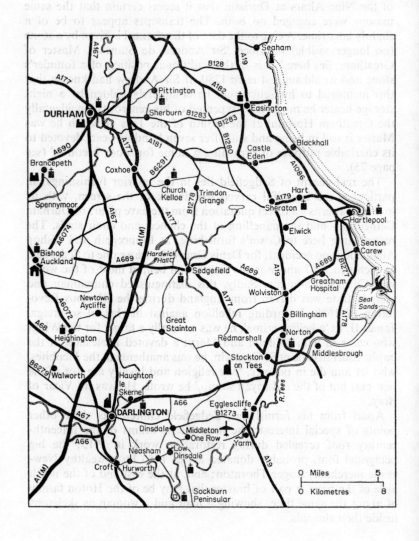

luxury hotel. Part of the grounds, including an ornamental lake, have been turned into a 'countryside park' ablaze with notices – DANGEROUS BUILDING, DANGEROUS BRIDGE, KEEP OUT. Paine's classical temple (1754/7) is among the lamented casualties of the years of neglect that have befallen this once great estate; the columns of the portico are still standing on two of its sides, but the roof is off and this beautiful building is now almost wholly ruin.

From Sedgefield take the A689 westward to join the A1 motorway in the direction of Darlington. Just to the right of the A1, near Newton Aycliffe, is **Heighington**, a village hiding itself from the main routes, not easy to penetrate but rewarding. Its beautiful church of St Michael, built by the Hansards of Walworth Castle, is set back in a corner of the green. Both the chancel and tower arches have mouldings similar to those in Durham Cathedral, with which they are almost exact contemporaries (1095). With the exception of the higher part of the tower (fifteenth century), the south aisle (seventeenth), and the north aisle (nineteenth century), the fabric is Norman. An unusual feature is a south doorway into the tower, the original entrance to the church. The pulpit from *circa* 1500 is the oldest in the county. The arms of the various families connected with St Michael's – Hansards, Jennisons and Surtees – can be seen on the hatchments of the tower wall and on the door curtain. The Surtees's pew is at the east end of the south aisle and their vault is in the churchyard. Robert Surtees, author of the classic *History and Antiquities of the County Palatine of Durham*, lived at Mainsforth near the present colliery village of Ferryhill. His equally famous kinsman, Robert Smith Surtees of Hamsterley, was the creator of Jorrocks, who made his first appearance on the literary and fox-hunting scene in the *New Sporting Magazine* in 1837.

From Heighington rejoin the motorway southwards and branch off to the left for **Darlington**.

This is, *par excellence*, the town for the railway enthusiast, for as all the world knows it was here that it all began at the opening of the Stockton–Darlington line, and *Locomotion Number One*, which on 27 September 1825 hauled the first public passenger/goods train from Shildon, will by now, after years on the platform at the Bank Top station in Darlington, probably have been moved to the newly opened railway museum at the North Road station, a Mecca for every devotee of Steam.

Darlington's involvement arose naturally out of the growth of the long-established coal trade from the Durham and Northumberland mines. The first engineering experiments in steam transport, such as George Stephenson conducted at Wylam and Killingworth collieries, were aimed at speeding up the movement of coal wagons underground and at raising them to the surface, but attention soon came to be directed also to movement from the pit-heads to the ports. Two Quakers with coal-mining interests, Jonathan Backhouse and Edward Pease, wanted a railroad as opposed to the alternative project of a canal, and convinced many local business men of the advantages. An Act authorising a railway was passed through Parliament in 1821; a Company was formed, with the inspired choice of George Stephenson as its engineer; and three and a half years after the first rail was laid the line was open.

In Darlington's museum in Tubwell Row, close to the town centre, there hangs a spirited picture of the scene on the great day, painted many years later by a local artist, John Dobbin, from a sketch he had made at the time. *Locomotion* is seen proceeding grandly over a viaduct drawing a long train of coal trucks, open trucks packed with standing passengers, and the superior closed carriage modelled on a stage coach called *The Experiment* containing the Company's officials. General excitement and wonderment is expressed on the faces of bystanders on foot, in farm wagons and carriages, as the new age passes proudly by. A horseman preceded the train, which managed to get up twelve miles per hour at the beginning of the journey and then the unbelievable speed of sixteen as it neared Stockton. Neither terminus is still in use, though Darlington's old North Road station can still be seen up Station Road and has been turned into a museum in time to celebrate the hundred and fiftieth anniversary of the opening of the line. The matter seems to be at present unsettled, but it may be that by the time these words are printed Dobbin's fine painting and many of the old photographs, models, prospectuses, uniforms and tickets relating to the railway in the **Tubwell Row** museum may have been transferred to **North Road** along with *Locomotion* itself – all that can be said with certainty is that wherever it is shown the material is unique and marvellous. Incidentally, a working replica of *Locomotion* has been built for the anniversary and after it has made a world tour it will probably find a final home at the Beamish Open Air Industrial Museum (see page 88).

The centre of Darlington is the usual English mixture of antiquity heavily overlaid with Victorian building and almost swamped under modern concrete and glass. The beautiful spire of its parish church is seen against a backdrop of a ring road and the cooling towers of a power station: they get on surprisingly well. Darlington in fact is far more sympathetic than many similar towns. Its main street is built on two levels: the raised High Row, still retaining some of its eighteenth-century houses, facing the charmingly tatty Victorian market. The official handbook to the town proudly announces plans to remodel this attractive building, though the clock tower at least is to be retained. A great deal of senseless destruction has already occurred. In Crown Street the Edward Pease Public Library maintains an efficient information service, and one can only hope that by the end of the century there will be something left to show the tourist.

The **Parish Church** (closed on Tuesdays) is one of the finest in the North and no lover of ecclesiastical architecture should miss it. If Durham Cathedral is almost wholly Norman, Darlington is as completely Early English. It took slightly longer to build: sixty years against Durham's forty. All its windows, with the exception of those in the aisles and in the crossing tower, are plain lancets, with no new-fangled tracery. The nave was completed in 1220, and from the presence of composite pillars and vaulting shafts at its east end was probably intended to be stone-vaulted, but this idea was abandoned, and what we have now is a splendid fifteenth-century wooden roof. The aisleless chancel (restored 1864) and the south transept are in the same style: the north transept, though built at much the same time, is plainer. The glass is all mid- or late-Victorian, but of exceptional standard and adds greatly to the beauty of the church. The altar-backing, by the same local artist, John Dobbin, who painted *Locomotion* on its viaduct, is mosaic and may not appeal to all tastes. It certainly did not appeal to the Dean and Chapter of Westminster Abbey for whom it was made. When they rejected it, it was cut down to more modest proportions and erected here.

The most unusual feature in the church is the recess for an Easter Sepulchre to house the representation of the Entombment which was often set up in medieval times during Holy Week: a more imposing version of the Easter Garden or Christmas Crib of our own day. Usually only temporary wooden structures were erected, or use might be made of an existing tomb recess, but during the fourteenth century it became customary to have purpose-built ones, as here.

Darlington was a collegiate church: therefore, as might be expected, the fifteenth-century chancel stalls dedicated to the comfort of infirm and elderly canons are opulent and rich with 'poppy-head' decoration at their ends and good misericorde seats. The view looking back into the nave from the chancel arch presents a serenely formal effect of grey stone. The reverse view from the west towards the high altar through the soaring chancel flanked by the matching transept arches must also have been very fine. Unfortunately it has been wholly ruined: first by a rood loft of 1381, then by a lower arch put in by Sir Giles Gilbert Scott in 1863, with organ pipes above it.

As is so often the case with our northern churches, the internal furnishings, apart from the woodwork, do not amount to much. The worn effigy of a woman on the south wall of the south transept is supposed to be of Berengaria, Coeur de Lion's Queen. The only possible connection seems to be through Bishop Pudsey, who built the church and had associations with Richard, though by no means always friendly ones. A Celtic cross and a Saxon sun-dial in the north transept and a Cosin-type wooden font cover complete the decoration. But it is in the splendid austerity of its Early English style that the attraction of the building lies.

Another historic church stands alongside the A66 – the main Darlington to Teesside road – St Andrew's at **Haughton le Skerne**. Awkwardly placed at the junction of two busy roads, in spite of its solid Norman tower it is not very attractive externally, but is very richly furnished with seventeenth-century woodwork. From the west end there is a fine view towards the Norman chancel arch and the identical pulpit and reader's desk that flank it, along the two rows of box pews with their regimented poppy-heads aligned like crosses in a war cemetery. There is a good font cover surmounted by a dove, and at the entrance to the chancel a brass showing a lady in late Elizabethan dress, Dorothy Parkinson, who died in 1593. It is accompanied by some touching commemorative lines in verse:

> Here lyeth she whose birthe whose life whose end
> Doe all in one hir happy state commend
> Hir birthe was worshipfvll of gentle blood
> Hir vertvovs life still praised for doing good
> Hir godly death a heavenly life haith gained
> Which never cann by death or sinn be staned

As a convenient base for touring the county Darlington provides a good alternative to Durham, lying as it does on the main line between King's Cross and Edinburgh, near a motorway, and served by two excellent hotels: the *King's Head* in the centre of the town, and *Europa Lodge* on the A66 going south, a former country house which was chosen by Willie Whitelaw for his conference with the Ulster leaders. A lively, dynamic place, Darlington has a thriving daily newspaper of its own, the *Northern Echo*, one of whose editors was the controversial journalist and social reformer W. T. Stead who went down with the *Titanic*. The town is also fortunate in having open country on its doorstep, particularly to the south, where the Tees ambles its way through the watermeadows in a series of loops and 'S' bends, nearly doubling back on itself around the **Sockburn Peninsula**, a strangely remote place to find near the perimeter of a busy airport and within a dozen miles of the huge Teesside conurbation. A turning along a cul-de-sac in the village of Neasham leads into the heart of it, where the metalled road gives out and only a farm track serves the last half mile to the ruined church by the river and the ancient home of the Conyers family.

This was the country of the Sockburn Worm, a splendidly voracious serpent of enormous size that terrorised the neighbourhood, perhaps in emulation of its more famous cousin at Lambton. Tradition has it that it was slain by good Sir John Conyers, using the ancestor of the falchion which his descendants presented annually to the bishops of Durham on Croft bridge in token payment of rent of their estates and which hangs today in the Monks' Dormitory at Durham. The lords of Sockburn escaped with such token payment supposedly as a reward for Sir John's services in the matter of the Worm, but more probably because of the help which another Conyers, Sir Roger, gave to the bishop in 1140 when the rest of the local nobility failed to support him against the Scots. The Worm, in the form of a wyvern with its head severed, still survives in the municipal arms of Darlington. It was at Sockburn that William Wordsworth met his future wife, Mary Hutchinson. Coleridge was in love with her sister Sara, and she was the subject of one of his poems, with implicit references to old Sir John:

> She lean'd against the armed man,
> The statue of the armed Knight;
> She stood and listen'd to my lay,
> Amid the lingering light.

When recently I was approaching this blissfully sylvan spot I heard below me a furious barking and baying. I thought the otter hounds must be out, but it was a kennels packed with lively and attractive dogs of all shapes and sizes, prominent among them almost as many dalmatians as in the Disney picture. 'This is the one that bites,' the lady who breeds them remarked to me, indicating a Jack Russell that was eyeing me in a purposeful kind of way. I was glad to see she had it securely tucked under one arm. The pink sandstone church of **All**

71

Saints just behind the wire which the more athletic animals were trying to vault in their excitement is now a total ruin, though some of the gravestones and the effigy of a cross-legged knight are preserved in what was once the Conyers chapel alongside the nave. The local impression is that this is the monument of Sir John, the wyvern slayer, who died in 1395, but Pevsner rejects this, saying the dating is wrong.

To reach this charming and forgotten part of the world take the road south out of Darlington as far as Croft (in whose rectory Lewis Carroll lived as a boy), turning left before the bridge (where Henry VIII's sister Margaret was greeted by the local nuns on her way to her marriage with James IV of Scotland) for **Hurworth**, one of the most elegant and beautiful of villages. Beyond it, following the course of the river, is **Neasham** where one turns down the cul-de-sac of Sockburn Lane. Visiting this area demands use of an Ordnance Map, for road and river endlessly twist and turn and there are very few bridges. Not far from Neasham, hidden deep in the lanes between the river and the Teesside airport, is the hamlet of **Low Dinsdale**, with a manor house and tiny twelfth-century sandstone church (restored 1875). Unfortunately it is usually locked. Another village I would strongly urge the visitor to find is **Middleton One Row**: a curve of elegant houses overlooking the wooded valley and placid waters of the Tees.

From here, going eastward along a minor road to Aislaby, or alternatively by the much busier and uglier B1273 from Dinsdale Station to Urlay Nook, the visitor reaches the bridge over the Tees at **Yarm**. Its very attractive main street, reminiscent of Aylesbury or Amersham or indeed Stockton before it grew too big, is one of the most charming in the North, and its *George and Dragon* inn has a plaque to commemorate an early meeting of those enthusiasts who were later responsible for the building of the Stockton–Darlington Railway. Facing it on a bluff on the north side of the river is one of the most agreeable of small Durham churches at **Egglescliffe** (not to be confused with Eaglescliffe further up the Stockton road). What is more, it is that great rarity in this part of the world, a church that is kept open – or at least it was when I was there. It can be reached by road, but perhaps the more attractive approach is to ask at the *Blue Bell* inn for permission to leave the car in its car park and walk along a path uphill to where St Mary's stands on its wooded plateau between the valley of the Tees and the agreeably-named Nelly Burdon's Beck. Windows and west tower are of the fifteenth century; the south door is Norman. However, the real treasure of the church is the seventeenth-century woodwork in the Cosin manner. Seen on entering, the effect is very striking against the background of white-washed walls. The box pews in the nave are a bit institutional, like a number of courtroom docks laid end to end, but there is a glorious screen under the chancel arch and the choir stalls are real beauties. A restored pulpit and wooden roof complete the sumptuous show. In the two-bay south aisle is a much worn effigy of a cross-legged knight, and there is another in the porch. Here notice also the rudimentary outline of a human face on the capital to the left of the door. The churchyard with its shady trees is flanked by a number of attractive brick houses and the *Pot and Glass* pub. There are fine views over the Tees valley and of the large Victorian railway viaduct of 1849.

Ahead, to north and east, best approached by the A19, lies the vast industrial complex of the new county of Cleveland, stretching along both banks of the river and including within its boundaries the towns of Middlesbrough, Stockton on Tees, Billingham and Hartlepool. An economy originally based on coal was later developed and diversified to include iron, steel, shipbuilding, chemicals and light engineering to form one of the most dynamic growth areas in the country. Anyone who wants to study industrial Britain can find his raw materials here in abundance. But the other side of the coin of prosperity is seen in the mass of urban development, one town spilling over into the next and swallowing the fields and villages in its way. Yet the scene has power and in certain lights a sombre beauty, and embedded in it are architectural gems surviving from an age – not so very long ago – when Billingham was a village, and the most mushroom of Teesside towns, Middlesbrough, had a population (at its first census in 1801) of twenty-five.

Middlesbrough, though the real heart of the conurbation, does not belong to this Guide, being Yorkshire by origin. Its neighbour across the river is **Stockton on Tees**, a much older community whose history goes back to the thirteenth century when its castle, guarding the river crossing, belonged to the bishops of Durham. It chose the losing side during the Civil Wars and paid for it when the Roundheads ordered this amenity to be pulled down. 'Old Noll in his day out of pious concern/This castle dismantled, sold all but the barn,' some versifier wrote. The barn referred to was in existence until comparatively recently. Stockton, however, kept its ancient market, which was established in 1310 and is still held in the High Street. This wide thoroughfare enclosing the eighteenth-century town hall at its centre must once have been one of the most imposing in the North: at first glance it still is. But most of the Georgian houses that lined it have been swept away and the present shop fronts are vintage Marks and Sparks. The parish church of St Thomas dates from 1710. Sir Christopher Wren seems to have been asked for his advice about the building, and most of that advice was rejected, even down to the choice of basic material – Sir Christopher suggested stone: Stockton got brick. The new modern hotel in the High Street, the *Swallow*, has a room commemorating the town's most useful citizen: John Walker, chemist and druggist, who in 1825/6 invented what he called 'friction lights', the first ancestor of the safety match. The fascinating story of how he came to do so is told by Doreen Thomas in her excellent booklet *Strike a Light* (Teesside Museums Service) which can be bought at the *Swallow*'s reception desk. In 1827 Walker started selling his invention commercially, but since he was too public-spirited to patent it most of the immediate profits of his ingenuity rubbed off on a Mr Samuel Jones who marketed the matches under the name of 'Lucifers'. No less a person than Michael Faraday visited Walker in his shop and later publicly saluted his 'Instantaneous Light Apparatus'. Contemporary with John Walker is the **Ticket Office** of the old Stockton and Darlington Railway at 41 Bridge Street. The office has now been re-opened as a museum to coincide with the one hundred and fiftieth anniversary celebrations of the Line. No railway enthusiast should miss it (Tel. 62803).

The seemingly endless housing on the town's northern outskirts becomes more attractive as it approaches **Norton,** a smart commuter village, very ornamental with a double row of trees and some pleasant classical houses grouped around greens. At one end is the church, the mother church of Stockton, and near to it a pond, a living reminder of a quarrel between a medieval rector and his flock. It seems that the villagers were granted rights to a market and chose to hold it on Sundays on land very close to the church – proof in itself of a somewhat unharmonious relationship. The Rector retaliated by flooding the land and the base of the market cross his parishioners had erected. And there in the middle of this man-made pond the cross remained for centuries. Its base now supports what is optimistically called a fountain, though it is more a trickle of water. Far happier relations exist today. Some of the glebe land was sold as a site for a housing estate, and by mutual agreement its new streets are named after past rectors. So even the market cross seems to have been forgiven.

The **Church** itself is mostly transitional, of the late twelfth century, but shows interesting traces of Saxon work in the lower stages of the crossing tower, with its deep-set triangular-headed windows, and in both transepts, particularly the north one. The nave is Transitional. An unfortunate twentieth-century restoration has put in low windows in the aisles, filled with dingy glass. The chancel was rebuilt in the thirteenth century and then again in 1496, when the upper stage of the tower was added. Under the crossing is one of the finest monuments in the county: the early fourteenth-century effigy of a knight in chain mail with crossed legs and a shield bearing the arms of the Blakiston family. However, no Blakistons lived in the vicinity in those times, and what seems to have happened is that when they came to Norton they purloined the effigy (probably that of Sir Roger Fulthorpe, whose arms appear over the cusped arch at his head) and replaced the device on his shield with their own, thus getting themselves a Crusading ancestor on the cheap. Seated at the knight's feet is a bedesman reading his prayers and near by a dog and a lion fighting. Most piquant of all are the face and hands of a tiny, grotesque figure peering over the top of the shield. In the churchyard is buried the safety match inventor, John Walker. His tombstone is a replica, the original having been removed to the Preston Park Museum. Stockton's Ropner Park with its lake is worth a visit.

From Norton take the road towards the coast to Wolviston and bear right on the A689 for the **Hospital of God** at **Greatham**. It was founded by a bishop of Durham, Robert de Stichill, for the care of forty 'poor brethren' in either 1272 or 1273 on lands that had belonged to Simon de Montfort but were granted by the Crown to the bishopric on the great rebel's death at Evesham. The Hospital then fell on hard days and was reconstituted in 1610 to house thirteen poor unmarried men of advanced age. By Victorian times its finances had improved to such a degree that the numbers were restored to forty, and now women pensioners are also cared for. Some institutional gates and railings surround a green, white with snowdrops in early spring and shaded by ancient trees. On the right-hand side of the green is the one-storeyed **Hospital** by Jeffry Wyatt (1803), which Pevsner unkindly derides as 'undeniably mean in size and finish', reserving particular scorn for its 'starved bell turret'. It is certainly on the small side, but to my mind very appealing. Straight ahead, at the end of the tarmac drive, is the restored and largely rebuilt Master's House; to the left, to the west of the parish church, the **Chapel**, rebuilt in 1788 and most sympathetically restored in the 1960s in blue and white with red furnishings by Francis Johnson of Bridlington.

With a fine flourish of medieval trumpets Robert de Stichill dedicated his hospital 'to God, to Blessed Mary, and to Saint Cuthbert, for the good estate of the founder, for the souls of all Kings of England, of the prelates of York and Durham, of the monks of Durham, of the people of Saint Cuthbert, and for the souls of all the faithful departed.' Though his buildings in their Georgian shape and elegance would greatly have surprised him, the good bishop would certainly have felt himself at home had he been able to attend in the spirit at the dedication ceremony of the new Hospital Almshouses on 7 June 1974, almost exactly seven centuries after his munificent gift to the poor of the diocese. His successor in the Durham see addressed the Architect, the Master Builder, and then the Foreman of the Works in turn, asking them if they were satisfied that the plans had been made and carried out with care, and the craftsmanship to be honest and good and worthy of the Foundation. The Foreman duly replied: 'Indeed it has been our just pride to do this work soundly and carefully.' Only then did the Bishop pray: 'May Almighty God, who hath given thee a will, and skill to do these things, of His mercy accept your work to His glory, and the benefit of this foundation, through Jesus Christ our Lord.' How de Stichill would have relished the style. But the new almshouses, so soundly blessed, are as up-to-date as new techniques can make them. They take the form of twelve two-person flats, four three-person bungalows and three single-person bungalows, all centrally heated by low-pressure hot-water radiation, with double glazed windows, tiled bathrooms with non-slip finish and safety handles, french windows on to a paved terrace, emergency lighting, television aerials and laundering facilities. The total cost was £152,000. I should add that the Hospital is private. Prospective visitors should write well beforehand to The Agent, The Estate Office.

One last word for the Greatham area itself, which has been producing salt commercially since the twelfth century and is today the home of *Saxa* and *Cerebos*. Close by on the coast are **Seal Sands**, a haven for migratory birds, now increasingly threatened by industrial expansion on Teesside.

Ahead lies **Hartlepool**, the result of a shot-gun wedding between the very ancient community of Hartlepool proper and West Hartlepool, its mushroom nineteenth-century neighbour and supplanter.

West Hartlepool has the docks, a golf course, Ward Jackson Park, one of Britain's two dahlia testing grounds, two sailing clubs, a maritime museum, the excellent and imposing *Grand Hotel*, and, on its traffic island, Christchurch, built in 1854 by B. E. Lamb, a hotch-potch of every conceivable style and one of the oddest churches in England. It has also a handsome sea-front at **Seaton Carew** offering a vast expanse of sands, with splendid views along the coast to the cliffs and Cleveland Hills on the Yorkshire side of the Tees estuary.

'Old' Hartlepool, as it was usually called before the amalgamation which it fought for many years to prevent, is a small decayed fishing town on a headland overlooking the entrance to the harbour. From the Seaton Carew promenade or from the sea its line of surviving houses looks extremely picturesque, like an early Victorian print, but far too many of them have been ruthlessly pulled down and the new housing developments inland are the result of thoroughly in-sensitive planning. In medieval times this was the most important haven on the north-east coast and therefore a place of considerable wealth. Here Bishop Pudsey fitted out his vainglorious ship to go crusading and Edward I's ambassadors embarked for Bergen to fetch the ill-fated 'Maid of Norway' to succeed her grandfather on the Scottish throne. It was here too that the forces of Philip II of Spain were expected to land to support the Catholic rising of the Northern Earls. But its history goes back much further than that: to St Aidan's foundation of the monastery of Heruteu, of which St Hilda, or Hild, was abbess for eight years before moving on to Whitby. It is because of her royal blood (she being related to the kings of Northumbria) that the present abbey choir enjoy the privilege of wearing red cassocks.

However, it was its connection with the Bruce family, originally 'de Brus', that secured Hartlepool its later importance. Members of this Norman clan which came over with the Conqueror and later produced the famous Robert, victor of Bannockburn, built most of the abbey **Church** we now see. Standing proudly on its headland under a strong, squat tower, it looks far too grand for its surround-ings – the small scatter of picturesque eighteenth- and nineteenth-century cottages, some of them dressed in fisherman's black, that face the sea, hemmed in to the west by modern housing estates, and not another building of any authority in sight, apart from the ancient Sandwell Gate and fragments of the town wall. From the landward side the place has a secretive, shuttered air. It has always been a community of strong parochial flavour, isolated even from its own harbour and incurious about the world – to such a degree that during the Napoleonic wars a monkey washed ashore from a wreck was supposedly hanged as a French spy. For many years its inhabitants had to endure the derision of their neighbours in cries of 'Who hung

77

t'monkey?' till they became decidedly touchy on the point. Indeed, the visitor would be well advised to keep off the topic of monkeys in this neighbourhood. Nowadays the town seems to be shrinking still further in on itself; its population is falling, many people preferring to live in West Hartlepool for its shops and entertainments. This is a great pity, for so potentially attractive a town, with the sea and shipping on its doorstep and boasting a charter from King John, surely deserves a better fate than to fade away as someone's poor relation.

Its **Abbey Church of St Hilda's** is undoubtedly a beauty: one of the best 'Transitional' buildings in the North. It fortunately survived the bombardment of the towns by elements of the German fleet in December 1914.

With the exception of a chancel of 1924 by W. D. Caroe – a thoroughly sympathetic work based on a study of old plans and prints – and of a crumbling Norman doorway, the church is almost wholly of the period 1185/1215. The two sides of the nave are dissimilar. The piers on the north are all uniform; while on the south three are alike, but the other two show differences from their neighbours and from each other. Again, the arches on the south side have nutmeg decoration on the hood moulds and are obviously older than those to the north.

Both chancel and nave are aisled, and the aisles have transverse arches which (unusually) extend into the chancel, the probable reason being that there were once chantry chapels at their east end. The clerestory is particularly fine: the treatment in nave and chancel is quite different. From the massive external buttresses of the tower and the blocked arches at the west end of the church it rather looks as though at some stage it was intended to extend in this direction and build a west transept, but perhaps the money ran out. As it stands, St Hilda's is in all conscience big enough: it could be the cathedral of Teesside if it were more centrally placed. A thorough restoration in the twenties of this century will have preserved it for some time yet, but it is hard not to see for it a fate similar to that other one-time home of St Hilda: the ruined abbey at Whitby in just such a position by the sea.

Hartlepool has a further distinction of which the municipal guidebook rightly boasts – the natural fluoride in the water makes it the despair of local dentists. Dental decay rates are only 50% of the national average.

Near Hartlepool are the commuter villages of Elwick and Hart. Elwick's wide green makes it by far the prettier, but **Hart**, on the

main road back to Durham, has the mother church of the area: a
squat building with a Norman tower tucked secretively away among
the trees. There was a church here in the eighth century which may
have been visited by Bede, and traces of it can be seen in Saxon
stonework and a triangular-headed window (or possibly doorway)
above the present chancel arch, vestiges of a tower above the arcades
of the north aisle, and a blocked window half way down the wall of
the nave. The corbel heads are Norman. Norman also is the wonderfully solid font near the south porch made from one block of stone.
The north arcades and the chancel arch are fifteenth-century. The
south arcade may be from 1600 and suggests Moorish influence in
the bow shape of the arches above their capitals. Built into the west
wall is a Saxon sun-dial and beneath it two stone columns found on
the site, similar to those at Bede's Jarrow and Monkwearmouth. The
fine ninth-century Saxon cross head was turned up by the plough of
a local farmer in 1967. Under the early Norman tower arch is the
remarkable fifteenth-century font, decorated with primitively carved
heads and symbols of the four evangelists. It is still in use. Hart is
fortunate in having its pre-Reformation stone altar-slab with the
usual carved crosses to represent the five wounds of Christ. The
church also owns a chalice of 1571 and an Elizabethan Bible, known
here as the 'Armada Bible', because in celebration and thanksgiving
for the great victory someone, during that summer of 1588, jotted
down his own observations in one of the margins.

From Hart the quickest way back to Durham is along the A19,
turning left on to the A181 at the old and very elegant brewery
opposite Castle Eden golf course. A slightly more roundabout route,
continuing along the A19, takes in the fine Early English church of
St Mary at Easington. Again, a detour for the specialist in church
architecture. The return to Durham would then be along the B1283.
The coastline between Hartlepool and Seaham has some dramatic
cliffs but is chiefly famous for its coal mines, some of them running
far out under the sea. Names like Easington and Horden are famous
among the Durham pitmen.

Chapter 4

Durham Circular – to Gibside

Take the A1 going north out of Durham. Some six miles along it is **Chester le Street**, once Roman *Concangium* situated on the *Vinovia* (Binchester)–*Pons Aelii* (Newcastle) spur, a branch of the main military road from York to Hadrian's Wall. Nothing now remains of the fort, though various inscriptions and tombstones have been found here. The town has been swamped by mediocre modern building but still has character and from a distance is redeemed by the beautiful spire of its **Parish Church**.

This stands on ground hallowed by the presence of the body of St Cuthbert, brought here from Lindisfarne on its wanderings in 882. It lay buried for a hundred and thirteen years before the monks guarding the sanctuary took to their travels again in fear of Danish raids, and during this time Chester le Street became a place of importance. The early history of the present church is shadowy until 1286, in which year Bishop Bek gave it collegiate status with a dean and seven prebends. Most of the fabric dates from the thirteenth century, though the north and south walls of the chancel are older, as evidenced by the Early English sedilia and piscina.

The one hundred and fifty-six-feet-high **Spire** was built in 1400 and is the finest in the county. Just to the left of the west doorway is a curious window carved out of a single slab of stone. It is in the wall of the 'anchorage', itself an unusual feature, with four rooms, occupied in 1383 by a hermit, John de Wessington. By 1630 it had become an almshouse for poor widows, whose running battle with the curate who wished to evict them and occupy it himself was recorded in the churchwarden's book. The local community, determined to support its widows, paid for a female protector and, eventually, for three male protectors when the curate became more militant. Some of the entries make poignant reading: 'Payd to Izabell Car for watching with the poor widowes in the ancharidge for feare of some displeasure done them by Mr Willis, 8 pence'; 'Payd when the churchwardens went to Durham when Mr Willis procured a warrant to duck the poor widowes, 6 pence'.

The door knocker at Durham
Cathedral, one of the finest examples
of Romanesque-style metal work of
the twelfth century

Statue from Biddick Hall, Lambton
Park: the Lambton Worm being
slain by Sir John Lambton, on
whose legendary heroic action and
broken oath the famous ballad is based

The Durham Miners' Gala.
Lodge banners in procession
approaching Elvet Bridge
during their annual
celebrations, held on the last
Saturday in July

The 'Guysers' in the New
Year's Eve tar barrel
procession at Allendale

Inside the church is the squint in the upper room of the anchorage which enabled the occupant to watch the altar in the south aisle. Here there is an ornate thirteenth-century doorway and in the north aisle a plainer one of similar date. The Lumley Chapel, which was originally at the east end of the north aisle, was pulled down in 1837 and replaced by a chapel by Bonomi which inside is not obtrusive but on the outside looks like an interloper. The approach to it up the north aisle is flanked by the remarkable **Effigies** placed here by the Elizabethan antiquarian John, Lord Lumley to honour his family: some of the greatest oddities to be found in a Christian church. Three of them – numbers three, four and ten, counting from the east end – are genuine medieval (and probably Lumley) monuments which he got permission to remove from Durham. Number ten, a knight in chain mail holding a bird in his bosom, is particularly fine. All the rest are faked-up Elizabethan imitations, headed by one Liulph, the legendary founder of the Lumley line, in such profusion that some of them had to have their feet cut off to squeeze them all in.

From the family church of the Lumleys it is only a short distance to their castle, which is reached by turning south on to the A1 from Chester le Street and then, after a mile, sharp left up the hill. **Lumley** is now in the booming medieval banqueting business and has recently been converted into a luxury hotel. It looks too good to be true. However, make no mistake: it is one of the most perfect fourteenth-century castles in the North, the only developing hand before the tactful modern alterations being that of Sir John Vanbrugh in the 1720s.

The west front, which contains the banqueting hall, stands grandly in its park among the trees, looking across a golf course and the Wear valley to Chester le Street steeple. The east front and present main entrance face the thickly wooded ravine of the Lumley Burn, and from here the castle looks much as Sir Ralph Lumley must have known it at the end of the fourteenth century when he fortified his existing home and built the great gateway leading to his quadrangle/ courtyard with its powerful angle towers. The block opposite the entrance is the oldest part of the building and encloses the original gateway, an extremely beautiful one; the wings and the east front on to the burn are Sir Ralph's additions. The Tudor round-headed windows and the armorial shields are the work of antiquarian Lord John who so packed the church at Chester le Street with his statuary. Not satisfied with ordering stone effigies of ancestors at so many to

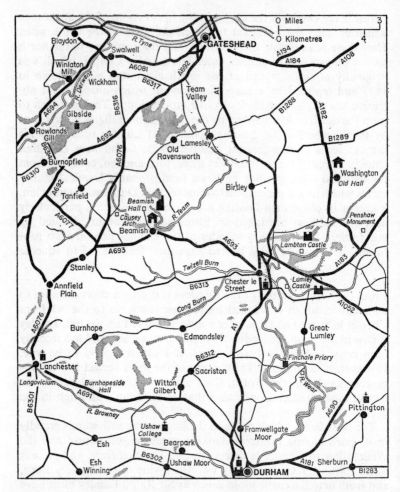

the yard, he also provided a gallery of equally fictitious paintings for his castle – an example later taken up with enthusiasm by the Scots at Holyrood House. This kind of fetishism so provoked King James I and VI that, on a visit to Sir John, after listening to the Bishop of Durham eulogising on their host's remote forbears he burst out: 'Oh mon, gang nae further: let me digest the knowledge I ha' gained, for I didna ken Adam's name was Lumley.' The fine fireplace in the barons' hall is also the work of this pedigree-loving lord.

In 1721 Richard Lumley, first Earl of Scarborough, invited Sir

John Vanbrugh to stay with him to plan alterations for 'state, beauty and convenience'. Vanbrugh, who preferred the grandeur of the North to what he called the 'tame, sneaking South' and thought Lumley 'a noble thing', was happy to oblige and the plans were quickly put into effect. A drawing of 1728 shows the castle as it is today. The west front was given an outside staircase a raised platform and a new doorway with a line of oval lights above. On the south front, in the interests of 'convenience', modern windows replaced the Tudor ones and a new staircase was built, giving inside access to the first floor at the expense of spoiling the symmetry of the courtyard into which it juts. The beautiful library is entirely to Vanbrugh's design, as is the banqueting hall (apart from the stucco decoration, which is the work of Italian artists). Below is one of the finest medieval kitchens in England.

Two miles from Lumley as the crow flies is another baronial extravaganza, **Lambton Castle**. Return to the A1, turn north, and immediately after Chester le Street take the A183 in the direction of Sunderland. The walls of the estate soon appear on the left-hand side of the road, standing much higher than the norm. The explanation for this becomes apparent at the entrance to the **Lambton Lion Park**. Over its two hundred acres roam not only lions but elephants, baboons, hippos, giraffes; and near the picnicking ground and the restaurants is a Pets' Corner and a 'Bear Reserve' for the children.

The castle itself is dramatically situated high above the north bank of the Wear, but unlike Lumley is not a genuinely ancient building. It was put up in 1797 as a mere hall on the site of an Elizabethan manor house and only changed its appearance and name in 1833. But if the castle is not old the Lambton family certainly is. Its most influential member was the first Earl of Durham, known as 'Radical Jack', a colleague of Lord Melbourne's in Queen Victoria's first Whig administration and the author of the famous 'Durham Report' on Canada which foreshadowed the growth of the self-governing Dominions and started that long and comparatively peaceful evolution of Britain's empire into a Commonwealth. Radical Jack was the hero of the Durham pitmen and after his death a grateful county built him a Grecian monument on a hill top, but it was a much earlier Lambton who made the name a household word and part of northern folklore, the hero of the ballad *The Lambton Worm*.

Whisht! lads, haad yor gobs,
An' aa'll tell ye aal an awfu' story,
Whisht! lads, haad yor gobs,
An' aa'll tell ye aboot the Warm.

It was a beast that started from small beginnings, a tich of a worm
petulantly thrown down a well by 'young Lambton', who had hooked
it in the Wear instead of the salmon he had hoped for. By the time he
had returned from the Crusades it had grown into a serpent of
gigantic size that milked the local cows and terrorised the neighbourhood. When sated with food it would curl itself round a rock in the
river or round the crest of Penshaw Hill. After consulting the local
witch, John Lambton learned that he could only kill it by wearing
armour covered with steel blades which would slice it to pieces when
it wound itself around him, and by tackling it not on dry land but in
the water, where the current would carry away the slivers before they
could miraculously grow together again. In return he must vow to
kill the first living creature he set eyes on after the destruction of the
monster: otherwise no Lambton heir for nine generations would die
in his bed.

The young man swore the oath and slew the Worm. He had
arranged with his father for one of his hounds to be slipped to
him once the deed was done: the sacrifice. Alas! in his excitement
the old man forgot and hurried to the river bank, so that it was on
him that the hero's eye fell as he climbed sword in hand from the
Wear.

Clearly a version of Theseus and the Minotaur, but with a novel
twist to the tail; for whereas in the Greek legend it is the returning
Theseus who causes his father's death by failing to change the black
sails of the ship for white, here it is *old* Lambton who by forgetting
to loose the hound brings down the curse on the heads of his luckless
family. For of course young Lambton cannot bear to kill him.

Whisht! lads, haad your gobs,
An' aa'll tell ye aal an awfu' story . . .

John's son is supposed to have drowned near the chapel where his
father swore the fatal vow. Sir William Lambton was killed at
Marston Moor, fighting for his king in the Civil Wars: his son,
another William, also fell in battle, at Wakefield in 1643. There was a
General Lambton who suffered torments in his last illness but was
unable to die until his pleas for release were answered and he was
lifted out of bed. The ninth heir was Henry Lambton MP, and on

26 June 1761 he brought the long roll-call of victims to its end by collapsing and dying – in his coach.

Near by, towards Sunderland, is the conical shape of **Penshaw Hill,** the Worm's habitat when on dry land; and on top of it now stands the monument to Radical Jack Lambton commemorating, with the due solemnity of the time, the distinguished service he rendered to his county as 'an honest, able and patriotic statesman and as the enlightened and liberal friend to the improvement of the people in morals, education and scientific requirements'. The architects of this splendid tribute to Whiggery were John and Benjamin Green, who built Newcastle's Theatre Royal, and here there is the same Grecian influence, for Penshaw is a copy of the Temple of Theseus in Athens. It sounds ridiculous but it looks magnificent, crowning its hill-top and, outlined against the sky, a landmark for miles around. The road to Sunderland runs very close to it, and for the energetic it is no great climb up the litter-strewn hill. However, my strong advice to the traveller is to pass by and keep his illusions, for at close quarters the temple is a mess, its massive pillars defaced with graffiti and a chain-wire fence enclosing it now that the foundations have been declared unsafe. One of these days it will simply tumble down.

Keep Penshaw at a distance, therefore, and turn left off the A183 on to the Gateshead road, the A182, for **Washington Old Hall,** a site no American at large in the north of England should willingly forgo, for it was the home of five generations of direct ancestors of the first President of the United States. The family – then spelt 'de Wessyngton' – came here in 1183, and a junior branch of it remained in possession till 1613: forty-three years later George Washington's grandfather emigrated to the colonies and the story began. The Hall's connection with the United States is still very strong, for it was largely with American money that it was rescued and restored in the 1930s; the American flag is flown here on Washington's birthday and on Thanksgiving Day, and an annual ceremony takes place on the Fourth of July.

Though there are traces of twelfth-century work, the present building is basically a small seventeenth-century manor house surviving in a village on the outskirts of a 'new town' development. The contents and the associations are what attract. There is some good Jacobean panelling in the drawing room, a striking portrait of the first President painted on drum parchment by John Trumbull of Salem, Massachusetts, two busts by the French sculptor Houdon, and a fan presented to Martha Washington by Lafayette. It is suggested in the Hall's brochure that the three stars and two stripes in the arms of the de Wessyngtons could have provided the inspiration for Old Glory, the United States flag. It is a piquant thought that the flag of liberty might be derived from this family of hard-nosed feudal lords.

From Washington continue six miles along the A182 for **Gateshead** at the south end of the Tyne bridges that link it with Newcastle, its twin town within the new Tyne/Wear conurbation. It is a large industrial workshop full of bright new building and high-rise flats, hotels and offices. If it lacks pretensions to charm and presence, it is a hundred times removed from the place so starkly described by J. B. Priestley in his *English Journey*, written at the depth of the Depression in the 'thirties. It has a fine park at its centre, complete with a lake and museum, and an interesting fourteenth-century church cowering under the girders of the giant George V bridge. Robert Trollop, who built Newcastle's Guildhall, is buried here, and there was once a statue of him in the graveyard pointing proudly across the water at his handiwork. The view from this point of the towers and spires of Newcastle rising above the squalid litter of its quayside is still very fine, though only a pale reflection of the city as shown in eighteenth-century prints. Those who like the bustle of a waterfront might care to cross over on foot by the low-slung Swing Bridge on the site of the Roman *Pons Aelii*. It sets historic Newcastle in perspective and in a sense explains Gateshead too, serving its bigger and more famous partner which now could hardly exist without its buses, car parks, residential area, shopping centres and hotels on the less cluttered side of the Tyne. A creative, progressive place, Gateshead was the home of Sir Joseph Swan, the inventor of the incandescent lamp, and of that unparalleled and never to be forgotten comedian, Stan Laurel. Here the first Tyne steamboat was launched on 21 February 1814. On 19 May it began to run a passenger service between Newcastle and South Shields. By November the faithful craft had become known as *The Perseverance*.

From Gateshead follow the A6081 westward along the Durham bank of the Tyne for Swalwell, and turn left here on to the A694 towards Rowlands Gill for **Gibside**, now alas only the ghost of the superbly planned Georgian estate it once was. From near Winlaton Mill the motorist can pick out on the opposite hillside a massive column standing on its own, the desolate, decaying mass of the

Hall (1603/20), the Banqueting House (1751) and the shell of the Orangery. That these fine buildings should have been allowed to fall into ruins is a sad commentary on all concerned. Fortunately, the jewel of the whole complex, Gibside **Chapel**, remains – one of the most ravishing small buildings in England.

To reach it, leave the A694 at Winlaton Mill at the National Trust signpost. Resist the impulse to follow its direction too faithfully into a caravan park, but stick to the road, and after three-quarters of a mile turn left at another Trust signpost up a cart track. From the car park a wicket gate leads to the wide, grass avenue lined with Turkish oaks, at one end of which stands the one hundred and forty-foot-high **Column** to 'British Liberty' (higher than Nelson's in Trafalgar Square) and at the other the **Chapel**, which will immediately remind admirers of Palladio of his **Villa Rotunda**. It was built in 1760 by James Paine as a mausoleum for the Bowes family and was consecrated as a church in 1812. It is kept locked, but there is a key at the charming small house next door, among the trees.

The Chapel is in the form of a Greek cross, of which the entrance forms one arm, the other three being semicircular apses with tunnel vaulting. Under the cupola at the centre stands the altar, and at each corner are box pews for the family, tenants and staff, with elliptical pews in the two side apses for outsiders, a typically patrician arrangement. The pews are made of cherry wood, but the three-tiered pulpit with its sounding board is of mahogany, Victorian by date but clearly as Georgian in spirit as the rest of the building.

The family for whom this wonderfully harmonious tomb was erected was in life anything but peaceful and orderly. A strain of 'Gothick' fantasy ran through it, as can be seen to perfection in the Bowes Museum at Barnard Castle (see page 320). The creator of Gibside was George Bowes, who planted the woods under the direction of Capability Brown, built the banqueting hall and the orangery and, in 1754, set his estate workers to erect the famous column. He was for thirty years a Whig MP, and this probably explains his honouring of 'British Liberty' in so quaint and typical a fashion. He also planned the avenue and was turning his attention to the chapel when he died. It was his only daughter and heiress who by her marriage in 1767 to John, ninth earl of Strathmore, linked the Bowes and Lyon families, from which sprang Queen Elizabeth the Queen Mother. Left a widow at twenty-seven with five children to bring up, the 'Unhappy Countess', as she came to be called, married an Irish adventurer and friend of the Prince Regent, Captain Stoney, whose outrageous attempts to make her part with her estates by kidnapping and other brutalities eventually led him to gaol for life. The ruined orangery which lies beyond the car park seems perfectly to reflect her sad and troubled spirit. On my last visit there, in the autumn of 1973, I heard a rumour that this small and lovely building is to be restored. It had better be done quickly.

From Gibside make across country for Burnopfield, Stanley and then the Chester le Street road, the A693, for the open-air **Industrial Museum** at **Beamish,** the first of its kind in Britain. By the turn of the century it will undoubtedly be one of the sights of Europe, for the North-East was for long the trend-setter in industrial techniques, and where else could you hope to find another such accumulation of the detritus of a vanished age. The plans are made, and the fortunate visitor to Beamish will one day be able to take a tram ride through the streets of a small Victorian town, visit a colliery of that era, and watch a demonstration of horse husbandry at a Dales farm. It is already possible to take a retired Gateshead tram for a short, nostalgic ride along the boundaries of the Beamish park. But today's visitor to the open-air section of the museum can walk a long way along dusty tracks and see very little except a row of old cottages and a car park. If you can find them, there are some remarkable sights – the rebuilt Rowley railway station (1867), the eighteenth-century home farm and its gin-gang, a very elementary use of horse power, and a gigantic steam excavator of 1931 – but to enjoy Beamish now the visitor would be well advised to make straight for **Beamish Hall** (included on his ticket), where he can have tea or a drink in an Edwardian bar before inspecting the smaller items of the collection.

The Hall is a handsome building of 1803, much enlarged and altered some ninety years later. As the museum's guide-book so rightly points out, its elegance and the handsome grounds that surround it form a remarkable contrast to the neighbouring pit village of Stanley and help to explain some of the legacy of bitterness that still bedevils industrial relations to this day. The exhibition area occupies only part of the Hall and is cramped; it can be impossibly crowded at the height of the holiday season. But the showcases are fascinating: vintage typewriters, photographic equipment, old newspapers and posters, ledgers for the coal trade out of Newcastle, late Victorian cottage interiors, a schoolroom of the 1920s, and a complete chemist's shop which once stood in Finkle Street, Stockton, containing a splendid array of bottles and items once owned by John Walker, the inventor of 'friction lights'. Most poignant of all are early photographs of pitmen and one of the original trucks used in lead mining, made especially narrow to negotiate the tracks that burrowed into the moor. Indeed, Beamish is in many ways a humbling experience: enough to put our own complaints to shame. On the way out is the stable block, which displays some early fire-fighting equipment, the glorious gleaming brass of the 'Nelson', coaches, carriages, and a hearse, in its tender and fussy way one of the most touching exhibits of all. In the neighbourhood is a still earlier industrial marvel: the **Causey Arch**. Built by a local man, Ralph Wood, in 1727/9, this single-span stone arch, flung across the eighty-foot-deep ravine of the Causey Burn to carry the horse-drawn coal trucks of the time, is the world's first railway bridge, a century before the Stephensons. Like Beamish it can be visited from Chester le Street.

Return westward along the A693 for Stanley and left here for **Lanchester**, a pleasant village grouped around a green. It was once Roman *Longovicium*, a stronghold on the military road from York northwards to the Tyne. Built in AD 122 by the Twentieth Legion (*Valeria Victrix*), it superseded the near-by forts at Binchester (*Vinovia*) and Ebchester (*Vindomora*) which had been constructed at the time of Agricola's thrust into Caledonia. It was sacked some seventy years later when the tribes over-ran Hadrian's Wall and was not restored till 240, when it became the home of a mixed force of infantry and Swabian cavalry. An altar to the Swabian goddess Garmangabis can still be seen in the porch of the parish church. From 240 the fort was in constant occupation till the final withdrawal of the Romans from Britain. The site of *Longovicium* is half a mile south-west of the village on the Wolsingham road, but there is little to see. It served for centuries as a handy quarry for local builders, and a group of its monolithic pillars support the arches on the north aisle of the church's nave.

Lanchester's **Church** is internally one of the most attractive in County Durham. Whitewashed walls set off the stonework of the Norman chancel arch, the wooden ceiling and the three deeply inset east lights. The chancel was originally twelfth-century work, rebuilt in the thirteenth, and much of the interest lies here. There are six unusual head corbels at the east end used as stands for candles, two of which are mitred and one crowned, reminiscent of those in the Chapel of the Nine Altars at Durham. The doorway into the vestry has a worn but still beautiful tympanum, with a seated figure of Christ supported by two angels. In 1283 Durham's Bishop Bek (always on the look-out to counter and out-do the power of the Prior and regular clergy) created a deanery and college of canons at

Lanchester. There was need of them, for the parish was ten times larger than it is today. A chapel was added to the north side of the church and two new windows were put in the south wall of the chancel, the most westerly of which contains some thirteenth-century glass, with scenes of the Annunciation, the Adoration of the Magi, and the Flight into Egypt. Some of the fifteenth-century woodwork of the Canons' stalls survives. Windows in the south aisle commemorate that now almost forgotten pioneer of the railway age, William Hedley, builder of *Puffing Billy*'s sister, *Wylam Dilly*, which first ran from Wylam Colliery to Lemington Staithes in the year before Waterloo and soldiered on till 1862. Hedley's home, **Burnopside Hall**, still survives as a hotel, to the right of the main road from Lanchester to Durham. Just before Witton Gilbert a minor road to the right leads to the Catholic college of **Ushaw** (see p. 61) on the outskirts of the city.

Chapter 5

From Durham to Sunderland and South Shields

❧

Take the A690 out of Durham for **Houghton le Spring**. Few people visiting it would guess that until 1821 it was an old-fashioned market town. In that year a mineshaft was sunk in the vicinity and the character of the place completely changed. Only a handful of the older buildings remain. One healthy survivor from the very distant past, however, is the Houghton Feast, which lasts a week, starting on the first week-end after 29 September. It still attracts large crowds.

The imposing stone gateway to the parish church once marked the boundary with the rectory, which started life as a fortified tower house, was rebuilt in 1670, was given east and west wings in Georgian times, and now serves as Council offices and its garden as a public park. The living was an extremely lucrative one and attracted a number of outstanding men. It became a kind of forcing ground for high office, and, besides many deans and bishops, produced two archbishops of Canterbury, William Sancroft (1678) and Thomas Secker (1758).

The church of **St Michael and All Saints** has the unusual feature of a two-storey chantry chapel of the late fifteenth century, once free standing, now attached to it at the south-east. Traces of Norman work in the church proper can be seen in one of the windows in the north wall of the chancel, in the narrow doorway and the delightful tympanum with animals locked in deadly combat. Most of the rest of the fabric dates from the thirteenth century. The eight lancet windows in the south wall of the chancel are very deep-set and attractive; the two most easterly are nineteenth-century insertions. Most interesting architecturally are the west windows in both transepts, showing an early attempt to develop tracery. The arches are made from a single stone set below another in which a quatrefoil window has been cut: the first faltering step towards the perfection of this art as seen in the east and west windows of chancel and nave. The south transept is full of interest. On the east wall is a brass showing Margery Bellasis at prayer with a quiverful of children

91

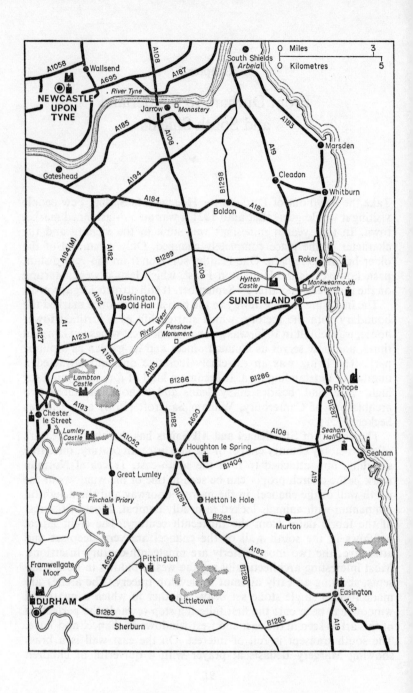

behind her. They form a gloomy little group, particularly the girls, who seem already to be bewailing their lost dowries, with eight lusty brothers to be fed. Margery was widowed for fifty-eight years, dying at the age of ninety in the year before the Armada. She was a friend of Houghton's most famous rector, Bernard Gilpin, whose table tomb stands close by her brass. Like his great-uncle, Bishop Tunstall of Durham, Gilpin tried to hold himself aloof from the religious confrontation of his times and devoted himself to administration and good works. A stipend of four hundred pounds a year – a fortune in terms of Tudor money to which today's equivalent would be something over £13,000 – enabled him to keep open house, entertaining Lord Burghley at one end of the scale and the poor of the parish at the other. He kept and educated twenty-four boys in his house, many of them going on to Oxford and Cambridge at his expense. He travelled his vast parish tirelessly and even penetrated into darkest Tynedale and Redesdale along the Scottish border, becoming known as 'The Apostle of the North'. With the help of John Heath, a wealthy Londoner who had bought up large estates in Durham, he founded the Kepier Grammar School which carried on a useful life until the 1920s. The school building can be seen east of the church, much altered, and near by are almshouses built in 1660 by a rector who was a relative of 'Leveller Lilburne' of Commonwealth times. They were derelict when I last saw them, in 1974, and one can only hope that some modern use can be found for them.

From Houghton the direct route to Sunderland and the North is along the A690. However (along a slight detour), just to the north of the mining town of **Seaham Harbour** and overlooking the bleak sea waves, is **Seaham Hall**, where Lord Byron married his 'Princess of Parallelograms', Annabella Milbanke, daughter of the local squire. A more unlikely venue for the nuptials of a Romantic poet could hardly be imagined, and the weeks he spent there with his intense young bride and his backwoodsman of a father-in-law played their part in the disastrous separation that was to follow, bringing about Byron's social disgrace and permanent self-exile from England. The marriage at Seaham was a step on the road that led to the death at Missolonghi and, through Byron's vast European fame, to the liberation of Greece from the Turks. The Hall, in whose drawing room the marriage was performed by special licence, is now a hospital, but the grounds with their fine trees still retain a park-like air.

Close to the Hall but nearer the sea is the old parish church of **St**

Mary's, described by Pevsner, who allots it a full page, as 'one of the most worth-while small churches in the county'.

Those in a hurry would be advised to give it a miss, for it is a target for vandals, is therefore kept locked, and the key has to be fetched from some distance off at the farm – first turn left off the coast road beyond the Hall. Inside the church is very dark, and there are no electric lights to switch on. It gives no great impression of age, though the small windows in the nave and the nave walls themselves are either late Saxon or very early Norman – even Pevsner cannot be sure. The chancel and tower were added in the thirteenth century. The most interesting feature is the damaged **Piscina** on the south wall of the chancel, in one alcove of which is the shape of an upraised hand, the third and little finger bent down. Under the tower arch is a print of the church as it must have looked in Byron's time, and alongside it a replica of the marriage register with the signatures of bride and bridegroom.

From the outside, if the visitor keeps his back firmly turned on the derelict vicarage and looming industrial developments to the south-east, St Mary's still makes a striking picture. Services are held once a month and the visitors' book is surprisingly well filled, but as with so many old Durham churches like Pittington and St Helen Auckland, the final impression is discouraging. The old community around church and hall has been quite supplanted by **Seaham Harbour** to the south, with a parish church of its own and two Methodist chapels. This was the constituency of Labour's first prime minister, Ramsay MacDonald. The harbour itself was built in the 1830s by Lord Londonderry, who had been overcharged at Sunderland for the shipping of coal from his collieries at Rainton and wanted a new outlet. It took only three years to build.

Just inland from the coast to the north and about half way to Sunderland is the old **Pumping Station** at **Ryhope**, the finest single industrial monument in the North, as the Trust that now runs it justly claims. Built at a cost of £9,000, it produced three million gallons of water a day for almost exactly a century before it went out of commission in July 1967. The Trust's brochure gives its specifications:

> The engines are double compound rotative, with Watts parallel motion and centrifugal over speed cut-outs. The cylinders are steam jacketed and were originally clad in timber, later replaced with asbestos. The HP cylinder is $27\frac{1}{2}$ in bore by 5 ft stroke and

the LP cylinder 45 in bore by 8 ft stroke. Steam supply was at 35 lbs psi with condenser vacuum 26 in. The beam of each engine is of double construction, 33 ft between pump rod centres and weighing 22 tons. Cylinder and pump rods and auxiliary equipment drives are taken direct from the beam in the sequence: staple well pump, LP cylinder, HP cylinder, cooling water pump, main trunnion, boiler feed water, air pump, connecting rod to crank and flywheel, and main well pump. The valves are double beat Cornish type, driven by cam-operated push rods, the cams being shaft driven from helical bevel gears on the main crank. Each valve can be manually operated from the control position. Pump strokes are counted by a pendulum system incorporated in the counter boxes attached to the beam. The crank shaft carries a 24 ft diameter 18 ton flywheel which can be barred over by using the rack mounted on the wall behind it. Originally the engines ran at 10 rpm, delivering 40,000 gallons per hour against a head of 243 ft (77 gallons per stroke). Latterly they gave 26,500 gallons per hour from 6 rpm. The pump barrels contain flap valve buckets with strokes of 10 ft 8 in, one bucket being driven from each extreme end of the beam. Water was lifted in two stages, the first discharging via an adit to a staple well, from where the staple well and pump drew water and completed the lift by discharging to a surface reservoir.

The Victorian genius was perhaps best expressed in its technology, and Ryhope Station is not only a functional object of high efficiency but also, inside and out, a thing of beauty. Its interior gleams like an engine room of a great liner, but there is also about it something of the air of a cathedral. In shape and grouping of buildings within an ordered landscape there are distinct traces of Regency good taste. It is now maintained by volunteers who run it with the encouragement of the Sunderland and South Shields Water Company.

A couple of miles to the north lies **Sunderland** astride the mouth of the Wear, next to Newcastle the largest and most important town in the North-East, the administrative centre for a district council with a population of three hundred and fifty thousand within the much larger Metropolitan County.

If industrial history can be romantic then Sunderland's certainly is. The 'sundered land' (sundered either from the mainland or from its once world-famous monastery of Bishop Wearmouth – a matter of doubt), it was listed in 1183 in the Boldon Book, the Domesday

Book of the Durham bishopric. Ships were built here for the campaigns of the Hundred Years' War. Yet centuries passed before it even became a parish in its own right. The turning point came during the Civil Wars, when in opposition to staunchly Royalist Newcastle it took Parliament's side and reaped its reward by cornering the coal-carrying trade to London – till then a Tyne monopoly. The coal was brought from the pits to the river staithes in trucks, was then loaded into Keels (flat-bottomed boats carrying about twenty tons), and rowed downriver to the sea-going colliers which could handle cargoes of up to four hundred tons. A natural development was for the Wearsiders to build their own keels and colliers: and so the foundations were laid for the enormous expansion of Victorian times. By 1857 the historian of Durham, William Fordyce, was calling Sunderland 'emphatically the first ship-building port in the world'; in case this sounds like provincial trumpet-blowing, statistics show that at the turn of the century, along with the Tyne yards, it was responsible for every third ship launched around the globe. During the Second World War half Britain's merchant ships came from the Wear, and next to the Clyde this is still the premier ship-building centre in the British Isles.

Coal itself was another element in Sunderland's growth, in emulation of collieries along the rival rivers of Tyne and Tees. Ten years of hard labour from 1826 to 1836 went into the sinking of the local Monkwearmouth pit. The seam lay deep, but no deeper than the determination of the owners who proclaimed: 'We'll go on till we sink down to Hell, and then if we don't get coal we'll get cinders.' When at last the seam was reached, local patriotism found expression in triumphant song:

> You may talk of the coal of the Tees and the Tyne,
> The Wallsend so good and the Primrose so fine,
> But I would engage to drink up byeth the rivers
> If Wearmouth Wallend waddn' beat them to shivers.

Always like Gateshead an enthusiastic town, Sunderland followed up its coal fever by a craze for railways. Its Member of Parliament for many years was George Hudson, known as 'the Railway King', who endeared himself to his constituents by buying up the Durham to Sunderland line at par when the shares were standing at only half their value. This energetic entrepreneur and wheeler-dealer did a lot for the town by building its South Dock, and even after a shares scandal forced him to resign from his companies he continued to be returned to Westminster by the faithful electors. It was he who was largely responsible for the building of **Monkwearmouth Station**, designed by Thomas Moore,* son of a local blacksmith; and a magnificent building it is to find in such parts and for such a purpose – a flourish of neo-Grecian with a huge Ionic portico. The municipality, belatedly rediscovering this treasure on its doorstep, has recently cleaned it and turned it into a museum, which Prince Philip opened in May 1973. For the enthusiast now celebrating the one hundred and fiftieth anniversary of the birth of railways this must be one of the most intriguing buildings in England. It stands on the left-hand side going north out of the town centre, just beyond the modern bridge over the Wear. The design for the first bridge on this site, incidentally, was the work of Thomas Paine, author of *The Rights of Man*, who had originally intended the bridge for Philadelphia. When opened in 1796 in the presence of vast crowds it was the biggest in England, and was to be long celebrated on Sunderland pottery.

Since those days Sunderland has diversified and redeveloped itself to take in light as well as heavy industry, being particularly strong on glass. Pyrex dishes are made here. It has docks and a harbour covering one hundred and thirty acres lying within the arms of two elegantly curving stone piers, the **National Music Hall Museum** in its Civic Theatre (formerly the **Empire**), an **Art Gallery** containing a magnificent collection of antique silver and of local early-nineteenth-century **Lustre Ware** (far and away the best of its kind made in England at that time), and a handsome Civic Centre by Sir Basil Spence. But its most cherished possession is undoubtedly Roker Park, home of Sunderland Football Club, one of the most prestigious in the Football League and, as everyone locally will remind you, the FA Cup winners of 1972/3. Near the Library is a monument to another local hero, Jack Crawford, who, at the Battle of Camperdown against the Dutch in 1797, shinned up the mainmast of the British flagship to nail Admiral Duncan's colours to the mast. Enthusiastic crowds turned out to cheer him and other victors of the great day at a grand parade in London, but Jack Crawford was an absentee, having apparently preferred to spend his time with a light of love.

Down the tangle of streets opposite Thomas Moore's station lies an attraction of a rather different kind: **Monkwearmouth St Peter's**,

---

*Pevsner says the architect was John Dobson: it is certainly very Dobsonian in design. However, Dobson's daughter makes no mention of it in her list of her father's buildings, and the attribution to Moore seems to be correct.

one of the most historic churches in Britain. The best way to reach it is to turn right immediately after crossing the bridge; if you pass the turning and get as far as Monkwearmouth Station you have to continue some distance down the one-way street and then work your way back south. Not everyone will be able to direct you, for to many Sunderland people St Peter's is a long time ago. However, if you persist you will eventually find yourself in an area of modern flats and radial roads, with below you in its grass compound the tall and narrow tower against a backdrop of cranes and shipping. Even as late as a century ago its surroundings were unspoilt, and very pretty it looks in prints of the time, surrounded by its grave-yard and a cluster of red-roofed cottages. Nowadays, imprisoned behind its railings, it has a forlorn and apologetic air for a church which has just celebrated its thirteen-hundredth anniversary and was once famous throughout Christendom.

In 664, the Council of Whitby, called by King Oswy of North-umbria, decided that the tenets of the Roman rather than the Celtic (Lindisfarne) Church should be followed, thus linking the North irrevocably with mainland Europe. One of the young nobles accom-panying the King, Benedict Biscop, chose to adopt the monastic life and visit Rome, which he did four times before becoming a monk at Lerins in France and returning home to found a monastery along the lines of those he had seen on his travels. He persuaded Oswy's son, Ecgfrith, to give him fifteen acres of land, and on it he built St Peter's church (much of whose fabric dates from that time) and a monastery whose ruins lie under the grass. The French glaziers he brought back with him produced here and at Jarrow the earliest glass (apart possibly from York) ever seen in an English building. To this monastery as a boy came Bede, though a few years later he went with Prior Ceolfrith and a band of monks to found the sister house of St Paul's at Jarrow. Monkwearmouth became renowned as a seat of learning, and from the joint monastery, among many other works of scholarship, came the *Codex Amiatinus* (*circa* 716), an illustrated Latin version of the Scriptures, now in the Laurentian Library in Florence. However, at the time of the Viking Raids Biscop's foundation fell on evil days and its later history was ob-scure until it emerged in 1083 as a Benedictine cell of Durham. It was dissolved in 1536.

A walk down the path gives an excellent view of the Saxon west wall and traces on the tower of a sculptured figure, apparently of Christ, one of the oldest in the country. The tower is an extension of the porch: the later sandstone blocks can be distinguished from the limestone below. The division between the two types of stone can be seen marked by the line of the steep gable roof of the porch above the second string course. To raise a tower of this height on walls only two feet thick was a daring and remarkable engineering feat, and it seems clear that the work was pre-Conquest.

A Saxon tower, then, above a Saxon porch. It is unlikely, however, that any of this is as early as Bede's time, for what he calls 'the porch of entry' was probably of one storey with a west entrance archway only. Now there are three archways, so alike that they must almost certainly have been built at the same time, slightly later than the rest of the seventh-century fabric. The tunnel vaulting, which until recently was thought to be the earliest in Britain, has now been shown to be a later addition. Original or not, the porch is of the greatest interest. To protect it from vandals it is now railed off by a grille, and can only be entered from inside the church through the nineteenth-century north aisle and then through a door which was originally a window in the west wall. Once there one can see vaulting, balusters, and the curious carvings. Similar work is preserved in the glass cases at the east end of the north aisle. The aisle itself is of course a much later addition to Biscop's Saxon church, whose west wall still stands much as his masons built it. Its measurements of thirty feet by eighteen and a half feet indicate the slim proportions of that church, which probably ended just short of the present chancel arch. The chancel itself is fourteenth-century and may cover the ruins of a lost church – St Mary's. The modern glass in St Peter's is by the local artist L. C. Evetts: extremely interesting and attractive work designed to let light in. Just opened is a chapter house, including a lecture room with accommodation for exhibitions and a tourist information centre. The hope is to give visitors a graphic view of the church's past back to its foundation in 674.

If this exhausts the attractions of Sunderland for the visitor, the local residents have other causes for pride in their go-ahead town. Roker and Whitburn sands are fine and attract a large bucket-and-spade population during the summer months. St Andrew's, Roker's parish church, is highly praised by Pevsner. And one cannot leave the area without a word for **Whitburn** itself, the town's stockbroker belt but also a village of beauty and charm. Newcastle has nothing to touch it; indeed, few industrial towns anywhere in Britain have.

Four miles west of the city centre on the B1289 to Washington are the ruins of **Hylton Castle**, a late fourteenth-century fortified manor house, its tower blazoned with heraldic shields. Hylton used to have a celebrated ghost, the 'Cauld Lad', a serving boy killed by his master in a fit of rage, but no one has reported him for many years now. Poor spectre, he would find the environment of the castle greatly changed and his wails would hardly be heard above the traffic. Not my favourite ruin.

Just to the north, along the coast road, is one of Nature's marvels: the vast limestone redoubt and archway of **Marsden Rock**, whose crannies house a population of kittiwakes and many other sea-birds. The bars at **Marsden Grotto**, cut out of the cliffs overlooking the bay, are a man-made attraction, a little too contrived for some tastes but certainly dramatic. The coastline hereabouts must once have been among the grandest in England. In a sense it still is – as anyone can see who follows the coast road to South Shields sands and looks across the estuary to the ruins of Tynemouth Priory high on its cliff above the sea and the long grey arms of the stone piers that enclose the Tyne.

Chapter 6

From South Shields to Whitley Bay

❧

South Shields is not everyone's idea of a seaside resort, though it is
nowadays very much in this way of business, with its amusements
and excellent sands, and I must declare a strong liking for the place,
having spent many a happy day there as a boy, emerging from a tent
to plunge into the North Sea in the teeth of a howling gale.

From the shore and from the long grey pier that guards the entry
into the Tyne there is a grand view over the estuary to the headland
on which stand the ruins of Tynemouth Priory. It is one of the best
seascapes in the country. The town itself is no longer attractive,
though at the centre of its rebuilt market square is the charming if
rather decrepit town hall built in 1768, facing St Hilda's Church,
whose tower dates from the same year. In the museum attached to
the public library is the world's first lifeboat to the design of William
Wouldhave, who introduced a number of revolutionary features in
the use of air cells and cork for buoyancy. As a result of a number of
shipwrecks off the mouth of the Tyne a committee of investigation
had been formed, and it duly considered Wouldhave's model. It
came down against it, and with the help of a local boat builder,
Henry Greathead, produced a prototype of its own, using Wouldhave's basic ideas, but for which Greathead got most of the credit
and a sizeable reward from the government. Yet the original conception for what almost exactly a century ago became the standard
lifeboat was Wouldhave's.

Lovers of shipping and of the bustle of a busy estuary should take
a stroll northwards from the town hall to the Tyne ferry pier, only a
stone's throw away. The ferry provides by far the pleasantest way
of crossing into Northumberland, but to take it would mean missing
an important attraction on the south bank at Jarrow. In any case,
before leaving South Shields no one interested in Roman works
should fail to visit its fort of **Arbeia**. Take the road that leaves the
market-place going south exactly opposite the town hall until you
reach the ABC Cinema; then turn left immediately into Baring Street.
At the top of the hill (the Lawe) on the right-hand side is the red-

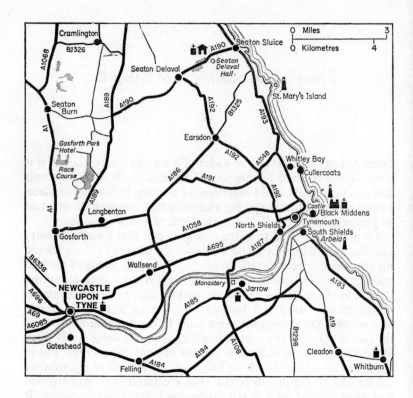

brick museum and behind it the camp.

Here, as might be expected at the most northerly port of Roman Britain, was a store depot comparable to Richborough in Kent. There have been three such buildings on the site, the earliest from the time of Hadrian, and they can be distinguished by their different coloured stone. The fort was used for stock-piling for the Severine campaign in Caledonia and was garrisoned by the Fifth Cohort of Gauls, until in the fourth century it became a base for goods to be transported up the Tyne to the Wall and the Gauls were replaced by the *Barcarii Tigrisienses*, the Tigris lightermen, more used to river navigation. If these *Barcarii* really came from the neighbourhood of Basra and Baghdad, what on earth did they make of the South Shields weather!

For all but the specialist admirer of granaries *Arbeia* is visually the least attractive of the Roman camps, but in the Museum are some very fine tombstones which contrariwise are among the very best in

102

the North. One is inscribed to 'Victor', a Moor, twenty-year-old freedman and trooper of the first cavalry regiment of Asturians, whose comrades 'dutifully attended his funeral'. Another, raised by one Barates to his freedwoman wife, carries a touching inscription in Palmyrian script: 'Regina, daughter of freedom. Barates. Alas!' The sculptured stone shows Regina holding a distaff and sitting in a high-backed chair, her trinket box on her right, her work basket and balls of wool on her left. A Roman officer's sword with bronze inlay was found under one of the ramparts of the camp. It dates from between 197 and 205 and is interesting technically because the blade is pattern-welded and proves what until this discovery was unknown, that the Romans used this process of forging together rods of malleable iron and steel. To the layman the fascinating points about it are the inlays: one of an eagle bearing palm branches, and on the other side the god of war. A mirror in the showcase allows an all-round view.

South Shields was the birthplace of Walter Runciman, later Lord Runciman, who formulated the plan to placate Hitler, by ceding him the Sudetenland in 1938.

From Shields take the Gateshead road for **Jarrow**, once a great shipbuilding town, then during the 'twenties and early 'thirties the symbol of the Depression which spread like a blight over this whole area of the three rivers, Tyne, Tees and Wear. A plaque at the entrance to the town hall commemorates the Jarrow Marchers of that now almost forgotten campaign to awake the conscience of the nation. To the survivors modern Jarrow must be a great improvement, with its new housing, roads, schools, and imaginatively-planned pedestrian precinct, but no one pretends that many tourists would visit it if almost exactly thirteen hundred years ago an enterprising priest had not built a monastery here and if there had not come to it from the sister house at Monkwearmouth a boy who was to become one of Europe's greatest scholars and the first English historian; the Venerable Bede.

'Why Jarrow?' is the thought that springs illogically yet inescapably to mind as, turning right just before the Tyne tunnel, at the signpost pointing to **St Paul's Church**, one dodges between the petrol storage tanks and a huge timber yard to reach the once-sylvan spot by a stream where the *Ecclesiastical History of the English People* was written and completed in 731. This famous book was not Bede's only work: he was a lifelong Biblical scholar and writer of Commentaries. Dedicated by his family to the spiritual life at the age of seven, transferred to Jarrow in the train of Prior Ceolfrith at twelve, it was in this monastery that he spent the rest of his life, and here he died and was buried. He later suffered at the hands of a relic collector from the monastery at Durham, a monk named Aelred, who made off with his bones in 1022 and re-interred them in St Cuthbert's tomb. To own relics in those days was like owning Old Masters now: a point of prestige if not a hedge against inflation. It brought in money too in the shape of pilgrims. After further adventures, as we have seen, Bede's bones were given a final resting place in Durham's Galilee Chapel.

Parts of the priory church of the first abbot–Ceolfrith–still stand. It was founded by Benedict Biscop in 684, and its construction probably owes much to the work of French masons whom he is known to have brought here. The present chancel was the nave of the Saxon church, whose own narrow chancel, which must have resembled that still standing at Escomb, has now disappeared. The small rounded windows in both north and south walls are original. The tower, which was raised towards the end of the eleventh century, is now the crossing tower, a Norman nave having been added. This nave was destroyed in 1786 and the one we now see is the work of Sir Giles Gilbert Scott. These changes of function and identity make Jarrow difficult to take in, and perhaps the safest policy is to stick to the Saxon chancel and ignore the rest. The so-called 'Bede's chair' is a fourteenth-century impostor, but the dedication stone of the monastery can still be seen in the church, dated 23 April 685, the year after St Cuthbert became bishop of Lindisfarne.

Traces of this monastery and of another important building by the banks of the Don have recently been excavated under the direction of Professor Rosemary Cramp of Durham University; they have been extraordinarily fruitful. Traces of door frames, plaster and painted plaster were discovered, and fragments of coloured glass, the earliest yet found in Europe. Exhibits from these digs, along with models and plans of the buildings, will be on view in the near-by museum that is being created inside the restored eighteenth-century **Jarrow Hall**, which will also provide an information and rest centre with a restaurant. Biscop's foundation, which stands at the beginning of organised Christian worship in these islands, will therefore take its rightful place in the modern age.

From St Paul's it is only a short journey through the Tyne Tunnel (highest score one thousand vehicles an hour) to **North Shields**, which is in Northumberland. This was the birthplace of the Victorian artist Myles Birkett Foster (1825-99) who as every encyclopaedia informs us could draw before he could talk. At sixteen he was a popular wood engraver, whose work was often featured in the *Illustrated London News*, but later turned to watercolours. North Shields, however, has only a tenuous claim to him, for he left at the age of five, spent most of his life in London and died in Weybridge, which is emotionally and culturally a long way from the Tyne.

Nowadays North Shields means, first and foremost, fish. Its quays along the river are smelly but colourful and to be recommended to all those who like the atmosphere of trawlers and nets and a busy port. The town above was once agreeably full of Georgian and Early Victorian red brick, and Pevsner has devoted a lot of space to it, including one of his famous perambulations, but this must have been before the bulldozers moved in. Its neighbour to the west is **Wallsend**, the Roman *Segedunum* and eastern terminus of Hadrian's Wall. There are hardly any traces of it left. The town is the home of Swan, Hunter and Wigham Richardson's shipyards, whose office block is one of the better modern buildings on Tyneside. Wallsend coal has long been famous.

North Shields' neighbour to the east is **Tynemouth**, a seaside resort and dormitory for the Newcastle commuters: one of the pleasantest of Northumbrian towns, with an extremely bracing climate.

The best view of it is from the South Shields sands across the estuary, with the walls of the ruined priory on its headland and Dobson's large column carrying John Graham Lough's statue of Admiral Lord Collingwood standing against the skyline above the long, grey arm of the north and south piers. The entrance from the west is more prosaic until you are almost in the centre of the town. To the left, however, are the charming Tudor-style almshouses of the Tyne Master Mariners' Asylum, built in 1837 by John and Benjamin Green, who gave Newcastle its Theatre Royal. Further on is a statue of Queen Victoria, much above average for such works. To the left again is Huntingdon Place and rows of elegant terraced houses; to the right, towards the sea, the wide and largely unspoilt Front Street, much as it was when Charlotte Brontë stayed at Number 57 with Harriet Martineau. A turn down Trinity Chare and through an archway past the *Royal Sovereign Hotel* (named after Collingwood's flagship at Trafalgar) opens up an agreeable view over Prior's Park and tennis club lawns (once the site of the Prior's fish-pond) to a jumble of good red-brick Georgian terracing and the Admiral heroically on top of his plinth. Better still, use the *Royal Sovereign*'s sun parlour which overlooks the same view.

Facing the seaward end of Front Street, behind the quaint clock tower and pant (erected 1861), is the **Castle** and the ruins of the **Priory**, once one of the most impressive in the north.

No trace now remains of the first monastic building here which dated from the seventh century. It was to suffer appalling losses – in 865, during one of the Danish raids, all the nuns who fled to it for shelter from St Hilda's at Hartlepool were massacred. Nevertheless it survived for upwards of three hundred years, largely because of its prestige as the guardian of the body of St Oswald, the victor of Heavenfield, buried behind its high altar. By 1008 it was abandoned; St Oswald's tomb was lost; and roofless and deserted it remained till in 1075 it was given to the monks of Jarrow, who promptly and very providently rediscovered the saint's body. Refounded after the Conquest by the Norman earl of Mowbray, it was to grow into the Priory whose ruins we see today.

The **Castle** was built later, as the strategic importance of the site, which is surrounded on three sides by cliffs, sank into the military consciousness and the Scottish raids began. Its most hectic period was during the Civil Wars of Charles I's time when it was besieged by General Leven's Scots. After its surrender it was repaired and garrisoned by Parliamentary troops under Colonel Lilburne, who later changed his coat and went over to the King. It had therefore to be reduced all over again – Lilburne paying for his temerity with his life. Parts of it are still in military occupation today.

Of Northumbrian castles it is not among the most attractive. Some of the thirteenth-century walls are standing, but the tunnel-vaulted archway of the barbican is of later date – 1395 – probably copied from similar work at Alnwick. On either side are guard-rooms; ahead, another tunnel-vaulted passage leads to the gatehouse proper, with more guard-rooms flanking it. The presence of an inner barbican shows how aware the builders were of the need for defence in depth on this side. Entrance to the gatehouse/keep was originally by drawbridge, but now by a ramp up to the small door on the first floor. Beyond is a lobby. On the right is the great hall, to the left the kitchen, where in the south wall the fireplace, oven and drains are still visible. Above is the great chamber, from where a spiral staircase leads down to rooms on the south side of the barbican. The whole complex is more extensive than appears at first glance. It needed to be, for here was the second line of defence against the Scots in case the northern fortresses fell. The similarities with the castle and cathedral of Durham on *their* promontory are evident, though here of course everything is on a smaller scale.

After the fustian gloom of the castle the ruins of the **Priory** on its windswept cliff-top comes as a refresher. In its early days it was a by-word for its wealth, and the church and monastic buildings still give some impression of this.

Only a few traces remain of the Norman church which succeeded the Saxon one. It had a short aisled nave of seven bays. The solid square stones of the period can be recognised on the outer wall on the south side, and there is also a walled-up doorway leading to the cloister just to the west of the thirteenth-century replacement. On the north side of the nave the east bay with its Norman capital and pier is well preserved. The crossing piers still stand: they once supported a square lantern tower.

In 1190 the nave was extended westward by the addition of three bays with octagonal instead of earlier cylindrical pillars. But it was at the east or seaward end that the grandest and most lasting changes were made. Apsidal chapels gave way to a much wider aisled choir of five bays with a flat wooden roof. A four-bay vaulted presbytery was then built out eastwards, and it is the east and south walls of this building that stand so magnificently today, a landmark for miles. The east wall, which is seventy-three feet high, impresses from the outside by its sheerness and simplicity. It has three long stepped lancets, then two small lancets and a central vesica, and at the top another large and finely proportioned lancet. Inside it is much more decorative. There is blank arcading along the plinth, groups of seven shafts divide the windows, and there is dog-tooth ornamentation both on the arches and the string course. The south wall has an arcade similar to that on the east, only here with the addition of a tomb recess, possibly of a hermit, St Henry of Coquet, who was buried here in 1127. (This extraordinary man was a Dane who had fled from his own country to escape an unwanted marriage. He is said to have grown all his own food, tilling the soil even when he was on crutches, and eating only three days a week.) The higher stages of the south wall differ from those of its neighbours. Its lancets are set lower and it has three matching round windows above. Jagged against the sky are the outlines of two windows of a unique upper chamber which was built over the vault of the presbytery and the flat roof of the choir, no one knows for what purpose. The last

107

addition to the priory was the **Percy Chantry** under the east wall, built in the mid-fifteenth century. It is a low chamber with intricate vaulting and sculptured bosses, now rather worn. The arms of the Percys and Delavals can be distinguished on the walls. It was restored by John Dobson in the nineteenth century and provides the only shelter on the site in which to catch one's breath when the wind is blowing off the sea.

The **Conventual Buildings** and living quarters, attached by custom to the south side of the church, are large but almost totally ruinous. The shape of the cloister is marked out on the grass. One can clamber through the warming room, past the lavatories with their Norman walls and stone-lined drains, and go downhill to the prior's chapel and great hall where guests were entertained. The whole area within the walls was once a self-contained township, with its own water supply, stables, poultry yard, bakehouse, brewery, storehouses, kiln and gardens overlooking the east cliff. In the seventeenth century a lighthouse stood just to the north of the present one, which looks rather self-conscious among so many ruins. Its presence is very necessary, however, for just off the headland lie the treacherous Black Middens which have caused many a shipwreck. After the loss of the steamship *Stanley* with twenty-six lives in November 1869 the people of Tynemouth formed a Volunteer Life Brigade, the first in the country, firing a rocket line, the ancestor of the breeches buoy. The cliffs by the lighthouse make a splendid look-out point in good weather from which to watch the shipping entering and leaving the estuary. The beaches north of the headland are a summer playground – the Long Sands at the popular end contrasting with the more staid King Edward's Bay.

A little further up the coast is the tiny fishing harbour of **Cullercoats**, which in Victorian and Edwardian times had a markedly individual seaside flavour which it has not quite lost. It is the most intimate and endearing of the Tyneside resorts but has to yield pride of place on the tourist ladder to its next-door neighbour, **Whitley Bay**, the North-East's Southend without the pier; one cannot call it its Brighton, since Whitley Bay has no pretensions to architecture, apart perhaps from its domed 'Spanish City', where generations of young Tynesiders in search of amusement have been entertained. The town has a number of good hotels. The sands are even more extensive than at Tynemouth – though I expect Tynemouth will deny it – and from the prom there is an impressive view up the coast to the lighthouse on St Mary's Island, which can be reached from the mainland at low tide. There is a popular Ice Rink. A flower show is held in August and an angling festival in October, the largest of its kind in Europe. In 1811 a hoard of Roman jewels and coins was found in the neighbourhood. They are now in the British Museum.

Introduction to Northumberland

❧

Now that we are in Northumberland, a word about its geology, reflected in its varied landscapes from the Cheviots to the Simonside hills and the coal measures of the south-east.

As in Durham, so here: the high ground is in the west. The dominant feature is the Cheviot range, a line of rolling whale-backed hills, all that is left of the active volcanoes that once poured out their rocks and lava over a tract of countryside between the Coquet and the Tweed and from Wooler to the Scottish border near Jedburgh. Into this lava mass later eruptions threw up a central thrust of granite, which was eventually exposed through weathering on the heights of the central *massif* – shorn of its surface peat, it can be seen in ravines such as the Bizzle and the Henhole on its northern flanks. The lava outflow grows only brackens and grass. To the north, east and south, lies a Cementstone belt providing rich farming land in the Vale of Whittingham, shut in by an outer rim of Fell Sandstone that forms another crescent: this time an escarpment of rugged heather-clad heights facing inwards towards the Cheviots across the plain for the whole of its length.

This system of concentric rings radiating from the volcanic centre of the *massif* is continued from north-east to south-west by a wide belt of Limestone, through which outcrops another visually dominant feature: the basalt ridge of the Whin Sill, on whose crests the Romans built part of their Wall north of the Tyne and later military engineers the great fortresses of Dunstanburgh and Bamburgh on the north-east coast. Beyond the limestone, still travelling outwards and eastwards, lies a narrow segment of Millstone Grit (mixed sands and shales), and then the Coal Measures that fill in the south-eastern corner of the county: a triangle with its base along the Tyne from its mouth to Wylam, and its apex just south of Amble at the mouth of the Coquet. Much of this is good agricultural land. In the south-west, between the North Tyne valley and the Cumbrian border, a countryside of rolling fells and the conifers of the Forestry Commission overlies the rocks of the Scremeston Coal Group, which

111

sounds industrial but in fact is blissfully rural.

One of the charms of Northumberland is the enticing way its landscape is laid out for the visitor from north or south. Crossing the Tweed from Scotland at Coldstream or Berwick the line of the Cheviots looms handsomely on the south-western horizon; and from the plain near Newcastle, looking north, this same view is seen in reverse, with the addition of the sharp skyline of the Simonsides guarding the Coquet above Rothbury. No matter where you are in Northumberland, hills of some kind are always present. And from any eminence on their eastward-facing side the sea appears. From the central *massif* the views are vast: to Skiddaw, Cross Fell and the Solway in the west, and on really clear days beyond the Eildons to the Pentlands and the Grampian Mountains near Stirling.

Yet even at its most grandiose it is a familiar landscape which men have fashioned and cultivated. The Iron Age camps lie thick around the Cheviots, well above the thousand foot contour lines on Yeavering Bell, and the Roman Camp at Chew Green stands at the head of Coquetdale in some of the most remote country in England. The sheep graze everywhere: a pack of foxhounds hunts the Cheviot itself. The desolate, almost soil-less Farne Islands, where the Whin Sill reaches the sea, were the last home of St Cuthbert. The fells near Chillingham are roamed by a herd of wild white cattle whose origins are lost in time: and from those same hills you can see the caravans massed along the coast at Beadnell. It is a land of castles – indeed Camden wrote of it, 'There is not a man amongst them of the better sort that hath not his little tower or pele' – but many of these towers and peles have been converted into comfortable homes and farms. It is a county where the old mixes harmoniously with the new: a county of contrasts, still astonishingly unspoilt and large enough to cater for most tastes.

Chapter 7

From Whitley Bay to
Seaton Delaval and Newcastle

❧

For the visitor at the coast Newcastle is only a step away along a choice of roads leading into either Gosforth or the city centre. However, this would be to miss a splendid building slightly to the north. Turn therefore along Whitley Bay's breezy esplanade, past the lighthouse to **Seaton Sluice**, whose harbour was created by the Delaval family for the export of their coal and, later, glass. The pier was built by Sir Ralph Delaval in 1660. John Seymour gives an interesting account of the commercial drive of this extraordinarily talented family and of their development of a viable harbour on this stormbound coast. The harbour was last used commercially in 1871. The old octagonal customs house designed by Sir John Vanbrugh is still standing – though rather forlorn now in its environment of streets and pubs – and a mile away inland is one of this architect's most superb creations, **Seaton Delaval Hall**.

From the road there is a good view of the north front, which is much more restrained than the much-photographed elevation at the south. In today's cult phrase, it 'keeps a low profile': a central mass between wings and pavilions. From this side the eye can easily take in not only the detail but also the elegant proportions of the house and its stepped skyline. At the same range from the south the high portico with its flight of steps and vast Ionic columns refuses to go into one ensemble with the smooth walls that flank it; the great mass is too dominant, and is really built to be seen at the end of a vista from far off in the grounds – now forbidden country.

The Hall (open May to September) was built by Vanbrugh between 1718 and 1729 for Admiral George Delaval, who gave his architect *carte blanche* to spend as much as he liked. If Sarah, Duchess of Marlborough had been as generous or understanding she would have spared herself and Sir John much bickering over Blenheim. Unfortunately neither Vanbrugh nor the Admiral lived to see the completion of the wonderful building that resulted from this collaboration between genius and generosity. Bad luck has always dogged it, often in the shape of fire which damaged the main block and one of the wings at various times.

The central block is a shell, but some of the state rooms in the west wing are furnished and on view. This west wing is now the stage for medieval banquets which take place nightly except on Sundays. Booking well ahead is essential (Tel. Seaton Delaval 481759). In the grounds are a mausoleum (1776) and the splendid stable block; also the twelfth-century **Chapel,** now the parish church, built by Hubert de la Val who went on the First Crusade. On no account miss this marvellous little building which is best approached by a drive leading off the main road a hundred yards to the west of the Hall. Press the button in the porch to light the nave and dazzle your eye on entering with a view of the two superb Norman arches – chancel and apse – standing one behind the other and set off to maximum effect by the plain white walls. Note the stone shields on the west wall which must have formed part of a tomb chest, also the effigies of a knight and a lady on either side of the altar – perhaps Sir Eustace Delaval (1258) and his wife Constance de Baliol or Sir Henry (1272, the year of Edward I's accession) and Mary de Biddleston. A rope in the sanctuary keeps one away from them, but they have from the distance a monumental and not very appealing look a far cry from their lively Hanoverian descendants.

The family fortunes were founded when Guy Delaval came over with the Conqueror and then married his niece, a helpful relationship to have when England was being parcelled out by its new ruler among a syndicate of adventurers. One of Guy's descendants, Gilbert, was a signatory of *Magna Carta*; and the family luck continued down to the eighteenth century when coal was found under the estate and the harbour was built at Seaton Sluice to export it. Till then the family's main home had been well inland at Dissington, but they sold it to a cousin of Admiral Collingwood to concentrate their energies nearer the coast and the source of their wealth. Inventive genius ran in the family – one of them, Edward, later Lord Delaval, the last of his line, was associated with Benjamin Franklin in the development of the lightning conductor – and also a long tradition of service to their country, particularly at sea, but they also developed talents of a more Hellfire Club persuasion, culminating in the exploits of the devil-may-care brothers Sir Francis Blake Delaval and Lord Delaval, which provided the material for a recent BBC serial. The jokes they perpetrated on their unfortunate house guests included beds that suddenly dropped through the floor into tanks of water, and the use of sliding walls which could be drawn up into the ceiling at appropriate moments after the ladies and gentlemen had retired for a night's pleasure in one another's rooms, so leaving them exposed to public view. Talented to a fault, the brothers and their sister persuaded Garrick to let them take over Drury Lane on one occasion to play *Othello*, an extraordinary choice for such natural comedians. Sir Francis Blake Delaval took up fortune-telling professionally, to the scandal of even that permissive age, but since his skills in this art helped him to trick and marry a rich wife, his friends could hardly have accused him of wasting his talents. Unfortunately the male line of this ingenious family ended in 1814, and it was through the female line that the estate came to Jacob Astley, later Baron Hastings, in the possession of whose descendants it still remains.

From Seaton Delaval the main road to the north runs through Cramlington and Bedlington, and those in a hurry to reach the beautiful coastline beyond Amble should take this way. Our route is along the A189 for **Gosforth,** now a suburb of Newcastle. Here is the luxury *Gosforth Park Hotel*, a golf course and golf range, and the **Racecourse,** one of the very best in the North, where in June is run *The Northumberland Plate*, sometimes called 'The pitman's Derby'. For details of meetings consult The Secretary, High Gosforth Park Co. Ltd., Newcastle NE3 SHP. (Tel. Wideopen 2020.) In Gosforth's church of St Nicholas was married Edward Barrett Molton-Barrett, father of the poetess Elizabeth Barrett Browning, and the model for the monster-parent of *The Barretts of Wimpole Street*. A couple of miles further down the road is **Newcastle upon Tyne.**

Few towns in Britain have a more cloth-capped image than the Geordie capital. Its original rise to prosperity was based on wool, but since Plantagenet times coal has been worked in the neighbourhood and the collier trade from the Tyne was in full swing in the days of the first Elizabeth. Under the Stuarts ten thousand men were employed in its mines and in the keels and lighters that carried the coal to sea. 'Keel' was a Saxon word for 'boat', and the Newcastle keel-men were a famous fraternity. The river has long been a great ship-building centre – that doyenne of Atlantic liners, the *Mauretania*, came from here. It was the first English river to have a steam boat plying along it (on 19 May 1814), though in Scotland the Clyde can boast *The Comet*, launched two years earlier. A workshop, then.

Yet Newcastle has always had an aura, a mystique, over and

115

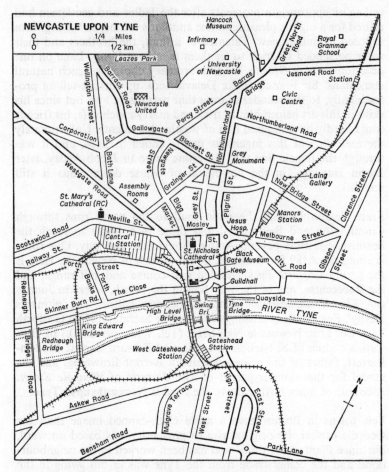

NEWCASTLE UPON TYNE

0   1/4   Miles

0   1/2 km

above its commercial importance. Camden called it '*Ocellus*', the eye of the North. John Wesley wrote of it in 1759: 'Certainly if I did not believe there was another world, I would spend all my summers here, as I know no place in Great Britain comparable to it for pleasantness.' Even as late as ten years ago a case could be made for saying not only that it was by far the most attractive industrial town in these islands but also that it contained an undamaged complex of streets, squares and terraces that would have been welcomed in many a spa. No one can any longer confidently lay his hand on his heart and repeat this now in the light of the horrors

116

which in the name of progress and the motor car have been inflicted on the city, but enough of it still remains to justify some of the eulogies of admirers, from Mr Gladstone to Sir John Betjeman, Ian Nairn and Nikolaus Pevsner, who has called it 'the best designed Victorian town in England and indeed the best designed large city in England'.

Most Geordies recall their heritage with pride, yet also with a certain apathy – 'canny Newcassel' will live for them as long as the Christmas lights shine in Fenwick's windows and *United*, the famous 'Magpies' in the black and white strip, can get to Wembley. They rightly applaud the clearing away of the dreadful slums and the huge rehousing schemes that have pumped back lifeblood into the town. Yet only now that the new roads that were planned to make Newcastle a 'motorway city' are visibly wrenching the place apart and making much of it into a desert do they seem to have grasped the scale of the destruction around them. No popular storm of protest arose when the classical facades of Dobson and Grainger's Eldon Square were ruthlessly rooted up to make way for a monster hotel – one that has never been built. Most people seem perfectly happy with the promise that it is now to become a 'leisure area'. The planned city centre is marvellously spacious and convenient, but many of its citizens reserve their real love for Northumberland Street (which could be any street anywhere) and only turn into Grey Street, that jewel among English thoroughfares, when looking for a parking meter. Nor do they bother much with that oldest part of their inheritance, the warren of 'chares' and stairs between the cathedral and the river. Yet to understand Newcastle and its history this is the place to be – on the Quayside near the Guildhall, preferably at dusk on a winter's afternoon, when the last gleams of sunlight are filtering through the superstructure of Robert Stephenson's High Level Bridge and lighting the huge coat-hanger girders of the George V Bridge downstream.

Here you are standing at what was once the commercial hub of the town, where its connection with the river is at its most visible and eloquent. The middle of the three bridges facing you – the interestingly-designed Swing Bridge (1868/76) which Pevsner unkindly scorns – stands on the site of the Roman crossing of the river and of the later stone structure of 1250 which for five hundred and twenty-one years provided the only real link between Newcastle and the Durham palatinate. Behind you is the seventeenth-century (but restored) Guildhall and some merchants' houses, relics of an old prosperity. As late as the seventeenth century the hub of the town was still down there in Sandhill and The Side, encircled by the river and its walls and huddled close for protection under the massive bulk of the Norman castle and the lantern tower of the parish church of St Nicholas, now the cathedral. In old prints the whole area teems with activity. It is much more of a backwater now. The north–south traffic on the George V bridge is moving – if not caught in the rush-hour jam – high above your head. So are the cars and buses on the lower tier of Stephenson's High Level Bridge and the trains that rumble directly above them. The words 'High Level'* supply the clue. Stephenson, given the industrial tools and techniques of the Railway Age, reversed fifteen hundred years of history and took his traffic by the short route from cliff-top to cliff-top, high above the river and the old rambling roads and stairs that had once provided the southern entrance to the town. In doing so he accepted and emphasised a trend that had been going on for years: the gradual shift of the town uphill and away from the Tyne.

Gradual, because though much new building had taken place on the higher ground - leaving fine memorials in David Stephenson's All Saints' Church, the same architect's Mosley Street (1784) and William Newton's Assembly Rooms (1774/6), the direct advance of building northwards was met by an obstacle right in its path: the mansion and ornamental grounds of a large private estate, Anderson Place, together with the adjoining Nuns' Field on the site of a medieval nunnery.

This immensely valuable property was offered by its owner to the city in 1826. Astonishingly the offer was refused. When a few years later the property was next on the market it was snapped up by a speculative builder by the name of Richard Grainger, whose nose for a deal was only equalled by a breadth of vision and taste surely unique in the field of property development. Trained in a provincial town at just the right interval in time behind Nash's achievements in London, he knew what to imitate and how to improve. Nash had faced his brick with stucco. Grainger would build in stone. Even in contemporary prints Grey Street has a more solid look than Nash's Regent Street, but it is just as graceful and its building line has far more variety: for a cardinal point about Grainger's development of central Newcastle is that it was the work of a number of architects, engaged within a general plan but given full scope to exercise their own individual talents.

When Grainger's models for his streets were first shown to the

*From 1771 there had been many proposals for such a bridge from a number of engineers before Robert Stephenson was finally chosen to construct it (1846/50).

public on 29 May 1834 they excited much admiration and, in the columns of the local press, even a sense of wonder that such things could be. Pride mounted as one by one, and in an astonishingly short time, the plans became translated into reality and people could walk around their fine new streets. When the 'New Markets' were finally completed in 1835 the public joy broke into vernacular verse:

> About Lunnen then, divvent ye maek sic a rout,
> For there's nowt there ma winkers te dazzel;
> For a bell or a market, there issent a doot,
> We can bang them at canny Newcassel.

> Ye see the wives naggle aboot tripe and sheep heads,
> Or washing their greens at a fountain,
> Where the young nuns used to be telling their beads,
> And had nowt but thor sins to be countin.

The *Newcastle Journal* went into similar if more decorous rhapsodies over 'this, the most attractive feature of Mr Grainger's splendid improvements'. Measurements were adduced to add to the public marvel. 'They exceed two acres in area, and are enclosed within a square of beautiful stone faced erections, replete with every convenience as shops and dwellings, 410 feet by 312 feet, designed with a chaste and classic elegance surpassing anything in street architecture hitherto witnessed in the neighbourhood. The stone is of the best quality and the mason work finely polished and executed in a very superior manner. The markets are the most magnificent in the world.' And so they probably were. They were also the largest in Britain, far surpassing Covent Garden: just as the new station with its classical portico was larger and grander than anything in that line to be found in the metropolis.

The plans for both these buildings were by John Dobson, whose name we shall meet time and again in the churches and country houses of Northumberland, and whose fruitful collaboration with Grainger is commemorated in two of the streets that meet at the Earl Grey monument. If you were to ask people today in the modern bustle of the town who had designed the buildings around you you would get some astonished stares but at least a fair percentage would at once reply: 'Why, Dobson and Grainger, of course,' and some would also remember the all-powerful Town Clerk of the time, John Clayton, Grainger's backer, who also has a street named after him in the centre of the town.

Substantial justice would thus be done to the men who between them did most to create the Victorian neo-classical centre of the city.

Not many could give a proper attribution to the superb Theatre Royal, designed by John and Benjamin Green, or to Benjamin's column commemorating the Earl Grey of the great Reform Bill which visually is as dominant to central Newcastle as Nelson's is to Trafalgar Square. Fewer still remember John Wardle and his assistant George Walker, whose work is everywhere about – on the west side of Grey Street, in Grainger Street, Market Street, Clayton Street and the Central Exchange – or Thomas Oliver, whose Leazes Terrace (1829/34), blessedly preserved by Newcastle University, is arguably the best thing in the whole city.

At the Leazes Oliver and Grainger had extended the boundary of the new development well to the north of the old wall line to the verge of the bumpy open spaces of the Town Moor. Slightly further to the east John Dobson planted St Mary's Place and the church of St Thomas the Martyr as part of the same northward thrust. The momentum of this movement has been sustained, for this northern fringe of the town now encloses four other elements vital to its well-being: Newcastle United's home ground in Gallowgate; the campus of the University; the near-by bus station in the Haymarket; and the new Civic Centre at Barass Bridge, placed at the furthest possible distance from the old Guildhall and Mansion House by the banks of the Tyne, at the northern exit from the town where it nudges towards its Jesmond and Gosforth suburbs and the motorist entering from the direction of Morpeth catches his first glimpse of the city in its elegant campanile crowned by the gilded carillon of its bell tower.

It follows from this that the visitor who wants to trace the chronological development of Newcastle through the centuries should start on the quayside under the walls of the Norman castle and work his way northwards.

There are reasons, however, why he should do just the opposite. In one sense it is Hobson's Choice, for though Newcastle is a compact town which can be crossed on a north–south axis at a brisk walk in well under half an hour from Civic Centre to Guildhall, a circular route will have to be followed by the visitor who wishes to take in its many attractions. But when he learns that most of the car parks are up-town and most of the restaurants and hotels down-town the arguments seem irresistible for starting in the morning at the top of the hill and breaking off at lunch-time at the bottom for refreshment before a leisurely climb back.

Start the perambulation, then, at the **Civic Centre**. The very name was long a bone of contention between the Socialist councillors who christened it and their Tory traditionalist successors who longed to re-dub it a Town Hall, but in the end nobly restrained themselves. Much derided for its acreages of glass, which can make an oven of it in hot weather, it stands at the centre of nothing except the swirling traffic stream: by far the finest building in Newcastle since Dobson and Grainger's time, and one of the most successful modern buildings in England. The best view of it is when approaching from the north, but it also looks well from the University campus. Internally it is the ad-man's dream of what civic grandeur should be, with its decorated plate-glass doors and red-carpeted staircase under an enormous chandelier. Like Coventry Cathedral, one of its outer walls is hung with statuary, but not alas Epstein's splendid 'St Michael'. It seems to be a Tyne god taking a shower and is allegedly the largest bronze figure since Bernini. It is no worse than the flying swans in the courtyard. The Civic Centre is still a marvellous building, and its carillon, playing its mid-day repertoire of *Bonny Bobby Shafto* and other Northumbrian folk-tunes, is the authentic voice of Tyneside.

Its neighbour to the west, standing on its own in a green open space, is the church of **St Thomas the Martyr**, consecrated in 1830 as successor to the old chapel of the Saint which had stood since 1200 near the site of the present Swing Bridge over the Tyne. The new site was chosen because it was on ground where the hospital of St Mary Magdalene had been founded by Henry I for the care of lepers. The architect of St Thomas's was John Dobson. Pevsner seems to dislike what he calls an 'ill-informed treatment' of the Early English style, including the open-work effect of the tower and the tall pinnacles at the east end, but Bruce Alsopp in his *Historical Architecture of Newcastle-upon-Tyne* finds this 'remarkable slenderness and refinement' a cause for praise. I cannot bring myself to like it, but at least there is space around it to enable one to look at it: an advantage denied to most of Newcastle's older churches.

Overlooking both St Thomas's and the Civic Centre from a mound to the north is the **Hancock Museum of Natural History**, which, with its Doric columns, also looks very Dobsonian in his lay manner, but was actually built by John Wardle in 1878, thirteen years after the master's death – a chaste classical interloper into the age of Victorian municipal Gothic. In the open space in front stands a statue to the first Lord Armstrong, the inventor, whose traces we shall cross again at Cragside near Rothbury and at Bamburgh. Internally the museum is very similar to that at South Kensington and contains a huge assortment (the largest outside London) of stuffed mammals, reptiles and birds, including the collection of heads donated by the naturalist Abel Chapman (who lived at Houxty on the North Tyne) and a white whale caught far off its normal Arctic beat near the mouth of the Tyne. The collection of birds is impressive and the presentation imaginative, if a little patronising. One showcase is devoted to the wild life of the Farne Islands – mostly birds including one very small and appealing rabbit with a coat nearly black in colour. This species of Farne rabbit is now extinct. Uniquely in Britain, the Hancock Museum has specimens of the wild White Cattle of Chillingham, that mysterious breed that may have been roaming the Cheviot foothills as early as Roman times and whose descendants still live on the Chillingham estates of the Earls of Tankerville. The two adults in the Hancock collection have been there for years, but the calf is a newcomer, the victim of a kidney disease. In the gallery above this group is a display of pencil and watercolour drawings by Thomas Bewick, the great engraver and author of three famous illustrated books on birds and mammals, who was born near Ovingham further up the Tyne but lived and worked in Newcastle.

The Museum is next to the University, which lies to the east. Cut into the bank above the road that separates them is a reproduction cave containing the skeleton and funerary ornaments of a **Bronze Age Burial** dated to about 1600 BC, discovered in 1930 at Blaydon across the Tyne. There is the skull, the body with its knees drawn up in the foetal position, the well preserved beaker. There are many older skeletons up and down the world, but I know of no more bizarre reburial than that of this very early Tynesider who had been lying in the grave two centuries before the birth of Tutankamun.

The **University**, once the 'modern' wing of Durham but now very much established in its own right, is best entered through the neo-Tudor gateway facing the Civic Centre enshrining a statue of Edward VII where one rather expects Henry VIII. The red brick is mellowing nicely and some of the quadrangles behind it have begun to have an Oxbridge air. The **School of Architecture Building** on the right is by W. H. Knowles (1911) – the gatehouse and the Queen Victoria Road frontage are his also. Some of the modern additions are easy on the eye as well as functional, notably the new **Arts Building** and the **Library**. And, understanding its true place as a seat of learning, the University has preserved and given a modern use to many of the older buildings on its periphery: some modest, as in Archbold Terrace, but some of high architectural importance, as in Leazes Terrace, which without this enlightened patronage would have fallen to the developers as surely as Dobson's Eldon Square.

Most agreeable about the Newcastle campus is the sense of community it shares with the town, so that no passer-by feels himself excluded or a stranger in an élitist establishment. The quadrangle provides a short-cut between the Civic Centre and the Royal Victoria Infirmary, and though Senate duly informs the public that there are no rights of way, of course it is often used by ordinary citizens of the town. Below the gateway is the **University Theatre**, whose production standards are rigorously *avant garde* but whose snack bar stands hospitably open to all. There are actually two auditoria, one of which houses what is virtually Newcastle Rep and which is largely dependent for its audiences on the town. This kind of liaison and interdependence is particularly valuable and is met with again in the **Museum of Antiquities** housed in Knowle's Gateway at the southern entrance to the university quadrangle, and run jointly by the University and Newcastle's venerable Society of Antiquaries. It contains mostly Roman work, including finds from the outlying forts of *Bremenium* (High Rochester) and *Habitancum* (Risingham). Particularly charming are Venus and two attendants bathing at a spring and a building inscription of the Twentieth Legion flanked by figures of a lugubrious-looking Mars and Hercules with his enormous club. There is a full-scale mock-up of the Temple of Mithras at *Brocolitia* (Carrawburgh) on the Roman Wall. The finest exhibit of all, however, is not Roman but Saxon – the shaft head of a cross, its sides carved with primitive but striking representations of Christ, of Christ healing a blind man, of adoring crowds, and part of a scroll. The bottom half of the cross is in the parish church of Rothbury (see p. 223).

No one interested in Rome should miss this excellent museum, if only as an introduction to Hadrian's Wall. And certainly no one interested in classical architecture as it survived into the 1830s should fail to take the short walk uphill to the north-west, behind the Royal Victoria Infirmary, to Thomas Oliver's **Leazes Terrace**. It is not the easiest place to find without a town map. Few casual visitors would suspect it was there, so tucked away is it, well off the main roads, and obscured on one side by the towering stands of Newcastle United's Gallowgate ground. Once the peer of Nash's Regent's Park Terrace, it had fallen on evil days before its recent rescue, and though it is being tidied up the effects are still patchy. In form it has been described as 'a square turned inside out' – actually a rectangle, with its longer frontages facing north-west and south-east. That to the south-east is now much the more agreeable, facing over sunken gardens well planted with trees towards the town which in true Regency style it keeps firmly in its place. It is surprisingly large even by London and Bath standards – eighty-six bays by twenty, by sixty-nine by twenty-one – built of three storeys with Corinthian pilasters and elegant iron balconies. The space inside the rectangle was even in its heyday, as Pevsner says, 'nothing but back yards', but the face it still shows to the world is the living proof of how large masses, treated with simplicity, even severity, with a minimum of decoration, can be used to obtain a grand effect that is never dull. When built (1829/30) it was seen as a centre-piece for other buildings subordinate to it, some of which still survive in Leazes Crescent, St Thomas's Square and St Thomas's Crescent, but now mixed up with modern development of a regrettable kind – as though garages and scrap-yards had somehow elbowed their way into Regent's Park.

At the Leazes you have reached the northern limits of Newcastle proper. Beyond it lies the **Town Moor**, where the Hanoverian army under General Wade camped during the alarms of the Jacobite rising of the 'Forty-Five. It is a large, open, untidy place. Harrogate with its Stray makes far better use of its lungs. On the Moor's southern verge at Gallowgate, as might be guessed from the name, public hangings used to take place, the last as late as 1844 when one Mark Sherwood suffered for the murder of his wife. When one remembers that Leazes Terrace had been standing for fourteen years at the time one sees that 'Civilisation' is a comparative term and that there was another side to the elegant ladies and gentlemen of the prints and engravings of the Age of Reason. In 1829, the very year when the building of Leazes Terrace began, a Jane Jameson was hanged near by on the Nuns' Moor for murdering her mother with a red-hot poker, and details of the execution have survived among the county archives. A sizeable company took part:

The town sergeants on horseback with cocked hats and swords; the town marshal, also on horseback, in his official costume; the cart with the prisoner sitting on her coffin, guarded on each side by eight free porters with javelins and ten constables with their staves; then came the mourning coach containing the chaplain, the under sheriff, the gaoler and the clerk of St Andrew's. The expenses were: To seven sergeants, five shillings each; twenty constables, three and sixpence each; sixteen free porters, five shillings each; for tolling St Andrew's great bell, two and sixpence; executioner, three guineas; halter and cart, three shillings; cart and driver, fifteen shillings; mourning coach, fifteen and six; nine horses for officers, five shillings each; summoning twenty constables, sixpence each; joiners' bill, two pounds, five shillings and three pence; allowance to joiners, six shillings.

Gallowgate, except to football fans going to the match, is not an attractive street, but at the bottom of it, almost engulfed by modern buildings, is the city's oldest surviving church, **St Andrew's**, whose bells had tolled for the unfortunate Jane Jameson. Externally, particularly when seen from the west, the squat tower has a huddled, almost apologetic air, as though overcome by the careless, hurrying world outside. Once, though, it played a heroic part in the life of the town, for during the Civil Wars a cannon was mounted in it and exchanged shots with the Scottish army encamped on the high ground at the Leazes. This was the one occasion when Newcastle fell to a besieging enemy, and St Andrew's was badly damaged in the process. For a year thereafter no services were held in it, and its bells were silenced for the best part of a century. The tower has been much restored.

Internally St Andrew's is more interesting, far and away its most impressive feature being the very tall chancel arch with its chevron decoration dating from *circa* 1160. The window at the south-east corner is Early English and was put in in the middle of the thirteenth century when the length of the chancel was doubled. The roof is much older than it looks, having suffered an insensitive restoration in 1844. There is a squint in the north wall of the sanctuary which may have been used by lepers from the hospital of St Mary Magdalene, who could see the high altar from this spot without mixing with the congregation. The nave is original twelfth-century, though the roof line was once considerably lower than it is now. The arcades are Norman in style. The transepts are so short as to be almost non-existent; they were added in the thirteenth century. Of particular interest is the baptistry, which contains a medieval font cover, considered to be one of the finest in England, and a *Last Supper* by Luca Giordano – 'and his associates', the Guide to the church adds with perhaps undue modesty, for there seems no doubt that Giordano painted at least part of it.

Newcastle's medieval **Walls**, which date from the reign of Edward I, followed the present line of Gallowgate at the northern boundary of the town, turning to the south-west just above St Andrew's church. They formed a formidable barrier, seven feet thick, with a parapet and merlons protecting a sentry walk twenty-five feet high, and defended by a ditch and a series of semi-circular towers and turrets, so that no part of the system was out of bowshot of the garrison. As late as the 1540s Leland could boast that Newcastle's 'waulls' surpassed anything of the kind in England and 'most of the cities of Europe'. Some traces have survived nineteenth-century rebuilding, and where Gallowgate meets Percy and Newgate Streets is the best place for the visitor to start. One of the turrets stands in St Andrew's graveyard, and a long section of the curtain is preserved in West Walls off Gallowgate, including the **Morden Tower**, now used for poetry readings, and the Durham and Heber towers where the fortifications swung south-west towards the Tyne. Though nothing like the equal of York or Chester for completeness, Newcastle's walls are among the six best examples of medieval defence works in the country.

Further down Gallowgate once stood Eldon Square, now almost entirely demolished: a remarkable act of official vandalism, for this beautiful terrace with its side wings had been among the earliest and finest fruits of the Grainger-Dobson collaboration. Even before its summary execution it had been allowed to run down and to accumulate a rash of lamp posts, statues and other ornaments which would greatly have pained its creators; in charity we must believe that it was the shop-soiled image that the planners saw in their mind's eye when they set the bulldozers to work. They did their town a great disservice all the same.

The fourth and open side of Eldon Square was formed by Blackett Street, and directly south of it once lay the gardens and mansion of Anderson Place. Here for ten months in 1646 Charles I was held prisoner. The ground is now covered by the fine streets of Grainger's 'Tyneside Classical', as Lyall Wilkes and Gordon Dodds have so aptly called the developments of the 1830s in their book of that name.

Pause for a moment at the eastern end of Blackett Street under Benjamin Green's one hundred and thirty-five-foot-high **Column** crowned by a parapet on which stands Baily's **Statue** of the hero of the great Reform Act, the second Earl Grey: a splendid focus for Grainger's 'new' town. Above and behind one's head is the remarkable Art Nouveau fantasy of **Emerson Chambers**. In front on a large triangular site is the domed **Central Exchange**, built 1836/38 by Grainger to the design of John Wardle and George Walker. It has a central arcade which dates from 1905 – a real Milanese *galleria*, if on a small scale, lined with shops and faced with shiny brown tiles: a striking and strangely satisfying effect. Diverging from their junction at the foot of Earl Grey's column run the two finest of Newcastle's streets: Grainger Street to the right, Grey Street to the left, descending the slope towards the Tyne.

We now begin the circular part of the tour. Start with **Grainger Street** and leave Grey Street for the final climax and *coup de théâtre*. Enough can be seen of the latter from here to whet the appetite for the even finer prospect uphill. **Grainger Street** is straighter and less subtle, though I know good judges who regard it at least as Grey Street's equal; it is certainly a fine classical prospect for anyone who keeps his eyes firmly above the line of the shop fronts and concentrates on the elegant proportions of the upper floors. It shows at its best looking up the slope from the station. A particularly appealing factor – and proof of the detailed care taken by the designers – is the way Nun Street and Nelson Street, leading at right-angles off it to the west, are closed in by shapely bow-fronted pubs (though the one in Nelson Street is admittedly a bit off-centre). Also to the west is the **Grainger Market**, built to Dobson's design in 1835 to general acclaim. At the bottom of the street is the impressive frontage of the **Trustee Savings Bank** by John Watson (1861). Opposite it is **St John's Church**, which gives an impression of great age with its black, worn stone and attractive tower, somewhat swamped like St Andrew's by modern developments. There was probably a Norman church on the site, and we can see an indication of this in the Norman arch of the window in the north wall of the chancel, which itself is the oldest part of the building and appears to contain Noman stones. But basically the church is thirteenth-century, with alterations and additions in the fifteenth. These were due to the generosity of Robert Rhodes, at one time Member of Parliament for the town, who died in 1474 and whose most prized gift to Newcastle is the lantern tower of the cathedral. At St John's we have his arms and an inscription, '*Orate pro anima*', 'pray for the soul,' on two bosses which show that here too he was intent on beautifying his native town. St John's tower with its high-pointed arch was built in the thirteenth century, but much of its attraction, especially when viewed from the chancel, comes from the vaulted roof behind it, which seems to have been built with Rhodes's money and carries one of the bosses mentioned above. The other is on the gable outside the south transept, which seems also to have been his gift. An unusual feature is the early fifteenth-century west aisle of the north transept, and it is this which gives the building an open and spacious air that could not be guessed at from outside. There is little stained glass, but one window in the north wall of the chancel contains fragments dating from 1350 to 1850, and above the centre of the left-hand light is the earliest known representation of the arms of the town: three castles on a red ground. There are also two fine examples of woodwork: the Jacobean pulpit (*circa* 1610) and the font (1690), the cover of which is much older, probably from about 1500.

From here a short detour up the Westgate Road leads to the **Old Assembly Rooms** (1774/6, by William Newton in the style of Nash). The building was dedicated in the true spirit of the age to 'the most elegant recreation' – and elegant it was, particularly inside, where the ballroom challenged comparison with Bath and York. It is now being redeveloped as an 'entertainment complex', which may strike a chill into some sensitive hearts. Yet a fine building which had been falling into decay should have life breathed back into it; and the great room on the first floor, with its chandeliers, its walls and ceiling in blue and cream and its apse in a delicate shade of powder pink, is still undeniably splendid.

The bottom of Westgate Road is as good a place as any in which to end the morning's sightseeing and look around for lunch before tackling the cathedral, the castle and Quayside. There is a wide choice in a small radius to suit every pocket – the posh *Swallow* and *Station* hotels, *The Royal Turk's Head* in Grey Street, from where the Edinburgh coaches used to start, the *Hadrian*, off the station platform, the Italian *Roma* in Collingwood Street, the *Empress* next door to the cathedral, and just above it three good Indian restaurants (the *Rajah*, the *Koh-i-Noor* and the *Golden Bengal*), *Pumphreys'* in the Cloth Market, and the unique *Balmbra's* from where the revellers set out in the most famous of all Tyneside ballads:

> Aw went to Blaydon Races,
> t'was on the ninth of June,
> Eighteen hundred and sixty-two
> on a summer's afternoon;
> Aw tyeck the bus from Balmbra's
> and she wis heavy laden,
> Away we went along Collingwood Street,
> that's on the road to Blaydon . . .

The races, alas! are no longer held, but *Balmbra's* bar and its music-hall (strictly known as *The Oxford*) were restored to their old glory in 1962 on the centenary of the great day and still keep alive much of its flavour. On the quayside are the *Moulin Rouge*, the *Red House*, the *Cooperage*, opposite the Swing Bridge, in a converted fifteenth-century building, and across the water in Gateshead the large *Five Bridges Hotel*.

Resuming just downhill from the Assembly Rooms and the pleasant County Court building at the bottom of Westgate Road, one is faced with John Dobson's **Central Railway Station**, surpassing any other terminus in the country outside of London. For his revolutionary use of curved ironwork in the ribs of his roof Dobson won a medal at the Paris Exhibition of 1858, but what remains in most visitors' minds is the splendid classical *porte cochère* facing Collingwood Street. The opening ceremony was performed on 29 August 1850 by Queen Victoria and the Prince Consort in the presence of a huge concourse of ticket-holders segregated into their various enclosures – First Class (two platforms – pink tickets); Second Class (one platform – white); Third Class (one platform – blue); and Fourth Class (no platform – buff). A century and a quarter later Newcastle remains proud of its station, and the Council have even refrained from knocking down the portico in the course of the 'improvements' in this part of the town.

Going eastward along Collingwood Street past hideously insensitive rebuilding one sees to the right the neo-Grecian front of Newcastle's Literary and Philosophical Society building by John Greene (1822) on the site of the old town house of the Earls of Westmorland. Its library and lecture rooms have seen most of the great Tyneside figures, from George Stephenson, who lectured here on the Geordie safety lamp, to his son Robert and the first Lord Armstrong. Here in February 1879 Joseph Wilson Swan demonstrated his incandescent electric lamp, and in the following year the Lit and Phil became the first public building to be lit in this way.

Further along still is **St Nicholas's**, since 1822 Newcastle's **Cathedral**. Its splendid open-work lantern tower was completed in 1448, slightly earlier than the similar crown of St Giles in Edinburgh. Perched dizzily nearly two hundred feet above the pavement on top of its tower, it is a triumph of ingenuity, daring and grace: an astonishing legacy from an age that was about to plunge itself into the fatuities of the Wars of the Roses. It has had other uses than that of pure decoration. When in 1644 in Charles I's time the besieging Scottish Army threatened to bombard it unless the town surrendered, the Cavalier commander, Sir John Marley, replied that if St Nicholas's tower fell it would not fall alone, and promptly marched his Scottish prisoners up aloft. No shots were fired at it, and in gratitude someone wrote a poem:

> Stout Sir John Marley
> Who fought late and early:
> Though the garrison lived and fed rather barely,
> O what a brave knight was Governor Marley.

The parish church of so important a town naturally played its part in history. Marley's master, Charles I, worshipped here during his not too rigorous imprisonment in Anderson Place. John Knox preached from its pulpit and in typically dictatorial style banished its ungodly lectern, which later found its way back to where it now stands. Admiral Lord Collingwood of Trafalgar fame who was born nearby in one of the old houses in The Side was baptised and married here – his memorial tablet by Rossi is on the wall immediately to the right on entering.

Inside, St Nicholas's is an impressively unified thirteenth/fourteenth-century church with traces of earlier building and some Victorian restoration. It suffered at the hands of the Reformers, who broke up the glass of its east window, a few fragments of which can be seen in a roundel over the altar. Mercifully they seem to have overlooked the fifteenth-century font cover with its beautiful Coronation of the Virgin, and were too early in time to uproot the handsome Carolingian organ with its gilded angels which takes up nearly the whole of the north transept. The body of the church has some unusual features: its aisles are wider than its nave and there is an almost complete absence of capitals to the columns in the nave, at the crossing and tower arch. Bruce Alsopp praises the 'extremely clean' visual effect that results, but Pevsner seems rather disturbed by it and remarks peevishly that the treatment of the tower arch carries the concept to extremes. The fourteenth-century crypt chapel is worth a visit – it is still in active use as a chapel of rest. There are a number of monuments in chancel and aisles to local worthies. A curiosity is a showcase containing a sliver of oak said to be from the piers of the Roman bridge. As the accompanying text points out, the tree from which it was cut would have been standing in the time of Christ.

Just below the cathedral is the **Keep** of the 'new castle' which gave the town its name. Built by Henry II, it stands on a bluff commanding the river crossing on a site previously occupied in turn by a Roman fort and by the motte and bailey castle built by Robert, eldest son of William the Conqueror. It is a splendid piece of Norman military architecture, its massive blocks of stone washed baptismally clean of the Tyneside soot by order of the city council – I should imagine for considerably more than the £911 10s. 9d it cost Henry to build in 1172. Most of its curtilage was swept away when the railway was built; indeed, at one time it was in danger of being converted into a signal box; and nowadays the viaduct along which the London to Edinburgh trains grind by and the horrid presence of its neighbour, County Hall, have severely polluted its environment; but there are scale models on view inside which give a good idea of how it must have looked in the days when it was the key to the Border defences against the Scots.

Entrance is by the unusual stone stairway on the south face into a small museum on the second floor and then into the Hall, which apart from the brick vaulting and the roof is exactly as it was built eight centuries ago. On one wall is the receipt given by Roger of Stutevelle, Sheriff of Northumberland, on final completion, rendering account 'For work at the New Castle upon Tyne and for the gate of the said castle, four score pounds and seventeen shillings and one penny is accounted for, by the King's writ, and supervised by Roger of Glanville as ordered by the King – and he is quit.' They got value for money in those days, as one sees from the immense solidity of the walls. Downstairs is a guard-room and the well preserved Norman **Chapel**, rib-vaulted with zigzag decoration. From the roof, among the battlements added by John Dobson, there is a fine view over the city, which from this angle seems gripped in a tight noose of railway lines. It is hardly pretty or elegant, and contrasts sadly with the picture downstairs in the museum of Newcastle in Victorian times, but it expresses well the power that helped to build the town's fortunes as a centre of communications.

From the battlements one looks down on the only other surviving part of the medieval castle, the **Black Gate**, built in 1247 to strengthen the defences on the vulnerable western side. It wears a brick super-structure of a much more recent date which gives it a decidedly quaint *Snow White and the Seven Dwarfs* appearance, and appropriately it houses what is believed to be the world's only **Bagpipe Museum**, opened by the Duke of Northumberland in 1972. It is the collection of Mr William Cocks of Ryton. New excavations are at present being undertaken in the foundations to the west.

The gates in the railings to the east of the Keep lead into a court-yard, Castle Garth, on one side of which is the tasteless mass of County Hall, and on the other William Stokoe's fine Grecian **Moot Hall**, now the home of the Crown Court. It is a building for which I have great personal affection, particularly for the beautiful Grand Jury Room on the first floor which overlooks the Tyne. There used to be a fine view from the forecourt looking east to the spire of David Stephenson's All Saints' Church, a far more dominant build-ing than the cathedral and indeed the most striking thing in the Newcastle skyline seen from the south, but much of this has now been ruined by new building. The Moot Hall's frontage on to the river shows up splendidly in old prints, but it too is now largely hidden by modern developments on the Gateshead side.

From Castle Garth the best way to reach Quayside is by the flight of steps plunging downwards between the Moot Hall and a private car park or by the near-by and charmingly named 'Dog Leap Stairs'. Either will vividly remind you of the steepness of the Tyne escarpment and help to explain much of Newcastle's early history as a fortress. At the bottom the traffic roars and one can be marooned for minutes at a time on the island by the roundabout. On the north side of the street are some of the old mansions of the merchants who dominated the town: the best known is the five-storey **Bessie Surtees House**, scene of a famous elopement in 1774. The fortunate lover was an impecunious young man who later became Lord Chancellor. This is one of a group of houses of some distinction – notice also Number 43 (sixteenth-century, restored in the eighteenth), Number 33 (Derwentwater House), and Number 23 (the Red House, now a restaurant).

Across from them on the Quayside, with its back to the colourful panorama of the river and the bridges, is the **Guildhall**, an ancient foundation of 1316, rebuilt by Robert Trollop in 1655 in a style never seen before or since, and decently covered up a century and a half later by David Stephenson, W. Newton, and ultimately by Dobson in 1823. I cannot bring myself to like it in its present shape and can only regret the suppression of Trollop's attractively crazy scheme. Internally, however, its great hall (one end of which houses the most individual, not to say uinque, courtroom in the country) is a revamping of Trollop's work with an attractive though frail-looking hammer-beam ceiling.

The stretch of Quayside downstream from the Guildhall is a reminder of how much of Newcastle's business still depends on the sea, and a grand old jumble of wharves and warehouses it is. The housing is mostly next door to derelict, and on the higher ground above City Road the bulldozers have been at work, but for the visitor who perseveres there are unexpected treasures.

Beyond the **Customs House** (1776, restored 1840), up the narrow passage of Trinity Chare, is **Trinity House**, a kind of Tudor 'Port of Tyne Authority' that maintained the river and the lighthouses that came much later to be built along the coast, besides providing here a school and almshouses. Even in their present dilapidated state the courtyards of red and whitewashed brick, with their scrolls and inscriptions over the doorways, have the decorous charm one expects in such towns as Delft, and the Carolingian wood carving in the

132

chapel and the Georgian panelling in the hall are remarkably fine.
It could do with a face-lift; and that is what the near-by **Keelman's Hospital** has recently received. Another handsome Dutch-looking building with a domed clock tower of Queen Anne's time, it stands above the site of the old Milk Market and of the suburb of Sandgate outside the walls immortalised in the ballad of *The Keel Row*:

> As I came through Sandgate
> I heard a lassie sing:
> 'Weel may the keel row
> That my laddie's in.'

The restorers have also been at work on William Newton's **St Ann's Church** (1786) just along from it in City Road. Around these two fine buildings, in what was once a warren of tenements and warehouses, stretches a desert of rubble and new roads, and one must look hard and penetrate into the pedestrian underpasses that lie behind the Australian Centre at the entrance to the George V bridge to find the **Joicey Museum**, housed in the seventeenth-century **Holy Jesus Hospital**, with its range of thirty moulded brick arches and gables in the tradition of Sir Christopher Wren, cowering between a railway viaduct and a multi-storey car park.

It is worth the trouble, for the Joicey is an excellent museum, geared in particular to the young, who will be entranced by its models of old Newcastle, its collections of weapons and armour, the regimental rooms and a sequence of beautifully constructed tableaux showing the development of taste in furniture and décor from the time of the early Stuarts to the arrival of Art Nouveau. There is a Thomas Bewick room honouring the great engraver and author of *The History of British Land Birds* and *The History of British Water Birds*, who lived and worked near by at Amen Corner in St Nicholas Square. A lesser but nevertheless appealing Northumbrian artist is also well represented in the museum – the woodcarver Gerrard Robinson (born 1834), who built up a fashionable practice in London in mid-Victorian times before returning to Newcastle to die there at the age of fifty-seven. His romantic evocations of King Arthur out hunting in a forest and other Tennysonian fantasies are out of favour today, but there is a powerful realism in his carving of an otter hunt which suggests that his talents were not really suited to the romantic tastes of that age. For the benefit of schools, the museum has a class-room on the premises, equipped for the showing of films and slides, where some of the exhibits can also be handled.

Once dominating this whole area but now hemmed in with modern building is **All Saints** (1786), one of the most interesting of North-umbrian churches. Its architect was David Stephenson, who used the plateau site at the edge of the escarpment to show off his portico and steeple to best effect to visitors coming from the south. Pevsner prefers Stephenson's treatment to Gibbs's similar work at St Martin's in the Fields, and without question the elliptical church behind it is a gem – perhaps more a theatre than a place of worship, with its box-pews and gallery of Honduras mahogany under a plasterwork ceiling, but a perfect expression of its age. It is therefore not wholly unjust that after restoration it is to be handed over to secular use.

At this point, near the George V bridge and the bold and effective new treatment of this, the main traffic entrance to the town from the south, the return journey uphill begins with a short stretch of Mosley Street to the junction with **Grey Street**, which Gladstone on his visit to Newcastle in October 1862 thought 'our best modern street' and which nearly a century later evoked the admiration of John Betjeman as being superior even to Nash's work in London. For Pevsner it is 'the best of Dobson's city streets' and one of the best in England – praise that is well justified and open only to this one objection, that at least three other architects besides Dobson worked on it and it cannot in justice be claimed as his creation alone, though he certainly designed the eastern side of it as far as Shakespeare Street and the Central Exchange at its northern end. The secret of its attraction, as many others besides Betjeman have noticed, is that long curve ascending the hill, with the Grecian portico of the **Theatre Royal** balanced across the way by Dobson's domes on the **Exchange,** and the column of the **Grey Memorial** drawing the eye top-centre as sweetly as do the trees at the crossing in that great avenue painting by Hobbema. Though not quite what it was when Gladstone strolled there in its bright morning, it remains a most beautiful street; even the traffic has recently been thinned out by order of the Council.

A turn to the right at the monument takes you back into the hub of things at the busy junction with Northumberland Street. How-ever, continue across it into New Bridge Street to find on your left the neo-baroque dome of the **Laing Art Gallery**, a building of which Dobson would have approved. Along with the Joicey and Hancock Museums, the Morden Tower and the 'Lit and Phil', this is the shop window of the Northumbrian arts, but, alas! at any given moment a large number of its permanent possessions will be hiding in the cellars to make room for touring exhibitions which gobble up its severely restricted space. No doubt there are good reasons for this, but it is sad to miss the Carmichaels and the John Martins and the Richardsons which ideally should be present on its walls to support the Newcastle silver and the small but beautiful display of Beilby painted glass, most of it on loan from Squadron Leader John Rush, AFC, whose book on the subject has had a wide success. Even apart from the Beilbys, Newcastle glass shares with Bristol the distinction of being by far the finest British provincial glass; it was in high demand by the Dutch engravers. An expert on the subject told me that any Jacobean glass in a collection will probably turn out to be from Newcastle. At present the Laing has only one exhibit from this classical period, but it has a good collection of eighteenth- and nineteenth-century glass, including some attractive work by Sowerby and Company of Gateshead.

Next door to the Laing is the new city **Library**, an austere, grey building of undeniable power, forming one side of a pedestrian precinct. Wheeled traffic is forbidden, but one gets the impression that the pedestrians are not very welcome either, and it is a relief to escape into the cheerful crowds of Northumberland Street.

The libraries and the galleries represent one aspect of Tyneside, the skills of its artists. But the real genius of the place lies less with Bewick, great engraver though he was, than with George Stephenson and his son Robert, with Charles Parsons, who first applied the principle of the steam turbine to the propulsion of a ship, and William Armstrong, the inventor of the hydraulic crane and designer of the breech-loading gun.

For this reason – although the visitor who wants to sample Newcastle's more sylvan side can make the short journey to **Jesmond Dene**, with its charming waterfall and rustic bridge – the visit to Newcastle should end close to where it began, at the **Museum of Science and Engineering** in Exhibition Park. It is there that the local flavour is at its strongest. In a specially built gallery is Sir Charles Parsons's little *S.Y. Turbinia* which in 1894 revolutionised sea transport. 'The Fastest Vessel Afloat: Another Triumph for Tyneside Engineering', enthused the local press at the time. Later *Turbinia* was cheekily to show off her paces by gate-crashing Queen Victoria's Diamond Jubilee Naval Review – no one had asked her. In a neighbouring room is Sir Charles's *Auxetophone*, looking like a gigantic tuba to be played in some demon band. There are mechanical engines in profusion of every shape and size, manufactured tools, lathes, torpedoes, guns, printing presses, safety lamps and beautiful ships' models, including that of HMS *Nelson*, one of the 'Cherry Tree' class of battleship whose overall length was 'cut down by Washington' or, to be precise, by the Washington Naval Treaty; and of the best loved of all Atlantic liners, the *Mauretania*, which was built on the Tyne and held the Blue Riband for the fastest crossing for twenty-two years, from 1907 to 1929. There are also models of the *Rocket* and of *Puffing Billy*, which used to work at Wylam Colliery, and the actual locomotive George Stephenson built for the Killingworth Colliery. It is a collection worthy of a city whose voice, long muted, is now beginning once more to trumpet its achievements to the world. After all, Newcastle's first printing press was set up by no less a person than King Charles I, the man who also gave the town the motto it still bears on its coat of arms – *Fortiter Defendit Triumphans* Bravely it (the City) Defends in Triumph.

Chapter 8

From Newcastle to Morpeth

❧

From Newcastle the main route north is by the motorway and the A1 to Morpeth and Alnwick. It is a pleasant enough road but carries a lot of traffic. The route nearer the coast passes through Tyneside's industrial overspill, the fine 'new town' development at **Cramlington, Bedlington** (where the famous terriers originated) and **Ashington,** birthplace of the footballing Charltons, Jack and Bobby, and of their uncle, 'Wor Jackie' Milburn of Newcastle United who was equally worshipped in his day. This part of the world has long played a prominent part in industrial technology – for instance, the rails for the Stockton–Darlington railway were cast at Bedlington, and at Killingworth, now wholly redeveloped as a new town, George Stephenson designed the locomotive *Blucher* which first ran in 1814 – but it is certainly not the most scenic part of Northumberland. Further west, however, lie unspoilt country and a number of villages and fine houses on either side of the A696.

Take this road to **Ponteland,** which has an interesting church with a Norman tower and the remarkable *Blackbird Inn* (converted from a seventeenth-century manor house itself converted from a medieval pele) but is chiefly famed locally for its plush stockbroker belt of the Darras Hall Estate. Continue past the fine seventeenth-century red brick of **Higham Dykes** to Belsay with its arcaded street. **Belsay Hall,** a Greek Doric mansion of 1810/17 by Sir Charles Monck, is not at present open to the public but there are rumours that this situation may change. I must confess that I have not had the pleasure of seeing it, but Judge Lyall Wilkes, co-author of *Tyneside Classical: The Newcastle of Grainger, Dobson and Clayton,* tells me that it is a superb example of the neo-classical, perhaps a little too pure and geometric for some tastes, but of its kind almost without rival in Britain. There is also the fourteenth-century tower house of Belsay Castle.

Hereabouts are tempting diversions. Three miles due north on a minor road is the hamlet of **Bolam** and the church of St Andrew. There was once a sizeable village here; now only the big house, the vicarage and the church, forming one of the most seigniorial

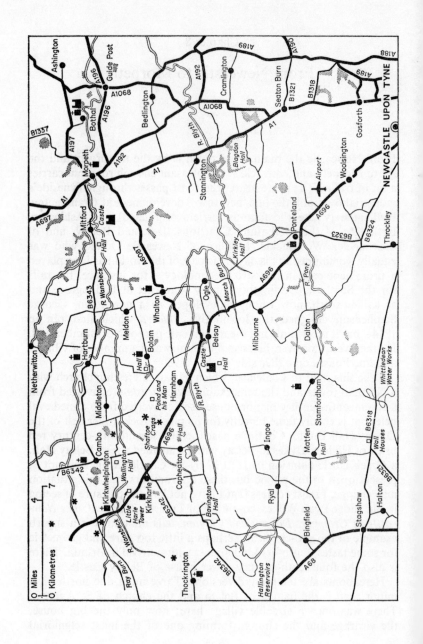

groups imaginable, the landscape of 'improvement'. The **Church** has a late Saxon tower with elegant bell lights and a Norman interior of great charm. It houses the crude effigy tomb of Robert de Reymes (d 1324), the builder of Aydon Castle and neighbouring Shortflatt Tower, which is lived in to this day. From the churchyard there is a fine view northwards to the line of the Simonside Hills, their crests sharp against the skyline. At the approach to the hamlet is **Bolam Lake**, now being developed as a Country Park.

A short distance along the minor road in the direction of Scots Gap a public footpath marked with a green signpost leads a mile to **Shaftoe Crags**, rearing themselves above the line of the A696. High on the crags is a large boulder known as 'The Devil's Punchbowl'. It was put to actual use as such at wedding celebrations of Sir William Blackett of Wallington in 1775. In the vicinity is a promontory fort and also a round barrow and standing stone called by the intriguing name of **Poind and His Man**. A much later arrival was the Roman road marked on modern maps as 'The Devil's Causeway' which ran through this countryside, perhaps on the line of much earlier tracks.

On the other side of the A696 and rather further off our route is **Stamfordham**, a pretty village built round a green, with a thirteenth-century church at the far end of it overlooking the low-lying country. In the chancel lie the effigy of a priest (probably the earliest in the county) and the legless figure of a knight who may be Sir John Felton, a survivor of the Battle of Otterburn Field in 1338 who lived to be High Sheriff. Arthur Bigge, private secretary to Queen Victoria and to King George V, lived here as a boy, where his father was vicar, and took the name of the village when he became Lord Stamfordham.

At this point one meets one of the problems facing those who write guide-books to Northumberland. There is so much of it and so much worth viewing. The moment one strays from any given route the complications are endless. From Stamfordham, for example, via **Ryal**, a minor road along a hill crest crosses delightful open country, with enormous views over the 'wild hills' or the Wannies, to the junction at the 'five lane ends' with the A68. The road passes close to the hamlet of **Ingoe**, which has a standing stone and hut circles near by. Bronze Age finds were made in the vicinity in 1860. On the far side of the A68, to the west of the *Tone Inn*, the adventurous motorist can find his way along gated roads to the Buteland Fells above Bellingham and the valleys of the Rede and North Tyne (see chapters 15 and 16). The sod banks on either side of the track are reminders of the old droving days. It is wonderful country for picnickers and lovers of solitude, but you must choose your weather and carry a good map. However, this is a digression piled on a digression and is to stray from east into central Northumberland.

Return, then, to Belsay and the A696. A few miles beyond the village going north a turn to the right (easily missed, for the signpost is set low) leads to **Harnham** – a ruined hall on a mound among the trees, backed by a group of farm buildings around a green; a most harmonious and beautiful spot. Here in the seventeenth century lived Katherine Babington, wife of the governor of Berwick and zealously militant daughter of the Roundhead general, Sir Arthur Hazelrigg, who had preferred the bill of Attainder against Strafford. The Restoration of Charles II and the return to power of the Anglican Church did nothing to daunt this fiercely Puritan spirit. For conniving with the local blacksmith (some say butcher's boy) to drag a vicar out of his pulpit in mid-sermon she was censured and later excommunicated (as was the blacksmith/butcher's boy), and when she died in 1670 her body was refused burial in consecrated ground. So she was laid to rest in a tomb in her garden at the Hall.

The simulation of a coffin is still there, though the real one was stolen for its lead in the eighteenth century and the bones scattered. But so forceful a lady could not be disposed of so easily; her spirit (strongly reinforced by a number of curious stone busts) still seems to brood over Harnham and the two grass terraces that descend to the grim little chamber where they buried her, the coffin lying on a stone shelf out of deference to an old tradition that the estates would pass out of her family if she was laid below ground. The pseudo-coffin, incidentally on its shelf, still conforms to this belief. There are two burial inscriptions. One seems to be contemporary and is carved in stone:

> Here lyeth the body of Madam
> Babington who was laid in this
> Sepulcher the 9 of September 1670
> My time is past as you may see
> I viewed the Dead, as you do me
> Or (ere) long you'll lie as low as I
> And some will look on thee.

The other is painted on wood – though by whom or at what date there is no record:

In hopes of future bliss, contented here I lie,
Tho' I would have been pleased to live, yet was not displeased
   to die.
For life hath its comforts and its sorrows too,
For which to the Lord of Heaven our most grateful thanks are
   due:
If it were otherwise, our hopes here would rest
Where nature tells us we cannot be blest;
How far my hopes are vain or founded well,
God alone knows, but the last day will tell.

I must add that Harnham is private land and permission to visit must be asked at the Hall.

A little further north, just to the left of the road, is **Kirkharle**, where Capability Brown was born. There is no memorial to him in the church. Another mile and a half further on, on the other side of the A696, is **Kirkwhelpington**, snugly secure on its mound. It has a church with an aisleless thirteenth-century nave, and in its churchyard is buried Sir Charles Parsons, pioneer of the steam turbine. Further back, just before Kirkharle, a minor road off the A696 leads to **Capheaton Hall**, which Pevsner calls one of the most interesting houses of its date and character in England, praising its 'endearing and provincial baroque'. Its architect was Robert Trollop, who built Newcastle's Guildhall. For Capheaton he received the sum of £500. This house is not at the time of writing open to the public but it shortly will be. There is an excellent description of it in Lyall Wilkes's *Tyneside Portraits*. It was the ancestral home of the Swinburnes and was often visited by the poet Algernon Charles Swinburne, who was born in London but was a Northumbrian to the marrow. Near by is Bavington Hall, seat of the Shaftos, one of whose sea-going ancestors inspired the famous ballad which the bells of Newcastle's Civic Centre still ring out daily over the city:

> Bobby Shafto's gone to sea,
> Silver buckles on his knee;
> He'll come back and marry me,
> Bonnie Bobby Shafto.

In this area also, three miles west of Bavington, is **Thockrington**, lost in the heart of the countryside. There was once a flourishing village here, but all that now remains is a farm tucked away among the trees and a church on the higher ground. With its top-heavy bell-cote supported by a neck of stepped buttresses against its west

141

wall, **St Aidan's** looks like a dead dinosaur lying along the outcrop of the Whin Sill. It is one of the most moving of Northumbrian churches, and one of the most surprising, for its ugly Stuart or Hanoverian outer shell masks the beautiful interior created by its Norman founders. An almost horseshoe-shaped arch leads the eye past the tunnel-vaulted chancel to a mirror-image of an arch above the altar. The effect is one of elegant simplicity. A relic from the past; yet by an agreeable irony Thockrington St Aidan's easily bridges the gap between mailed Norman knights and the Welfare State, for in its graveyard lies Lord Beveridge.

On the other side of the A696 a minor road leads to **Wallington Hall**, which can also be reached via Bolam. This is one of the very few great Northumbrian houses open to the public. Embedded in its cellars are the foundations of the pele tower which once stood on the site. The Fenwicks (a Northumbrian clan still very numerous and active in the county) acquired it, rebuilt it, and indirectly affected British history, for when Sir John Fenwick, last of his family to hold the hall, was executed in 1697 on a charge of plotting to assassinate William III, his horse, Sorrel, was escheated to the crown, and it was while riding it that the King was fatally injured when Sorrel, like a good Jacobite, stumbled over a molehill in the park at Hampton Court.

What we see today is substantially the house built for Sir William Blackett in 1688, the year of the Glorious Revolution. It passed in time to the Trevelyans and finally to the National Trust as the gift of Sir Charles Trevelyan, a member of Ramsay MacDonald's Labour governments of 1924 and 1929/31.

From the outside the house is elegant but severe – the frou-frou appears only in the stable block with its small classical dome. Inside all is opulent good taste. Outstanding is the superb plasterwork of the Italian *stuccatori* employed by Sir William Blackett during the remodelling of the building in the 1740s – a Reynolds portrait in the 'Saloon' of this portly country squire in an old brown suit and shovel hat, attended by his dog, perfectly displays the mixture of the rustic and the grandiose that marked the English gentry at the high tide of their fortunes. Sir William was in fact a man of considerable artistic taste and creative talent; it was he who planned the restoration of the house, created the park and gardens, and rebuilt the estate village of Cambo. 'Fabulous' is the only word to describe Wallington's collection of china, and some of the furniture is almost as good. Among several good paintings is one of Miss Susanna (Sukey) Trevelyan – said to be by Gainsborough but later altered by Reynolds

142

who painted out her wide-brimmed hat – some Romneys, Hoppners and Turners, and a panel of blue cornflowers by Ruskin, which he left unfinished after a dispute with his hostess, Lady Pauline Trevelyan, who dutifully finished the job and signed it, 'P.T.' This stands next to the 'Death of Bede' in the Central Hall.

It was this same highly gifted and artistic lady who, on Ruskin's advice, commissioned the most interesting artistic works to be found at Wallington: a set of eight murals in the Central Hall by a young Edinburgh-born admirer of the Pre-Raphaelites, William Bell Scott, a poet and painter who is now re-emerging after a century of neglect as an artist of rare talent. He was, wrote Dante Gabriel Rossetti, 'the best of philosophic natures, a man of the truest genius'. Christina Rossetti was in love with him and would have married him had he not been married already. The murals depict episodes from Northumbrian history, from the building of Hadrian's Wall to Grace Darling's rescue of the passengers from the *Forfarshire*, and, perhaps more successful, because of his time, an evocation of industrial Tyneside. Local worthies of every class and kind found themselves limned for posterity in situations and poses rather unlike themselves. In the most famous of the murals, 'The Building of Hadrian's Wall', Dobson and Grainger's friend and supporter, the Town Clerk of Newcastle, John Clayton, is the frenetic-looking centurion with the glittering eye and pointing finger, directing Ancient Britons to get on with it. Lady Pauline herself appears in one scene, wailing high on the cliffs as the Danes raid Tynemouth. In the Grace Darling picture the painter craftily included his mistress, Alice Boyd, aboard the wrecked vessel.

At another level, the most popular of all Wallington's attractions are the dolls' houses, including an enormous one presented to the Trust in 1970. The old kitchen is also interesting, though I personally feel that too many 'Downstairs' implements of all kinds have been crammed into it, making it more a museum than a room – a contrived element wholly out of keeping with the rest of this enchanting house. Lovers of literature will find in the Study the desk at which Lord Macaulay wrote his *History of England*. Woodcarvers should make a special point of seeing the two panels in the gallery by Thomas Kendall (1878).

The park and gardens are very fine. They contain the sole survivor of the first larches to grow in England, presented to Wallington as seedlings by the Duke of Atholl in 1738; also an artificial lake, an elegant bridge built by James Paine (1760) and some curious eighteenth-century griffins' heads brought from London. Capability

Brown was responsible for the landscaping but for some reason the National Trust's guide-book omits his name – almost a relief when one thinks of the number of Capability Brown parks up and down the country. To round things off, there is an excellent café next door to the stable block and clock tower. The Northumbrian Pipers' Annual Gathering is held here early in June, but those allergic to this kind of music should not allow themselves to be put off, for the Northumbrian pipes, which only developed from their Scottish ancestors in the seventeenth century, are much more subdued, even beautiful, with an Arcadian tone to them: first cousins of the pipes of Pan.

A mile north of Wallington on a ride overlooking the grounds is its model estate village of **Cambo**, which gets its name from Camhoe, a fort or camp on a hill. Capability Brown went to school here. The building still survives and boasts also the report book of one of its head teachers, William Robson, who used to write rhyming couplets about his pupils:

> The names distinguished by a star
> Were the most docible by far;
> And those with equidistant strokes
> Were second-handed sort of folks;
> But where you find the letter B
> A humdrum booby you will see;
> And where an exclamation set
> The rascals went away in debt.

In William Robson's time, of course, education had to be paid for. Cambo post office occupies what was once a pele tower nearly on the crest of high ground. Not as high as the church, though, from whose graveyard you overlook the green and unspoilt country rolling away on every side. The church was built in 1842 by Hodgson, the historian and vicar of Hartburn: with its aisleless nave, whitewashed walls, pine pews and plain glass in most of its windows it breathes an atmosphere of light and reason. The west tower was added in 1883, perhaps to provide a more imposing and conventional presence for the worshippers from Wallington Hall. Let into its inside wall are some old gravestones, one of them showing a woman whose feet are resting on the back of a dog that is brandishing its tail. The inclusion of a family dog on a gravestone was often used as a general symbol of fidelity.

Just to the north of the church the B6343 leads along the valley

144

Newcastle

Above. Bridges over the Tyne. *Below*. Grey Street, with the portico of Theatre Royal, designed by John and Benjamin Green, on the right, and the Grey Monument – the column by Benjamin Green, the statue of the second Earl Grey by E. H. Bailey

'The Side' – a plunging street typical of so much of pre-war Newcastle, now being relentlessly destroyed

The view from George V Bridge, showing many of the city's most notable buildings: Henry II's Keep, the Cathedral lantern tower of 1448, the seventeenth-century Guildhall, Bessie Surtees' house and the early nineteenth-century Moot Hall

to **Hartburn**, where in Roman times a timber bridge carried the Devil's Causeway over the stream. John Hodgson, the historian of Northumberland, was vicar here from 1833 to 1845. The medieval-looking pele tower on the left on entering the village is an eighteenth-century fantasy built by the parishioners under the direction of their vicar, Dr Sharp, father of that Granville Sharp who was one of the leading Abolitionists in the anti-Slave Trade Campaign and founding-father of what used to be called Sierra Leone. Its ground floor in those days was the parish stable; its upper floor housed the schoolmaster. Close by is the eighteenth-century vicarage standing above a curve of the Hart burn and the **Church** with its squat tower glimpsed alluringly through the trees.

The tower, which may once have been free-standing, is the oldest part of the fabric we now see. A few years ago a number of skeletons were found in its walls, and these have been dated to between 966 and 1166. A charter of King John in 1207 shows that at that time the church belonged to the monks of Tynemouth Abbey, but it later seems to have been taken over by southerners from St Alban's, called north to rescue the declining monastic life of the area. Some of the stresses of the rebuilding that followed can be traced at the junction of nave and tower, where the bulge in the stonework above the filled-in wall shows where the tower arch had proved too weak for its work. The tower itself in Norman times provided the living quarters for the priest, who climbed to his bed by a rope or wooden ladder – not till the middle of the thirteenth century was a stone staircase added.

Internally Hartburn's most striking feature is of the kind met with so often in Northumbrian churches, a chancel that inclines quite sharply away at an angle from its nave. Traditionally this is supposed to represent the droop of Christ's head on the Cross; though the present vicar of Hartburn suggests more realistically in his guide to the building that it is probably due here to the deficiencies of the local masons. The four bays of the nave with their graceful columns are thirteenth-century; one of them, the first pillar on the south side, has an unusual if not very elegant decoration of hanging bobbles. The south doorway into the church is very ornate and preserves a link with the Knights Templars, whose Maltese cross and daggers, the insignia of a provincial grand lodge, can be seen on the inside curve of the arch as you enter. The chest facing you as you step inside belonged to Oliver Cromwell and was used by him to carry bullion.

Near Hartburn are a number of large country houses: Shortflatt Tower, Bolam Hall, Angerton Hall, Netherwitton Hall and, outstanding among them, Nunnykirk, John Dobson's masterpiece. The most that one can hope for is a glimpse of roofs and chimneys across the fields, for all these are still homes in private ownership; but even without being told about them one could guess their presence from the complete absence of ribbon development, the peaceful, orderly landscape and the crookedness of the lanes that wander across it. Try finding your way without a large-scale map, for instance, from Hartburn to Whalton: you can easily end up in Mitford – which would be no particular hardship, since both are charming villages.

Whalton is the tidier, Mitford the more exciting. The stone-built Whalton houses embody a number of pele towers, but you would never guess at anything so uncivilised from their elegant Georgian facades behind tall hedges of beech and holly. The most dominant buildings are the creeper-covered hotel and the **Manor House**, beautifully redesigned by Lutyens – the church can hardly be guessed at from the centre of the village, though from the south there is a fine view of its massive early thirteenth-century tower on the rise of the hill. It has two distinctive features: a very short nave, which gives it a square, box-like effect, and a north aisle to its chancel. Traces of an earlier church can be spotted by the curious in the two-pointed stone niches on the south wall of the nave, evidently the remains of blocked lancet windows, and in the respond at that west end of the north aisle, where the Norman capital was left in place when the thirteenth-century rebuilding of the nave was undertaken. The church is usually locked, but the key is always available at the vicarage up the road. The village stages a Baal Fire ceremony on the evening of 4 July with folk and sword dancing: an event said to date back to Saxon times.

Compared with Whalton, which is all of one piece, **Mitford** is a Jekyll-and-Hyde of a place. If you come to it direct from Hartburn on the B6343 you will certainly want to hurry on to Morpeth. Just below the village, however, on a parallel road nearer the Wansbeck, you enter another world: fields and trees; a church spire; the bastions of a medieval castle; a Carolingian gateway; and the park and classical facade of a mansion built by John Dobson in 1823. This last is now unoccupied and will soon become derelict unless like near-by Matfen Hall it is bought by the Cheshire Homes or some similar charity. Massive, rambling and unloved, it has a forlorn, beaten look, unlike the jagged stump of the castle which still glares defiance from its mound. The church with its tall spire does not look old, though parts of it date from the twelfth century. Its priest's door on

146

the outside south wall of the chancel is of this period and one of the finest in Northumberland. Notice also the Norman pier on the western side of the north arch of the transept and the thirteenth-century lancet windows in the chancel. The feel of the church is, however, decidedly Victorian and mixes rather oddly with the ruined gateway of the now vanished manor house next door.

The village is the ancestral home of that talented and prolific literary family which has given us *The Pursuit of Love, Hons and Rebels*, and so many other lively works in addition to a treatise on the concept of 'U' and 'Non U'. An earlier member of the clan was Mary Russell Mitford, author of *Our Village*, who took to writing in desperation after her father had spent both his wife's dowry and her own twenty-five thousand pounds winnings in the Irish Sweep. Meadows Taylor, who wrote *Confessions of a Thug*, was also a Mitford through his mother; nor should we forget 'Drunken Jack' Mitford, one of Nelson's captains, who fell on evil days but still contrived from the workhouse to write that once famous but now almost forgotten book about his experiences, *Johnny Newcome in the Navy*.

'Whenever I think how I am to be happy again my thoughts carry me back to Morpeth,' wrote that Trafalgar hero Admiral Lord Collingwood; and when one looks at his eighteenth-century house in Oldgate, with the bridge over the river and the meadows on one side and the snug little street of Georgian facades shut in by the Clock Tower at the other, one understands what he meant.

Morpeth's reputation at large, however, for most Northumbrians has not been invariably as happy. 'You'll end up in Morpeth' is another way of telling someone that he wants his head examined, for here is the mental hospital; and here too for many years were the headquarters of the county Constabulary.

As late as fifty years ago this was a beautiful town, surpassing even Alnwick and Hexham. Traces, as in Oldgate, still remain, but they have to be searched for up alleyways and unfrequented streets. Morpeth's town hall in the old market-place was designed by no less a person than Vanbrugh, but it was rebuilt and ruined in the nineteenth century. Modern shop fronts have similarly disfigured Newgate Street, though the *Black Bull Inn* with its charming bow front has somehow managed to survive. Further down from it on the opposite side of the road the Old Chantry House still looks delightful and very spry after its recent shampoo. Originally it housed three chantry chapels; was then used as a Grammar School; and is now a factory. It is one of the few survivors of Morpeth's prime. However, the view from the adjoining bridges over the Wansbeck – one very ancient under its modern parapet – has gaiety and charm, as certainly has the Wednesday market and the gardens by the water-side, with the moored punts and the ducks which someone is always feeding, all of which stand in the shadow of the green mound of the castle, the 'High Hill' or 'Ha', built by William de Marley, who had 'pacified' the area for the Conqueror. A late fourteenth-century gatehouse still stands above the municipal gardens facing the crenellations which housed the police headquarters before it moved to Ashington.

Another de Marley, Ranulph, concerned about the redemption of his soul, founded the abbey of Newminster about a mile upstream. This was to grow into one of the richest monastic establishments in the north, owning the forest of Kidland in the upper Coquet valley beyond Rothbury; but not much survives of past glories.

The same may well be said in some not too distant future of Morpeth's parish church of **St Mary's** which stands inconveniently out of town on the southern outskirts, ringed by housing estates and an ugly, untidy graveyard. And this is a crime against the environment if not against God, for St Mary's, reminiscent of Hartburn in its roof line, is a brooding and impressive church, and its East window contains the finest medieval glass in Northumberland, a county sadly deficient in such work. Let us not make too much of it. The richness here is nothing in comparison with windows in many other parts of Britain, but lovers of good glass should spare a few minutes for this modest but beautiful work which somehow escaped Scottish raids and the iconoclastic fury of the Puritans.

In the graveyard is buried the famous Suffragette, Emily Wilding Davison, who, on the day of the 1913 Derby, threw herself at the feet of the King's horse, Anmer, as the field rounded Tattenham Corner, and died of her injuries four days later.

She had been born at Longhorsley in 1872, and after graduating from London University joined Emmeline Pankhurst's Women's Social and Political Union, in which she swiftly graduated to the militant wing which was making itself beastly to the British male by chaining itself to railings in Downing Street and committing outrages against property deeply shocking to the public opinion of the time. A woman of heroic, perhaps excessive, temperament, she was several times imprisoned; went on hunger strike; underwent the pain and indignity of forcible feeding; on one occasion locked herself in her cell, which was thereupon flooded by hosepipe by order of the visiting magistrate; on another, threw herself from the gallery of Holloway Gaol on to the safety net below; concealed herself like Guy Fawkes in the precincts of the House of Commons, though not apparently with the aim of blowing it up but only of interrupting its debates; and horse whipped a Nonconformist minister whom for some extraordinary reason she had mistaken for Lloyd George. Huge crowds turned out in the streets of London to see her funeral procession pass, the coffin escorted by a praetorian guard of Suffragettes, and at Morpeth these scenes were repeated on a scale quite astonishing for so remote a provincial area. But then Morpeth, with its mining hinterland to the east, is far more radical than it looks: a staunchly Labour constituency. Come to think of it, if only she had been born a little later, Emily Davison would have made a very acceptable and lively Member. Yet, sad to say, the centenary of the birth of this brave and extraordinary woman passed almost unnoticed, even by her spiritual descendants of Women's Lib.

Morpeth was the birthplace of another celebrity: William Turner, who introduced scientific botany into Britain in his *New Herball* (1551). The town stages the annual gala of the Northumbrian miners. At the other end of the time scale, like Yorkshire's Ripon, it sounds a nightly curfew, but an hour earlier, at 8 o'clock.

Chapter 9

From Morpeth to Alnwick

❧

If Northumberland is fortunate in its fells and valleys it also has a coastline, nearly eighty miles of it from Tynemouth to Marshall Meadows Bay beyond the Tweed, the northern two-thirds designated an area of outstanding natural beauty. There are only some small rashes of urban sprawl and a few caravan sites to break the long sweep of sand and dune and basalt cliff of Swinburne's *A Jacobite Lament*:

> We'll see nae mair the sea-banks fair
> And the sweet grey gleaming sky,
> And the lordly strand of Northumberland
> And the goodly towers thereby;
> And none shall know but the winds that blow
> The graves wherein we lie.

The southern section between the Tyne and the Wansbeck is fairly industrialised. **Blyth** has no pretensions to be other than a workaday port, though its waterfront is not without interest to those who love ships. Between Ashington and Morpeth, however, is the rural oasis of **Bothal**, containing some charming cottages with latticed windows, a splendid small church and a castle overlooking a curve of the river Wansbeck.

There has been a house or hall (*botle*) here from pre-Conquest times. It was fortified by Richard Bertram in 1345, extended in 1576 and again in the nineteenth century, and still serves a useful purpose as a guest house of the Welwyn Electric Company. It is closed to the public. An intimidating notice, 'BEWARE OF DOG', should not prevent one from getting a glimpse of the tower gatehouse at the top of the drive. By taking a public footpath to the river, skirting the walls, you can see two stone figures on the battlements similar to those at Alnwick, and get another view of the castle from the opposite bank of the river which can be crossed by modern stepping stones.

St Andrew's Church is open to all in its peaceful wooded churchyard sloping down to the Bothal Burn, one of the most charming of Northumbrian settings. Should the entrance gate ever be shut the vicarage is conveniently opposite. The most striking outside feature is the heavily buttressed rounded bell-cote, which probably dates from the thirteenth century. A nave with north aisle and a small south chapel was built at this time, followed by the chancel. Much alteration was done in the fourteenth century when the south chapel was extended to form a south aisle, the aisle walls were raised, and the lovely deep-set square-headed windows were put in. Fragments of pale yellow and soft blue medieval glass in the tracery heads greatly add to their beauty. The clerestory was added in the fifteenth century. The chancel is sombre, with wooden stalls, a Jacobean altar rail, and the same beamed ceiling as the rest of the church. The east windows are disappointingly modern, but on the south wall there is a charming and unusual piscina with protruding basin, fluted inside, and a trefoiled sedilia, both of the thirteenth century. An unusual recess in the north-east angle of the north aisle remains a mystery. In the south aisle is the alabaster **Tomb** of Baroness Bertram and her husband Sir Ralph Ogle (1516). No doubt for centuries the pride of the church, it is now disgracefully defaced with graffiti. Sir Ralph lies in chain mail, his feet cushioned on a dog, his head resting on his bull's-head crest; the Baroness, in flowing robes beside him, has a more orthodox tasselled cushion upheld by two esquires. The tomb chest with the figures of mourners and angels is in better condition.

Nearer the coast are **Woodhorn** and **Newbiggin by the Sea**. I have to confess that two attempts to visit them were rudely met, while still some distance off, by the appearance of thick sea fret reducing visibility to a few yards. On my third assault the weather relented to provide a halcyon day, but alas! the two churches I had come to see were locked and I failed to find any keys. However, the interior of **St Mary's** Woodhorn is said to have a particular fine thirteenth-century effigy of Agnes de Valence, sister-in-law of Edward Baliol, King of Scotland. I understand that the church has been declared redundant and is only used for worship at the great festivals of the Christian year – its new role under the care of the Wansbeck District Council is as a meeting place and concert hall. The Council offices are in Ashington: (Tel. 814444). As for **Newbiggin**, it has always been a favourite with Geordie writers and is a cheerful little town grouped around the thin sickle of its bay. Its parish church stands aloof from it on a headland under its thirteenth- or fourteenth-century spire, one of the only two such spires in the county. On a calm sunny day, with

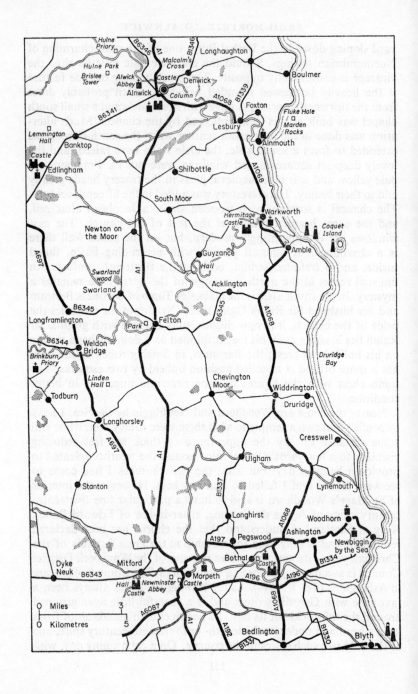

the murmur of the sea breaking on the rocks below, its crowded grave-yard can be a strangely reassuring spot: the distant pubs and boarding houses and the serried ranks of caravans lend a companionable air. Pevsner says complimentary things of the interior of this church, and I can only regret that its charms have evaded me. Through the Vicar's kindness I now learn that the key can be had at 28 East View from the Churchwarden, Mr Sampson, a great enthusiast and authority on this attractive building.

North of Newbiggin's Beacon Point lie the six miles of **Druridge Bay**. The sands and dunes are splendid, but inland the country has been ravaged by open-cast coal mining. It will look much better one day when the soil has been put back, but at present will attract only those who come to the shrine of Big Geordie, a mammoth excavator which weighs nearly three thousand tons. North of the bay is **Amble**, picturesquely placed at the mouth of the Coquet, with Coquet Island and its lighthouse (1841) just offshore. The three Trinity House keepers are also bird conservationists, protecting the nesting of the eider duck, whose southernmost breeding point this is. Amble, once a prosperous port, is now in search of a new identity as a boat-building, yachting and caravan centre.

Across the river lies **Warkworth**, one of the most exciting small towns in Britain, graced with a medieval bridge and toll house, a castle of great distinction, a Norman church, and the Hermitage, cut out of the solid rocks on the river bank. Small though it is, Warkworth has played a star role in history. Commanding the crossing of the Coquet, a stronghold here would be of obvious military importance, and in Saxon times a castle came to be built on the mound where now the late-fourteenth-century keep towers dramatically against the skyline. King John stayed here in 1214. The rebuilt Norman castle passed in time to his great-great-grandson, Edward III, who sold it to the Percy Earls of Northumberland. Hotspur was brought up here as a boy, and Shakespeare used it as a setting for scenes in both parts of *Henry IV*. Turner painted it. During the Jacobite rising of the 'Fifteen the rebel commander, the third Earl of Derwentwater, dined with several of his companions at the *Mason's Arms*, where an inscription on a beam in the bar records the event. Warkworth was the first market town in which the Old Pretender was proclaimed, and in its church of St Lawrence prayers were said for him by the Catholic army chaplain, the Protestant vicar having refused to perform this office.

When the Jacobites sat down to their dinner at the inn they paid no attention to the **Castle** high on its mound above them: it had long since fallen into ruins. Yet it remains today, as it was then, the dominating feature of the town. The best of many views of it is from a boat on the river, from the church porch at the bottom of the long street descending the hill, or from the new bridge over the Coquet on the road to Alnmouth, where, looking back, the huge bulk of the keep rises beyond the medieval toll-gate. It is a view almost impossible to overpraise. And the castle is just as fine at close quarters.

The car park is at the west entrance, beyond which a bridge over the moat leads to the ticket office and custodian's lodge. The Gate Tower is Norman (1191–1214). Moving east, the remains of the chapel, solar, kitchens and hall are to the left, and straight ahead the bases of the ruined pillars which once lined the nave of the castle church. The most impressive building still standing in the outer ward is the Lion Tower, with the heraldic emblem of the Percys still in a fair state of preservation. The **Keep** at the seaward end is one of the finest examples of its kind in Britain: a fortification thought to be impregnable to the siege artillery of the time that was also the creation of a great artist, working at the moment in the late fourteenth and early fifteenth centuries when the seeds of domestic architecture were being sown in the unlikely and troubled soil of the Border country.

From the massive windows of the Keep the visitor has views over the mouth of the Coquet to the lighthouse on the island and inland along the dark weed-strewn river which flows at the foot of the castle bluff. The main hall has a minstrels' gallery and a chapel which even in ruins are great correctives to the notion usually formed of a medieval castle as a place fit only for violence and barbarism. But that the days of greatness did not last long and were already over in Tudor times is clear from Shakespeare's 'Induction' to *King Henry IV Part II*, where he makes 'Rumour' speak very disrespectfully of Warkworth, calling it 'this worm-eaten hold of ragged stone' – a gross historical howler in the context of the fortress that Hotspur knew.

Long before the Percys had come to England, and probably before the building of the wooden palisades of the first Saxon fort, a chapel had existed at the foot of the hill by the banks of the Coquet. In 737 the Northumbrian king Ceolwulph (the man to whom Bede dedicated his *History*) gave the site and the building already on it to the monks of Lindisfarne. The Danes destroyed it in 875; the Scots did the same for its stone successor in 1174, the year when King William the Lion is said to have massacred three hundred villagers who had taken sanctuary within its walls.

Northumberland is rich in Saxon work – the crypt at Hexham, the towers of Corbridge, Bywell St Andrew, Warden and Ovingham, to name only a few – but what is rare in the county is a nearly complete Norman church. Here at Warkworth we have one, and a beauty it is. The north wall of the nave with its buttresses is Norman entirely, and it is from this angle that the visitor should take his first close look at the exterior of this fine building – from the graveyard under the copper beeches, with the placid stream of the Coquet sliding by. It is one of the most restful places imaginable, even at the height of the summer season when the pleasure boats are out on the river and the caravan camp at Amble is bursting at the seams. What even the buttresses cannot conceal, however, is the bulge in this north wall that is reaching dangerous proportions – and where in so small a community is the money to be found to save it? The rest of the church, seen from the west or from the south, the town side, where most visitors first see it, looks a great deal trimmer. The tower is twelfth-century, the spire that tops it fourteenth.

Inside, **St. Lawrence's** is a gem. The nave is ninety-feet long, the longest Norman nave in the county. The south aisle was built by the Percys somewhat later, in the fifteenth century, and is still covered by the beams of the original lead roof – a space full of air and light and graced in the east window by a few fragments of medieval glass. Best of all, however, at the heart of the church, is the chancel arch, seeming to bend inwards like a horseshoe, and the truly superb twelfth-century vaulted chancel beyond it, one of the finest of its type in Britain, its ribs marked with zigzag decoration on a model evolved a few years earlier at Durham. Even restoration in mid-Victorian times has not done much to impair a shrine very much in keeping with the Crusader who lies in effigy on his tomb in the south aisle, holding in his hand the heart that may have been buried in the Holy Land.

Legend, perhaps? The Crusades and the men who fought in them seem to belong to an era out of time. It is much easier to understand the matter-of-fact Romans of the third century than these pilgrims in armour of the eleventh, twelfth and thirteenth who crossed seas and deserts both in pursuit of an ideal and ever-hopeful for easy riches. Nor in matters of faith should we forget the animal creation. For what of the sagacious dog – a pointer – belonging to a Mr Edward Cook of Togston, that travelled with him across the Atlantic, got lost out hunting in the woods near Baltimore, and found its own way back to Warkworth to greet its astonished master on his return

155

home? Mr Cook is buried in the churchyard, the author of what must be the first of all shaggy dog stories.

Warkworth's most surprising marvel, however, is **The Hermitage** which lies on the north bank of the Coquet and is best reached during the season by ferry. Tickets should be bought at the Castle where directions will be given. It is also possible to reach this remarkable place by a riverside path on the far bank.

The word 'Hermitage' has an austere sound, and the legend attached to it of the young lord Bertram de Bothal, who accidentally slew both his brother and his intended bride and in penance gave away his worldly goods to pray for salvation by the banks of the Coquet at this spot, seems to match the Latin inscription just inside the entrance: '*Fuerunt mihi lacrymae panes nocte et die,*' 'Tears have been my portion day and night.' The truth, however, is that Warkworth Hermitage is quite spacious and in its time provided a home not for any hermit but for a chaplain. It dates from the early fourteenth century, contemporaneous with the high tide of the Percy fortunes, though the first written record of it is in 1531, when it was granted by the Earl of Northumberland to one George Lecontre, described simply as 'a priest'. Traces of a garden and of a loggia above the stream testify to the comforts that once attached to this strange and secretive place.

Three miles further north the small town of **Alnmouth** can be seen on the right, very picturesque, almost continental, with its gaily painted houses following the curve of the estuary to the sea. It boasts the foundations of a Saxon church, St Woleric's, an earthwork on Beacon Hill, and the remains of an ancient harbour, now silted up and covered at high tide; but Alnmouth's present appeal depends on its fine beach of firm sand stretching as far as Marden Rocks and on its two golf courses, one on the links near the centre of the town, the other on the cliffs at **Foxton Hall**, where even the unfortunate who hooks or slices his drive into the sea can have the consolation of seeing grey seals disporting themselves offshore, the most delightful and attentive audience imaginable. There is even a 'Fluke Hole', not one of the eighteen but a deep hole in the sea bed, and marked blue on the Ordnance maps. Near by at **Boulmer** are the austere silver towers of the RAF installations behind barbed wire. **Boulmer Haven** was once a great smuggling centre for gin. In the pub, *The Fishing Boat*, is a spirited painting by A. H. Marsh of the women of Boulmer pulling the local lifeboat through the sands to a launch. Lifeboats are still a living issue here, for the RNLI boat has recently been withdrawn from service and has been replaced by Boulmer's own. It is a perilous coast.

Five miles inland to the north-east is **Alnwick** (*A'lain wick*, the town on the clear water) lying at a river crossing in the narrows of the coastal plain where the Cheviot foothills elbow closest to the sea, and thus the natural choice for the medieval capital of the earldom of Northumberland and the fortress of its leading family, the Percys. It had been an Anglian, then a Norman settlement, and one of its fascinations is that in the present pattern of streets you can still see the groundplan of the medieval village of thatched cottages grouped around a green, at whose focal point now stands the cobbled market-place and the Northumberland Hall. Bondgate Without, Bondgate Within, Pottergate and Bailiffgate (Baileygate) overlie very ancient tracks, later to be squeezed inside defensive walls, of which the **Hotspur Gate**, built by the son of Shakespeare's hero, survives to delight the eye and infuriate the motorist, at the southern entrance to the town.

The burgesses got their first charter under Henry II, their rights to a market from Henry VI in 1464, in which year they completely re-built their parish church. But not till the eighteenth-century Enlighten-ment did the street frontages take on their present shape. The first Duke of Northumberland, a notable 'improver', led the way by re-building the castle and the estate farms, planting woods and hedges, and then turned his attention to the town. In 1773 he replaced a medieval bridge over the Aln by the elegant **Lion Bridge**, designed by John Adam, who was also responsible for the **Denwick Bridge** of the same year. On the north-western outskirts the first Duke also built the **Pottergate Tower**, which originally had a spire similar to St Nicholas's in Newcastle. Learning from his example, the burgesses began to replace decayed housing with the fine classical residences and shops that now line Bondgate, Narrowgate and Market Street, and crowned things in 1771 with a new town hall in Finkle Street.

The dukes of Northumberland continued to be considerate and liberal friends of the town that lay under their wing. A pleasing rivalry developed. In 1814, to celebrate the ending of the Napoleonic Wars, the second Duke raised a Peace Column in the grounds of Swallowfield House south of the Clayport road. Not to be outdone, two years later the Percy Tenantry Volunteers put up a monster eighty-foot-high **Column** surmounted by the Percy Lion just south of the Hotspur Gate on the Alnmouth road, sometimes called 'The Farmers' Folly'. The tale goes that the local farmers stuck it up here in gratitude to the second Duke for reducing their rents in a time of agricultural depression; whereupon, remarking that he had no idea they had so much money to spare, he promptly put them up again. There is unfortunately no truth whatever in this agreeable story, but the column was certainly erected by a grateful tenantry and carries a laudatory inscription to say so. The architect was David Stephenson, who also built All Saints in Newcastle. Duly gratified by this testimonial to his benevolence, the second Duke responded in 1821 with the Cannongate Bridge taking the Eglingham road over the river, and two years later the classical **Northumberland Hall** at the centre of the market-place.

There is no more delightful small town in the county than Alnwick and few to beat it in England. As at Berwick, hardly an ugly house or shop front intrudes. Old customs here die hard. There is an annual Shrove Tuesday football match. Bull baiting took place in the market-place as late as 1783, and for centuries the new freemen had to take part in a gruelling initiation on St Mark's Day, 25 April, involving a horse race, an ale-swilling contest and an obstacle race over flooded ground, supposedly as a penance imposed on the town by King John, who while hunting in the vicinity fell off his horse into a bog the citizens had omitted to drain. The custom ceased in 1854, but the St Mark's Day junketings have now been transferred to near-by Hedgeley Moor to mark the anniversary of a battle in the Wars of the Roses. Indeed, if Alnwick has a fault it is perhaps its too devoted dedication to the 'Ye Olde' industry, which reaches its climax in the town in the first week of July during the annual Fair, a determinedly medieval mock-up in fancy dress which won the British Tourist Board's Award for 1973. So you know what to expect. It brings in the crowds and the money, so who am I, a comparatively recent resident of Northumberland, to criticise? A fringe exhibit is a display of bottles in the *Cross Keys Inn* which has stood untouched for one hundred and fifty years under the shadow of a curse on anyone who lays hands on them.

However, Alnwick is not only a museum of antiquities and branch of International Show-biz. It is a serious working town: the home of the world-renowned fishing tackle firm of Hardy Brothers. The excellent Bondgate Gallery above Sanderson's Wine Shop features the work of living artists. The charming old *White Swan Hotel*, tucked just inside the Hotspur Gate, is a haven for visiting Americans; it has a lounge lifted from the White Star liner, the *Olympic*. Even the castle, which propagandists are inclined to label 'the Windsor of the North', houses a Teachers' Training College, now also to be axed.

The **Castle** is nevertheless the reason for Alnwick. In 1095 the Norman family of de Vescis built a stone keep by the banks of the Aln on a mound which was probably already fortified. The building one sees today had its origins in 1309 when the Percys bought the land from the Bishop of Durham, who had filched it from his own ward. The family had come over with the Conqueror's nephew and took their name from a village in Normandy which had probably derived it from the word *'percée'*, 'a clearing in the woods'.

Their history is the history of the Border country. In the remote, wild valleys of the Tyne and Rede if any writ ran it was Percy's, not the King's. These earls had one outstanding gift: the talent for survival. Time and again in the course of their long history they made rash decisions, were killed on battlefields, executed on scaffolds, lost their lands and titles and even ran out of heirs; but there were always heiresses, and somehow or other they clung on, to emerge in the nineteenth century even more influential than they had been in the fifteenth.

To catalogue them would be wearisome. The greatest of their line was certainly Hotspur, who had fought in arms against the Scots at the age of twelve and who got his name for his impetuosity in mounting a freelance invasion of France. He came to a bad end: killed at Shrewsbury fighting as a rebel against the king he had helped on to the throne. But such was his fame as the mirror of Border chivalry that an impediment in his speech, making him roll his 'rs', is supposedly the reason for the Northumbrian burr, a very different kettle of fish from 'Geordie' and one of the most piquant and poetic of accents. Anyone who supposes such obsequiousness of the rough-riding Border clans can suppose anything, but it is at least a pleasant fancy.

During the Wars of the Roses the Percys went up and down on the seesaw. Usually they took the Lancastrian side. Two of their earls lost their lives for the cause in battle at St Albans and Towton. Prudently they became Yorkists. Still more prudently after Bosworth Field (on which for once they did not fight) they became supporters of the new Tudor monarchy. It did them little good. The fourth Earl was murdered while collecting unpopular taxes for his royal master; the sixth was unfortunate enough to fall in love with Anne Boleyn, lost her to that importunate wooer, Henry VIII, and had to plead sudden illness to avoid sitting on the court that later condemned her for adultery. The King was vindictive and no gentleman. Under Elizabeth his Catholic allegiance and participation in the northern rebellion of 1569 cost the seventh Earl his head on the block, and his two successors spent long terms of imprisonment in the Tower of London for suspected treason. Through the over-enthusiasm of a cadet member of the family the Percys even found themselves implicated in the Gunpowder Plot, and as a result of their disgrace their castle at Alnwick fell on evil times. It was used by Cromwell in 1650 to house six thousand Scottish prisoners taken at Dunbar; they were held in the middle bailey for eight days, during which half of them died from hunger and exposure. In the 1680s the fortress was becoming ruinous when a Percy heiress came to the rescue by a timely marriage to the Duke of Somerset. Two generations later another daughter of the clan married an enormously wealthy Yorkshire baronet, Sir Hugh Smithson, socially beneath her but a great land improver and developer who got a reversion to the title of Earl of Northumberland and lived to become its first Duke. With his arrival Alnwick was restored along with the Percy fortunes, never more flourishing than they are today, when their representative – almost alone of modern dukes – is a kind of local constitutional sovereign, a miniature of the British monarchy itself.

From the centre of Alnwick the castle is invisible; it does not dominate its environment like Windsor or many much smaller fortresses. From Bailiffgate, opposite its barbican, it does not even look easily defensible, in spite of the stone warriors perched on its battlements – sometimes credulously supposed to have been put there to confuse and alarm the Scots. The stream – the Bow Burn – which once protected it on this side now runs underground, and it is only from the eighteenth-century **Lion Bridge** over the Aln at the northern entrance to the town that the castle gives any impression of power. This was the view that Turner chose for his famous painting of it by moonlight, and it is still one of the great sights of the North.

In essence the **Castle** as it now stands consists of the central Keep (much altered) on a mound surrounded by beautifully kept lawns within a curtain wall strengthened by a series of towers and turrets. In summer the view from the north terrace is a pastoral scene which would have delighted Constable – the river flowing through the water meadows and under two elegant eighteenth-century bridges, the woods on rising ground, and mares and foals cropping the grass below the battlements.

One enters through the stable quarters which house two state coaches and a number of interesting photographs. The main entrance – the **Barbican** – is now the exit for visitors touring the castle. It is on your left as you enter the outer bailey. It was built by Hotspur's son in 1440. The outside arch carries the Percy shield with lion

Alnwick Castle from Lion Bridge

Warkworth Castle: a view from the north bank of the River Coquet

Lindisfarne Castle from the west, taken from the nineteenth-century drawing by G. Balmer

Norham Castle, morning, by J. M. W. Turner

rampant and under it the family motto, *Esperance en Dieu*, borrowed from another family into which a Percy heiress had married, the Counts of Louvain. It has square projecting towers on either side and there are flanking towers also to the inner gatehouse. Originally there was a drawbridge here over a ditch. Beyond the Barbican is the **Abbot's Tower** (1309) which now houses the beautifully dressed military museum of the Royal Northumberland Fusiliers. There are remarkable records from the American War of Independence, also trophies and relics from the Indian Mutiny and the Omdurman campaign, including a whip whose handle was cut from a tree in the garden of Gordon's palace at Khartoum. Next to the Museum on the north wall is the rebuilt **Falconer's Tower**. From this point the best course is to return to the Barbican and continue the tour of the wall in an anti-clockwise direction past the **Clock Tower** and the **Avener's Tower**, both eighteenth-century replacements, to the four-teenth-century **Auditor's Tower** connected to the **Middle Gateway** (1309) giving access to the Inner Bailey. On your right to the south the curtain wall continues with the nineteenth-century **Warden's Tower** and a round tower at the south-east corner. The wall then turns northwards embodying the remains of a small watchtower known as **Hotspur's Seat** and beyond two fine towers, the fourteenth-century **Constable's Tower** in original condition and the **Postern Tower** which contains an **Archaeological Museum**. Passing beyond it on to the nineteenth-century terrace with various cannon you can glimpse at its base the small postern gateway, the only other exit from the castle in medieval times.

The **Keep** itself is entered over a wooden bridge, once the site of a drawbridge. To the right is a stretch of the moat which once sur-rounded the whole area. On either side are octagonal towers built in 1350 carrying on their battlements the original stone **Figures** in realistic poses. One man is drinking from a bottle; another is winding a crossbow. A Norman arch leads into the inner courtyard of the castle, in which stands a fourteenth-century **Well** and its original winding gear. This precinct has twice been altered: the first time in 1755 by Robert Adam to the order of the first Duke. His elegant fan-shaped entrance stairs, Gothic plasterwork and gilding were, how-ever, anathema to the fourth Duke, obedient to the earlier strictures of Sir Walter Scott who had visited the castle in 1827, finding much of the décor 'meagre and poor' and the 'fine old pile' itself dis-figured by the absence of a central tower to dominate the landscape.

The fourth Duke had visited Rome and Florence and had admired the combination he had found there of solid, grim exteriors and the brilliance of Renaissance work inside. Alnwick must follow suit. High up above the Keep went the great **Prudhoe Tower** which would have enchanted Scott. And to embellish the castle's rooms a highly gifted team of Italian artists and craftsmen were imported to teach their skills to the local work force. At the height of the improvements three hundred and forty men were employed here. The effect is certainly splendid, the transition from austerity to opulence beautifully contrived. The stone-flagged stone-walled entrance hall, sporting an armoury of weapons used by the Percy Tenantry Volunteers at the time of the Napoleonic Wars, leads towards a staircase, each step of which is formed by a single stone; but look up and the vaulted ceiling is rich with Italian stucco and the walls are of coloured marble. The guard-chamber at the stair-head has a mosaic floor and marble balustrades, yet still retains a proper sense of austerity. Beyond it the library and private rooms belong entirely to the world of the Italian Renaissance as seen through the eyes of nineteenth-century Italian painters, carvers and *stuccatori* working in a northern clime at the dawn of Victorian Gothic. Alert eyes, trained and directed by the castle's guide-book, will catch constant references to the homeland: a quotation in the drawing-room frieze from Giulio Romano's work in Castel San Angelo, decoration in the music room reminiscent of St Peter's, and a dining-room ceiling based on the Basilica of San Lorenzo outside Rome.

It is a matter of individual taste, but I find the effect of so much opulence and so much crowding of furniture somewhat indigestible. There is none of the elegance here one finds at Castle Howard or within the area of this Guide at Raby, except in the **Library** which occupies the entire first floor of the Prudhoe Tower. Its bookcases of oak inlaid with maple hold sixteen hundred volumes, including the *Sherborne Missal* (1400), the *Northumberland Household Book* of 1512, and a copy of Caxton's *The Recuyell of the History of Troye*, the first book to be printed in English. In the **Dining Room** a glass showcase displays the uniform worn by Colonel the Hon. Henry Percy when he brought the first news of Waterloo to London. Alongside is the velvet sachet given him at the Duchess of Richmond's famous ball in Brussels and used by him to carry Wellington's historic despatch to the government. To complete the scene, a gallery of paintings, mostly Italian, were bought entire from a private collection: notable among them a Canaletto study of the Castle in 1752, well before the fourth Duke's improvements.

The Castle is best visited on a Wednesday or Sunday, for then you will also have access to the three-thousand-acre **Hulne Park**, landscaped by Capability Brown, 'the Capability Villain' as Sir Walter Scott was later to call him for his substitution here of clumps of birch and fir for the oaks of an earlier time. The modern visitor, however, will find little cause for complaint, for this is one of the most blissfully beautiful of parks, rising from the lush meadows to the moorland of Brislee Hill and containing the picturesque ruins of two quite separate monasteries and a splendid folly on Brislee Hill. Not least of its attractions is the fact that the motor car is banned and one must explore on foot. Entrance vouchers should be obtained from the castle's ticket office.

The main entrance is at the end of Bailiffgate just left of the Wooler road, and should the visitor wish to climb to the **Brislee Tower** this is the route to take. It is a seventy-eight-foot column probably designed by Robert Adam for the first Duke from which he could survey his pleasure park and vast estates.

Premonstratensian **Alnwick Abbey**, known locally as Cannongate Abbey, lies close to the town and is best reached by a gateway in the park wall on the left of the Wooler road. It is a visit for the specialist, for nothing survives above ground except a gatehouse. Yet this was a foundation that boasted twenty-two canons and was the proud possessor of Simon de Montfort's toe, a relic reputed to have great curative powers. The house chronicle kept by the monks is now among the Harleian MSS at the British Museum, but, alas! these worthies seem to have led very dull, exemplary lives. After the Dissolution the Abbey came into private ownership, was for a while the home of one of the Wardens of the Marches, and in the eighteenth century was bought by the first Duke of Northumberland.

Hulne Priory, lying deeper into the park, has much more to show of itself and is situated in one of the most beautiful valleys in Northumberland. No discerning visitor to Alnwick should dream of missing it. A warning note, however – it takes some finding. Follow the Wooler road for two and a half miles with the park wall on your left all the way. The gate comes upon you very suddenly. It is marked 'No entrance', but on Wednesdays and Sundays will be open. Cars can be parked inside. A track then leads downhill, forking left through woods with the river below and the Brislee Tower straight ahead on its hill, backed by the masts of the RAF Signal Station. It is a walk of about half a mile.

Hulne Priory was one of the earliest Carmelite monasteries in Britain, dating from *circa* 1240. The Abbot of Alnwick Abbey had his tower inside the castle to retreat to in times of trouble. The Prior of Hulne and his monks were more exposed to attacks by marauding armies and were therefore given a curtain wall and later a tower, both of which survive, though the tower's first floor was heavily Gothicised by the first Duke. Splendidly solid defensive walls are a rarity in priories; here they lend the place great distinction. Entrance is through a gate at the south-west. A visitor may wander around at his will, provided he remembers that the tower and the Gothic summerhouse built by the first Duke are private and that there are other occupied dwellings within the perimeter.

Of the **Priory Church** the south wall of the nave and chancel survives virtually intact, including a fine three-stepped sedilia. So does the west wall, but the rest of the complex is much less easy to read. Hulne Priory is one of the extremely rare instances where a reading of Pevsner is not a help but an actual hindrance. The five straight windows he mentions in the vestry simply do not exist, though he accurately points out the unusual facilities provided in this room in the shape of a two-tiered trough for making of wafers for the Communion service. A south transept is apparently separated from the church by walling. The jumble of buildings in this Arcadian setting is perhaps better enjoyed than comprehended, but a south transept apparently cut off from its crossing with nave and chancel is certainly an imponderable. There are two fine gateways through the curtain wall: one to the south, undoubtedly Tudor, the one to the east, eighteenth-century. The Duke's chief agent on a notice at the public entrance comprehensively disclaims any responsibility in case various arches and stones fall upon the visitor's head. It is a risk most people would willingly run to view this extremely beautiful place.

There is a stone near the Forest Lodge entrance to the park remembering William the Lion, taken prisoner here in 1219. An earlier King of Scots, Malcolm Canmore, who was killed besieging Alnwick in 1093, also has a cross, a medieval one, restored in 1774.

The **Parish Church of St Mary,** like the castle and the Park, stands on the northern outskirts of the town. The one-time presence of a Norman church on the site is suggested by stones with zigzag pattern above the chancel arch, but nothing else of it remains. The south arcade dates from the early fourteenth century, the north arcade with its ornate octagonal columns from perhaps fifty years later, and a small oblong window showing a pelican, the only medieval glass, may have been part of a narrow north aisle which has now vanished: the rest of the fabric is from the second half of the fifteenth century when the Wars of the Roses were raging in the North – the only work of this date outside of Tynemouth Priory and the fortified town of

Newcastle. So here is a Perpendicular church almost entire, with a sturdy tower and six splendid south windows, buttressed and embattled. An unusual feature is a turret in the south-east corner which may have lodged the vicar and served also as an observation post as late as the Napoleonic Wars.

Inside, the church gives an impression of great width, owing to the presence of two chancel chapels. Note the octagonal pillars, the most easterly of which on the north side is known as the 'Hotspur Pillar', being marked with Percy insignia. Opposite it the south-western pier shows an angel holding a shield bearing the arms of Bishop Bek. The chancel is packed with pews, but none of the woodwork is older than the 1850s, when those reserved for the ducal party and staff were carved by local craftsmen trained at the castle. Surprisingly enough there are no Percy tombs or monuments, since none of the Earls died at Alnwick and the Dukes have their own chapel in Westminster Abbey. However, the castle is probably represented by a monument of a lady in a wimple, believed to be Isabella, widow of the last of the de Vescis barons. At the west end are two figures dug up in 1818: one of them probably a representation of the church's benefactor, Henry VI, the other, pierced with arrows, St Maurice, martyred by the Danes. The **Carved Chest** at the west end of the north aisle is fourteenth-century Flemish work, one of the earliest and finest examples in the whole country. The town has another large church in St Paul's (1846) by Anthony Salvin.

A short trip out of Alnwick can be recommended to all those with particular interest in architecture, who at **Edlingham** (pronounced 'Eglingjum', but not to be confused with Eglingham, pronounced almost exactly the same) will find one of the finest of Northumbrian tower houses.

The Clayport road towards Rothbury leads over a hill, from whose summit is a fine view northwards of the Cheviots and of Lemmington Hall, listed in the fourteenth century as the Touris de Lemmaton, transformed into a mansion in Georgian times and recently restored. A couple of miles further down the hill **Edlingham** appears on the rising ground to one's right: a nicely composed group of a Georgian rectory, a few cottages, a church, a tower and the ruins of a railway viaduct.

There is no visible footpath to the **Tower** and the visitor must brave various four-footed beasts and a cunningly placed bog in order to reach it. The ground floor has silted up and entrance is on the first floor into the hall. Ribbed vaulting mounted on caryatids as corbels reaches up to embrace two floors, and there are caryatids also to embellish the great fireplace. The building, far grander than other comparable structures of its kind, dates from the fourteenth century: it is now in a sad state of decay.

Its one-time owner, Sir William de Felton, is buried in **St John's Church** just uphill from it. It is a small, mainly Norman church. The chancel arch and the south porch (which has tunnel-vaulting, rare in such a building in the North) is late-eighteenth-century. The north aisle is late-twelfth-century. Though the tower is more modern it still has a fortress look about it.

The Rectory was the scene almost exactly a century ago of a famous armed burglary for which two Alnwick poachers were sentenced to penal servitude for life. The judge who tried them, J. Manisty, had been born in that very house. After serving ten years the convicts were released and given a Queen's pardon when two other men confessed to the crime. This miscarriage of justice played its part in the creation of a Court of Criminal Appeal. (I was told the story by the grandson of the solicitor who worked to have the case reopened, and was later able to use it in *The Massingham Affair*.

Serving this whole area and convenient also for the coast, four and a half miles north of Alnwick, is a YHA hostel at Rock Hall in an historic mansion built during the reign of Henry VII.

Chapter 10

From Alnwick to the Farne Islands and Bamburgh

❧

From Alnwick the A1 leads northwards through Belford, well inland, a route only for those in a hurry. It is far more pleasant to
follow the minor roads closer to the coast through Longhaughton
(which has a church with Norman tower and chancel arch) and the
charming country around **Howick Hall**, the home of the Earl Grey
who carried the great Reform Act of 1832. The Howick gardens are
open to the public from Easter till September, from 2–7 p.m. Near
by at Fallodon lived Sir Edward Grey, Foreign Secretary in Asquith's
'government of all the talents'. Sir Edward, a great countryman, is
said when in London to have opened letters from his gamekeeper
before turning to the far less agreeable despatches of his ambassadors,
but one should not on that account blame him for the outbreak of the
First World War, which he did his civilised best to prevent. The
excesses of the Kaiser's Germany were alien and inexplicable to that
refined, aristocratic and supremely Whig spirit, which still survives in
Northumberland in a proliferation of great houses and estates.

Beyond Howick as far as the Tweed the countryside is quite
unspoilt. On one side lies a plain of rich farming land merging into
the upland pastures of the Cheviots; on the other the road veers
towards the sea and the stark outcrop of the Whin Sill at **Cullernose
Point**. About a mile further on turn right through a stone gateway
for the tiny fishing village and harbour of **Craster**, strongly reminiscent of Cornwall. Craster kippers are famous. Smoked over oak
chippings, they have a subtle flavour of their own: together with the
ubiquitous, scone-like stotty cake, one of the few Northumbrian
specialities. The Craster family still live in Craster Tower. They had
been here certainly since the twelfth century and were probably here
before the Conquest. The present head of the family, Sir John, who
has a fishery protection vessel named after him, is a well-known
naturalist, and indeed this coast is a joy for those who love watching
fulmers, oyster-catchers, redshanks and gulls of many kinds.

Craster should be visited for another reason, since it offers an

167

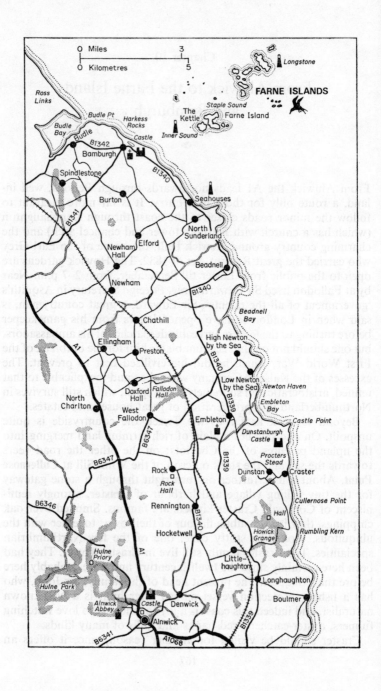

O Miles 3
O Kilometres 5

Ross
Links

Longstone

FARNE ISLANDS

Budle Pt   Harkess
Rocks

Budle
Bay   Staple Sound
Budle   The   Farne Island
       Castle   Kettle
B1342   Inner Sound
Bamburgh

Spindlestone   B1340

Burton

                    Seahouses

                    North
Newham   Sunderland
Hall   Elford

Newham   Beadnell

                              B1340

Chathill   Beadnell
                              Bay

Ellingham
        Preston   High Newton
A1   by the Sea

                              B1340

Doxford Hall Fallodon   Low Newton
              Hall   by the Sea   Newton Haven
North
Charlton   West   Embleton
           Fallodon   Bay
                      Embleton   Castle Point

                              Dunstanburgh
                              Castle
                    B6347   Procters
                                     Stead
              Rock   B1339   Dunstan   Craster
              Rock
              Hall   Cullernose Point

B6346   Rennington
                              Hall
                                            Rumbling Kern
              Hocketwell   Howick
                                  Grange

                              Littlel-
              Hulne   haughton
              Priory
                                     Longhaughton
Hulne Park
                                          Boulmer
        Alnwick
        Abbey   Castle   Denwick
                              B1339
              Alnwick
B6341
                    A1068

ideal starting point for a glorious mile-long walk through the fields along the seashore to the ruins of **Dunstanburgh Castle**, high on its dolomite cliff. Even Warkworth is tame compared with it. The huge round bastions of the **Gatehouse/Keep** dominate the scene like settings for some northern Camelot, for Dunstanburgh is the largest of Northumbrian castles, covering eleven acres. On the north the vertical drop to the sea made defensive walls unnecessary, and it was only the southern approach that required guarding in strength. For this reason the original gateway on this vulnerable flank was converted into a keep, which in its final development stood five storeys or eighty feet high and contained both the living quarters and the front line of defensive works – a most unusual arrangement for a medieval fortress where the keep was usually central to the ground plan and protected by powerful outer walls.

The interest of Dunstanburgh visually as a castle therefore diminishes once one has passed under this enormously impressive gate and emerged into the empty spaces of the bailey, with only a thin curtain of walls and two towers to draw the eye. The Margaret Tower to the east with its majestic views over the sea and the rocks below was the site of the latrines – proof, if any were needed, that the medieval mind was very matter-of-fact and not much given to the romantic spirit. On the western side the Lilburn Tower provides another superb view towards the distant folds of the Cheviots and northwards to the rock on which stands Bamburgh Castle beyond the coastal plain.

So obvious a strongpoint as Dunstanburgh must have appealed from the earliest times, and indeed there is reason to suppose that it was one of the many tribal centres of the Britons whose traces lie thick on the ground around the Cheviot *massif*. Most of the castle we see today was built between 1313 and 1322 by Thomas of Lancaster, a grandson of Henry III. It was John of Gaunt who turned the gatehouse into a keep in 1380. Later, during the Wars of the Roses, it became one of the main Lancastrian strongholds in the North. Henry VI's tigress of a queen, Margaret, captured the place after her defeat at Towton; lost it to the Yorkists; re-captured it; then lost it again to Warwick the Kingmaker after that other defeat at Hexham along the Devil's Water in 1464. A hundred years later it was in ruins, and so it has remained. The only legend attached to it is neither Yorkist nor Lancastrian but belongs to an earlier time, relating how a knight, Sir Guy the Seeker, home after fighting the Moors in Spain, is overtaken by a storm while riding past its walls, seeks shelter, and at the witching hour of midnight is shown by a giant into a secret chamber where an enchanted princess lies sleeping on a crystal bier. Only by the use of either a jewelled sword or an ivory horn hanging in the chamber can Sir Guy release the lady. Perhaps remembering Roncesvalles and the ballad of Roland and Oliver, he chooses to blow the horn. Poor booby, he has chosen wrong. Failing to wake the sleeper, he drops senseless to the ground, comes to next morning outside the castle gates, to spend the rest of his life wandering around the walls, haunted by thoughts of lost paradise and of his own stupidity – a good Northumbrian twist to a story which elsewhere usually has a happy ending, but here, on this wild coast, suits the vision of a tortured spirit roaming the cliffs to the dull booming of the sea. Something of this high romantic quality must have appealed to Turner, who (as visitors to the recent London exhibition will have noticed) painted it a number of times during his life.

Back at Craster, *The Choughs* provides home-made teas and has a shell museum and curio shop upstairs.

Inland from Craster at **Dunstan** is a group of buildings known as Proctor Steads or Dunstan Hall, consisting of a pele tower and hall built of stone from Dunstanburgh Castle, with the date 1652 carved on a lintel. The famous medieval schoolman and theologian Duns Scotus – from whom the word 'dunce' is unkindly said to have been derived – is supposed by some to have been born here. An often-quoted manuscript in Merton College Library asserting this fact apparently does not exist, but though the great scholar's name does not appear on the college rolls he certainly went to Oxford, and the parish of Embleton quite close to Dunstan is in Merton's gift.

Embleton itself is attractive in its own right, with its vicarage and vicar's pele which figured in the list of fortified 'tourris' in 1416 – compare the similar tower in the churchyard at Corbridge. The church was built about 1320 on a Norman site, but in the nineteenth century was twice restored, once by Dobson, a great town-planning architect but less at home with churches, as one sees in his east front at Hexham Abbey. The coastal walk to Dunstanburgh can be undertaken from here instead of from Craster: it is only a mile and a half and the Dunstanburgh Castle Hotel provides a convenient base. There is a golf course that follows the coastline right up to the walls of the fortress, and just to the north of it the charming hamlet of **Low Newton by the Sea**, or **Newton Seahouses**, with its open-ended square of cream-washed cottages around a green on the beach of Newton Haven. The only trouble with the place – or rather its

170

salvation – is that there is hardly room to park more than a dozen cars. What it has escaped is only too glaringly obvious in the villas and huge caravan site to the north of it at **Beadnell**, which has splendid sands, a tiny harbour, some eighteenth-century lime kilns preserved by the National Trust, and a hotel, the *Craster Arms*, sporting very grand armorial bearings on its handsome facade, but the village is the victim of its own attractions on a holiday coast. To its credit it possesses a feature on the cliffs called 'Nacker Hole'. For the collector of such items there is also Football Hole and Snook Point.

Beyond it, **Seahouses** is a queer mixture. The modern shop fronts and the chips-with-everything face it shows to the traveller on the main road are painful to a degree. But go down the slope to the harbour and in an instant everything is changed; it could be the coast of Fife or Cornwall before the great invasion. Not that Seahouses turns its back on the tourist – far from it. But the picturesque beauty of the quays and the harbour with its fishing boats is irresistible. There is a fine local fleet of these motor vessels and also a number of clinker-built Northumbrian cobles, of which John Seymour gives a detailed and fascinating description. Along the curve of the waterfront the conversions of the old fishermen's houses are eye-openers of what an enlightened builder can do by way of conservation, and he was a local man too. From the top of the hill at the south end of the village is a fine view over the harbour to the Farne Islands with their two lighthouses, one white, one red, and in the background the romantic bulk of Bamburgh Castle on its rock. From Easter till the end of September, weather permitting, boats leave Seahouses for the islands at 10 a.m., 2 p.m., and at the peak of the holiday season at 5. There is a choice of tour operators, whose huts are down on the quayside, but even so during the school holidays it is wiser to book ahead. The modest sum of 50p was being charged in 1975 for the round trip of between two and a half to three hours; this must soon be due for revision. There is also a twopenny surcharge sternly exacted on embarkation by the harbour board and a National Trust landing fee of ten pence collected at Inner Farne. However, no one is likely to complain that he does not get value for money.

Farne (*Ferran*) is a Celtic word meaning 'Land'. There is precious little of it apart from rock and a diminishing layer of topsoil on these easternmost extensions of the Whin Sill – twenty-eight islands visible at low tide, fifteen when anything of a sea is running. The best view of them is from Lindisfarne further up the mainland coast, from where they can be seen extending like a long broken promontory into the sea in two distinct groups: **Inner Farne** with its satellites; then the mile-long gap of Staple Sound; and beyond it a maze of rocks in the shape of a letter 'C', with the lighthouse on Longstone and the outriders of Northern Hares and Knivestone furthest out. Many of the names are striking – Big Scarcar, the Bush, the Bridges, Knocks Reef, Wideopens, around Inner Farne; Megstone, Oscar, Glororum Shad and Fang in Staple Sound; North and South Wanses, Big and Little Harcar, Blue Caps, Sunderland Hole and Nameless Island in the outer group, at which point the cartographers obviously gave up.

All this is a nature reserve; and standing like sentinels on the rocks and on ledges where the cliffs are sheer are sea-birds in profusion – eider duck, shags, cormorants, terns, oyster-catchers, kitti-wakes, guillemots – and puffins, with their boozy music-hall comedian beaks. Most of these species seem to prefer the smaller and least accessible rocks, but the grey seals, like their tamer fellows in zoos and circuses, are true exhibitionists and congregate chiefly in the waters around Inner Farne where they can be seen to best advantage by the public and can rubberneck on them in return. 'They're just like wee dogs,' I heard a voice remark on one occasion as the whiskered, inquisitive heads – more like blown-up rubber toys than those of actual animals – came popping out of the water around the boat. Sad to say, there are far too many of them: they are a menace not only to the fishermen whose salmon they take off the mouth of the Tweed but also to each other, and they are being severely culled – each cull arousing passionate outcries among animals lovers in the correspondence columns of the Newcastle press.

The tour boats go first to the **Longstone**, where half an hour is allowed for a visit to the red and white tower of the **Lighthouse** made famous by Grace Darling. Grace was a girl of eleven when it began duty in 1826; she was twenty-three when, just before dawn on the morning of 7 September 1838, peering from the window of her small circular room she became aware that a ship had gone aground on the Big Harcar half a mile away to the west. As the light improved survivors were seen clinging to the rock. Her younger brother was on a visit to the mainland, and there was no one but herself to help her father, the lighthouse keeper, to launch their coble to the rescue of the passengers of the luxury steamer *Forfarshire*.

No one knows for certain what the weather conditions were that morning. Most of the artists who have depicted the scene have shown seas so mountainous that no coble or other small rowing boat could have lived in them. Others have pointed out that this is fairly enclosed water and that the *Forfarshire*, her boilers out of action and dependent on sail, may have foundered less from the storm than because her master (who was not among the survivors) had mistaken the Longstone light for the one closer inshore. The tremendous hullabaloo that greeted the rescue, causing even *The Times* to wonder editorially if in fact or fiction there had ever been another such instance of female heroism, brought its own backlash of jealousy and ill-feeling among the seafaring community in Seahouses, whose lifeboat, with Grace's own brother aboard, had arrived on the scene only to find the nine survivors had already been taken off in two batches to the Longstone in the Darlings' coble. And this unflattering version of events found support in the fact that the lighthouse keeper himself made no mention in his log or in his private journal of his daughter's part in the affair. Clearly he regarded the rescue of passengers from a shipwreck as all in the day's work. Yet the legend has survived all disparagement, and the modern tourist, standing in Grace's bedroom or in the museum at Bamburgh, sees her as Victorians did, as the heroine that she undoubtedly was in life – incidentally a tragically short one, for four years after the wreck of the *Forfarshire* she died of consumption, probably hastened by her ordeal.

For the modern visitor a typed notice, strongly reminiscent of the kind found in army barracks or fire stations, hangs in Grace's room to record some of these events. The historical records show that neither father nor daughter would have expected anything more, probably not as much. Yet no less a man than Wordsworth once apostrophised her in lines more typical of Alfred Austin than of the poet of Lakeland:

> And through the sea's tremendous trough
> The father and the girl rode off . . .

The manager of a London music hall offered her large sums to appear (twice nightly) rowing her boat across the stage. This offer was rejected. The Darlings were professionals of another kind: they were lighthouse keepers. And the lighthouse itself, quite apart from the *Forfarshire* saga, is immensely impressive. Put into service in 1826, hit by a German Heinkel in 1941, it was rebuilt and electrified in 1951. The tower, to which one climbs by a circular stair and then by vertical iron-runged ladder, stands seventy-five feet above the high tide mark. The light – a single white flash every twenty seconds – can be seen fifteen miles away, and there is also a radio beam. Two thousand watt electric filament lamps (with a five hundred watt standby) project the beam: power is supplied by diesel generators. From the tower it is exactly like being on the bridge of a ship at sea, with the Big Harcar rock on which the *Forfarshire* went aground seemingly quite close and the mass of Bamburgh Castle in line behind it. The jagged teeth of Dunstanburgh Castle can be seen far down the coast to one's left, with the Wellsian towers of the RAF station at Brislee on the moors above Alnwick a few degrees nearer centre, the cluster of Seahouses in the foreground, Holy Island to one's right, and as a backdrop the shapes of The Cheviot and Hedgehope to complete what must surely be one of the most spectacular of English views.

The tour proceeds to **Inner Farne**, once the home of St Aidan and later of St Cuthbert, who was summoned from it in 684 by King Ecgfrith of Northumbria to become Bishop of Hexham. He then exchanged his bishopric with Eata in 685 for that of Lindisfarne, but after two years in office returned to Inner Farne to die. Once again the feature of the island are appealingly named: Farne Haven (where the boat puts you ashore), St Cuthbert's Cove, St Cuthbert's Gut, The Churn, Wideopen Gut, The Stack. The chapel named for the Saint was built in 1370, centuries after his death, and was extensively restored by Archdeacon Thorp in 1848. For the occasion the Archdeacon brought here part of a screen from Durham Cathedral, a superb piece of seventeenth-century woodwork. Next door, Prior Castell's Tower, a typically Northumbrian pele, probably stands on the site of Cuthbert's cell, and formed at one time the quarters of the Benedictine monks who had established themselves on the island in 1255; the ruins of their guest house (now called for some reason Fish House) can be seen a little nearer the landing in the cove.

At the south end of the island is another lighthouse, painted a gleaming white in contrast to the dullish red of the Longstone. It is not on public view, but most visitors come to this spot to see the precipitous cliffs of **The Stack** and the teeming bird life which at nesting time fills every ledge and cranny.

NESTING BIRDS
YOU MUST NOT
GO BEYOND THIS NOTICE

the National Trust's warning boards proclaim, and as far as one can see both sides observe this prohibition to the letter. The best time to see the birds is late spring and early summer, seal calves in November and December. In conclusion the Farnes provide one of

174

the most rewarding outings anyone could wish for, and I would urge all but the congenitally sea-sick to make the trip.

Beyond Seahouses the coast runs north-west towards Budle Point, with sandy beaches backed by links and dunes which tend in August to be crowded, for it is an ideal place for camping. This holiday coast culminates at **Bamburgh**, a charming village dominated by a castle that is visually one of the most exciting in Britain, reminiscent from a distance of Edinburgh, but with the added attraction of the sea right under its walls.

Purists may find fault with Bamburgh. But overweight and over-restored though it may be, there can be no doubt that it is everyone's ideal of what a castle should look like, and the proof of it lies in the way film-makers have flocked to it. Some of the most memorable scenes in *Becket* were shot here. Elizabeth Taylor's arrival to watch her future husband at work in the title role caused almost total chaos among the pursuing pressmen and a public unused to such excitements. More recently Ken Russell came here to make *The Devils*. Plantagenet England, Bourbon France, it obviously makes no difference – the place is irresistible, particularly when seen across the sands from the Harkess Rocks: a Gustave Doré engraving of a castle in Spain.

Bamburgh is a very ancient site. Recent excavation has revealed that the Romans used it, and the likelihood is that tribes much earlier had recognised the defensive advantages of a one-hundred-and-fifty-foot-high rock covering eight acres, perched above the sea and the plain. There is some archaeological evidence to suggest this; in which case Bamburgh may claim to surpass York as the oldest continually inhabited site in Britain.

Its name is supposed to be derived from *Bebba-burgh*, 'Bebba's Town', after the wife of the Saxon king Ethelfrith. It was the capital of the kingdom of Bernicia in the sixth and seventh centuries, at a time when Christianity was establishing itself in the north. St Aidan died here, on or near the site of the present parish church. The Anglo-Saxon Chronicles describe it as a strongly fortified city, not very large, 'being of the size of two or three fields, having one entrance hollowed out of the rock and raised in steps after a mar-vellous fashion'. So its strength was clearly recognised even in these very early times. In its church, according to Bede, was preserved the incorrupt right hand of St Oswald which Aidan had blessed during one of the pious king's distribution of food and alms to the poor. This relic was stolen during the troubled times that followed the

decline of the Saxon kingdom which ended in the sack of the town
and castle by the Danes. After the Norman Conquest Bamburgh
became once more a fortress of great importance, and the roll-call
of famous names associated with it is long indeed. William Rufus
besieged it. King John lodged in it, as did his son, the youthful
Henry III, who carried out large alterations on the site. It was visited
by Edward I, by Edward II after Bannockburn, by Edward III,
who left his wife Philippa of Hainault here to enjoy a peaceful seaside
holiday somewhat interrupted by the appearance of a Scottish army
outside the walls. It was occupied by the Lancastrians under Queen
Margaret; formed for a time the capital of Henry VI's sadly shrunken
kingdom; and was finally captured for the Yorkists by Warwick the
Kingmaker, being the first English castle to fall to the new heavy
artillery.

Later its importance declined, until in the early eighteenth century
its ruins were bought by Lord Crewe, Bishop of Durham, whose
trustees after his death carried out a wholesale conversion and set
up a girls' school on the site, together with a granary, an infirmary,
a lighthouse and a hostel for shipwrecked seamen. The costs of this
early experiment in Welfare were so exorbitant that in the nineteenth
century the castle had to be sold to the great inventor, the first Lord
Armstrong, who embarked on another wholesale restoration to
'Gothicise' a place which in its primal origins had been almost contemporaneous with the Goths.

These reconstructions by Lord Armstrong and the Crewe trustees
are, I fear, largely the castle we see today. It is still tremendously
impressive, but the closer one comes to it the smaller the effect.
Apart from the **Keep**, which with minor modern alterations to its
windows is much as Henry II built it about 1164, the second largest
in the Border country, traces of the original structure are hard to
find. Parts of the curtain wall and the one dividing the east from the
west bailey are medieval, as are the ruins of the chapel, and there is
some Norman stonework in the east gateway. But the rest is more a
projection of the Romantic Imagination than the real castle destroyed
by Warwick's guns in 1464. The grey stone predominant in large
sections of the present fabric (as opposed to the native pinkish stone
used by earlier builders) marks Lord Armstrong's reconstruction and
was brought here by wagon from his Cragside estate near Rothbury.
Even the guided tour of the castle is now concentrated chiefly on the
rooms his architects created, and though a visit to the ground floor
of the keep is included the visitor not on the *qui vive* may easily find
himself shown out at the end of it without even a glimpse of its most

interesting feature, the splendid arch of the Norman doorway which is set, most unusually, at ground floor instead of first floor level. Pevsner finds this to be proof of the sense of security induced in its occupants by the impregnability of the site: the castle guide-book is worried about this departure from the normal. But Norman it is, and perhaps the best thing in Bamburgh.

The conducted tour of the building is hardly worth the money, though this is no reflection on the guides. The first Lord Armstrong was a great engineer but the rooms he commissioned are grandiose without being interesting. The visitor is shown some fine furniture – the best of it French – and a collection of weapons and armour. In one room he is asked to visualise a secret chamber (no longer extant) where General Tom Forster, the incompetent joint commander of the Northumbrian rising of the 'Fifteen, was hidden after his sister, the famous Dorothy, had engineered his escape from London. To put the Hanoverian authorities off the scent, pending his transfer to France, a mock funeral is supposed to have been arranged for him; but, alas! he is a character who obstinately refuses to come to life in any capacity, even as a bogus corpse. In the so-called Knights' Hall, a room straight out of *Morte d'Arthur*, is an oil painting, *The Card Players*, by von Honthurst, and I gleefully recognised that one of the school is holding five aces. The castle also contains a stunning Annigoni of the present Lady Armstrong. Only the ground floor of the Keep is shown.

Bamburgh **Village**, for all its vast popularity at the height of the tourist season, remains unspoilt, its triangular green surrounded by Georgian and Victorian cottages, the *Lord Crewe Arms*, and a coffee house called *The Copper Kettle*. Further up the slope from the castle is the house where Grace Darling died on 20 October 1842.

The **Parish Church** stands at the west end of the village on rising ground overlooking the sea. It has a squat tower of four stages and an extremely long chancel with eight lancet windows in pairs. An historic church this, from its connection with St Aidan for whom it is named. He had been called to Northumbria by King Oswald after the Christian victory at Heavenfield near Hexham; his mission, to resume the conversion of the country which had been interrupted by the defeats of the previous reign at pagan hands and the flight of that earlier missionary and mass-baptiser, Paulinus. For some reason Aidan has never received the popular acclaim and respect so freely given to St Cuthbert (a true folk figure like St Patrick), but up and down Northumberland there are a number of churches named for him, and historically he is an even greater figure, the founder of the Christian kingdom in the North. The present chancel probably stands on the site of the rudimentary Saxon church of Aidan's time, and according to Bede it was outside the west wall of that building, under an awning or tent, that he died on 31 August 651, worn out by his self-imposed austerities and his untiring missionary work. In the present tower is a wooden beam which is supposed to have supported the awning and, according to Bede, possessed miraculous fire-resistant qualities – highly necessary, since on two occasions the church was thoroughly sacked by the Danes. The traditional spot where he died is in the north-west corner of the chancel under a window dedicated to a later ecclesiastic and has been marked by a hideous modern memorial lantern.

Internally Bamburgh St Aidan is spacious, the tower opening into the nave and its south aisle through two pointed arches. Its best feature is the sixty-foot-long chancel with three early thirteenth-century lancets at its east end. On entering in the wall to one's right is a square opening with a stone tracery screen, the squint, which gave a view of the altar to that part of the congregation sitting on the south side of the nave. Near the priest's door is a recess dating from the fourteenth century in which lies the figure of a knight wearing rowel spurs. On the north wall is a memorial tablet to the Forster family, whose traces we have crossed in the castle and will again at Blanchland, together with the helmet, breastplate, sword and gloves of another member of that clan, Ferdinando Forster, treacherously murdered by one of the equally prolific Fenwicks at Newcastle in the days of Queen Anne.

The north aisle of the nave was built at the end of the twelfth century and probably antedates the piers and moulded capitals of the south aisle by nearly a century. Also in the north aisle are two monuments, one to Grace Darling and another quite stupefying one erected by Catherine Sharpe to the memory of her clerical husband, to whom she is seen looking adoringly upwards – a piece of statuary only possible to Victorian taste and verging on the sacrilegious. There is also a crypt, like that at Hexham discovered by accident, containing Forster family coffins, including that of Dorothy and her brother Tom. The churchyard, which has splendid views towards the Farnes, contains Grace Darling's grave and a monument to her, sited so that it can be seen from ships passing along the coast.

Across the road from the church is the **Grace Darling Museum**, opened in 1938, the centenary year of the wreck of the *Forfarshire*. It consists of two rooms, in the first of which is the actual coble used in the rescue, an open rowing boat twenty-one feet long by six feet wide. Near by is the famous painting by J. W. Carmichael and H. Perlee Parker, loaned by Newcastle's Hancock Museum; and on the wall facing you are three Carmichael watercolours which help to explain the big sale-room prices now being reached for works by this artist. Also in the first room is a selection of books written about the rescue, almost all of which are accompanied by a stern cautionary word to the effect that their authors were prejudiced, inaccurate, uninformed or plain ignorant of the facts about which they were writing. The Royal National Lifeboat Institution and the village of Bamburgh never seem quite to have forgiven their great heroine for hogging too many of the headlines and obscuring the fact that Bamburgh was the site of the world's first lifeboat station. Everyone should care, for this was the beginning of something that has saved countless lives. Yet I am afraid the visitor, penetrating into the second room of the museum, with its stiff representations of the Darling family, the letters written in reply to perhaps the first fan mail in history, the notebooks, the faded locks of hair, will be remembering not a national service, however praiseworthy, but the village girl who became the heroine of the Carmichael painting.

Chapter 11

From Bamburgh to Holy Island

🌱

North of Bamburgh the B1342 skirts the village's golf course beside the sea and then the almost landlocked **Budle Bay**, which looks inviting but contains stretches of mud among the sands (particularly near Budle itself) and like much of this coastline should be treated warily on account of the tides, which can be treacherous. North of the bay are the long **Ross Bank Sands** which can be reached via Elwick or Ross links, and then the crescent of **Fenham Flats** and **Holy Island Sands**, famous for their wild-fowling and part of the Nature Reserve that stretches from Budle to Goswick. Permits required for shooting can be obtained from The Nature Conservancy, 13 Windsor Terrace, Newcastle upon Tyne, NE2 4HE. Certain restrictions apply: all dogs must be controlled and nesting birds left undisturbed. Inland is **Belford**, which has an excellent hotel, the *Blue Bell*, also a church with a Norman chancel, and a little further north the twin villages of East and West Kyloe lying under the wooded **Kyloe Hills**, from which grand views are to be had over the Cheviots and the sea. There is an earthwork on top of one of them. The main attraction of this coast, however, is of course **Lindisfarne**, or **Holy Island**, which is reached by turning off the A1 at Beal.

> Dry shod o'er sands, twice every day,
> The pilgrims to the shrine find way;
> Twice every day the waves efface
> Of staves and sandalled feet the trace,

wrote Scott in *Marmion*. For this small, box-shaped island, with the long snout of The Snook thrust out from it like the nose of a duck-billed platypus towards the mainland, was the power-house of the Celtic branch of Christianity and home of St Aidan, who came here from Iona at the bidding of King Oswald of Northumbria in 634.

As a Victorian bishop once remarked, it was not St Augustine but Aidan who was the true apostle of England, and his ministry of seventeen years undertaken from his small oratory at Lindisfarne is among the most fruitful in missionary history. Yet on Holy Island,

180

as on the Farnes, it is not Aidan who is remembered but the shepherd boy from the Lammermuirs probably born in the year after Aidan's arrival from Iona – St Cuthbert. Why this should be is not easy to understand. A recluse by nature and so much a hermit by profession that he found the island of Lindisfarne too worldly and retired from it, first to its offshore islet of Hobthrush and then to the still more remote fastness of Inner Farne, Cuthbert by tradition seems to have been one of the most spiritual of saints, the very opposite of the busy and practical St Aidan. Summoned to be bishop at the age of fifty by appeals from King Ecgfrith, he served for barely two years before returning to Inner Farne to die. Nevertheless, something about him, some inner quality of sanctity and kindliness, left an impression in folk memory that has never been effaced. Livingstone had that quality; and there is a distinct resemblance between that astonishing last journey as his body was carried by his African servants to the sea and the long wanderings of Cuthbert's followers with his coffin up and down Northumbria till they found a final resting place for it at Durham. The fossilised remains of the creatures called 'crinoids' which once lived on the bed of the ocean and are sometimes washed up on the shores of Lindisfarne are still known locally as St Cuthbert's 'beads', and the eider duck as St Cuthbert's 'chicks' – a St Francis-like touch which is wholly in keeping with the image we have of this unworldly man whom the world revered. It may be heresy to say so, but later generations have tended to idealise and exaggerate this side of the Saint's nature – he could hardly have survived the dangerous times in which he lived if he had not had political acumen. For a new view of those times and of the men who lived in them I recommend *St Wilfrid at Hexham* (Oriel Press, 1974), particularly the essays by D. P. Kirby and D. H. Farmer.

The old pilgrim route Scott wrote of in *Marmion* lay from Beal directly across the sands to Chare Ends near Lindisfarne village – a three-mile crossing marked with guide poles and furnished with refuge towers in case of danger from the tides. The villagers' pony traps and in course of time their ancient tourist taxis made the shorter crossing to *terra firma* at The Snook and then followed the sands close inshore to the same landing at Chare Ends. A sizeable stream, The Low, had to be forded even when the tide was right out and caused tremendous rusting to the chassis of the local cars. Now all these hazards are things of the past, and the modern tourist crosses in comfort on a good tarmac road which bridges The Low and emerges on the island at the tip of The Snook after a journey of about a mile. However, since it is still just possible to be caught by the

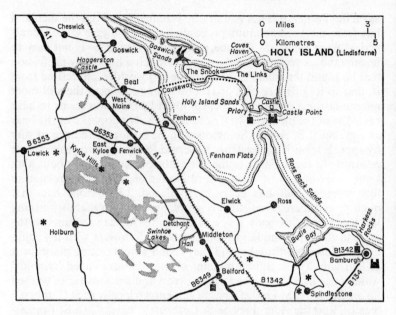

tide, a refuge platform is provided at the bridge and large warning signs at the entrance to the causeway remind the visitor that for an hour or two on either side of high tide Lindisfarne is still an island and the road submerged to varying depths.

'Holy Island from the mainland,' says Pevsner censoriously, 'is not at all an impressive sight,' and certainly from the mainland below Beal at high water on a grey day there is little to be seen but a line of dunes with a few huddled buildings in the distance. But when the tide is out, and the huge expanse of sand lies glistening in the sun or under a thin covering of water from which rises a forest of poles on every side, there is no more extraordinary place to be found in Britain – indeed, one must go to the Venetian lagoon between Burano and Torcello to find a similar desolation, with the suggestion beyond it of great buildings and a culture reaching back centuries.

Once ashore on the island the road leads two unexciting miles to the dour village which faces the harbour. The more active may prefer to reach the same point by walking along the north shore of the Snook to Coves Haven and then southwards along a beautiful rocky coastline interspersed with sandy beaches. It is a great place for seals, and the mud flats around the Snook are a paradise for the bird-watcher. Then turn inland for the village. Standing close to the end

182

of the Pilgrims' Way across the sands are the parish church and the ruins of the Priory. Leave them till last: they are at the heart of Lindisfarne. To start with it is best to get some idea of their setting; and to do this one has only to do what most visitors do instinctively, and make for the pinnacle of the castle on its rock, the dominant feature of the island. There is ample parking space on the links except at the height of the summer season when crowds almost over-run the place.

From here the scene is splendid in any weather. But if I could choose a day for the visitor it would be in the early autumn, as I last saw it, with a sea fret over half the island, blocking the view northwards towards Berwick and showing only the ominous grey of the surf, but with the sky clearing towards the south, so that Bamburgh Castle and the lighthouses on the Farnes are bathed in a blue radiance. The light changes on such a day with bewildering rapidity, as the mists move down the coast, blotting out the islands, while inland the sun touches the crests of the Cheviots. On that last occasion a rainbow seemed to come within touching distance; the pastel shades of sea and sand and dunes varied from moment to moment.

Inshore lies the haven with its seaweed and anchored craft – a few fishing boats and yachts nowadays, but once the great herring fleets that fished the east coasts of Scotland and England. In the first Elizabeth's time there would be merchantmen and sometimes a squadron of the Queen's ships. It was to protect them that the **Castle** was built towards the middle of the sixteenth century. It is tiny compared with Bamburgh across the bay, but very distinctive from the conical shape of the rock to which it clings. Like the very grand Elizabethan fortifications at Berwick it came into the world late in the day, when the enemy against which it had been erected – Scotland – was about to supply England with its ruling house. So it underwent no great sieges and its garrison tended to be a couple of dozen men under a non-resident captain. In 1715 it was actually captured by a couple of Jacobites, Launcelot and Mark Errington. Launcelot had gone there to be shaved by the Master Gunner; noticed that most of the defenders were absent; returned with his nephew, Mark, on the pretext of having left his watch-key behind; and summoned the astonished barber with the words, 'Damn you! the castle is ours.' However, no Jacobite reinforcements arrived in response to exultant signals to the mainland, and next day the castle was recaptured by loyal troops and the Erringtons were marched off to Berwick Gaol. This was not the end of their adventures, for they succeeded in burrowing their way out to freedom, disposing of the

183

earth from their tunnel in an oven – quite in Colditz style. Launcelot later kept the *Salutation Inn* in the Fleshmarket in Newcastle and is supposed to have died of grief at the news of Culloden. The castle suffered no more such *coups de main* and became in time redundant. It continued to be garrisoned till the end of the Napoleonic Wars, but it is only in very recent times, after it passed into private hands and was imaginatively restored by Lutyens, that it has become once more a place of importance, a magnet for visitors to wander in and admire its romantically placed rooms on the crest of the rock. The castle and the whole island, incidentally, provided the setting for Roman Polanski's controversial film, *Cul de Sac*.

Back in the village the ruins of the **Priory** make altogether more serious viewing, for this is one of the greatest buildings in the North. It is built of red Goswick sandstone. Unlike the similar churches at Hexham and Brinkburn it was only once attacked by Border raiders so that no great call on the imagination is required to recreate a Benedictine foundation of the twelfth century. In fact, until the dissolution of the smaller monasteries in 1541 the Priory remained in almost perfect order and until the middle of the eighteenth century still had its great central tower. The old Saxon monastery and church had been derelict for over two hundred years when in 1093 the site was given to the see of Durham for the formation of a new cell. One of the monks by the name of Edward seems to have been given the task of rebuilding, and it was his decision to clear the ground completely and start 'new from its foundation'. The link with the mother house was in such circumstances bound to be close, and it is not surprising that the priory church we now see greatly resembles Durham Cathedral, where building started about the same time. It is of course very much smaller. When first built it was one hundred and forty-two feet long, measured from the original rounded apse (whose foundations can still be seen) to the west door, compared to Durham's three hundred and seventy-five. Very early on – probably between 1140 and 1150 – the chancel was lengthened and given a square end, but otherwise alterations were few.

The chancel had only two bays and no aisle; the nave was one hundred feet long with north and south aisles that were separated from it by arcades of six rounded arches each, of which the only two surviving can be seen on the north side. The piers of the nave are alternately cylindrical and compound, the ornamentation on the cylindrical columns being very similar to those at Durham. Both transepts had semi-circular apses on the east side – an unusual feature. The north transept has a large north window. Rising diagonally

184

above the crossing is the beautiful soaring forty-four-feet-high arch
known as 'the rainbow', and one can see why, for it stands alone,
its twin having disappeared along with the tower that it supported.
Perhaps the finest thing of all is the Norman **West Doorway**, the
ceremonial entrance to the church. From the early seventeenth
century on, when everything of value was stripped from the building,
until 1821, when some clearing of the site took place, this doorway
was buried in rubble and has therefore been preserved from weathering and stone robbers. It is very reminiscent of the Priors' doorway
at Durham, and the decoration between its three orders of columns
suggests that it could not have been built before 1135. On each side
it has a plain arcade above a window, and from inside the building
one can see that it is the pierced centre of an open gallery of five
arches. The projecting turrets are shafted at the angles.

Having built their church to the glory of God,

> A solemn, huge and dark red pile,
> Placed on the margin of the isle,

as Scott says of it in *Marmion*, the Benedictines of this newly established monastery turned their attention in the thirteenth century to
permanent buildings for their own needs. As was common practice,
these were attached to the south transept, and being of grey stone,
contrast strikingly with the red sandstone of the church.

To the south of the nave was the cloister separating the domestic
and residential buildings. The remains of it are fragmentary. On its
west side lay the cellars, the pantry, the larder with a stone-lined pot
probably used as an ice-house, the brewhouse, bakery and kitchen;
and here we can see on the outer wall the traces of six small lancet
windows. Over these buildings were no doubt rooms for the lay
brethren. To the east, with its vaults on semi-circular supports, was
the chapter house where readings from the rule of St Benedict took
place daily; it was also used for formal meetings. Above was the
monks' dormitory with night stairs leading down into the church,
as at Hexham. In the early days the Prior would sleep here among the
brothers, but later he had his own chamber and adjoining it a guest
chamber over the warming room, which was the common meeting
place of the monastery. You can see the great fireplace here and one
above it on the first floor. This room led to the parlour where visitors
were received and also to the dining hall, few traces of which survive.
Between hall and kitchen is the thirteenth-century inner gate; its
outer court was surrounded by a battlemented wall. This gateway was
strengthened by a barbican in the fourteenth century, a reminder of

the constant danger of Scottish raids and unique for a monastery. The walls to the east were particularly stout and were protected to the north-east by a tower and on the south-east by an angled turret, or bartisan, probably built at this same time, when the western walls were also raised. Legend has it that in this bartisan a nun was walled up alive, but this probably arises from the story of Constance of Beverley which Scott tells in *Marmion*.

Before leaving the priory do not fail to visit the **Museum** which contains several interesting exhibits, including an eighth-century tombstone with Christian symbols on one side and pagan carvings on the other.

The priory's greatest treasure, however, is no longer here – the world-famous Lindisfarne Gospels. This, one of the most beautiful illuminated manuscripts in the world, was begun by the monks of Holy Island when Eadfrith became bishop in 698, only eleven years after Cuthbert's death. A note added some three hundred years later describes the making of it:

> Eadfrith, bishop of the church of Lindisfarne, he at the first wrote this book for God and for St Cuthbert and for all the Saints in common that are in the island. And Ethilwald, bishop of those of Lindisfarne Island, bound and covered it outwardly as well as he could. And Billfrith the anchorite, he wrought as a smith the ornaments that are on the outside and adorned it with gold and with gems, also with silver overgilded, a treasure without deceit. And Alfred, an unworthy and most miserable priest, with God's help and St Cuthbert's, overglossed it in English.

The writer added an interlinear English translation to this copy of the Gospels in the Vulgate. The beautiful cover referred to was presumably destroyed at the time of the dissolution of the monastery in 1541, but the manuscript survived and came into the possession of Robert Bowyer, Clerk of Parliaments under James I, was then bought by Sir Robert Cotton and passed with the rest of his library to the British Museum, where it is now kept. Its history throughout was chequered. It accompanied Cuthbert's body in its wanderings and is said to have rested on his coffin when he was finally buried behind the high altar in Durham Cathedral in 1104. According to legend it had earlier been lost in a storm at sea, when the monks had been attempting to seek refuge in Ireland for fear of the Danes, and had been miraculously washed ashore and restored to its guardians through the personal intervention of the Saint.

Immediately to the west of the Priory is the **Parish Church**, and it too is worth a visit, for it has some interesting and unusual features. The three rounded arches between the nave and north aisle date from the late twelfth century and have voussoirs of alternating red and white stone, a great rarity in England. Most of the church was built in the thirteenth century, and it has a very fine chancel with three stepped lancets in the east wall with buttresses between them. On the west front is an eighteenth-century bell-cote reminiscent of the one at Ford – a fine and individual effect. The carpets near the altar are reproductions of a page in the Lindisfarne Gospels worked in wool embroidery by the women of the island. The old stone stump in the churchyard was part of the original market cross which was replaced by a new one in 1828. The old stump was called the 'Petting Stone', over which newly married couples used to jump for luck. It still plays a part in village weddings, as does the local drink – mead – made from fermented honey and drunk in Saxon times for a lunar month after the ceremony (hence 'honeymoon').

Chapter 12

From Holy Island to Berwick on Tweed

*

The direct route north is through Beal to West Mains and then by
the A1 through Scremerston. To the right lies the huge expanse of
the Goswick and Cheswick Sands, from which the sea recedes almost
out of sight at low tide. Great care should be taken by anyone ventur-
on them, for the sea comes back very fast, as on the Solway coast,
and there are quicksands. There are other traps for the unwary, for
access by car from the villages of Cheswick and Beal is over un-
manned level crossings and there is always the possibility of having
one's outing interrupted by the arrival of The Flying Scotsman at
speed. Some of the beaches nearer Berwick are beautiful, especially
Cocklawburn, with its view along the coast of coves and grassy head-
lands, though for some unexplained reason this bay which rates two
signposts on the A1 is not shown on the Ordnance Survey map. Also
off the A1 near Beal is a 'country park' and vast caravan site at
Haggerston Castle. The big house itself, built in the 1770s and added
to by Norman Shaw, was pulled down in 1931, but a very tall, thin
and peculiar-looking tower survives among the trees.

Lovers of coastal scenery who are prepared to leave their cars and
walk will relish this area south of the Tweed. Yet the roundabout road
to Berwick that runs inland is also beguiling, and my advice at this
point would be to take it, through Lowick to Ford, Branxton, Etal
and Duddo Standing Stones. As an alternative, these places could
be visited on the southward run out of Cornhill on Tweed – in fact
there are a number of combinations of routes that can cover this
small but outstandingly beautiful and historic corner of Northumberland, and I can only plead that the one I have chosen, if not
the most logical, is the one that appeals to *me*. It has too this advantage, that it helps the motorist to follow the movements of the
rival armies before Flodden through the eyes of the Scottish commanders, marching to their doom from Ford and Branxton Hill.

Turning inland, our route after Lowick runs west along the B6353.
However, those interested in pre-history should branch south after
three-quarters of a mile on to the A6111 and after another half mile

turn right on to the minor road that straggles across country over
Bar Moor towards Kimmerston. Two miles later one arrives at a
large rock on the right-hand side of the road just short of the wooded
entrance to Roughting Linn Farm. It is covered with the mysterious
Cup and Ring Markings associated with Bronze Age culture and also
runnels in the stone leading down from the crest. For what purpose?
To carry away blood from a sacrificial altar? They certainly look
purpose made and not the effect of weathering. This is the largest
rock of its kind in Northumberland and is in every way fascinating.
Immediately to the west of it is a British Iron Age fort of perhaps a
millennium later, with four ramparts and forty-feet-deep ditches.
The position is a strong one, for where the ramparts stop protection
is afforded by a stream at the bottom of a ravine. The one mystery
is why the fort is built so close to the rock 'altar' of a much earlier
time which physically commands it. Were the Iron Age inhabitants
sheltering under the holy 'high place' of their ancestors? Or was there
some religious or mystical reason why they did not want to incorporate it into their perimeter? We will find a somewhat similar
situation at Lordenshaw (see p. 231) though here the fort is on a
higher elevation than the rock. At Roughting Linn the rock seems
almost a threat to the camp below it, but perhaps even tribal enemies
had a superstitious dread of using it. This whole area around
Doddington is full of prehistoric camps and rock markings, though
none of them is as easy of access. Those interested should see Pevsner,
page 138.

At the junction just short of Kimmerston a road to the right rejoins
our main route at **Ford**.

Ford is a 'model village' planned in the middle of the nineteenth
century by Louisa, Marchioness of Waterford, who in her youth
had been chosen 'Queen of Beauty' at Lord Eglinton's famous
tournament inspired by Sir Walter Scott. Widowed early in life, she
took to good works, becoming, according to one hostile critic, 'an
organisation for the relief of the undeserving poor'. Ford village is
part of the evidence of this. It has been much praised, and the view
down the slope of its one long street to the castle in its bower of trees
is attractive; but there is a cold formality about the planning that
somehow detracts from the evident good-will of its founder and
makes it a strangely depressing place. The **Village School** (1860) is
interesting, for it contains a series of watercolours (they are *not*
frescoes, as sometimes supposed) on Biblical themes by Lady Waterford herself, a follower of the pre-Raphaelites. Her friend Ruskin

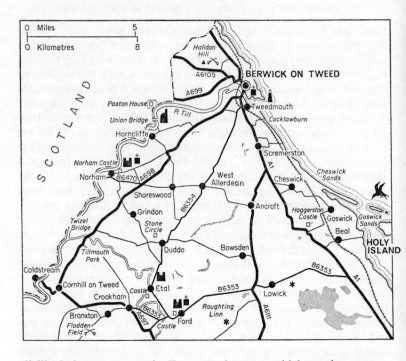

disliked them very much. 'I expected you would have done something better,' he told his admirer and acolyte discouragingly. Yet many will find these figures, drawn from village characters of the day, surprisingly impressive. People come to smile but stay to admire – Lady Waterford was a true artist who deserved much greater recognition than she got. The scenes depict Cain and Abel; Abraham and Isaac; Jacob and Esau; Joseph and his brethren; Moses in the bulrushes; Samuel; the boy David; the child-king Josiah; three infants; and a large painting of Christ blessing the children. The visitors' book contains among a host of signatures of celebrities those of Mr Gladstone, Sir Edwin Landseer, Earl Grey, and surprisingly enough that scourge of the Victorian ecclesiastical Establishment, T. H. Huxley.

Ford **Castle**, at the bottom of the hill, the home chosen by the Marchioness for herself after her widowhood and which she rebuilt very baronially in the 1860s, is now used by the Northumberland County Council. The earliest parts date back to Plantagenet times; but there is little point in whetting the appetite of the visitor who can get no more than a distant glimpse of its walls by trespassing a

190

little along the path leading from the church. There are other compensations, however, for facing you as you look south-west across the valley are the wooded slopes of Flodden Hill where the Scottish army camped before the battle in September 1513. In summer before the scything has begun the churchyard is ablaze with flowers – a most beautiful and restful spot. **St Michael's** itself dates from the early thirteenth century, though much altered in Dobson's restoration of 1853. Its most distinctive feature is the sturdy bell-cote which serves as a tower. Compare similar features on Holy Island and at Thockrington.

From Ford it is little more than four miles across country to **Branxton Hill** and the actual site of the battlefield of Flodden, fought on 9 and 10 September 1513, in which perished most of the chivalry of the northern kingdom. Older writers used to call it the Battle of Branxton, but for some reason it has been immortalised as Flodden Field, though Flodden Hill, where the Scots lay before the battle, played no further part in the struggle. Most of this country in the triangle between the rivers Tweed and Till is now rich agricultural land: it was then open heath with few trees. But the contours have not changed, and the motorist with an Ordnance Map will find it easy to follow the movements of the rival armies without even leaving his car.

King James IV of Scotland with a powerful force had been making raids into England, partly because this was the traditional Border sport but also as a diversionary measure to help his French allies, whose country had been invaded by Henry VIII. An English army under the Earl of Surrey and drawn chiefly from the northern counties had been hastily raised to drive them back, and in accordance with the fanciful dictates of late medieval warfare a challenge had been sent to the already retreating Scottish king to make up a battle somewhere on the Millfield Plain by 9 September at the latest. But when Surrey saw the ground his opponent had chosen on the south-east slope of Flodden Hill he thought better of an attack, and decided instead on a manoeuvre so risky that it could only be justified by success. Crossing to the east bank of the Till on a flank march around the enemy position, he moved north, sent his artillery back to the west bank by Twyzel Bridge (which still stands), forded the river with the rest of the army just upstream from it, and united his columns near the village of Branxton, where they now lay *between* the Scots and their homeland.

If James had come down from Flodden Edge and attacked his

191

enemy in detail during the course of this perilous march he might well have won. From the slopes where he was camped the movements of the English should have been plainly visible: and indeed there is a traditional spot some distance down the hill where he is said to have sat and studied them. On the other hand, the weather on the day of the battle was drizzly, and if there was mist and low cloud off the Cheviots some of the English moves may have been hidden from him until it was too late to intervene. There must have come a point, however, at which the King appreciated he had been outflanked, for the Scots army turned about and came down the northern slope of Flodden to occupy the crest of Branxton Hill on the line of its retreat march northwards.

Below them lay the English near the village itself, numbering about twenty thousand, the approximate strength of their own army also: and about 4 p.m. on 9 September – the expiry date of Surrey's challenge – the fight began with a disorderly Scottish descent from the hill-crest, perhaps induced by the ravages of the better-served English artillery. At first the Scots seemed victors on one flank; but part of their army held back, leaving the centre to be overwhelmed by superior forces of English spearmen and guns. Besides the King and his natural son, Alexander Stuart, there died twelve earls, fifteen chiefs of clans, a number of clergy including a bishop and two abbots, and perhaps nine thousand men. The English too lost heavily and Surrey was in no position to exploit his victory to the full; but for the Scots this was catastrophe. Sir Walter Scott's lines on the battle still preserve the sense of shock and horror that had seized his countrymen:

> Tradition, legend, tune and song
> Shall many an age that wail prolong:
> Still from the sire the son shall hear
> Of the stern strife and carnage drear,
> Of Flodden's fatal field:
> When shiver'd was fair Scotland's spear
> And broken was her shield.

Equally fine is Jane Elliott's famous ballad, whose music fills the air at Scottish gatherings: *The Flowers of the Forest*, a lament for the fallen. Close to Branxton village a footpath leads up to a mound and a Celtic cross of grey Aberdeen granite raised in 1910 on the spot where the King and his nobles fell. It is inscribed:

FLODDEN 1513
TO THE BRAVE OF BOTH NATIONS

There is an annual commemoration service and oration on the site. Riders come from the Scottish side of the Border and a piper plays *The Flowers of the Forest*.

From Branxton turn north on the Berwick road for **Etal**. The village, like Ford, has a planned appearance, with an eighteenth-century manor house in its park at one end of the single street and a ruined castle at the other. Its thatched cottages are now a rarity in Northumberland, though once upon a time thatch or heather was the norm for small houses throughout the area. As a result, Etal's cottages have often been over-praised; they would hardly be thought worth a mention south of the Trent. But there is a pretty pub, the *Black Bull*, with some tourist accommodation; and the ruined castle, which was recorded as being 'in very great decay' as early as the Border Survey of 1542, has a certain melancholy charm. No one has attempted to restore it or tidy it up: it has a genuinely owl- and bat-infested air. Once a fortress of some strength, it never recovered from the battering it got from James the Fourth's Scots. Yet Etal had its revenge; for it was across the old bridge over the Till, whose foundations can still be seen, that the captured Scottish guns were hauled southwards after Flodden. A right turn just before reaching the castle leads down a lane to the river, running dark and slow through meadows under the trees, crossed by a wooden footbridge: an Arcadian spot.

A little downstream, between Ford and Etal and reached by a minor road running south on the right bank from Ford Forge, is **Heatherslaw Mill**, one of the oldest water-driven flour mills in England with its machinery still intact. It was in business till 1946 and has now been preserved as a museum, complete with car park and café. The millers who were grinding corn here in an earlier building on the site at the time of the Hundred Years' War would be astonished to learn that nearly fifty thousand pounds is being spent, a substantial part of which is being met by such mysterious bodies as The English Tourist Board and the Ministry of the Environment. Lord Joicey of Etal Manor is the real fairy godmother behind the scheme.

Two and a half miles north of Etal on the B6354 lies the hamlet of Duddo ('Dod', a round hill: 'how', a height) whose castle was similarly hammered by the Scots and was later further undermined by workings in a coal seam. It is of no particular interest today, though it looks romantic in the distance. At the T-junction in the village turn left, passing a handsome Georgian house, and when you come to the end of the plantations on your right you will see through a farm gate a cart track leading uphill to **Duddo Standing Stones** on the hill-top just over a mile away. When crops are growing it is not permissible to visit the circle, though a good view can be had by walking up the track towards them. Permission in any case should be asked from Duddo Farms Ltd. There are at present five of these stones standing, the largest one two feet high and broad in proportion, and they formed part of a forty-foot circle that once enclosed an ancient British burial ground. See them if you can, for they are among the most impressive things in Northumberland, giving us a remarkable insight into the strength of faith or superstition that drove these remote ancestors of ours to drag and erect them here on this height looking towards the mass of the Cheviot Hills across the Millfield Plain, said to be the site of one of King Arthur's early battles. Deeply furrowed by the ravages of the weather, they now seem in further danger, for it looks as though someone has taken a substantial hack at the base of one of them, revealing the red sandstone core.

Seven miles away, via East Ord and Tweedmouth, is the north-eastern limit of our tour at **Berwick on Tweed**.

> A bridge without a middle arch,
> A church without a steeple,
> A midden heap in every street
> And damned conceited people.

These lines on **Berwick** have been ascribed to Robert Burns, but there are a number of other anomalies he missed out. The town lies in England: its county – Berwickshire – is in Scotland. Its football team plays in the Scottish League. A municipality numbering some twelve thousand people, its Mayor is yet held to be the third most important civic dignitary in the country, or rather had this status until the recent government reforms. Sometimes part of England, sometimes part of Scotland, changing hands no less than thirteen times, it managed for a while to be a semi-sovereign entity of its own, being mentioned separately in royal proclamations and Acts of Parliament, and according to one legend is still at war with Russia over the little troubles in the Crimea which the peace delegates forgot to wind up on Berwick's behalf when the firing stopped.

Whatever it may or may not be, it is without doubt the place, second only to Durham, which no visitor to Northumbria should miss: in Pevsner's words, 'One of the most exciting towns in England, a real town with the strongest sense of enclosure, a town of red roofs

194

and grey houses with hardly an irritating building anywhere, and a town of the most intricate change of levels.' Apart from the truly horrible bus station, other facts bear Pevsner out: he is no lone enthusiast. The remarkably intact Elizabethan fortifications are accepted as the earliest of their type outside Italy and are among the four finest to be seen north of the Alps. The town contains a higher proportion of listed buildings – one in ten – than anywhere else in Britain; indeed, the whole zone within the walls is a preservation area; yet this is no museum but the thriving communications and commercial centre for the large triangle between Alnwick, Kelso and Edinburgh that makes its living in the valleys of the Tweed and its tributaries.

The approach over the estuary from the south is disappointing. To your left the graceful rounded arches of Robert Stephenson's **Royal Border Bridge** (opened in 1850 by Queen Victoria and Prince Albert) show up splendidly, imperially, like some great Roman aqueduct, but the parapet of the modern road bridge is too high to allow a view downstream to the old Bridge, a most beautiful Jacobean structure which took twenty years to build and still does its job of carrying the downtown traffic across to Tweedmouth. This middle bridge dates from 1925/28. It has its defenders, and concrete can be used to great effect by engineers of taste and genius. This has not happened here, and the siting between two works of extraordinary quality and grace only adds to its ungainliness – Berwick's ugly duckling, which fortunately most visitors fail to see since they are liable to be travelling along its back.

Pevsner suggests that visitors should start their 'Perambulation' from the Town Hall in Marygate. I would dissent from this for two reasons. The spire of this fine building, which can be glimpsed from almost anywhere along the ramparts, provides a constant focus of attention and interest for people making the round tour; and the café on its ground floor, stocked with Scottish scones and baps and cakes, with cream and jam, is a splendid spot in which to rest your legs after the walking is over. It should be saved up till last. For this reason start at the north end of the Jacobean **Bridge**, where the English Gate and its guardhouse stood till 1825, and where you can see the elegant and subtle curve of the arches and parapet leading over the Tweed. At this point the main channel of the river runs close to the north bank; therefore the second nearest to you of the fifteen arches is the highest and gives to the rest a delicately declining fall. You yourself are on **Quay Walls**, another curving line, this time of houses, with high ground behind you but giving unexpected glimpses of streets sloping down to the river level below your feet.

Quay Walls could become a slum. Some of its eighteenth- and early-nineteenth-century houses are already derelict, and under a less alert and enlightened Council could have been swept away to limbo in some town redevelopment scheme. Berwick happily understands the need to guard its heritage, and its Preservation Trust is busily at work acquiring some of these ravaged buildings, not individually of outstanding architectural importance, but part of a pattern of great interest and charm. Others have already been reclaimed – like the admirable Customs House with its arched windows and Venetian doorway. The whole adds up to a grand jumble of terracing, boatyards, red pantile roofs and plunging streets, along one of which one can discern the elegant and gaily painted *King's Arms Hotel*.

Going east and anti-clockwise along Quay Walls one reaches the classical terrace of Palace Green overlooking the mouth of the river and the long mole on its northern bank; then the tall 'Lion House', built in the 1820s, with two stone beasts *couchant* (probably Siamese brought to Berwick by a ship's captain) which for the benefit of small boys who stay out late are reputed to come down from their pedestals to prowl the ramparts after dark. Just to the south is an untended garden, where there are a number of ice-houses which have been in continuous use since 1723. They are easy to miss, as a mound in the garden obscures them from view. In summer the scene is bright with blobs of colour from the sails of yachts. There are few signs of the salmon, whose netting during the season, 15 February–14 September, provides a livelihood for many people in Berwick and whose presence up-river makes the Tweed one of the finest sporting rivers in Britain. The depredations of the grey seals from their breeding grounds on the Farnes and of the urban poaching gangs with their cars and high explosive are among the problems that plague the local fishermen, the landowners and the magistrates – this is a tough area still, for all its bland appearance.

A little further on the **Ramparts** begin – like some smaller and handier Lucca without the horrors of Italian traffic pounding by. Before the Second World War many of the gun emplacements were lined with cannon. Patriotically they were given for scrap to help the war effort, but Berwick darkly suspects that they are still in existence somewhere, perhaps in Edinburgh or London. All that remains is one Crimean cannon which was a gift to the town – a decidedly ambiguous one, since it arrived at its destination fully primed and loaded and capable of knocking off the Town Hall steeple at the drop of a match.

But it is the **Elizabethan Fortifications** that really make the town unique: the first-fruits of sixteenth-century Italian military engineering at that moment in time when the fortified castle and city wall had become useless against the power of the heavy gun and some other kind of defence work had to be developed. The result was the low-profiled, earth-topped, star-shaped citadel, with projecting bastions providing all-round fire from its cannon to cover the wide, deep moat surrounding it. Such fortresses, which sprang up throughout Europe, particularly in the Netherlands, northern Italy and northern France, were to hold their own with modifications down to the time of the Franco-Prussian War. But why, one may ask, at Berwick?

Because, almost throughout its history, the town's strategic position at the mouth of the Tweed had made it a key point in the duel between England and Scotland and Scotland's partner of the 'Auld Alliance', France. It was a prize worth having. At the height of its prosperity in the thirteenth century under Scottish rule it was described by the Lanercost Chronicler as 'a city so populous and of such trade that it might justly be called another Alexandria, whose riches were the seas and the water its walls'. Nor was this idle boasting, for in 1287 the Customs of Berwick provided Scotland with a sum equal to almost a quarter of the total for the whole of England, and its continued eminence as a port is vouched for by the special mention made of it in the famous Navigation Acts down to the days of the elder Pitt. 'One of the greatest and most beautiful towns in England,' wrote a French observer in 1762. The struggle for possession of such a pearl was almost continuous for three centuries. King John set fire to it. It was in Berwick in 1292, in the hall of the castle whose ruins now lie under the railway station, that the barons and prelates of the two kingdoms under the presidency of Edward I finally awarded the crown of Scotland to John Baliol. Some years later, when Baliol rebelled against his overlord, King Edward stormed the town and slaughtered some seven thousand people inside it. It was he who ordered the building of the fortifications known as 'the Edwardian Walls', stretches of which still stand to the north of the Elizabethan ramparts. Captured by the Scots after Bannockburn, Berwick was besieged in turn by the English by land and sea. In his epic poem *The Bruce*, written some fifty years after the event, John Barbour, Archdeacon of Aberdeen, has a passage where he describes how the besiegers built a 'sow' of stout timber to protect the sappers and miners as they worked away at the foundations of the walls, and how this engine was destroyed by a giant stone hurled from a catapult inside the town. Mr A. A. Douglas, himself a direct descendant of Robert Bruce's most trusted lieutenant of the same name, has provided us with a spirited modern translation of Barbour's verse:

> Direct upon the sow it crashed;
> In pieces were the main beams smashed!
> In terror all the men ran out.
> Then the defenders gave a shout:
> 'The sow is farrowing! Hurrah!
> Now we can see what swine ye are.'

Long after the Bruce, Berwick continued to be a bone of contention. It played its part in the campaign that ended at Flodden, and it was here that the body of James IV was embalmed after the defeat. So it was natural that in the dangerous years that followed her accession Queen Elizabeth should have wanted to have Berwick fortified *à la mode*. It cost her a pretty penny and must have caused much heartburning in that parsimonious soul. And amusingly enough she got no value for her money, for in her time Berwick was never called upon to undergo a siege. When eventually during the Civil Wars the fine new fortress was summoned to surrender, it did so at the first shot.

The shape and scope of these Elizabethan fortifications can easily be grasped without a map – Windmill Bastion at the most easterly point facing the sea; Brass Bastion at the north-east angle; at which point the line makes a sharp turn to the south-west past Cumberland Bastion to Meg's Mount overlooking the Tweed. You can walk all the way on a pleasant grassy promenade with fine views over the sea and river and at one point over the busy Castle Gate. For a closer look at the system **Brass Bastion** is an ideal spot, providing one can find the perambulating official who carries the keys and can borrow his torch to grope one's way through the narrow underground tunnel into the open, where the guns once stood with their plunging field of fire into the moat. Not to be recommended to those given to claustrophobia or without a light of some kind: otherwise a fascinating experience, in the course of which one can picnic like d'Artagnan and the Musketeers in that famous scene in the bastion at La Rochelle. **Cumberland Bastion** (again if you can ever find the person with the key) is the viewpoint recommended by John Seymour, who gives a fascinating description of the whole system of fortifications as they existed in their prime. He also describes the Edwardian Walls to the north of them, traces of which exist between Brass Bastion and Northumberland Avenue and on the river side, just south of the railway station. Near this point there is a riverside walk that passes under Stephenson's superb Royal Border Bridge.

Apart from the fortifications and the bridges and the agreeable ambience of the town, there remain three buildings of special interest: the Town Hall, Holy Trinity Church, and the Ravensdowne Barracks, all of which can be reached in a matter of a few minutes from any point on the ramparts, for one of the chief joys of Berwick is its compactness.

The **Barracks** lie opposite Windmill Bastion. The home of the King's Own Scottish Borderers and of their regimental **Museum**, this is the oldest barracks still in active use in Britain: sometimes attributed to Vanbrugh or to Andrew Jelf, architect to the Ordnance Department in the years immediately after the Battle of Blenheim. The courtyard is of considerable distinction, best seen through the entrance gate with its fanlight and royal coat of arms looking towards the steeply pitched roof of the classical south wing. The **Museum**, to the left on entering, contains a collection of weapons and uniforms and personal relics of Earl Haig, the British Commander-in-Chief of the Western Front during the First World War.

Holy Trinity, the parish church, adjoins the barracks, huddling beneath the brutally aggressive Victorian Gothic spire of the Presbyterian church on Wallace Green, without doubt the most appalling thing in Berwick. Holy Trinity itself has neither spire nor tower; Cromwell would not allow one; though it has two rather regrettable pepper-box turrets in lieu. It is that great rarity, a church built during the Commonwealth, between 1648 and 1652. By rights it should be a dark and depressing building, as from the outside I fear it is. Certainly its packed graveyard under the trees is dour enough to have gratified even John Knox, who is sometimes said to have preached from its pulpit, though in fact his chaplaincy was at an earlier church some distance away. Even inside, the effect must at one time have been ponderous, with wooden galleries facing into the nave and a third at the west end (which still survives and is used on ceremonial occasions). It must have been a church deeply in thrall to the Puritan obsession with sin – indeed, 1972 saw the tercentenary of a strange event centred on one of its clergy, who, after delivering a sermon in passionate denunciation of the Devil and the Scarlet Woman and all their works, collapsed in the pulpit and was carried home to his manse, where lay the body of his wife whom he had brutally done to death. Now that the side galleries have been removed the interior of Holy Trinity breathes a very different spirit: with its Venetian windows patterned in a chequer-board of black and white edged with blue and red, and the graceful Tuscan columns and arches of the nave, it is as restful and elegant a church as one could hope to find anywhere. Built by command of the Puritan governor of the town, Colonel George Fenwicke, by John Young of Black-friars, it is said to resemble the rather earlier City of London church of St Katherine Cree. A chancel was added in 1855 and the clerestory windows were changed from round-headed to Venetian style; but the restoration is not intrusive. The reredos is an early work by Lutyens; the pulpit is Cromwellian; and some of the stained glass roundels in the west window are by Netherlands craftsmen probably about the time of the Spanish Armada. An unusual feature is the long rounded arch in the wall of the north aisle of the nave which in Cromwellian times, when high altars were anathema, may have housed the Communion table and given a surprising twist to the normal orientation of a church, never mind to the necks of the worshippers in the north gallery.

There remains the **Town Hall** or Guild Hall in Marygate, which I have left till last out of respect for its tea room and gift shop. Up-stairs on the top floor, in stark contrast, the old town gaol has been preserved, complete with monster keys and stocks, much as it was in Hanoverian times. For that matter, Berwick Town Hall is not internally one of the most luxurious of buildings and its lavatories must rank as about the most rudimentary in the kingdom. From Marygate, however, looking down the hill, it is quite another matter, for few municipal buildings have more style or command of their environment than this mid-eighteenth-century building with its Tuscan portico at the top of a flight of steps and its one-hundred-and-fifty-foot-high belfry which can be glimpsed from practically any-where in the town: from the ramparts, Quay Walls, and perhaps best of all from the London to Edinburgh trains as they glide over Robert Stephenson's great bridge nearly as high as the steeple itself. One Joseph Dodds, who carried out the building (1754/60), vain-gloriously signed himself over the main door as architect, but the design was by S. and J. Worrell of London.

Really serious tourists may want to inspect what is left of the ancient castle between the river and the railway station, but it is hardly worth the trouble. Students of military history will be drawn to **Halidon Hill**, two and a half miles north-west of the town, where in 1333 a Scottish army trying to raise the siege of Berwick was decimated by the English archers. Berwick still retains the ancient custom of boundary riding, once universal throughout the Border country, in which the citizens re-assert their territorial claims. The Berwick riders are sent on their way rejoicing with stirrup cups of cherry brandy and whisky in equal proportions!

Chapter 13

From Berwick to Cornhill on Tweed

✤

Both to the north and south of Berwick is beautiful coastline. To the north, almost on the coastal border with Scotland, are the cliffs above **Marshall Meadows Bay**; to the south, close by **St John's Haven**, is a romantic cave, its entrance curtained by a waterfall. Both are worth a visit.

Two main roads follow the Tweed westward from Berwick: the A699 north of the river and the A698 south of it. Ideally start with the northern route, which allows an opportunity of taking in the site of the Battle of Halidon Hill and then skirts the grounds of Paxton Hall. The Paxtons, balanced precariously on the Border where their lands were vulnerable to predators on both sides, barely managed to survive till the union of the Crowns, but thereafter thrived, and it was one of their clan, Sir Joseph, who built London its famous Crystal Palace for the Great Exhibition of 1851. The village near by was noted once upon a time for 'drunken old wives and salmon sae fine', also for the celebrated Victorian ballad, *Robin Adair*, of which two versions exist, the older and homelier being the one for me:

> Paxton's a fine snug place, Robin Adair.
> It's a wondrous couthie place, Robin Adair.
> Let Whitadder rin a spate
> Or the wind blow at ony rate,
> Yet I'll meet thee on the gait, Robin Adair.

Half a mile further on turn sharp left, doubling back towards the east to cross the Tweed by the **Union Chain Bridge**, built by Sir Samuel Brown in 1820. Brown was the inventor of the wrought-iron link which he had patented three years earlier, and in this elegant structure we have the first suspension bridge in the country, earlier even than Telford's work at the Menai Straits. Its total length suspended is four hundred and thirty-two feet, its width eighteen feet, and it stands nearly seventy feet above high water level. In the bend of the river, which makes a wide turn at this point, Charles I pitched his camp in 1639 on his way to meet the Scottish Covenanters.

The Tweed is a beautiful river throughout its length and the scene at Union Bridge is nothing less than idyllic, with the prospect of the wooded grounds of Paxton Hall rising on their bluff beyond the stream.

Further west along the south bank of the river, beyond Horncliffe, lies **Norham**, whose castle and church are among the great sights of the Border country: little wonder that Turner chose to paint it so often.

The **Castle**, which holds the high ground at the entrance to the village, was once the chief northern stronghold of the bishops of Durham, whose jurisdiction was independent of the surrounding countryside. It follows the normal motte and bailey plan, but the large size of the inner ward and the unusual width of the outer ward reflect its additional role as a bishop's palace, providing accommodation far in excess of what would be required by a local baron.

The situation is magnificent – a grassy mound, guarded on the north and west by the steep banks of the Tweed and on the east by a ravine. Ranulf Flambard built himself a timber fortress here, but it was only after the reconquest of Scotland by Henry II and the rebuilding of the crown castles of Newcastle, Bamburgh and Wark in stone that Bishop Pudsey followed suit by strengthening this northern outpost of the bishopric. Of his castle (1158/74) the most outstanding remains are the West Gate (often called Marmion's Gate) facing straight down the village street, and the splendid red sandstone **Keep** in the inner ward. Its east and south walls had to be particularly strong because they formed part of the curtain wall, as at Dunstanburgh, but the north and west walls facing into the ward were much flimsier and were honeycombed with small rooms and staircases. This was a three-storey building with a solid vault divided by a five-foot wall and a smaller one on the first floor. The wall walk was at about the same height as the tallest of the present remains – ninety feet. In 1422/5 for some inexplicable reason it was decided to add two more storeys. Every precaution was taken to strengthen the fabric. A dividing stone wall was built on the second floor, the west wall was shored up and all the hollows filled in, but the structure simply would not bear the weight and the whole of the north wall collapsed.

Norham, as we have seen, was a dual-purpose building. The Keep was where the Constable lived. The bishops had their palace in the north-east corner of the inner ward. The remains of their sixty- by thirty-foot great hall with its three doorways to buttery, pantry and service passage were part of a sixteenth-century rebuilding. The great oven is still in existence. In front of the hall stands the well-head, all that remains of the draw-well that must have had machinery and superstructure attached. Back over the wooden bridge are buildings to the left in the moat. These were to do with the water supply, and the miniature swimming baths with sloping floors were probably used for washing horses. Water from the moat ran out into the river underneath the fifteenth-century chapel on the right. Here we are in the outer ward with its beautifully kept lawns rising to the remains of the curtain wall and turrets backed by splendid trees: the vulnerable point in the defences where constant repairing and rebuilding went on throughout the castle's active life.

Norham was a vital link in the defence of England against the Scots, and whenever there was the least doubt about the loyalty of the bishop the King would take over and the castle would be given a royal Constable and garrison. This happened between 1174 and 1198 and again between 1208 and 1217. Throughout most of the thirteenth century there was peace. But a storm was brewing. It was here that Bishop Bek entertained Edward I and his court when as overlord of Scotland the King claimed the right to dispose of its crown. Here sat the arbitration court with thirteen hopeful candidates before it, including John Baliol and Robert Bruce 'the Claimant', grandfather of the victor of Bannockburn; though it was not at Norham but at Berwick that the fateful choice in favour of Baliol was made. It marked the end of the peaceful times and by 1318 the line of the Tweed was under constant pressure from the Scots. Northumberland was laid waste and the siege of Norham by King Robert Bruce lasted for almost a year. The outer ward was captured, but was retaken after three days and the siege had to be lifted. The following year the Scots tried again. It was during this campaign, as every reader of Scott knows, that Sir William Marmion arrived at the castle with the gleaming helmet given him by his lady with orders to prove his valour in the most dangerous place in England. He was given the opportunity to do so by the Constable, Sir Thomas Grey, who urged him to ride out alone against the foe. 'May I deny my God if I do not rescue your person alive or dead or perish in the attempt,' Sir Thomas remarked encouragingly to the champion, the first of the fall guys. I have always admired the fine flavour of that phrase 'alive or dead'. At any rate, in his gleaming armour and his lady's helmet, Marmion charged out on his war horse by the west gate, was bowled over by the Scots, and then rescued on cue by the Constable, bleeding but alive.

Norham has other claims to chivalric fame. Some say that it was here that the gallant Edward III rescued Lady Shrewsbury's garter, rebuked his sniggering courtiers and founded the famous Order with its motto, *Honi soit qui mal y pense*. However, the honour seems more properly to belong to Wark on Tweed. It was at Norham certainly that John Knox, scourge of 'the monstrous regiment of women', met his future wife, Marjory Bowes, daughter of the governor of the castle. But by that time the place had fallen into decay. In 1571 Queen Elizabeth granted it to her cousin Henry Carey, Lord Hunsdon, Lord Warden of the East March, who was followed in the captaincy by his three sons; but in spite of the near relationship not a penny could any of them extract from the parsimonious Queen, not even to build 'a poor cottage' for themselves within the walls. With the Union of the Crowns Norham's function entirely ceased and it was left as a quarry for local builders.

From the castle a wide street leads downhill to the village green and its stone cross, whose base is medieval. Here one bears right and then left past the council houses to the **Parish Church** dedicated to St Peter, St Cuthbert and St Ceolwulph, in its bower of trees.

There was a church here or near by in Saxon times, built in 830 by Bishop Egred to house the remains of King Oswald and of St Ceolwulph, who himself had been a local king before taking the cowl. The church as it now stands is the creation of Bishop Flambard, built at about the same time as the first castle on the hill, but heavily restored in 1617 and again between 1846 and 1852. From the outside it looks as though two separate buildings have been stuck end to end – on the left, one of the nineteenth century, with its regrettable tower and porch; on the right, the south chancel wall with five exquisite windows whose friezes continue from the arch across the buttresses. Here and inside one can visualise the power and solidity of the Norman work from the evidence of what remains: the five round-headed arches in the south aisle with their zigzag frieze; the huge circular piers with capital decoration reminiscent of that in Durham's Galilee Chapel; the three-shafted piers of the chancel arch; and the beautiful windows in the south wall of the chancel, shafted, with a three-tier decoration of their arches similar to that in Pudsey's hall in Durham Castle. In contrast, those on the north side are plain. The Norman apse at the east end was taken down in 1340; the chancel was then extended, and the east windows date from this time. Of a slightly earlier date (1320) is the recessed tomb of a knight on the south side. Particularly interesting are the vicar's stall and the pulpit with the royal arms which were originally in Durham Cathedral. The wood carving was done in Cosin's time after the Restoration. This great traditionalist would have been pleased to know that the ceremony of blessing the salmon nets at Norham still takes place every February.

The direct route to the west out of Norham lies across the river towards Swinton. Double back therefore for a mile or so eastward on the B6470 to the junction with the A698, where a sharp turn leads to the Cornhill road. Three miles along it lies another historic bridge, this one dating from the fifteenth century: the same structure over which the Earl of Surrey's vanguard and artillery clattered on the eve of Flodden. Sir Walter Scott describes it in his poem:

> From Flodden Ridge
> The Scots beheld the English host
> Leave Barmoor Wood, their evening post,
> And heedful watched them as they crossed
> The Till by Twizel Bridge.
> High sight it is and haughty, while
> They drive into the deep defile;
> Beneath the cavern'd cliff they fall,
> Beneath the castle's airey wall.
> By rock, by oak, by hawthorn tree,
> Troop after troop are disappearing,
> Troop after troop their banners bearing

– to emerge on the 'opposing hill'. Clearly Scott had studied the ground and **Twizell Bridge** itself which crosses the ravine of the Till in one spectacular leap. To appreciate the daring of its builders and the beauty of the bridge itself, turn off the main road at its eastern end and along the track that runs beside the river, where the span is seen against the sky and the ivy-covered 'folly' of the castle in its woods. Beneath the arch flows the Tweed's main tributary, the Till, a slow and enigmatic stream whose waywardness is legendary:

> Tweed said to Till,
> 'What gars ye rin sae still?'
> Till said to Tweed:
> 'Though ye rin wi' speed
> And I rin slaw,
> Yet where ye droon yin man,
> I droon twa.'

206

The meeting of the waters is about a mile upstream from the bridge, opposite Tweedmill on the B6437. Till (which in its upper reaches is the Breamish) is a Northumbrian river throughout its length. But the border-line between the kingdoms hereabouts runs down the centre of the Tweed's channel, leaving Coldstream in Scotland and Cornhill in England.

Coldstream does not therefore strictly concern us. It has famous associations with the Guards' regiment formed here by General Monk, for whom the river was another Rubicon. By crossing it, out of his command, he was signalling his rejection of the Commonwealth, and it was not long afterwards that he declared for Charles II.

Cornhill, much smaller than Coldstream, is not an interesting village, but has a two-star hotel, *The Collingwood Arms*, and near by, in its own extensive grounds, is the luxury *Tillmouth Park Hotel*, one of the finest in the Borders, with fishing along three miles of the English bank of the Tweed and two miles on both banks of the Till. The whole of this north-east corner of Northumberland can be covered from a base in either of them.

Chapter 14

To the Cheviots and Rothbury

✣

All the way north on the coastal route past Bamburgh to Berwick the motorist will have been aware of the line of the Cheviots along the western horizon, and once he has made the turn into the Tweed valley towards Coldstream he will see them in fresh perspective, now almost directly ahead and spread in a wide arc beyond the valleys of the Till and the Bowman Water.

By most standards they are minor hills. Nowhere, even on The Cheviot itself, is the three-thousand-foot level approached, and few of the heights are over the two-thousand-foot mark. But just as the Lake District fells can look impressively Alpine at times, particularly under snow, so the Cheviots on closer acquaintance belie their puny size.

They cover four hundred square miles of ground, running on a line from south-west to north-east, from near Newcastleton in Scotland on the Liddel Water to Wooler, some forty miles away on the edge of the coastal plain. The north–south axis is much narrower, amounting at Carter Bar and the Note o' the Gate to a mere coll, but it is considerably deeper than this around The Cheviot itself – it is fifteen miles as the crow flies from Peat Law beside the Coquet to the northern slopes of the *massif* above Kirk Yetholm.

These are hills of igneous rock, their central core being of pinkish granite forced up from the depths by volcanic action and surrounded by a wider area of lava, weathered and smoothed into the familiar conical or rounded contours during the Ice Age and now grass covered. In the true Cheviot country there is little bracken and almost no heather, in remarkable contrast with the Simonside Hills across the Coquet valley. Outcrops of rock are rare, except in the ravines of the Bizzle and Henhole. At the centre, The Cheviot (2674 ft) is the highest point in the range but in many respects its least typical hill, its crest a featureless bog which has been the despair of generations of fell walkers. Radiating from it like the spokes of a wheel are a number of streams: the Usway and Alwin burns, tributaries of the Coquet; the Breamish; and in the north-east the Hart-hope and College burns which go their respective ways by the Bowmont and Wooler Water into the river Till, which itself is a tributary of the still grander Tweed. The lower slopes of the hills provide grazing for the flocks of Cheviot, Blackface and cross-bred sheep that find their markets in the small Border towns. There is no industry and very little afforestation except along the upper reaches of the North Tyne and the Rede where the countryside is being sub-merged under vast acreages of spruce. Much of the range is within the Northumberland National Park, which gives protection from most despoilers, if not from the Forestry Commission. It is good walking country, providing views which can take in glimpses of both the Irish and North Seas, the Pentlands, Lammermuirs, Eildons, and in very exceptional conditions of visibility the Highlands beyond the Forth. If not overblessed with wild life (as are some of the forests in the North Tyne valley) the bare hillsides of the *massif* are home to the wild goat, many specimens of bird, both brown and mountain hares, and foxes in profusion. Several packs of fox-hounds share the country, most notably the 'College', based on the valley of that name, which works regularly above the two thousand-foot contour lines and thinks nothing of killing its foxes on the summit of The Cheviot itself. Similarly, though vegetation is scant, botanists have found a number of rare specimens on these heights. Specialists should consult *The Flora of the Three Northern Counties* by J. W. Heslop Harrison and G. W. Temperley, which forms chapter XIII of *The Three Northern Counties of England* (Northumberland Press Ltd.) and *Geology of Northumberland and the Borders* by Dr Douglas Robson in the Transactions of the Natural History Society of Northumberland, Durham and Newcastle-Upon-Tyne, Vol. 16, No. 1, New Series (Dec. 1965).

To the general visitor who wants to walk the Cheviot fells, fish the streams or simply enjoy the landscape from his car, one may offer certain tentative advice. The approach from the western side I deal with in a later chapter. This sector includes the most dramatic road crossing of the range at Carter Bar. But on that summit the Cheviots, apart from the drear slopes of Carter Fell, are the last thing one notices – it is the glorious view northwards to the Eildon and Pentland hills that really takes the eye. The western side of the range has one good hill – Peel Fell – and some entrancing valleys – the North Tyne, the Rede and the Tarset, Tarret and Chirdon burns – but it has not been improved visually by the new forests which tend to blur the skylines and spoil the views. And from this side only a

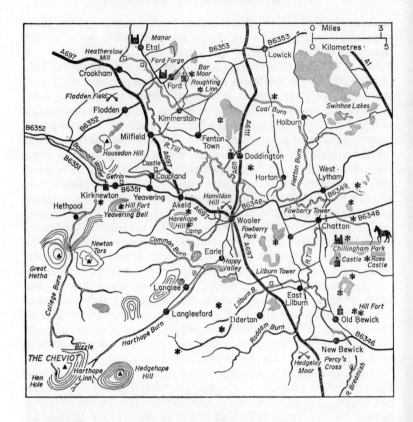

few footpaths and forestry tracks approach the central *massif*. Those
that exist (including part of the much publicised Pennine Way) are
marred by the fact that between the Rede and the Coquet valleys
lies the Redesdale All Arms Training Area, a large tract of ground
where it is very unwise indeed to wander when the warning red flags
are flying, as they do during much of the summer. For this reason
alone the best of the Cheviots for the tourist is not to be found
among the western foothills.

Approach, then, from other directions. At the southern end the
Coquet river carves deeply into the range. To the north, opposite
Kirk Yetholm at the end of the Pennine Way, is the cleft of the
College Burn. Between these extremes are the two blandest and for
the motorist the most convenient introductions to the hills: the
valleys of the Breamish and the Harthope burns. Conveniently

placed as a base for the visitor are Cornhill on Tweed and, going south, the small market towns of Wooler and Rothbury.

For the Bowmont Water and the Breamish valley, **Wooler**, on the A696, the main Coldstream–Newcastle road, lies closest to the range. It has a very agreeable family hotel in the *Tankerville Arms*. All the low ground hereabouts under the bluff on which the town stands was in prehistoric times a lake, and in the fields close to the hotel the old shore line can still be made out. Called sometimes the 'Great Glendale Lake', sometimes 'Wooler Lake', it once extended over the whole area now bounded by the main roads to Berwick and Coldstream and the high ground above Ford; and around its flanks lay a ring of hut circles, barrows and standing stones, many traces of which survive, notably on Horsdon Hill, on the shoulder of Harehope Hill, and on **Yeavering Bell**, where remains of a Celtic pre-Roman fort and township of a hundred and thirty timber-built huts with a stone rampart covers a wide area of the summit. These hillsides and their close neighbours have other claims to attention. At the foot of **Horsdon**, only just outside Wooler town, is the **Pin Well**, once used for May Day ceremonies along 'coins in the fountain' lines. **Yeavering Bell** (1182 ft), just south-east of Kirknewton, is among the very best of the Cheviot Hills for views: a thoroughly satisfying peak, easy to climb and accessible from the main road. The summer palace of the Saxon king Edwin, Gefrin, lay at its foot – there have been very fruitful recent excavations of the site. Humbleton Hill (977 ft), two miles north-west of Wooler, was the scene of a battle fought on 13 September 1402 in which Hotspur took his revenge for his defeat at Otterburn, capturing the Earl of Douglas and many other Scottish nobles. It also brought about his own downfall, as Shakespeare tells us in *Henry IV Part I*, for when the King demanded the handing over of the captives (very valuable ones in terms of ransom money), Hotspur fell into a rage at this greed and ingratitude after all his services to the usurper, freed his captives in exchange for their promises of armed aid, and went into open rebellion – a road that led to his own death in the field at Shrewsbury.

'Windy Wooler' itself is a small, unpretentious town, lying conveniently on one of the main routes to Scotland but mercifully spared by a by-pass from the worst of the traffic pounding along to Coldstream. It has no buildings of particular merit and is best regarded as a base from which to explore the surrounding countryside. Near by, though not on view to the public, is Lilburn Tower, once the home of Admiral Lord Collingwood, Nelson's colleague at Trafalgar. Typically Northumbrian in its brevity was the hero's letter recording this event after he had succeeded to the command of the fleet – 'There was a battle on the 21st and we obtained a victory.' Best of all, however, Wooler serves the fishermen who have rods on the Till and the walker who wants to climb The Cheviot, which lies only nine miles away, part of it along a metalled road that follows the course of the **Harthope Burn**.

For some reason Wooler provides no signpost to help you here: you have to chance your arm and strike out south-westwards, then after a mile and a half turn right where mercifully there is a sign directing you to Earle. The road is perilously narrow, with only the occasional passing-place; yet he would be an insensitive motorist indeed who would want to hurry along this lovely valley, with the burn to his left and ahead of him the looming shapes of the hills – **Hedgehope** on one side, **The Cheviot** on the other, with a saddle joining them, for they are really all one hill. At **Langleeford Farm** the public road ends. There is room for a few cars under the pines. Here Sir Walter Scott stayed in 1791, fishing the streams and absorbing the Border lore; and along this road in 1728 came Daniel Defoe on his celebrated climb of The Cheviot, which he feared would be a pinnacle surrounded by precipices on every side. The summit is in fact a large heart-shaped morass of soggy peat in what was once the crater of a volcano: easily the least attractive hill-top in the range, though the routes up to it by the Harthope and College burns are grand enough to make up for any disappointment. In December 1944 an American Flying Fortress crashed with its bomb load on the summit. Before the bombs went off two shepherds, guided by their sheepdog, Sheila, found four of the crew alive and sheltering among the peat – Sheila won the Dickin Medal, the animal's VC, for her share in the adventure.

If the hill is to be climbed, I would opt for the route up the Harthope, bearing right at Langleeford under Scald Hill. It is the easiest ascent. The real tigers of fell walking prefer a route further north under Watch Hill to Broadstruther Farm and Goldscleuth, a really 'out-by' dwelling where the steep part of the climb begins. Others claim that easily the finest of all routes to the top lies from Kirknewton, along the College Burn, and then over the wildest and most dramatic landscape on The Cheviot's flanks, where the two deep ravines of **The Bizzle** and the **Henhole** have been carved into the rock. **Kirknewton** is an intriguing starting point in its own right – on the wall behind the lectern of its Norman (but restored) church is a carving of **The Virgin and the Magi,** the latter tastefully arrayed in kilts. In the graveyard is buried Josephine Butler (d 1906), the social reformer and crusader against the white slave trade. This whole area is rich in character and memories of the past. Near Hethpool, where the road up the College Burn gives out, a number of oak trees survive from the days of Admiral Collingwood, who was constantly concerned with the probable fate of the nation if the timber for his ships was not kept in good supply. Hethpool Tower probably dates from the reign of Henry I. Terracing on a near-by hill is a reminder of the Ancient Britons who grew corn here. The oddly named 'Henhole' has been well described by Sydney Moorhouse in his *Companion in Northumberland* as a 'stair of tumbling waterfalls'. It is the source of the College Burn and an eerie place, particularly on an autumn afternoon when the mists are coming down over The Cheviot and the wise walker turns for home. Henry Tegner, who knows it well and has recorded his impressions in his *Charm of the Cheviots,* recalls also its legendary history as the home of the Northumbrian fairies (a less publicity-conscious breed than the Dartmoor Pixies, but anxious to do their best tourist-wise for their native county), along with one or two personal experiences calculated to cause a prickling of the scalp. This is certainly the route for the experienced fell walker and lover of the wilds. For the less ambitious, Yeavering Bell provides a panoramic view for less trouble. Auchope Cairn (2382 ft), south-west of The Cheviot on the Pennine Way and the border with Scotland, is another wonderful vantage point, with views on a clear day far into the Highlands. Another hill, Housedon, inspired the nineteenth-century Northumbrian poet Robert Story to write:

> Pours the spring its earliest green
> Upon Hoseden still?
> Are the milk-white hawthorns seen
> Upon Hoseden still?
> Does the tall and grove-like broom,
> With its moist and yellow bloom,
> Shed a glory and perfume
> Upon Hoseden still?
>
> Rest the light and downy cloud
> Upon Hoseden still?
> Is the sky-lark's carol loud
> Upon Hoseden still?

Is the cuckoo seldom dumb?
And the wild bees, do they hum,
As of old, to sip and hum
Upon Hoseden still?

Shades of Rupert Brooke! Had Brooke perhaps been reading Story when he came to write of Granchester?

This northern sector of the hills by no means exhausts the attractions that can be covered from Wooler. Three miles directly north of the town is the village of Doddington lying under the steep slopes of Doddington Moor. The whole area abounds in intriguing place names – Sweet Haugh, Dod Law, Luntie Well, Biteabout – and also in British camps, earthworks and hut settlements. The maps in George Jobey's *Field Guide to Prehistoric Northumberland* show their remarkable density along the river Bowmont on the northern slopes of the *massif* and in the Breamish gorge around Ingram. Three-quarters of a mile south-west of Hethpool on the heights of **Great Hetha** is a hill fort with stone ramparts, and there is a standing stone circle in the College valley. Not all these sites are easy to approach, and only specialists will find much visible reward for their labours apart from the views and the bracing moorland air. **Doddington** itself has a thirteenth-century church, much restored, with a chancel at the *west* end. This strange state of affairs arose in the nineteenth century, when a thirteenth-century west chamber was put to this use following the rebuilding of the east chancel by Ignatius Bonomi. Perhaps his alterations did not gain approval! There is an early Norman font.

Five miles south-east of Wooler and of much wider appeal is one of Northumbria's unique sights: the famous herd of **Wild White Cattle** on the estates of the Earls of Tankerville at **Chillingham**. Here is a game reserve with a difference, for the descendants of *Bos Taurus*, the wild ox, have been roaming the Cheviot foothills at least since the twelfth century, when the park was enclosed, and may have been here when the Romans came. Twice in recent times the herd has come perilously close to extinction: in 1966 when an outbreak of foot and mouth disease was sweeping over Northumberland, and during the severe winter of 1946/7, when all the young cows succumbed and it was feared that the rest were too old to breed. The numbers fell to a mere thirteen, but by some miracle of natural adaptation the reproductive span of the females was extended and new calves were born. At the last count – December 1974 – the herd numbered fifty-one, twenty-four of which were bulls, a higher ratio of males to females than usual.

The Chillingham herd are genuinely wild creatures, normally shy of man, but if startled or in defence of their young they can be extremely dangerous. For this reason visits to the park may only be made under supervision of a ranger. Enquiries should be made at the estate office in the village – it is well signposted. It is a great advantage to bring binoculars, since one cannot approach too close to the herd. Sometimes it has come down to the low ground and can be quickly reached; sometimes it is in the hills and a good deal of walking is entailed; but it is well worth it, for in their natural surroundings of woodland and crag and fell the cattle are a thrilling sight. The herd is ruled by a king bull, who alone exercises marital rights over the cows until challenged by some younger male. The fight is seldom to the death, but in this harshly ordered world any sick or maimed beast is doomed. Newly-born calves are hidden in the bracken – if they are touched by human hands their fate is certain, for their mothers will abandon them. The cattle are not entirely white, having a black muzzle and reddish ears. Thomas Bewick provided some dramatic studies of them, but the most vivid and charming are the drawings made by Landseer and Count d'Orsay when they stayed at Chillingham Castle in the 1830s – drawings brought together for a recent exhibition at Agnew's in London but now, alas! dispersed. A famous illustration of 1872 shows that big-game hunter, Edward Prince of Wales, standing triumphantly beside the carcass of a bull which he had shot – allegedly from ambush under a hay cart. There were derisive verses in Geordie about his feat at the time:

> He's a warrier, ye knaa, and the papors are full
> Iv a terrible encoonter he had wiv a bull!
> He slowtered the bull, but his critics will say
> That the Prince was cuncealed in a bundle iv hay;
> And that it was ne feat at a' te lie hid
> And slowter the bull in the way that he did;
> But some folks are selfish an' winna hear tell
> Iv ony great feats unless dune be thorsel.

The cattle are now under the protection of a society, The Chillingham Wild Cattle Association Ltd, of which the dowager Countess of Tankerville is patron. Anyone can join. The booklet containing the late Earl of Tankerville's extremely interesting paper on the herd can be obtained from The Warden, The Warden's House, Chillingham, Alnwick.

Chillingham Castle is now uninhabited and is not open to the public – one must content oneself with tantalising glimpses through the railings along the rides between the trees. But among the elegant buildings of the estate village is the **Parish Church of St Peter** containing one of the finest medieval tombs in England. The church, with its plain bell-cote of 1753 and its Norman nave, is simple and unpretentious. Note the unusually deep-set windows to north and south, the raised chancel (to allow a burial vault below) and the highly effective modern treatment of the east window with its iron cross. The north transept contains a font of 1670 with a Jacobean cover, the south transept the fifteenth-century **Tomb** of Sir Ralph Gray and his lady who served both the Lancastrian and Yorkist kings and lie in alabaster effigy surrounded by a sumptuous décor of saints and angels. He has a small, neat moustache, and is an unexpectedly natty figure to find in armour clasping a sword: his wife wears gorgeously flowing robes and a Flemish head-dress. A realistic if macabre touch is struck by the small caskets at their feet containing skulls and crossbones and an hour-glass. Indeed, Sir Ralph came to a sad end – captured in arms defending Bamburgh Castle against the Yorkists and executed by them. The Grays, a family of Norman origin, have owned Chillingham since the Middle Ages, though now in the female line and in the name of Bennet, earls of Tankerville. Due east of the park are the remains of the hill fort of **Ros** (or **Ross**) **Castle** which belongs to the National Trust. It is worth the climb if only for the view, a great favourite of Sir Edward Grey's when he was living at Fallodon.

From Chillingham the southward route leads along a minor road towards Eglingham. Just before the hamlet of **Old Bewick** a lane to the left at a wayside cross takes you to one of the most attractive small churches in Northumberland, hidden away among the trees. It was founded by Queen Matilda, wife of Henry I, in memory of her father Malcolm, King of Scots, who had been killed near by at Alnwick. It was later in the possession of the powerful Tynemouth Priory which owned so much land in the North. The oldest part of the fabric dates from the twelfth century. Damaged (most ungratefully) by the Scots, it was restored in the fourteenth, thereafter decayed, and was severely taken in hand in 1867 by a Mr J. C. Langlands, whose other memorial is the cross where the lane joins the road. On entering, be sure to find the light switches which are to the left just inside the door; otherwise in the gloom you will miss the full beauty of the Norman chancel and apse arches and the apse itself behind them, now colourfully restored in a motif of stars on a blue

216

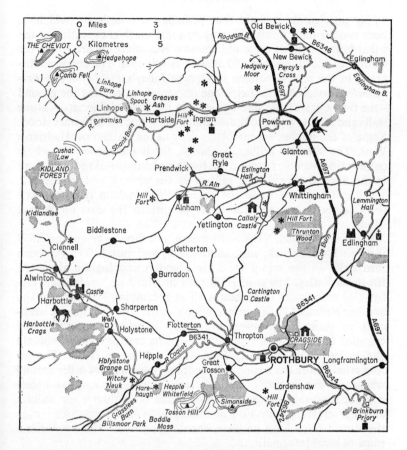

ground with bands of red and gold lettering below. Tragically, apses
fell out of fashion in the North. Usually they were knocked down and
replaced with square east ends. Even here, from the outside, you can
see how the objectionable shape was squared off. But internally the
apse was left untouched, and what a charming and impressive finish
it lends with its three tiny windows and elegant curves.

On the high ground immediately to the east of Old Bewick village
and approached by a farm track on your left is a **Pre-Roman Hill
Fort.** In aerial photographs its circular defences look remarkably
like a woman's bra, and even more remarkably like the ring markings
one finds carved on rocks associated with the earlier Bronze Age
culture – to such a degree indeed as to tempt the layman into the

217

wildly unscientific thought that perhaps these designs could have been rudimentary forms of a map or some magical evocation of the tribal home. Not all these old Cheviot encampments are worth the trouble of the climb, but Old Bewick is splendid. The aerial photograph in the second volume of George Jobey's *Field Guide to Prehistoric Northumberland* helps one immensely in reading the ground – the twin circles lying side by side and the three visible sets of stone walls and ditches rising to the central arena where the huts once stood. Some of the ditches are almost as deep as the Vallum on Hadrian's Wall. The site was brilliantly chosen, for it commands the whole countryside for miles around – a touching testimonial to its strength is the Second World War pillbox at the eastern end of the hill. The views are superb: of the Vale of Whittingham lying between the Cheviot massif and the lesser heights to the east on Bewick Moor.

From Old Bewick – the word means 'bee farm' – rejoin the A697 through New Bewick, turn south on it, and just before Powburn turn right on the minor road for Brandon and **Ingram** along the **Breamish Valley**. The road is liberally provided with picnicking lay-bys and culminates at **Ingram** itself in a camping and caravan site and the National Park's Information Centre. Though busy at weekends in summer, however, the valley is seldom uncomfortably crowded and is extremely beautiful – at its best perhaps in autumn and in late May and early June when the broom is out. The **Information Centre** has a shop attached: the only place for miles around where you can be sure of an ice cream. The main room has a scale contour sand-table map of the hills which is invaluable for walkers and a fascinating collection of photographs and showcases – even the stuffed birds have an alert, encouraging look. The curator is a mine of local information.

To many the Breamish Valley is the jewel of the National Park, and Ingram's **Church of St Michael** tucked away among the trees above the stony bed of the stream makes a picture worthy of Constable. There is a fine close-up view of it to be had from the garden enclosed by a yew hedge which is a memorial to the Allgood family, whose tracks we shall cross again at Simonburn in the North Tyne valley. The tower, which was shorn of its spire in 1884, has a sullen, offended look; the lower part of it is early Norman while the upper is thirteenth-century, but though its stones date from those times the whole structure was pulled down and re-erected during the Victorian restoration work. The tower arch inside is of the eleventh century and is the church's most notable feature; the responds below it lean outwards as though they are being slowly crushed by the weight of the arch above – a striking and strangely beautiful effect. The chancel arch is fourteenth-century and there are other traces of medieval work in the arches and arcades; but the building was severely damaged in a Scottish raid, was in ruins by the mid seventeenth century, and in its now reconstructed state somehow fails to live up to the expectations one forms of it at first sight from across the river.

For most people Ingram means a base for exploration of the hills that press around it on three sides. Close by are ancient round barrows on Ingram Hill, a thick cluster of Romano-British settlements on the heights above the valley, and traces of several promontory forts. The most impressive is **Brough Law,** with its two massive stone ramparts dating from about 400 BC perched steeply to the left of the road above the Breamish gorge. The only feasible approach is to leave the car in the car park half a mile west of Ingram and to take the track leading up to the left. By this route one can also reach another ancient settlement on Haystack Hill.

The public road up the Breamish ends at Hartside Farm, and one must leave the car. About three-quarters of a mile further on, at the corner of the second plantation on the right, is a tin hut, and on the fells a short distance above it are traces of the walls and stone hut circles of the largest Romano-British village in Northumberland, **Greaves Ash** – like Old Bewick apparently a twin affair. There is also what seems to the layman a ceremonial sunken entrance at the southern end running between high banks; but Mr Jobey in Part 2 of his *Field Guide* does not term it such.

To the inexpert eye Greaves Ash is not very impressive, and I would invite the visitor at this point to climb the fells above it, from where a splendid view can be had of the waterfall of **Linhope Spout** gushing down the hillside like water from a gigantic hydrant. I can hardly recommend too highly the walk to the Spout itself, which is reached by a signposted track from the big house at Linhope in the valley below. It is at its finest in late autumn, when the dull gold of the bracken and the glitter of the leaves of the birch trees around the waterfall make an unforgettable picture. So do the hills, for the track is leading into the heart of the *massif*. Walk Number 8 of *Ramblers' Cheviots* (Harold Hill, Newcastle, 1969) takes in the high country of the upper Breamish towards **Hedgehope**, the second peak of the range. The Cheviot itself can be reached along this route by the determined walker, but is better approached further north by the routes already mentioned. Hedgehope is much the more satisfying hill, more of a peak and less of a bog, and offering grandstand views of its larger neighbour and of the Northumbrian coast from Blyth to Berwick.

Returning eastward down the Breamish to the A697, turn right southwards and then right again on the yellow road that leads back into the hills through **Glanton**, where there is Britain's first **Bird Research Station**, a more appealing place than its name implies. From Glanton the road runs on through Mile End, Great Ryle and Prendwick to **Alnham**. Unless one keeps a good look out one can pass within a couple of hundred yards of this charming place and miss it altogether. An elderly signpost points the way to its church and the beautifully restored pele tower next door to it which was once its vicarage (now privately owned). The parish is in plurality with Alwinton and Holystone and serves about five hundred and fifty souls in one hundred and twenty square miles of country. The mound covering an ancient castle stands on the hillside facing the pele. The church, long ruinous, was restored in 1870. It probably dates from 1200, but little remains from medieval times apart from some gravestones on the floor – two on the north side inscribed with swords, the male symbol; two to the south of women with the traditional scissors or shears – and a fifteenth-century arch which may have housed a tomb. The general impression the church gives is still remarkably un-Victorian – particularly effective is the view, looking west, of the dark pews, the dark beams in the ceiling, and the windows of plain glass in geometric designs, as though the original builders and worshippers here have imposed their own vision of things on their successors. Architecturally one of the least exciting of Northumbrian churches, Alnham rivals even Old Bewick in its remoteness and its sense of a piety now lost to us. To the west of the hamlet is a British fort on **Castle Hill** and traces of a far more ancient palisaded settlement at **High Knowles** – an expedition for specialists only.

From Alnham, double back through Little Ryle and Yetlington to Callaly. It looks complicated on the map but the mileage is small. Alternatively cut out Alnham altogether and take the much shorter route from Glanton through the vale of Whittingham, noted for its fertility and once upon a time for its fair, celebrated in an enigmatic ballad which begins:

Are you going to Whittingham Fair?
Parsley, sage, rosemary and thyme.

220

> Remember me to one who lives there,
> For once she was a true lover of mine.

Whittingham's pele tower and church have been heavily restored, but it has some pretty cottages grouped round a green and a stream and in the *Castle Inn* an old posting house for the Newcastle to Edinburgh coaches. Turn right at the agreeable small statue of a man and his dog, which recalls one of the earls of Ravensworth, whose estates are near by at Eslington Hall.

Two miles further along the road, just beyond the hamlet of Callaly and easily missed, a sharp turn to the right leads to **Callaly Castle** (Caer-law-ley: the pasture near the hill camp), one of the few great houses in Northumberland that can be visited by the public. The surrounding countryside is very beautiful, and besides visiting the house and gardens one can climb the half mile through the woods to **Castle Hill**, where there is an early British camp with earthworks and the foundations of a medieval castle that was never completed. A legend recites how the local baron decided to build his hall on a hill, but his wife preferred the comforts of a more protected home in the valley and, Penelope-like, employed servants to pull down by night what her lord had laboriously put up by day. Eventually her arguments prevailed:

> Callaly Castle built on the height
> Up in the day and down in the night,
> Builded down in the Shepherds' Shaw
> It shall stand for aye and never faw'.

The first pele was built on the present site and parts of it are incorporated in its fabric.

Originally the manor was held direct from the crown on a service tenure of Drengage, the rental being an oak tree for the King's hearth, to be delivered to Bamburgh, nearly twenty miles away, on every other day from Whitsun to Lammas. This has been commuted for an annual payment of £3 which the present owner still makes to the Queen. In medieval times the manor was held by the Norman family of Clavering which claimed descent from Charlemagne. They were staunch Cavaliers in the Civil Wars, which cost them dear in men and money, and they later 'came out' with the Jacobites in the 'Fifteen. In 1876 their heiress, having married into the ancient Norfolk family of the Pastons, sold the estate to the grandfather of the present owner, Major Browne.

One's first impression of Callaly is of a classical building that somehow fails to satisfy the eye. This is natural enough, seeing that the house with its three fronts is an architectural conundrum which has been remodelled and built on too often for comfort. The core of it is by that elusive and excellent craftsman, Robert Trollop, who built Newcastle's Guildhall and whose masterpiece is at Capheaton. I find it more sympathetic inside than out. The drawing room, probably designed by Paine, is a room of the greatest beauty: a perfectly thought-out eighteenth-century *salon* with matching balconies at either end and exquisite plasterwork by the same team of Italian *stuccatori* that was employed at Wallington. Comical plaques of George II and George III in fancy dress proclaim the Jacobite sympathies of the Claverings, as do the two plaster frames left empty in the place of honour awaiting the coming of the King from 'over the water'. The chimney had a false flue that was used as a priest's hole, and in the course of repairs in 1962 certain religious tracts came to light in it. These are now displayed in a glass case in the most original of all Callaly's rooms – the pavilion or music room, once an open courtyard but later roofed over to house a collection of *objets d'art* which are now in the British Museum. The most striking piece of furniture is a huge ironwork spiral staircase which reaches right up to the roof. It was made by Walter Macfarlane and Company of Glasgow and is of exceptional quality. Heads of animals line the walls, row upon row, including a Chillingham bull and cow killed by the grandmother of the present owner on a trial run prior to the Prince of Wales's great safari of 1872. As you enter, a huge Alaskan bear confronts you on one side; on the other is a python, shot by the same intrepid sportswoman, whose vast travelling trunk used on her honeymoon is also on view. There are several other rooms on show, including the large banqueting hall, originally intended as a chapel and now used for Hunt Balls. It has some fine Gobelin tapestries depicting the amours of Henry IV of France with Gabrielle d'Estrées, but is otherwise tasteless, a vulgar piece of Victorian baronial.

From Callaly take the minor road that keeps close to the hills past the ruins of **Cartington Castle** (a Cavalier stronghold which fell to the Roundheads in 1648) to Thropton and down the Coquet valley to **Rothbury**.

The sole disadvantage here is that since the vintage *County Hotel* was converted some years ago into a Holiday Home there has been a distinct lack of tourist accommodation in the town. There is an AA two-star establishment, the *Coquet Vale*, and the one-star *Queen's Head*. There is an Information Centre at the bus depot. The town itself, with its large triangular green, is certainly one of the pleasantest in Northumberland, beautifully placed on a reach of the Coquet (next to the Tweed the premier salmon river in the county) under the fine escarpment of the Simonside Hills on the south-western skyline. It has a dramatic feature at the Thrum, east of the town, where the Coquet rushes impetuously through a narrow gorge.

From very early times Rothbury was an important centre, and with the arrival of the Normans its importance increased. Its manor belonged to King John, who gave it in 1205 to Robert Fitz Ryan along with the right to try malefactors in his own court – a spot called Gallowfield between Rothbury and Thropton marks the site where the executions took place. Later, Rothbury came into possession of the Percys. Licence to hold a market was granted by Edward I in 1291. This king's activities in the north against the Scots brought retribution to the town in the shape of William Wallace's army, which camped in the near-by forest during its raid into Northumberland after its victory at Stirling Bridge. The Jacobite forces under the Earl of Derwentwater passed this way during the rebellion of the 'Fifteen. For two hundred years horse-racing took place on the haughs beside the Coquet, but unfortunately these meetings which made Rothbury a great centre for the sporting fraternity have now been axed.

Nowadays the stamp and sense of history may be ebbing somewhat from this ancient and charming town, but much still remains. **All Saints Church** (thirteenth-century, largely restored in 1850) would be unremarkable in itself but for the **Anglo-Saxon Shaft** (*circa* 800) supporting its font. The head of the shaft is in the Museum of Antiquities at Newcastle, but what one sees here is alone worth the visit. Two sides of the shaft are covered with stylised decorative patterns; the third displays a splendid lion and other predatory beasts entwined in a kind of tree of life motif; while on the fourth is a primitive **Ascension** (probably the earliest ever carved in Britain) with the figure of Christ supported by angelic hands, and apostolic heads below like so many coconuts or woods on a bowling green. From the pulpit Bernard Gilpin, 'the Apostle of the North' who did so much to tame this wild hinterland, once quelled a famous riot in church – the episode forms the subject of one of W. Bell Scott's Northumbrian murals at Wallington. It was a tough neighbourhood in which even the women were militant, as proved in the parish records by a sentence of excommunication passed on one Elizabeth Brown for beating a churchwarden while he was in the execution of his office. Outside of office hours this was presumably no offence.

223

More ancient even than the cross are the barrows, forts, earth-works, hut circles and standing stones that surround the town at Tosson Burgh, Old Rothbury, Soldiers' Fauld, Bickerton, Mount Healey, Debton Moor, Whitefield Moor, Garleigh Moor and the very important site at **Lordenshaw** (see page 231). Ordnance Survey Map Sheet 71 is an absolute necessity for anyone who wants to pin-point these very early traces of Man's settlement in the valley: few ordinary road maps mention them, nor do the signposts. These settlements lie very thick on the ground: part of a pattern of de-velopment that was later to include the Roman highway which left the main northern route into Caledonia at Rochester in Redesdale (on the present A68), crossed the fells to the Coquet at Holystone, and continued through modern Sharperton, the Tyrwhitts, Lorbottle, Callaly and Bridge of Aln, to join another Roman track (marked on today's maps as 'The Devil's Causeway') running north from Bewclay on Stagshaw bank to Glanton and aimed towards the crossings of the Tweed.

Clearly from the beginning Rothbury has always been a favoured area, and so it has continued into modern times. The elegant little town itself is one proof of this, and another is near-by **Cragside**, the extraordinary mansion created in 1870 by Norman Shaw for the engineer and inventor, the first Lord Armstrong. Shaw, who built London's Scotland Yard for the Police, was an extremely gifted and inventive architect. Pevsner calls the site 'Wagnerian', and so it is, perched among the rocks and crags above the Coquet. The house itself (which is not open to the public) is a remarkable interpretation of Tudor black and white and of the Tudor Stone house, perched dizzily on top of one another. Shaw is said to have drawn the plans in a fit of inspiration in one day: I am afraid it looks like it. Pevsner, however, loves it, and certainly the scheme is daring and god-like enough in conception to match its rugged site. Local opinion at the time of its creation was also deeply impressed, to judge from some verse in praise of it:

> And on yon brown and rocky hill
> See princely Cragside lies,
> Where boundless wealth and perfect taste
> Have made a paradise.

The money was there all right, as we have seen in Lord Armstrong's other extravaganza in the great hall at Bamburgh. Paradise indeed (and open to the public) are the **Cragside Gardens**: one thousand four hundred acres thick with rhododendrons which in late May and

June are in their full glory. Splendid too is the big ornamental lake below the house, its reeds mirrored in the placid waters. Walkers can wander for hours through a romantic landscape; while the indolent motorist has been provided with his own circular (one way) tour of the estate and with parking spaces for picnics by the banks of an upper lake. He had better keep a sharp eye open for the proper but very inconspicuous exit lane on leaving, however, or he could conceivably go on circling Cragside gardens for ever. The pressure of death duties and of rising costs has recently forced the present Lord Armstrong to consider selling part of the estate for new luxury housing, causing no little controversy to environmentalists in the neighbourhood. This idea has now been dropped and the hall and grounds are to be taken over by the National Trust. Appropriately, there will be in the hall an exhibition of the inventions of the first Lord Armstrong and of Joseph Swan, who lighted Cragside with electricity for him, the first private house after his own to be so lit.

Three miles east of Rothbury are the well preserved ruins of **Brinkburn Priory**, lying in a sheltered meadow in a loop of the Coquet. It was founded around 1135 by the lords of Mitford for a colony of Augustinian canons, suffered greatly from Scottish raids, and was suppressed in 1536. Its church, however, was beautifully restored in 1857 by a Newcastle architect, Thomas Austin, and it is now kept up by the Department of the Environment. Built at the same time as Hexham Abbey, during the late twelfth and early thirteenth century, it is a remarkable example of the transition from Romanesque to Gothic. Of the lancet windows at the east end, for instance, the top tier is in the earlier style. The triforium has rounded lights with a round encircling arch above the pointed arches of the nave, and the north doorway is Romanesque, though the gable above it is Gothic. But what will strike most people is the beauty and peace of the setting and of the surrounding woods. Some people have professed to see a likeness to Fountains Abbey, but of course it is far less grand and the real resemblance is to Finchale. Near by are the remains of an old water mill, and when the river is low the foundations appear of the Roman bridge that once carried the Devil's Causeway across the Coquet.

Rothbury is also the most convenient starting point for a tour of the upper reaches of its river, celebrated in Roxby's *Fishers' Guide* of 1826:

> I will sing of the Coquet, the dearest of themes,
> The haunt of the fisher, the first of a' streams.

Take the Thropton road and fork right at this village for Sharpe-
ton. Cross the river here for the short detour to **Holystone**. It has a
pleasant pub, *The Salmon*, from whose car park a short stroll
through the fields and along the burn brings you to **The Lady's Well**,
a survival from the early days of Christian civilisation in the North
which still supplies the village with its water. The well – a large
trough in a grove under the trees – stands beside the Roman track
which ran from *Bremenium* in Redesdale to the coast. It was walled
in and given approximately its present shape in medieval times. The
name 'Holystone' came into use early in the twelfth century when a
priory of Augustinian nuns was founded here: the wall itself was
repaired some six hundred years later and given a statue and a cross
(standing in the middle of the pool), on whose plinth an inscription
records that Paulinus the Bishop baptised three thousand Northumbrians here at Easter in 827. Unfortunately there is reason to
suppose that Paulinus was actually far away in York at the time. The
village was also the home of a Northumbrian character or 'worthy',
Ned Allen the weaver, who figures in a charming ballad by Robert
Heaton, a local schoolmaster:

> Here lies Old Ned in his cold bed,
> For hunting otters famed;
> A faithful friend lies by his side
> And 'Tug 'em' he was named.
> Sport and rejoice, ye finny tribes
> That glide in Coquet river,
> Your deadly foe no more you'll see,
> For he is gone for ever.

In the vicinity are the standing stones known as 'The Five Kings',
four of which are still erect among the grass and bracken, and also,
if you can find it, 'Rob Roy's Cave', probably a piece of Border
conning by Sir Walter Scott.

Soon after Holystone, going north, the valley road enters the
Northumbrian National Park close to the village of **Harbottle**
(Here-both – the bothy or station of an army). Its castle, traces of
which still stand, was built for Henry II on the site of the third oldest
Saxon stronghold in Northumbria. In the troubled years of Border
warfare and raiding it was the last outpost on the English side, the
headquarters of the Warden of the Middle March, surrounded within
a radius of six miles by no fewer than sixteen pele towers, which tell
their own tale. The family mottoes of the Border chiefs are eloquent
in themselves – 'Best riding by moonlight' was that of the Buccleughs;

'We'll hae moonlight again' was that of Wat o' Hawden. The favourite raiding period was in October, while the cattle were still out on the high fells and in prime condition. Throughout the area the principles of Jeddart (Jedburgh) Justice applied – 'Hang a man first, then try him at the Assizes.' In Tudor times a tight system of watch and ward was organised throughout the Borders: all fords and passes in the Cheviots were guarded and sentries (working on a roster system) were posted on the hills. They were not always very effective, if we are to judge by a stirring ballad by Joseph Crowhall:

> Hue an' cry – hoond an' horse – ca' to the fray,
> For the Scots hae been Rotbarie way i' the murk
> An left na a galloway, sheepe, hogge or stirke,
> Fired a' the haudins an' harried the Kirk,
>   Au faur waur them a';
>   Oh! wae ti'll us wae,
> The Meenister's missin', they've lifted him tae.

Robert the Bruce had come this way in 1311, and in 1318 Harbottle Castle itself fell to the Scots. However, there were intervals of peace, and Harbottle was to witness one of the key events in the eventual reconciliation of the kingdoms, for it was here that the widowed Queen Margaret of Scotland, re-married to the Earl of Angus, gave birth to a child, another Margaret, who was destined to become the mother of Darnley and grandmother of James the First and Sixth. In the times of its prosperity under the early Tudors the castle had a garrison of a hundred men at eightpence apiece. Its captain got four shillings a day, the drummer a shilling. However, by 1584 it was officially listed as 'decayed', and after the Union with Scotland under Queen Anne it fell into complete disuse.

Instead of a living fortress, the village today boasts a craft centre and a pub and a four hundred-acre wild life reserve (the illustrated booklet for which can be obtained from the Hancock Museum in Newcastle). It looks very tame, but the remote and craggy country surrounding it is steeped in legend, and rumour has it that the thirty-foot-high Drake Stone (estimated to weigh two thousand tons) on Harbottle Hill was used within living memory for black magic rites. Near it is a rather gloomy and sinister lake in a hollow of the hills. Even the lighter side of Harbottle life seems to have taken a slightly macabre turn. In Victorian times the local doctor kept a famous greyhound which won the Waterloo Cup and had a memorial tablet erected to it in its owner's garden. It was called 'King Death'.

*

Three miles further up the valley is **Alwinton**, a hamlet consisting of a post office-cum-store, a few houses and a pub. Nevertheless, in October it is the venue for one of the most colourful sheep shows in the North. During the Middle Ages it was one of the most important junctions on Clennel Street, from which radiated tracks across the hills towards the Tweed. Alwinton's church – which should surprise no one with experience of these valleys – is the best part of a mile away from any visible parishioners, and in the middle of nowhere. Set into the hillside, with delicious views from its graveyard, **St Michael and All Angels** is a haven of peace. The dead in that gracious and beautiful spot easily outnumber the living for miles around. It is a huge and crowded graveyard for so remote a place. Even the path to the main door is paved with gravestones. To one's right as one approaches is a building labelled 'Hearse House'. The hearse itself is still around – it was last used in 1940 and no doubt would be used again if the local farmers would only get off their tractors and breed a horse sturdy enough to pull it.

Inside, this is one of the most distinctive of Cheviot churches, for due to the slope of the ground its chancel stands at the top of a flight of steps, high above the nave and the crypt, the burial vault of the Selbys of Biddlestone Hall, supposedly the Osbaldistone Hall of Scott's *Rob Roy*. The Selbys 'came out' in the 'Fifteen with the Jacobite army which concentrated on near-by Plainfield Moor – it was a staunchly Catholic area, as may be seen from the 'Papist' lists kept in Newcastle by a watchful and nervous government. Much of the church is nineteenth-century restoration work, including the attractive black and white roof. There are relics of earlier times in the western part of the church, which dates from the eleventh or early twelfth century: a chancel window of the same date; a fourteenth-century south-east window and piscina; and a thirteenth-century window and piscina in the north aisle which also houses some classical table tombs of the Clennels of Clennel Hall. Alwinton's vicars have seldom enjoyed a wholly peaceful life – one sixteenth-century incumbent found himself evicted from his vicarage by some rampant parishioner who proceeded to turn it into an ale house. This work of Mammon has perished, but the village's present pub, *The Rose and Thistle*, once visited by Sir Walter Scott, is very much alive and a great venue for motorists, shepherds, fishermen and fell walkers bound for the upper Coquet valley and the Cheviot heights. It must be the jealous, grudging, parochial feeling of one who lives up the rival North Tyne that makes me carp a little at this river once one has passed beyond the noble reaches above Rothbury and come to the headwaters. To my mind there is a constricted feel about it. The fishing is strictly private, with boards constantly proclaiming the fact; the valley is also hemmed in to the west by the Redesdale All Arms Training Range; and though the road connecting it with the A68 penetrates deep into the heart of the hills, it is effectively a cul-de-sac and impassable beyond Chew Green when firing is in progress.

In spite of this the Coquet is a splendid river, acclaimed by generations of anglers:

> Oh! come, we'll gae up by the Traws
> Where the burnie rins wimplin' and clear,
> Where the bracken and wild heather grows
> And the wild rose is sweet on the briar.

All around one are the traces of ancient settlement. Just north of Alwinton near Clennel Street there is a hill fort, and another lies under Clennel Hill. Opposite Windyhaugh the monks of Newminster Abbey used to have a fulling mill: here we are on the western border of the forest of Kidland, under monastic control from 1181 to 1536. Below Windyhaugh is a deep pool known as the Wedder Laup ('leap'), where once a sheep stealer tried to escape from his pursuers by jumping the stream in spate with his booty slung around his neck; he fell in and was drowned. Kidland is still wild country, quite close to the Cheviot *massif* with its attendant hills – Windy Gyle, Bloody-bush Edge (named for what battle or raid?), Cushat Law, 2020 ft (a Cushat is a ring dove), and Woolbist Law (Woolau – a place for cattle). Russell's Cairn on Windy Gyle marks the spot where in 1585 Lord Russell was treacherously killed by the Scots on a day of truce. If the right bank of the Coquet is forbidden ground, the left bank provides a paradise for the fell walker. The Ramblers' Association's guide, *Ramblers' Cheviots*, recommends two circular routes in the area, one of them from Alwinton to Cushat Law, the second to Windy Gyle on the Pennine Way. The Cushat Law walk, starting from Alwinton village, passes Clennel Hall, built on the foundations of the pele that was once the home of this ancient family, skirts the site of Biddlestone Hall, and returns from the uplands to the waterfall of Linhope Linn. The Windy Gyle walk starts and finishes some distance up the valley near Windyhaugh Farm, once a fulling mill, where cloth was specially cleaned and thickened, and owned by the Kidland monks. From Windy Gyle (which can usually be relied on to live up to its name) fine views can be had of the two giants of the range, The Cheviot and Hedgehope, and at Uswayford the visitor can inspect the remains of a still used for making illicit whisky (known locally as 'innocent whisky'), proudly displayed as one of the chief attractions of the area on the National Park's official map.

The valley continues up to the headwaters which lie under the heights of Thirlmoor through a countryside of 'small green conical hills . . . like huge ocean billows', in the words of David Dippie Dixon, whose book on Upper Coquetdale, published long ago at the turn of the century and recently re-published in a handsomely illustrated edition (Frank Graham, Newcastle upon Tyne), is a mine of information as well as a labour of love. The course of the river, followed upstream, is first to the north, then after Windyhaugh due west, and after Blindburn, whose pool was a famous place for giant trout, south-west to the source of the Scottish border. Gemmel's Path, a remote track through the wilds, was one of the appointed meeting places of the English and Scottish wardens in Tudor times. It was also a convenient route for smugglers. Right at the source of the river, where the metalled road swings left and uphill into the Redesdale Range, is the Roman camp at **Chew Green**, described by Professor Ian Richmond, that outstanding authority on Roman Britain and editor of Collingwood Bruce's classic *Handbook to the Roman Wall*, as 'the most remarkable visible group of Roman earthworks in Britain'. The word 'visible' needs qualifying, however: the visitor coming up the Coquet can easily miss it altogether, close though it is on its plateau on the hill above him. Nor does it reveal much of itself to the visitor who scrambles over its mounds and ditches to the central area liberally sprinkled with Coca-Cola cans. To see the shape and cut of it as a man in a helicopter could do it is necessary to take the metalled road up the hill opposite it, which cannot be done when firing is in progress on the range. For this among other reasons I would most strongly urge visitors to this site (which from a distance is everything Professor Richmond said of it) to approach Chew Green not from the direction of the Coquet but from Redesdale Camp just off the A68, the Corbridge to Jedburgh road (see page 240). Arrangements should be made by telephone to find a day when no firing is taking place, but the trouble involved is well repaid by the finest scenic drive in Northumberland, with a bird's-eye view of Chew Green as a climax.

Chapter 15

To Simonside and Redesdale

❧

Rothbury lies at the divide between the granite and lava of the volcanic Cheviots and the rough sandstone of the Simonside Hills on the other bank of the Coquet. Here is some splendid walking country along the crests of Simonside itself (1409 ft), the twin Kate and Geordie crags on Ravensheugh (1385 ft), and Tosson Hill (1447 ft), the highest point in the range. In the neighbourhood is the remarkable Iron Age fort (later a Romano-British settlement) of Lordenshaw.

Cross the bridge to the south side of the Coquet and take the Hexham road, the B6342, rising steeply up a hill and then descending to the Northumberland National Park boundary stone on the right-hand side of the road, three and a half miles out of Rothbury. Turn right here along an unsignposted road, pass a red-roofed farm, and a quarter of a mile beyond it park the car by the roadside. You will see on your right a narrow grassy track marked by a couple of hawthorn trees. It seems extraordinary that so interesting a site should have no official signpost, but so it is. Follow the track uphill and turn right when you reach a low earth wall. Aim for the back of a small notice board which stands by a rock covered with **Cup and Ring** markings. A left incline here leads to the crest and **Lordenshaw Fort**, with its two entrances, protective ditches and circular banks. You can see within the enclosure the circular stone foundations where the huts once stood. To the north-east is an open stone burial cyst with cover stone nearby. From the fort there are fine views of the Simonside Hills, the Cheviot range, and to the east the sea at Druridge Bay and the slim pencils of the power station near Blyth.

A quarter of a mile further along the road to the left, well hidden in the trees, is the National Park **Car Park**, the starting place for Nature Trails in the hills. An experienced walker can keep to the heather as far as Elsdon.

The road running west up the valley on the south of the river leads to **Great Tosson**, picturesquely placed above the Coquet under the steeply rising heights. This area was reputed to be the home of a

231

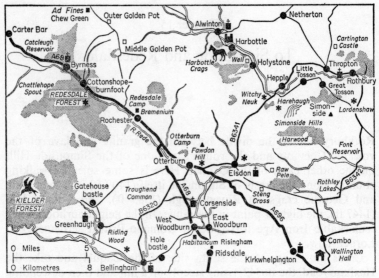

breed of mischievous elves called 'Duergars', perhaps by-products of the vast quantities of illicit whisky produced there during the eighteenth and early nineteenth centuries – one still, discovered by Excisemen in 1840, had a capacity of one hundred gallons a week. In his *Upper Coquetdale* David Dippie Dixon recorded particulars of a wedding about this time of a wealthy local farmer, William Donkin, at which twenty-five fiddlers and pipers performed before five hundred and fifty guests, who sat down to dinner and consumed one hundred and twenty quarters of lamb, forty-four of veal, twenty of mutton, twenty of beef, twelve hams, besides a quantity of chickens, brandy punch, hogsheads of wine and ninety bushels of malt brewed into beer. Great Tosson itself, however, is now so sober and respectable a place that even its fine old coaching inn, the *Royal George*, once a great place for cockfights, has become a farm. Above it is the far more ancient **Tosson Burgh**, an earthwork covering almost two acres. Bronze weapons (now in Alnwick Castle Museum) were found in the vicinity.

From the village two tracks lead steeply upward to the crest of **Simonside**, a feature almost as distinctive and visually dominant in the county as The Cheviot itself. Once up on the heights it is fairly easy going over the 'neck' of Simonside to the central plateau that includes the crags on Ravensheugh and the trig point and promontory fort on the summit of the slightly higher **Tosson Hill**. The views are

232

superb – southward over the plain towards Whalton and Morpeth; northward and westward to the Cheviots. W. W. Tomlinson, writing towards the end of the last century, describes it well:

> Wastes of heather and bracken broken by fissured sheets of dark brown peat; sweeping uplands of coarse and withered-looking herbage; level haughs; corn-fields and pasture lands; dells bristling with pine woods; their crags and green knolls . . .

to which I would add the new Forestry Commission plantations of spruce that have begun to spread across the hills.

Experienced walkers may want to return to the valley by another route; in which case they should cross the peat of Boddle Moss (but with caution and never in wet weather) and either take the track past the cairn to Hepple Whitefield or skirt the woods at Gunner's Box, past the two small tarns of Little and Dorden Loughs to the Rothbury–Elsdon road at Billsmoor Park. Great Tosson to Simonside is about a two-mile climb; Simonside to Tosson Hill via the Neck and Ravensheugh a little longer but on more level ground; from Tosson Hill via the Loughs to Billsmoor Park a roundabout and fairly arduous seven.

From Great Tosson the metalled road continues westward under the lee of the hills with the river making a series of meanders to the right. Across the water is the hamlet of **Warton**, once the home of the celebrated Warton Ox, which was exhibited in a caravan around the Border towns and when slaughtered in 1835 weighed two hundred stone and six pounds. On the fells to the left of our route, just before it joins the B6341 near the bridge over the Coquet, is the ancient hill fort of **Harehaugh**, and there is another fort near by overlooking the Coquet at Holystone Grange; it rejoices in the name of **Witchy Neuk**. Both are on private land and classed as 'for the specialist only'. **Hepple**, on the other bank of the stream, has the ruins of a castle which appears in a list of fortifications in the year of Agincourt – a brash newcomer alongside the Iron Age settlements in its vicinity.

The country hereabouts along the Coquet is well wooded and strikingly beautiful. After Billsmoor Park the road rises over Elsdon Common, from the top of which there is a quite superlative view back towards Rothbury and the Simonsides. To the west is much bleaker country as the road drops down to the village of **Elsdon** at the foot of the reverse slope.

Hae ye ivver been at Elsdon?
The world's unfinished neuk:
It stands amang the hungry hills
An' wears a frozen leuk.

So ran one old traveller's complaint after finding 'neither bed nor bite' there and having to kip down in a hay loft.

Should the Frenchers land in England
Just give them Elsdon fare;
By George! they'll sharply hook it back
And nivver come ne mair.

– which would be a gross libel on the modern village, a kindly and hospitable place, though it is true that only one pub survives of the many that lined the green in coaching days when this was one of the halts on the Newcastle to Edinburgh run.

Elsdon (Elles-dene – the valley of the waters) was once 'the capital of Redesdale when neither Scotland nor England existed', to use the words of one of the greatest of English historians, G. M. Trevelyan, who lived not far away at Hallington. From these Saxon times probably date the mounds of the **Mote Hills** just to one's left as one enters from Rothbury. Legend had it that the hills were occupied by a Danish giant, Ella. On the same site the Normans built a wooded motte and bailey castle in 1080, whose remains Pevsner regards as the most important in the county. In medieval times the lordship of Redesdale (whose first holder was one of the Umfravilles of Prudhoe) was held directly from the King. The lords had to swear to defend it 'for ever from wilves and enemies', no easy task, since the enemies were not only the Scots without but the unruly inhabitants within. In the thirteenth century England and Scotland agreed to divide the frontier lands into three 'Marches', with Wardens on each side to investigate complaints and crimes, arrest wrongdoers, and on a set day of truce to hold a joint court. Elsdon was one of the main centres of the Middle March, which stretched from the head of the North Tyne to Cheviot, and in the words of Sir John Forster, Warden in 1565, it was 'an evill countrie'. It is easy to see why this was so, for it was practically impossible to make an honest living there. The constant harrying and warfare that had continued from Norman times had devastated large parts of it; the soil was only capable of supporting sheep and cattle; and the ancient custom of Gavelkind caused the land to be divided up on a man's death among his sons, into plots too small for subsistence. Raiding and cattle 'lifting'

234

became therefore the order of the day. The reputation of those born in Tynedale and Redesdale was so notoriously bad that the Merchants Company of Newcastle ruled in 1564 that no one from that area could be received as an apprentice, the menfolk not being 'of honest conversation' – a regulation not rescinded till 1771. It is an illuminating fact that in the former parish of Elsdon, which stretched from Rothbury to Otterburn, only fortified peles now remain of houses built before the reign of Queen Anne.

The **Church** itself, however, has survived since 1400 on the site of a Norman one, traces of which can be detected in the pilasters of the west gable. Perhaps a Saxon church preceded them both, for the dedication, as at Bellingham, is to St Cuthbert, and tradition has it that his body rested during its wanderings at all the Northumbrian churches named after him. On the pillar nearest the porch certain scratches on the stone have been optimistically put down to the sturdy bowmen/swordsmen of Redesdale busily sharpening their arrows/swords during the services. But it is well accredited that the church was associated with great bloodshed. In 1810 workmen removing a mound of earth against the north wall of the nave came across a hundred skeletons packed together like sardines, and in 1877 a similar find was made under one of the chancel walls. The dead from Otterburn field brought for burial in consecrated ground? It seems likely, for a church was certainly in existence here at the time of the battle in 1388 and the foundations of the nave in the rebuilding work of 1400 are not as deep as elsewhere in the fabric, as though the diggers had not wanted to disturb the graves of those who had so recently fallen. St Cuthbert's has an extremely fine early-fourteenth-century east window, perhaps the more impressive because its tracery stands out against its background of plain glass. If you can find the Rector for the key to the vestry you will see there a charming Victorian painting of the window and of the church before its restoration in 1877. There is a Roman burial monument in the north aisle brought from *Bremenium* (High Rochester) that was erected by Julia Lucilla to her husband, a surveyor of roadworks. Three horses' skulls were found during repairs to the bell turret in 1877, and are now in a case at the west end of the church. An unusual though by no means attractive feature is the extreme narrowness of the aisles of both nave and transept, which are quadrant-vaulted. In the churchyard, not far from the porch, a gravestone records a death on 31 April!

Close to the church on the high ground facing the Mote Hills across a wooded glade is the fourteenth-century vicar's pele, now a private house in the ownership of Mr G. N. Taylor, Elsdon's historian and author of the excellent guide-book to the village.

Three miles away to the east on the crest of the old drove road at the **Steng Cross** is **Winter's Stob** ('stob' being a Northumbrian word for 'pole'), a replacement of the gibbet on which hung the corpse of William Winter, a gypsy, tried and executed at Newcastle in 1791 for the murder of an old woman who lived by herself at Raw Pele. His corpse, displayed and left to rot in chains within sight of his victim's house, was one of the last to be so treated in England. The handcuffs clapped on the murderer are still in the possession of the descendants of one of the constables who arrested him. Finding the suspect wandering among some whin bushes the officer advanced on him on horseback, calling out: 'You are my prisoner.' 'A poor prisoner you have of me,' Winter replied. Thousands of sightseers came to Elsdon to see the corpse, till the day came when the stench was too much for delicate nostrils and it was said that even horses would not pass the spot. When decomposition had set in the bones were sewn into a sack tarred inside and out. When the sack itself rotted the remains fell to the ground and were buried by local shepherds. Justice had still not done with Winter's memory however, for a wooden effigy was erected, and when this in turn fell to pieces a new one was put up in the 1860s. A carved head still hangs there. The principal crown witness to the crime had been a boy of eleven, Robert Hindmarsh. He lived the rest of his short life in constant fear of the vengeance of Winter's tribe, who on one occasion set on him as he was returning from Morpeth market. He died at the age of twenty-two.

Three miles due west of Elsdon is **Otterburn**, standing at the junction of four roads: the A68 and the A696, which run north from Corbridge and Newcastle respectively, meeting just above the village to form the route to Edinburgh over Carter Bar; the B6347 from Rothbury; and the B6320 to Bellingham and the North Tyne valley. A very convenient night stopping place for the motorist bound for Scotland, it has two good hotels, the *Percy Arms* and *Otterburn Towers*, and the excellently appointed Holiday Home at *Otterburn Hall*. Booking ahead in summer is essential. *Otterburn Hall* provides cricket, squash and tennis in its extensive grounds and a programme of evening lectures and discussion groups; *Otterburn Towers* is a Scottish baronialised antiquity in its own right; and the *Percy Arms* owns the fishing at Sweethope loch.

The village itself is world-famous as the home of Otterburn Tweeds.

The **Mill** itself stands on the triangle of ground between the narrow bridge over the Rede and the junction of the A696 and the B6320. It has been in existence for over a hundred and fifty years in the same elegant yet workmanlike building, owned by the same family, the Waddells. At the height of the summer season it is likely to be besieged by customers in search of skirt lengths, socks and tartan ties, but it is usually possible to arrange a conducted tour of the looms and processes of tweed making, an opportunity not to be missed. Needless to say, the display counters are extremely enticing. I have only one complaint – the beautiful featherweight mohair blankets which until recently could be bought in the annual May sale for as little as five pounds are now no longer made.

Apart from its mill, its hotels and the near-by Redesdale All Arms Training Area, the village also boasts the site of the Battle of Otterburn (sometimes confused with Chevy Chase) which was fought by moonlight in August 1388. The official spot marked on the Ordnance map is a mile or so out of the village to the north, where the 'Percy Cross' stands at the end of a ride in thick woodland. However, the whole matter is riddled with contradictions. The original commemorative stone was set up half a mile away. No one knows for sure the exact date of the battle. It involved historic personalities – for 'Percy' in this context means 'Hotspur' – yet the cross does not mark the spot where he fell (since in fact both he and his brother were captured in the fight) but rather the place where his victorious opponent, the Earl of Douglas, is supposed to have died, which should logically make it 'the Douglas Cross'. What is more, one school of opinion holds that the battle was really fought on the opposite side of Otterburn altogether, on Fawdon Hill, to the east of the Elsdon–Otterburn road, where it was sited on maps prior to 1750 and where the features of the ground seem much more in accord with those described by Froissart after talking with survivors from both sides.

Briefly, what seems to have happened was this. Part of a raiding Scottish army became detached from the rest and penetrated as far south as Durham, gathering loot as it went; attempted – not very seriously – to take Newcastle; exchanged insults with the English inside the town; captured Hotspur's personal standard in an affray; set off northwards by the drovers' road back towards Scotland; camped for the night in the neighbourhood of Otterburn; and was attacked at sunset by a much larger force under the vengeful Hotspur and his brother. Out-numbered, the Earl of Douglas decided on a daring move. Leaving his infantry of spearmen to hold the first onslaught of the English, he and a small body of mounted knights made a flank attack. In the course of it the Douglas himself was killed, trodden underfoot by the English spearmen, and then trodden over again as the Scots fought their way back to recover their leader's body and raise his battle-cry. The struggle ended in the capture of the Percy brothers and a disgraceful English rout.

Later, long after Froissart, this bloody and rather messy battle fell into the hands of the balladists. I speak with some feeling, for as a boy I was required by my father (a fanatic for Border lore) to learn the entire text of one of the many versions. However, there were compensations. Particularly was I struck by the fate of one English knight:

> For Witherington needs must I wayle,
> As one in doleful dumps;
> For when his legs were smitten off
> He fought upon his stumps.

Since then the Witheringtons – more properly 'Widdringtons' – have fought in many battles for their country and are still very much alive in Northumberland. I think the rugged warrior of their name who made such a mark on my youthful imagination is far nearer to the grisly truth of Otterburn field than much of the other minstrelsy that has grown up around it, with its sentimental *Morte d'Arthur* imaginings about death in medieval war. Take the Douglas's dying soliloquy:

> My wound is deep; I fain would sleep;
> Take thou the vanguard of the three;
> And hide me by the braken bush
> That grows on yonder lillye lee.
>
> Oh! bury me by the braken bush,
> Beneath the blooming briar,
> Let never a living mortal ken
> That ere a kindly Scot lies here.

Where the Earl actually fell is, as I say, a matter of conjecture. The Percy Cross was erected in 1777, rather late in the day, but since it appears that fragments of weapons and armour have been found in its vicinity it could mark the approximate site. But if I had been the commander of a Scottish army hurrying back home with stolen cattle and other property, having just insulted a virile and warlike foe, I would not have camped in the low-lying district along the Rede but on Fawdon Hill, where the walls of a deer park and the embankments of an Iron-Age fort would have provided ready-made shelter and protection.

Not everyone is interested in old battles; but I would strongly urge those who are to get hold somehow of a copy of Volume XXXV, Part III, of the Berwickshire Naturalists' Club *Journal* for 1961, which contains an enthralling reconstruction by Captain R. H. Walton. Along with other members of the Redesdale Society I have myself walked over Fawdon Hill under Captain Walton's agile direction – I must admit several lengths behind him and not always in earshot of his enthusiastic commentary. That Fawdon Hill is the site of the battle is his most decided opinion, and without succumbing to his arguments entirely I feel half convinced that he is right. The stone-littered 'graves' he points to on the fells could be those of sheep, but who would take such trouble to preserve sheep's carcasses from the foxes? And what are we to make of the extraordinary triple line of earthworks descending the fell to the east of Fawdon Hill? Some Iron Age work perhaps, connected with the circular camp above it on the hill-top? A more modern boundary line? A Roman dyke – it certainly has some resemblance to the remains of the Vallum along Hadrian's Wall? Or a turf wall, as Captain Walton has it, built by the Scots and their English prisoners in the hours after their victory as protection against the second English army, under the Bishop of Durham, that was advancing on them from the east? I find that hard to accept either: but let everyone judge for himself.

Our route from Otterburn runs due west into the North Tyne valley. But before taking it the visitor will wish to be reminded of the country further up Redesdale, going north along the A68.

At the entrance to **Rochester** (pronounced 'Roe-chester') a cul-de-sac branching off to the right between the war memorial and the one-time schoolhouse leads after a quarter of a mile to the hamlet of **High Rochester**, which is built inside the ruins of the Roman fort of *Bremenium*. This is one of those rare instances where a Roman site has been used by successive civilisations without its origins being wholly obliterated by later building. The stone blocks of what were once the walls and towers of the fortress can easily be picked out; and that the ground was used in medieval times is shown by the presence of a converted pele to the west of the present farm. This easy familiarity of old and new makes *Bremenium* one of the cosiest of Roman remains. The spring guns known as *ballistae* were mounted here, and two of the projectiles can be seen on a gable of the now converted schoolhouse whose porch is built entirely of Roman stone.

Rochester itself is strung out along the main road. But there is a charming footbridge over the Rede leading to the football ground and beyond it a hidden waterfall. Just to the north of the village on the A68 is the Redesdale Army Camp, whose artillery range sprawls across a large tract of country from the Coquet at Alwinton to the Scottish border at Brownhart Law. When there is no firing, permission is given for a visit along the old line of Roman Dere Street to the Roman camp at **Chew Green**. This is a journey of which it is impossible to speak too highly: marvellous in any weather except under heavy rain or when the clouds are low on the hills. Turn right off the A68 at the red-bordered Army signpost into the Redesdale Camp and get clearance at the headquarters hut (Tel. 083 02 658). Cross the cattle grid and at the fork in the road above a farm on one's right keep left. At the top of the pass above Featherwood Farm the views over The Cheviot and the Coquet basin are superb. The nearest comparison is of Salisbury Plain, but on a much vaster scale and quite free of traffic and clutter. Close to the road (one within a couple of yards of it) and marked by five-pointed metal stars on posts are **Middle Golden Pot** and **Outer Golden Pot**, freestone blocks that were probably sockets for Roman road markers, very necessary in winter on this exposed high ground. They sound more exciting than they look. Over the crest the earthworks of the Chew Green camp suddenly appear directly ahead, tilted at an angle on the hillside so that one can look down into them. Below runs the infant stream of the Coquet under the heights of Thirlmoor (1829 ft) and Brown-hart Law (1642 ft), on the top of which are traces of a Roman signal station. The works consisted of a convoy camp and a labour construction camp inside a fortified enclosure, with another labour camp on its northern side. The complex, almost thirty miles beyond the Wall and in the midst of this wild fell country, creates an unforgettable impression of the power and self-confidence of Rome.

Sheet 70 of the one-inch Ordnance Survey map is an invaluable aid to this expedition. From the camp a good metalled road runs down the Coquet to Alwinton and Rothbury (see pages 222–8) as an alternative to returning to the Redesdale Army Camp or by a parallel track over Cottonshope Head to the A68 and the Forestry village of **Byrness**. This has a pleasant small hotel (south of the village, to the east of the main road) and an information centre for those interested in the Forest Park. Byrness's **Church**, the smallest in the county, has some unusual stained glass, showing workmen and machinery, a commemoration of those who died in the construction

Bamburgh Castle

Domestic Architecture

Top left. The Saxon Church at Escomb

Top right. Early seventeenth-cent[?] bastle house at The Hole Farm, near Bellingham

Left. 'Blagroves', the Tudor villa[?] house at Barnard Castle

Above. Tower-house, *circa* 1300 – the Vicar's Pele at Corbridge

of the **Catcleugh Reservoir**, which begins a mile further up the road and continues nearly to the Scottish border. In its churchyard is a memorial stone to the Presbyterian minister of Birdhope Craig, Joseph Tait, who died on 9 November 1720. It has some charming verse on it, brought to my attention by the Bellingham and North Tyne local history group who have included it in their Survey of the graveyard:

> Marble to therive trust his name
> For Grateful Reidsdale will proclaem
> His worth in words of Endlefs Fame
> Whilst solid virtue without stain
> And Real piety obtain
> Thy Tair Remembered shall remain
> Ftrangers if pafsing this thou fee
> Think what a Minister fhould be
> And then conclude that such was he.

Byrness, in fact, despite its remoteness, is in many ways a most surprising spot, even to the extent of getting one of its place-names into the *Guinness Book of Records* with Blakehopeburnhaugh, whose eighteen letters supposedly make it the longest in England. However, this claim is hotly denied by neighbouring Cottonshopeburnfoot (nineteen letters). In the same valley Blakehopeburnhaugh supporters insist that theirs is still the primacy, since Cottonshopeburnfoot is clearly three separate words. The Cottonshopeburnfoot contingent retort that Blakehopeburnhaugh is self-evidently four. This particular dispute may well never be settled.

Byrness is also the roadhead of the recently opened **Forestry Drive** (toll) across the watershed into the upper North Tyne valley. Near the entrance gates a signpost points the way along a track marked with red-topped poles to **The Three Kings**: a walk of about a mile over rough ground, most of it uphill. The Three Kings (originally four, the largest now lying on the ground) are standing stones that once surrounded a cremation cairn dating from the middle of the second millennium BC. The whole subject is dealt with in learned and fascinating articles by Aubrey Burl and Noreen Jones in Volumes 49 and 50 of *Archaeologia Aeliana*, fourth series (Society of Antiquaries of Newcastle upon Tyne, 1971 and 1972). The three Kings are of special interest because they are among the very rare instances of this particular burial culture to be found outside of north-east Scotland and Perthshire. Incidentally, close to this route, at the Goatstones near Simonburn (see page 258), there is yet another of these 'four-posters', as archaeologists call them. The Byrness stones were probably never intended to be very grand – only a 'family-sized' monument, in the words of the joint authors of the paper – and in their present environment of half-cleared scrubland they have a lost and forlorn look. Think of them in terms of gravestones in a churchyard, but put up about the time of the happenings in the Book of Exodus, and you may have their measure.

Up Chattlehope Burn is the waterfall of Chattlehope Spout. Bateinghope Burn, a tributary of the Rede, was the scene of the murder of Percy (Parcy) Reed of Troughend. The tale of how he was betrayed to his enemies by the four 'faus-hearted Has' (Halls) of Girsonfield is the subject of a popular Border ballad.

If one returns to the A68 and reaches the top of the pass at **Carter Bar** there is a famous view over the Lowlands of Scotland to the conical Eildons at the centre of the scene. An incident in Anglo-Scottish beastliness known as the 'Raid of the Redeswire' took place on the fells near by. Its fourth centenary was celebrated in the summer of 1975 by a gathering of horsemen from both sides.

Chapter 16

To Bellingham and the North Tyne

✤

The direct route from Otterburn to Bellingham and the North Tyne valley lies over the desolate Hareshaw Fell. A far more attractive and rewarding approach is by West Woodburn.

Leave Otterburn on the Bellingham road and at the big crossroads at the top of the hill turn left on to the A68. After just under two miles a signpost points along a gated farm road eastwards to **Corsenside** and the church of **St Cuthbert** standing deserted, apart from one house, among the fields. The church guide (available near the entrance) tells us that the ancient name may have been 'Crossensyde', in memory of a monument put up to commemorate the Saint, whose coffin is said to have rested here. The building, which is now seldom used, is basically Norman. Pevsner says that the chancel arch is of this period, but the guide has a more interesting theory. The windows in the nave are Georgian additions, and very charming they look, with their plain glass centres and border decoration in red. The bell-cote is also a later addition, typically Northumbrian – compare Thockrington and Ford. There are some very attractive funeral monuments on the outside of the south wall of the nave, and one quite hideous one in red granite. There was once a sizeable village at Corsenside. The reason for its disappearance is unknown, though there have been suggestions that perhaps the Plague was to blame. The views from the churchyard are splendid, with the Wannies sharp against the skyline to the south.

After another three-quarters of a mile on the A68, on the right-hand side of the road and, owing to the height of the stone walls, easily missed, is a **Roman Milestone** recently erected by the local history society. We are nearly on the line of Roman Dere Street. Another milestone stands at the bottom of the hill in the village of West Woodburn, where the modern bridge crosses the river Rede. It is actually in the garden of the pleasant *Bay Horse Hotel* and shows signs of having been used as a gatepost.

On the south side of the river and reached by a gate nearly opposite the turning to East Woodburn are the grass mounds covering the

243

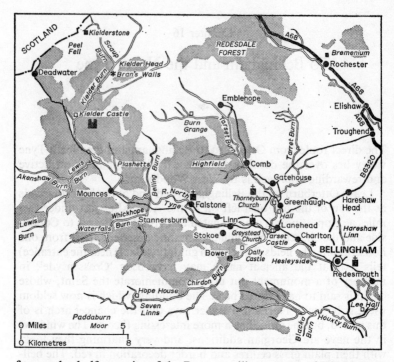

four-and-a-half-acre site of the Roman military camp of **Habitancum** (Risingham). The site was known to Camden, but apart from some amateur diggings in the early nineteenth century and the cutting of exploratory trenches by Professor Sir Ian Richmond in 1935 there has been no excavation of this large and important outpost in the wilds beyond the Wall. Professor Richmond found traces of a mid-second-century fort, of a rebuilding in 205 under Severus, reconstruction in 300 and a final rebuilding in 340. At one stage the garrison was the Fourth Cohort of Gauls, who were later at *Vindolanda*. The presence of Vangiones from Mainz and of Tyrolean units is also proved by altars and inscriptions found on the site.

Habitancum is cosily placed in a valley not far from the river which in Camden's day lapped its walls. A good deal of imagination is now needed to translate these bumpy fields into the stronghold of Roman times. A glance northwards helps to set the scene, for there the traces of the old military road can be made out running diagonally up the opposite slope. The masonry, some of which is exposed within the perimeter of the fort, is of exceptional quality and is said by experts

244

to be greatly superior to that of any other fort or milecastle in Northumberland.

A little further along the modern A68, still going southwards, in a field at the top of a hill on the right-hand side near the old railway station and rail bridge, is the lower half of a piece of heroic statuary of a soldier or more probably hunter familiarly known as **Robin of Risingham**. Sir Walter Scott's friend, the antiquary Dr Horsley, supposed that this was a representation of the Emperor Commodus in the role of the Roman Hercules. This is unlikely, since drawings of Robin before he was smashed up by a former landowner, infuriated by trespassing sightseers, show him to have been brandishing not Hercules's club but a hunter's bow, and having a quiver strapped to his back. However, the statue probably is Roman and may depict the local Celtic god Cocidius. A local tradition connected it with the Cain and Abel story of two brother giants who lived in the locality, one of whom poisoned the other when game grew scarce.

Hereabouts I fear I am drifting perilously far from the route I laid down for myself, but I must add that if the motorist with time on his hands cares to venture a little further still into the not very attractive moorland alongside the A68 he will see on his left Darner Quarry, which provided the stone for Edinburgh's George Street, then on his right an impressive piece of industrial archaeology in the ruined power house of the old ironworks at Ridsdale, then on his left again, near Waterfalls Farm, a Roman milestone lying on its side. It is of particular interest, first because it is one of the very few instances of such a stone in Northumberland that has survived to us entire, enabling us to see the full shape of its mushroom base, and secondly, because it was used as a mounting block by the Earl of Derwentwater at the concentration here of the Jacobite army at the outbreak of the 'Fifteen. But this really must be the moment for a halt and a return to our route.

Back in West Woodburn take the Bellingham road opposite the *Bay Horse*. After a couple of miles on the left is a fascinating **Bastle House** at The Hole Farm. The ground floor, as in all such buildings, was used for the cattle, and is still used as a byre to this day. It has a barrelled roof with a shaft in it to enable the farmer to climb to his living quarters, which he could also reach by an outside stone staircase. The first floor was divided into two by a willow and wattle screen, and this too survives. This is private property and permission must of course be asked. Better bring your gum boots.

Bellingham (pronounced 'Bellingjum' to confound the incomer) is the capital of the North Tyne, It has a population of just under a thousand, yet, believe it or not, in the quadrilateral between Hexham and Hawick, Haltwhistle and Alnwick, which would comfortably take in the whole of Surrey, it is the largest and indeed only town – and a town by royal charter at that.

Bellingham has always been a workshop. It is not a dormitory for anywhere nor a place of retirement. Through the centuries it has put its hopes into a number of industries and causes – cattle lifting in Tudor times; iron ore and coal mining in the Victorian heyday; nowadays forestry, the provision of services for the farming community and for the huge Redesdale Army Camp, a mart for the local sheep breeders, to which it has still more recently added a modest interest in tourism. The deserted iron and coal workings hover desolately on the fells above the town, but the pubs are booming, and will boom still more when the Kielder dam nine miles up-river is being constructed. The one-day Agricultural Show (held on the last Saturday in August), which in the days of the North Tyne railway brought the crowds from industrial Tyneside in their thousands, is not quite what it was, but it has survived as a great Northumbrian occasion. The nine-hole golf course, one of the most 'sporting' in Britain, has lately got itself a clubhouse in a converted farm, where those at the bar can watch their neighbours playing the ninth immediately below them across *two* enormous ravines. There is a thriving Amateur Dramatic Society and a branch of the Northern Arts Association – the Northern Sinfonia have been among recent visitors. Few other towns of its size could have boasted (if boast is the word) of the headquarters of a Rural District Council and of a Petty Sessional magistrates' court of its own. I use the past tense because the Council, if not the Petty Sessions, has been swallowed up in regional redistribution.

But if it lives in the present Bellingham is equally happy in its past, and indeed a very distant past, in the dawn of Christianity in these islands. According to tradition, the body of St Cuthbert was brought this way before finding a final resting place in Durham. The very interesting **Church** is named for the Saint and must often have been used by the parishioners as a refuge for themselves and their cattle when harried by mounted raiders from over the border, to judge from the cannon balls found in the roof during reconstruction and now exhibited inside. It has no tower. The chancel and chancel arch are thirteenth-century. But here for once it is not the early work that enthralls but rather the remarkable rebuilding of the nave and south transept in the early 1600s: the astonishing stone waggon-vaulting which makes of it a whitewashed cave and reflects in unmistakable terms the tough and enduring spirit of the place. It is one of the only two instances of this type of vaulting to be found in Britain.

In the churchyard a gravestone recalls one of the most famous of northern tales, of which James Hogg, the Ettrick Shepherd, left a spirited and most misleading account. The story dates back to Hanoverian times, its site Lee Hall, a couple of miles downstream, where one night a pedlar called with a large roll of merchandise, asking permission to leave it in the house while he went to find lodgings in the village. Just after midnight a maidservant in Lee Hall was awoken by a sound and called in help from a lad with a gun. In the moonlight flooding through the window the boy saw a movement of the 'Long Pack' propped up against the wall; fired point-blank into it; to be rewarded with a muffled cry and a spreading stain of blood. What happened to the pedlar, the other principal in this ingenious plot, is not recorded. What happened to the man inside the pack is uncertain too, for it seems that no bones lie under the gravestone in St Cuthbert's churchyard. According to one version this was no mere two-man attempt at burglary but part of a planned raid by mounted men, probably living in the neighbourhood, who later carried off the pack with the body of their confederate inside it – whether dead or alive the tale does not tell.

To return to the modern town. Its citizens are rightly proud of it and have shown this in a practical way by victories in the *Newcastle Journal*'s 'Best Kept Village' competition, but few of them would claim that it is beautiful, as Rothbury is beautiful. Though the main street has an interesting row of 'stepped' shops, no photograph of it has ever made it look better than functional. Yet some of the lanes leading down to the Tyne and the old Boat Yard are very attractive, and from the river bank there is a fine view downstream to John Green's handsome four-arched bridge of 1834. There is a Cuddy's (St Cuthbert's) Well, whose miraculous properties were once extolled and whose water (as the parish guide-book tells us) is still used at baptisms. There is much to admire also in the award-winning Westlands housing estate facing the rectory across a sloping green, Giuseppe Bonomi's St Oswald's (1839) at 'Catholic Corner', the touching Boer War memorial in Manchester Square, and the town hall with its deliciously Disneyland clock tower, outside which stands a remarkable gun captured during the Chinese Boxer Rising.

For the tourist Bellingham makes a convenient centre. Its only fault is that it is still light on accommodation. It has a youth hostel, but only one of its four inns is residential, and though a list of houses offering bed and breakfast is kept at the information office, none of this has kept pace with the town's increasing popularity. A new arrival, however, is the fully licensed residential *Reivers of Tarset* at The Comb, five miles away in the Tarset valley beyond Green-haugh, specialising in orienteering and country pursuits.

Much of this popularity comes from the week-end motorist from Tyneside and Wearside making the round tour by the North Tyne valley into the Scottish Lowlands and back over Carter Bar. But the golf, fishing and riding are also great attractions. Best served of all are the walkers. A National Forest Park Guide to the Border lists no fewer than twenty-two walks of varying length and toughness within the Park, nearly all of which can be tackled from a Bellingham base and five of which start from the town. To deal with them in any detail is impossible in a book of this kind; but the reader can take it that all are attractive in one way or another; that one of the most blissful of views – of the North Tyne from the crags above the Linn at Ridley Stokoe overlooking the Greystead–Falstone road – is not even thought worth listing in the Forestry guide; and that much of the remote and beautiful country on the left bank of the river and along the Tarset and Tarret burns can be explored from the comfort of a motor car. Nearer home a gentle mile and a half stroll out of the centre of Bellingham leads along a wooded glen to one of the most satisfying waterfalls in the North, the **Hareshaw Linn**. For the serious fell walker there is, besides all this, the **Pennine Way** which passes through the town.

And what, one may ask, is the Pennine Way? It is true that this brainchild, conceived in the '30s by Tom Stephenson of the Ramblers' Association and finally brought to birth by Whitehall and the National Parks Commission, is little known, even to some of the farmers and landowners whose fields it crosses. In his pictorial guide, *Pennine Way Companion* (published by Westmorland Gazette Ltd, Kendal, Cumbria), A. Wainwright, who has walked every yard of its two hundred and fifty miles from Edale in Derbyshire along the spinal cord of England to Kirk Yetholm across the Scottish border, sets out to display it to a wider public – and very well he does it with his sketches and his comments, not always kind. As he points out, 'Pennine Way' is really a misnomer when applied to the northern fifth of the track, since the Pennines stop at the Tyne Gap, and 'Cheviot Way' would have been a more appropriate name for the

sections north of it. But what does it matter? For at Bellingham –
one of the very few places where the 'Way' approaches a town or
village of any size – the enthusiast can set out on one of the challeng-
ing stages of a unique journey. Northwards, I fear, in the forty-five
miles to the track's end, lies some of the less rewarding country on
the route. In fact I would go further and say that these final sections
almost perversely seem to avoid the best of the Northumbrian
countryside – the Hareshaw Linn, for instance, and the Simonsides
– and choose instead to wander morosely over long whale-backed
fells till the 'Way' finally peters out (for no obvious reason) in the
hamlet of Kirk Yetholm. But there are still some marvellous places
along its length – the Roman camp at Chew Green and Roman Dere
Street, built by Agricola's legions; Windy Gyle and Auchope Cairn.
And southwards from Bellingham there are the delights of the Warks
Burn beckoning one towards the Roman Wall country, fourteen
miles away. Later we must of course return to the Wall and the
roll-call of military camps and milecastles along its length. The
Pennine Way out of Bellingham launches the tourist on perhaps the
best of all approaches to it – from the north, where the Caledonian
tribesmen of fifteen hundred years ago will have seen the sentinel
towers rising on the crests of Cuddy's Crag.

From Bellingham our route down the west side of Northumberland
turns south towards Hexham and the moorland border with County
Durham. Before taking it, however, I would urge the visitor with
time to spare to branch off for a while to follow the upper reaches
of the North Tyne through Kielder Forest to the Scottish border at
Deadwater. This wild and remote valley is about to be drowned
under the largest man-made reservoir in Europe: a project against
which local preservationists fought in vain. The peace of the valley
is thus doomed; though no doubt once the dams and the new roads
are built and the countryside has settled down to its new role as a
'recreation centre' it will recover most of its good looks. For the
next five years at the least, however, the section between Falstone
and Kielder will be greatly disrupted and constructional traffic is
certain to be heavy.

From Bellingham two roads run beside the river: one to the north
of it past Lane Head to Falstone where it joins its twin which has
kept to the south bank all the way. Both run through beautiful
country: the southern route is the more wooded and passes close
to the fine Georgian mansion of **Hesleyside**, home of the Charltons
(for centuries the chiefs of one of the four great local clans or

'graynes' – the Dodds, Robsons and Milburns were the others) and of the 'Charlton Spur', a piece of Tudor ironmongery which the lady of the house which stood at Hesleyside in those distant times would produce from under a salver at supper time instead of the expected roast, as a hint that the horses should be saddled at once and a course set for Scotland. The Spur forms the subject of one of W. Bell Scott's murals at Wallington romanticising grim and bloody events, for in their day the Tynedale men and those of the Tarset and Tarret burns were a lawless and formidable force among their own hills. One William Charlton had no fewer than two hundred armed retainers 'bound and bodily sworn on a book' always to take his part; and in 1538 an official report listed three hundred and fifty 'Tyndell thieffs', all with horse and armour, and one hundred and eighty-five foot thieves in the neighbouring valley of the Rede. Even the writ of the Percy earls did not often run in these remote parts. A far cry from the Age of Elegance and Capability Brown, who much later laid out the Hesleyside estate. Incidentally, Capability Brown, christened Lancelot, earned his nickname through frequently remarking of any great house he was invited to inspect that it showed 'capability of improvement'.

The road on the opposite north bank of the river runs parallel to the old North Tyne railway line whose embankments can often be glimpsed on the rising ground. On the far side of it, a quarter of a mile before the hamlet of Charlton, a footbridge leads uphill to the Romano-British settlement of **Riding Wood**, now no more than a group of large hollows in the ground with traces of stone walls lying under the trees. Only specialists in this field will find it worth the climb. It is on private land and permission would have to be got from the farm at The Ridings (the track to it leads off to the right, half a mile back towards Bellingham at the top of the bank). After Charlton the road rises over the fells before coming down to the valley again at **Tarset**, where a grass mound covers the castle of the Red Comyn, one of the greatest of the Scottish nobles. We must remember that all this country was part of Scotland as late as 1357, and that down to the end of the fifteenth century Tynedale and Redesdale were regarded even in London as an independent franchise, a law unto themselves. Later, when Tarset Castle passed to the English it was garrisoned in an attempt to keep the 'thieffs' in check. The locals greatly resented it and they had their way in the end. It fell into ruins, as did Dally Castle, a mile and a half away across the river by the banks of the Chirdon Burn. Rumour had it that a secret underground passage linked these strongholds: a highly unlikely tale. Incidentally, there is a splendid walk along the Chirdon into the Forest and out to the waterfalls of **The Seven Linns**.

This middle section of the valley is graced by several interesting buildings. At **Gatehouse**, on a minor road beyond Greenhaugh, are two bastle houses typical of the area during the days of the Border raids, one of them in a splendid state of preservation, and nearer the Comb another at the Black Middings. More accessible are two 'listed' churches from the decade after Waterloo at **Greystead St Luke** and **Thorneyburn St Aidan,** and further down towards Hexham, at Wark and Humshaugh, are two others of the same date: making four as like as peas in a pod. Upstream from them all, Falstone St Peter bears a remarkable likeness to them. The style is most conveniently seen at Greystead St Luke, whose small battlemented tower with three lancet bell openings overlooks the Bellingham–Falstone road and a pretty stretch of the Tyne. Inside it is plain and unfussy, with a flat ceiling, a fine tower arch of honey-coloured stone and all the hallmarks of the elegant, sensible proportions typical of its date. Thorneyburn St Aidan, on the Tarset Burn near the village of Greenhaugh, is more cosily furnished but darker. The architect of these five churches (with the possible exception of the one at Falstone) was H. H. Seward, who built them for the Commissioners of Greenwich Hospital.

A further oddity is that until the 1920s, when the Church Commissioners took over the buildings and the preferments to the livings were transferred to the bishops of Newcastle, all the rectors of the parishes had been naval chaplains put out to grass. For an explanation of such singular events one must turn to the history of the earls of Derwentwater, who owned much of the land up the North Tyne but lost it through too great a devotion to the Stuart cause that brought them 'out' in the Jacobite risings of the 'Fifteen and the 'Forty-five and ultimately to the block. The estates became vested in the Crown and were later granted to the Admiralty, which passed them on to Greenwich Hospital.

Other piquant oddities surround this unique group of buildings. Four of them were provided with near-identical rectories. Two of these have since been sold into private ownership – indeed, for twenty-five years I have lived in one of them myself. I can therefore vouch for the fact that they are well-found and shipshape, though mine is somewhat infested with bats. But the placing of the rectories and churches in relation to local geography and the spiritual needs of the district is perhaps the oddest and most inexplicable thing of all. The rectory at Falstone, for instance, is nearly a mile from its church. If the rector strays over his garden wall he is in the parish of Thorneyburn St Aidan. Thorneyburn itself was sited a quarter of a mile from the nearest human habitation and a mile from the nearest village, Greenhaugh, which was not to be in its parish anyway. At Greystead there was no village within sight: they simply stuck up a church by the roadside and hoped for the best. This seems a quaint arrangement: but wait a moment – the parish boundaries extend fifteen miles as the crow flies across the fells nearly to Gilsland in what is now Cumbria. It is a journey of forty miles by car.

Four miles upstream from Greystead the village of **Falstone** (probably from the Anglo-Saxon *Fausten*, a stronghold) will lie nearly at the foot of the projected dam for the vast new reservoir. Here the church was rather over-restored in the 1890s. It is outranked in seniority by its near-neighbour, the Presbyterian kirk, which dates from 1807 and is one of the oldest foundations of its kind south of the Border. The village must have been an Anglo-Saxon settlement, to judge from fragments of a cross found here with runes on one side and a legible inscription on the other:

> Eomar set this up for his
> Uncle Hroethbert – Pray for his soul.

It is now in Newcastle's Museum of Antiquities.

Beyond Falstone we enter the Forestry Commission's **Border Forest** which in fact consists of nine separate units on either side of the Cheviots covering one hundred and eighty square miles, the largest man-made forest in Europe. **Kielder Forest** itself is the largest in Britain, occupying forty-nine-thousand acres, mostly of Sitka and Norway spruce. Not everyone loves the way the trees have gobbled up the fells and blurred their skylines, but there is another side to the picture, and there can be no doubt that the Commission has not only brought much-needed employment to the valleys but also a genuine care for conservation. Some of the forest will be drowned when Kielder Water is built. At least one of the present Nature Trails – the one at Lewisburn along with its camp and caravan site – will also be a casualty, but there are others to the north, and much of the wildlife will probably manage to survive, provided the inclination is resisted to turn the whole area into a marina with power boats and water-skiing. At present wild goats, roedeer, foxes, badgers, otters, blue and brown hares, red squirrels, blackcock, red grouse, several breeds of duck, ravens, woodpeckers, meadow pipits, goldcrests, kestrels, oyster-catchers, skylarks, whinchats, nightjars, pied flycatchers, dippers, wagtails, snipe and even the occasional kingfisher, heron, peregrine falcon, grey goose and whooper swan can be seen, and there are hides where nature lovers can enjoy them at their leisure. Enquiries should be made at the Forestry headquarters in what was once a shooting box of the Dukes of Northumberland in **Kielder Castle**, where there is an information centre, tea room and charmingly arranged museum. The Duchess Drive Forest Trail that starts from here will lie above the lake, as will the twelve-mile private motor road linking the North Tyne valley with Redesdale at Byrness through some of the most remote country in England.

Kielder Village itself, at the northern end of the reservoir, may well get a new lease of life as a tourist centre. It is now exclusively a forestry village and one of the most isolated imaginable: there is not even a pub, though a thriving Working Men's Club and a really fine Community Centre have been built in recent years. Until the 1950s the North Tyne railway ran past the village, with connections to Hexham and Riccarton Junction, where passengers changed for Edinburgh or Carlisle, but even before Lord Beeching's arrival at British Rail the bureaucrats had axed it, and the local housewives must now depend on a bus service down the Tyne which might be appropriate to the wilds of Lapland. All that has been saved from the wreck is a viaduct, a splendid piece of Victorian railway engineering, which conservationists managed to preserve, though they failed to save the valley that lies below it. The waters of the lake will lap around its piers.

Village and castle are famous in legend as the home of a Border chieftain, the Cout or Colt of Kielder, gifted with a giant's strength and magic armour:

> In my plume is seen the holly green,
> With the leaves of the Rowan tree;
> And my casque of sand by a mermaid's hand
> Was formed beneath the sea.

In a delightful ballad Dr Leyden tells how the Cout ignores his wife's warnings and goes to dine with the wicked Lord Soulis in Hermitage Castle across the Scottish border. The Cout's men are fixed to their seats in the banqueting hall by a spell; only the Cout himself breaks free, but is caught and held down by the spears of his foes to drown in a pool which for many years was shown to visitors to Hermitage as 'the Cout's linn'.

253

The holly floated to the tide
And the leaf of the rowan pale;
Alas! no spell could charm the tide
Nor the lance of Liddesdale.

Swift was the Cout of Kielder's course
Along the lily lee;
But home came never hound nor horse
And never home came he.

The best of the tale, as one sees, really belongs outside the territory of this Guide, at Hermitage Castle, where the Cout's enchanted henchmen and their hounds must sleep on, like Barbarossa in his cave, till the ruined tower falls down. If they wake quickly, apart from the motor cars and the spruce on the fells, I do not think they will find their home valley above the reservoir so greatly changed, still green and russet, and the air still clear. It is fine walking country, best of all along the Border itself. A track from Deadwater crosses **Peel Fell** (1975 ft), from where on a clear day both the east and west coasts can be seen. The track leads on another four and a half miles to the enormous sandstone block of the **Kielder Stone**, through which runs the boundary line between Scotland and England. Legend has it that in the lawless days of the Border raids it was used as a post-box by the clans on either side. It is also supposed to be very unlucky to ride three times round it 'withershins' – that is to say, against the course of the sun. All this part of the route is marked with blue disks. A diversion (white disks) takes one to Knox Knowe ('Knowe' being a variant of the Anglo-Saxon 'knoll', a small rounded hill), with fine views over the Jed Forest to the north. From the Kielder Stone a route with blue disks leads four miles to Kielder Head, and a forest road (yellow) the same distance down the burn to Kielder Castle. Alternatively, another six miles along the actual boundary line from Knox Knowe brings one to Carter Bar and the A68 Corbridge to Jedburgh road (OS Sheet 70 in either case).

I should sound a warning note. Walks in the Border country as elsewhere in the Cheviots demand stamina, training and a good deal of care. The mists can descend very quickly on the fells and this is an area of high rainfall. Some of the ground is dangerously boggy. Proper equipment, including of course a compass and maps, should always be carried. The Stationery Office's *Northumberland National Park Guide No. 7* is essential reading. Another problem with such walks is that accommodation is in short supply, apart from hotels at Falstone, Byrness, Bellingham and The Comb and camping and caravan sites at Bellingham and Lewisburn (soon to be submerged). Kielder itself has nothing to offer except a youth hostel and the occasional bed and breakfast.

All the way from Bellingham we have been following the North Tyne, a dashing and beautiful upland stream on its pebbly bed. When beyond Kielder it reappears it has shrunk to a very small and modest burn winding its way through the bent-grass from the watershed at Deadwater, where at the Tyne springs, if you can find them, you can hold a great river in the palm of your hands. Swinburne knew all this country well and wrote hauntingly of it in *A Jacobite's Exile*:

> On Kielder-side the wind blaws wide:
> There sounds nae hunting horn
> That rings sae sweet as the winds that beat
> Round the banks where Tyne is born.

About a mile further up the streams are running the other way into the Liddel Water, which flows into the Esk and so to the Solway near Gretna Green. Northwards lies Roxburghshire and the Cheviot pass of the Note o' the Gate by which Bonnie Prince Charlie and the Jacobite army crossed into England on their march to Derby in the 'Forty-five. But that is outside the scope of this Guide.

So far we have been dealing with the upper valley of the North Tyne: it remains to follow it southwards to the Roman Wall and the junction with the South Tyne.

Take the B6320 out of Bellingham. The road rises up a long hill with the intriguing name of Pinch me Near, then drops sharply down Houxty Bank to rejoin the river. The country to the south is much lusher and some say an overcoat warmer than the upper reaches. Just after the bank, the house on the left, standing right up against the road, was the home of the naturalist Abel Chapman, at whose urging President Kruger of the Transvaal set up the famous game reserve of the Kruger National Park. Chapman's collection of trophies from the veldt are in Newcastle's Hancock Museum.

Wark on Tyne, a mile further on from Houxty, was for many years Scottish territory, and a local capital at that. There are the remains of a motte and bailey castle where the courts of the Liberty of Tyne-dale were held. Its manorial court leet met for the last time in 1920. The village looks a mess from the main road, which bypasses it, but at its centre there are some charming houses grouped around a

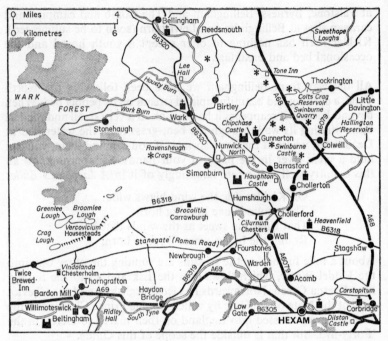

The map shows various locations including:

WARK FOREST, Stonehaugh, Greenlee Lough, Broomlee Lough, Crag Lough, Vercovicium Housesteads, Vindolanda Chesterholm, Twice Brewed Inn, Bardon Mill, Willimoteswick, Beltingham, Thorngrafton, Ridley Hall, Haydon Bridge, South Tyne, Low Gate, HEXAM, Dilston Castle, Corstopitum, Corbridge, Acomb, Warden, Fourstones, Stagshaw, Wall, Chesters, Cilurnum, Chollerford, Heavenfield, Humshaugh, Chollerton, Haughton Castle, Barrasford, Simonburn, Nunwick North, Ravensheugh Crags, Brocolitia Carrawburgh, Stanegate (Roman Road), Newbrough, Swinburne Castle, Gunnerton, Swinburne Quarry, Colwell, Hallington Reservoirs, Chipchase Castle, Birtley, Colts Crag Reservoir, Little Bavington, Thockrington, Tone Inn, Sweethope Loughs, Reedsmouth, Bellingham, Lee Hall, Houxty Burn, Wark, Wark Burn, B6320, B6318, B6319, A69, A68, A6079, A6305

Scale: 0 Miles 4, 0 Kilometres 6

green close to the bridge over the river. It has an excellent small
residential hotel, *The Battlesteads*, and two pubs, the *Black Bull* and
the *Grey Bull*. The pubs stand next door to one another, and are
now jointly owned, but continue under their separate names. The
parish church and its rectory, standing some way out of the village,
are the image of the other Seward works further up the Tyne. On
the hills above the left bank near Birtley (whose church has a Saxon
cross, *circa* 700) are traces of a number of British earthworks, one
appealingly named 'Good Wife Hot', another 'Male Knock Camp',
also a holy well and the Devil's hoofmarks where he incautiously
tried a leap too big for him and landed in the stream. It is an interesting fact that nearly all the prehistoric camps in this part of Northumberland are on the left bank of the Tyne. Was the river and the
undrained ground around it a good defensive barrier against the
tribes to the north and west?

From Wark, roads run downriver on either side of the Tyne. The
right bank route is the quicker, along the B6320, where at a sharp
bend under the shade of some ancient beeches a minor road leads
off to the right for **Simonburn**. For centuries, from the reign of

256

View from the Roman Wall at Winshields

Cheviot country near Wooler

The Old Border Bridge at Berwick, with the belfry of the town hall dominating the skyline

Edward II until the new parishes up the North Tyne were created in
the years following Trafalgar, St Mungo's Simonburn was the mother
church of the whole vast area between the Scottish border and
Hadrian's Wall, the largest parish in England. St Cuthbert's Bellingham was only its chapel of rest. When therefore the signpost at the
junction points to 'St Mungo's thirteenth-century church' it is in one
sense being unduly modest, for a religious foundation of some kind
has probably existed on the site since the days of the Northumbrian
kingdom of St Oswald. But in another sense I fear that signpost is
misleading. For the thirteenth-century vestiges inside the church are
barely visible to the naked eye: they amount to a piscina in the
chancel, some arches in the west end in the arcades, and some lower
courses of stonework in the nave level with the pulpit. All the rest
has been restored – first in the eighteenth century and then again in
Victorian times.

For all that, Simonburn is well worth a visit. The village itself is
charming – of Northumbrian villages only Blanchland is better. In
the autumn the terraced cottages with their plumes of smoke rising
at dusk against a background of a great screen of trees seem like an
echo of Jane Austen's England. Not a building is out of place. The
vicarage front is said to have been designed by Nicholas Hawksmoor
– I know few more beautiful or restful houses. And even that over-
restored and too prestigiously-minded church has charm. It is built
on a noticeable slope from west to east, so that one is looking down
into the chancel, which is very long and well-proportioned. An air
of Montagu and Capulet surrounds the place. On the left-hand side
looking towards the altar are the plaques and funeral tablets of the
Allgoods, the family that still owns the big house of Nunwick among
the beech trees. To the right are the corresponding inscriptions of the
Ridleys of Park End. And the Ridleys are still here too. This constantly happens with Northumbrian families: they are great survivors, very tenacious. And the family pews are still here also – in
the front row, to left and right, with specially carved backs to them.
The organ (which the guide to the church insists is much grander and
more melodious than it looks) was purchased from York Minster.
Best of all, to my mind, in the north aisle is the funeral monument of
Cuthbert Ridley, one time rector of St Mungo's, who is shown, a
bearded man with a Tudor ruff, kneeling with his children beside him
on a plinth inscribed:

> IN THE DAY OF JUDGMENT
> GOD BE MERCIFUL
> TO RIDLEY A SINNER

as moving a piece of monumental masonry as one could hope to find. In the eighteenth century one of Simonburn's curates was the well-known naturalist and lichenologist, John Wallace: also famed for the fact that his spaniels used to try to share the pulpit with him. During the Middle Ages the village's pele tower was an outpost of the Keepers of Tyndale. It was demolished in the eighteenth century by treasure hunters. The tithe barn has been converted into a modern house.

Another road opposite the Nunwick gates leads three miles west towards Stonehaugh to **The Goatstones** on Ravensheugh Crags: four standing stones that surrounded a cremation cairn as at The Three Kings at Byrness and part of the same Scottish culture of 'four-posters' that somehow or other found its way into the valleys of the Tyne and Rede (see page 241 and H. A. W. Burl's paper in *Archaeologia Aeliana* for 1971). Leave the car in the lay-by opposite the tiny cottage, go through the gate on the left-hand side of the road, and follow the rutted track half a mile uphill to the point where the stones suddenly appear to one's left at very close range against the skyline. Small though they are, their siting in these lonely uplands make them to my mind more impressive than Byrness's Three Kings. The views are grand. The cup markings in the stone lend an air of mystery. Invocations? To what gods? The near-by crags are also very impressive. Stone from them was used in the building of the Allgoods' elegant house at Nunwick.

From Simonburn down the B6320 it is only another four miles to the Tyne crossing at Chollerford. But unless the visitor is in a great hurry I would urge him at this point to go back into Wark, bear right into the village, cross the bridge, and then turn right again on the road that follows the left bank of the river. After one and a half miles **Chipchase Castle** appears on the right, a Northumbrian pele tower, once the home of the Keepers of Tynedale, added to and embellished over the years, in particular by the handsome Jacobean east front (1621). Its central porch is wholly of this date, but there have been several alterations to the windows on either side of it, and the present mullions are actually mid-Victorian, being by our old Newcastle friend, John Dobson. Chipchase is not open to the public, but this beautiful wing and the Georgian chapel in the park show up excellently from the road. The best view of the castle as a whole is from across the Tyne, but will escape all but the most observant, who will have to peer through hedges on the B6320 between Wark and Simonburn.

A little further down the left bank of the Tyne a left turn leads to the village of **Gunnerton**, and its **Church**, dedicated to St Christopher. From the outside, I confess, it looks very uninspiring, but it is something of a curiosity. It seems that a student architect by the name of Hall won a competition for a design for a small moorland church. Invited by the Rector of Chollerton to build it here, Hall set to work with local masons using local stone. Pevsner calls the result (1900) 'somewhat mannered', and indeed there are some remarkably unexpected features in the large, very 'mod' oculus window at the west end and the Byzantine slits of coloured glass high above the altar at the east. The chancel is raised three steps above the nave, from which lower level its woodwork looks uncommonly handsome. Hall went over from the Anglican ministry to Rome and ended his days as a hermit in Australia.

Gunnerton is also a taking-off point for some places of great interest which I have to admit are somewhat off our route.

From the road going uphill out of the village towards the A68 there is a striking view to the right of the steep, austerely grey escarpment of **Reaver Crags,** part of the Whin Sill. There is an ancient hill camp on the summit which will probably disappear eventually, since Barrasford Quarry on the far side is constantly nibbling away at the ridge. A little further up the road, almost completely hidden in the woods above a burn, is an artificial mound on which stood a Norman motte and bailey castle. This mound is now known as **Money Hill**, because some of the more credulous inhabitants got it into their heads that there was treasure to be found there and dug a large hole in its core. Alas for such enterprise! Nothing was found.

This road out of Gunnerton eventually joins the A68. Continuing our detour, turn right here and after half a mile, at a series of 'S' bends, left, along a private road leading to **Swinburne Quarry**, whose hard clean stone was used in building the vaults of the Bank of England. Some two hundred yards along it, on the top of a mound right up against the track, is the most easily accessible of all the ancient British hill camps in Northumberland. The site is naturally strong, with the ground sloping away on all sides. Artificial mounds and walls on the summit add to its strength. There are traces of what appear to be a defended entrance gate, but there is none of the large concentric rings of ramparts that mark the pre-Roman Iron Age camps. Their absence, and the camp's nearness to the old Roman road out of Corstopitum towards the Tweed, would seem to argue a Romano-British settlement that grew up under the wing and shadow of the imperial power. However, the presence within little more than a mile of a standing stone pitted with deep cup markings points to a very much earlier occupation of this tract of upland country. This **Standing Stone,** nearly twelve feet high and the tallest in North-umberland, is in the park at Swinburne Castle, on private land, so that the normal permission must be got in advance. How much earlier it arrived on the scene than the hut circles at the Quarry no one can say. It looks immensely old and impressive, its original red colour now grey with lichens, deeply weathered by the rain and winds of centuries. The day I was there hounds were running far off in the hills; there were the sounds of voices calling; and suddenly a small herd of roedeer came bounding across the fields under the trees. Near by one can see excellent examples of 'lynchet meadows', the ancient terracing, providing drainage from the higher ground and level strips for cereal crops, which marked Man's early attempts at agriculture in this area. Did the inhabitants of the camp at Swinburne Quarry use this ground? It seems quite possible.

From Swinburne the motorist who has followed this detour through Gunnerton can rejoin the main route by following the A6079 (the ancient 'Corn Road' from Hexham to Rothbury and Amble) at the hamlet of Chollerton. The visitor who has stayed on the riverside road, before reaching the same point, will pass through the village of Barrasford, where the bulk of **Haughton Castle** looms romantically across at him from beyond the stream. The ferry that used to ply here is sometimes said to have inspired the ballad *Waters of Tyne,* sung or played on the pipes at so many local functions:

> O bring me a boatman – I'll give any money,
> (And you for your trouble rewarded shall be)
> To ferry me over the Tyne to my honey,
> Or skull him across that rough river to me.

I think from the last line, however, that the ferry this verse refers to must belong further downstream, to the estuary. Haughton (a homestead on the haugh or river meadow) is like Chipchase still inhabited: a very grand country house. Its dungeons once featured in a grim story – of one of the old lairds of Haughton who, catching one of the Armstrong clan in the act of armed robbery, clapped him into his darkest cell, deep underground, rode off to a conference at York. Suddenly remembering that he had brought the only key to the dungeon with him, he galloped home, to find the robber dead with an arm gnawed to the bone. Armstrong's ghost was for long said to haunt the castle, one of a large gallery of Northumbrian 'boggles'.

The valley road joins the A6079 at **Chollerton**, which I mentioned above. Here the parish **Church of St Giles** is a great curiosity, for the pillars of the south arcade of its four-bay nave are Roman monoliths with Roman tooling, brought from the camp of Chesters (*Cilurnum*) in the twelfth century. The octagonal pillars of the north arcade are thirteenth-century work, as is the font, which has a Jacobean cover. The reredos and choir panelling are also Jacobean, and the organ is by Father Smith, a famous seventeenth-century instrument maker. One would never guess at such richness from the outside of St Giles, whose squat eighteenth-century tower is capped by the most comical Victorian tiled turret.

From the church turn right, southwards, towards Hexham. A mile and a half along the river bank is Brunton crossroads, surely one of the very few in the country where a B road has priority over an A road. (The route I am describing is on this A road, so beware. It is a famous accident black spot.) A right turn here over Chollerford Bridge leads to the *George Hotel* overlooking the river, one of the best and most convenient stopping places for visitors to the Roman Wall. For anyone with half an hour to spare, however, there is a rewarding detour up Brunton Bank from the crossroads on the B6318, going eastwards towards Newcastle. About a mile up the hill there is a modern cross on the left-hand side and a chapel in the fields behind it on the site of **Heavenfield**, King Oswald of Northumbria's victory over the forces of Cadwallon and the West Britons in 634. Pursued up the line of the old Roman road past Corbridge, Oswald turned here at bay and set up his standard of the Cross. His victory was followed by a swift evangelising of the North and was one of the key events of our early history. The exact spot was for a long time marked by a stone cross set on a Roman altar stone, probably not far from the present road. The cross has disappeared, but the heathen altar (*circa* 200) survives and can be seen in the small chapel (1737) that crowns the hill behind a screen of trees. The peace and simplicity of the place are deeply moving. Plain whitewashed walls are formed of massive blocks of stone. In the porch are some ancient slabs and carvings, including what appears to be a head of Christ. There is a fine view from the churchyard over the Tyne valley towards Chollerford Bridge.

Chapter 17

The Roman Wall

✖

The Roman Wall is one of Britain's greatest tourist attractions, and rightly, for nowhere else in Europe can such a system of fortifications be seen, and everything is within easy reach of hotels in a grand and unspoilt countryside.

Roman interest in Britain, briefly aroused by Julius Caesar's two raids, did not revive till a century later when the Emperor Claudius landed in search of a Triumph in AD 42. The first serious incursion into the North was made between 78 and 84 by the great governor Agricola, who had advanced as far as the Grampians with the evident aim of subduing the whole island when he was recalled by a jealous Emperor.

Such ambitions shrank under the hard realities of climate and terrain and Caledonian stubbornness, and by the end of the first century the northern frontier had fallen back to the narrow throat of England between the Tyne and Solway, where a number of forts on the lateral road of the Stanegate had been built in Agricola's time in the territory of the Celtic *Votadini* tribe. About the year 120 the most realistic and most travelled of Emperors, Hadrian, ordered the construction of a wall roughly parallel to the Stanegate but holding the high ground a little to its north. It was intended to be of stone throughout, but to the west of the river Irthing material for grouting ran out, and the work was completed in turf. Two years later Hadrian came in person to the ground; ordered the length of the works to be extended; moved up the garrisons from the Stanegate forts to the line of the Wall itself: and provided for a new defensive ditch, the *Vallum*, to be placed on its southern side. (*Vallum* is in fact what the Romans called the Wall. It was Bede who first called the *Vallum* by its present name.) The result was the creation of a formidable barrier stretching for seventy-two and a half miles (eighty Roman miles) from Wallsend to the Solway. It was to be fifteen (some say sixteen) feet high and ten feet thick, with a six-foot parapet with merlons, making the total height twenty-one or twenty-two feet; there were milecastles every sixteen hundred and twenty yards with signal towers between them, and at intervals much larger camps garrisoned by units of auxiliary troops.

These auxiliaries, drawn chiefly from the Rhine and the Belgic provinces, Gaul, Spain and increasingly Britain, were not of course irregulars but highly trained and battle-hardened professionals, formed into wings (*alae*) of cavalry, one thousand or five hundred strong, and into battalions of infantry or mounted infantry of similar size. The Legions, the real backbone of the Roman Army, were not stationed on the Wall (though the Second, the Sixth and the Twentieth largely built it). These élite troops were normally held in reserve, the nearest legionary fortresses being at York and Chester.

Hadrian's Wall was not simply an obstacle carrying a cat-walk for sentries, though of course it was that also. On the north side lay a wide and steep defensive ditch, except where a natural escarpment performed a similar purpose, as on the Northumbrian Whin Sill. South of the Wall itself and the military road that ran parallel with it was the *Vallum*, which doubled the role of boundary between military and civilian zones and defensive barrier in case of trouble from the supposedly 'pacified' tribes to the south. In time, as occupied Britain became more and more Romanised, this danger diminished and parts of the *Vallum* were filled in. There were sixteen forts in all. At the height of its power the Wall was manned by some twelve to fifteen thousand troops, around whose camps clustered the civilian settlements (*Vici*) of the local inhabitants who had provided the unskilled labour for the building of the fortifications and became increasingly identified with the *Pax Romana*, sending their sons to join the colours and themselves serving as blacksmiths, farriers, stonemasons, carpenters and armourers to meet the needs of a garrison itself rooted in the soil. Units of the Roman Army on the frontiers of the Empire seldom moved: they became assimilated to the country, just as the tribes became assimilated to them. These civilian *Vici* are among the most interesting of the remains that have come down to us.

The Wall was not built to be an impregnable barrier; it never aimed to keep out every marauding Caledonian. Massive though it was, its function was more that of a trip-wire which could slow down and unbalance any major enemy attack from the north while the regular forces of legionaries manoeuvred to meet it in the open field. From day to day it was also a method of frontier control, a means of regulating customs and trade, for by no means all the peoples to the north of it were hostile – the North Tyne valley, for instance, towards the end of the occupation, was quite thickly settled

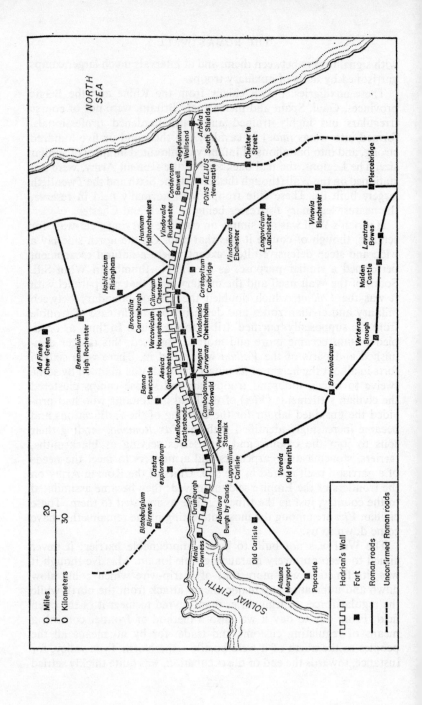

by tribesmen who seem to have been in regular contact with the Romans and may well have been veterans from the army. This hinterland was policed if not fully controlled by the imperial power. A string of forts in the wild fell country of the Cheviots was linked with *Corstopitum* (modern Corbridge) by Roman Dere Street. From Stagshaw above Corbridge another Roman road (marked on today's Ordnance maps as 'The Devil's Causeway') ran at a tangent off Dere Street to the north-east through Great Whittington and Glanton, crossing the Till below Horton and then running through Lowick to the mouth of the Tweed. Leaving Dere Street at High Rochester, a connecting track crossed the Coquet at Holystone and joined the Devil's Causeway near Whittingham. With the Stanegate, these roads provided better all-round communications in the North than was achieved again till late Hanoverian times. A series of signal stations completed the network, connecting the Wall with legionary headquarters at York and with camps as far north as the Eildons. Vetruvius tells us that grapes were grown at this time in Britain as far north as York; this points to a much sunnier climate, and, since the Romans used the heliograph, messages could have been flashed across these large distances in a matter of minutes in good weather.

So long as Rome was at peace with herself and her forces in Britain were kept up to strength the system worked well. For a while, during the reign of Antoninus Pius (about 138), no need was felt for defences in Northumberland at all, for the Romans were attempting the colonisation of the Scottish Lowlands by means of another wall between the Forth and the Clyde. This forward policy failed and a return was made to the Hadrianic line. And the peace imposed by great emperors did not last. When Rome once more fell prey to civil war the disturbances were reflected on the frontiers with dire results, and in 197, during the absence from Britain of its governor, Albinus, and of most of his British-based troops in an unsuccessful attempt to seize power in Italy, the northern tribes saw their chance, stormed the forts on the Wall and reached as far south as York, where the great legionary fortress was sacked and burnt.

It was a calamity in which thousands died, but Rome was still too powerful to be dispossessed by undisciplined tribesmen. The Legions returned, the situation was speedily restored, and the new governor of Britain, Senecio, was not only able to rebuild and strengthen the Wall but also reoccupied some of the outlying forts in Redesdale to the north. When the tribes reacted to this move with fresh attacks the Emperor Septimius Severus himself came to Britain, and so thorough was his pacification that the tribes were effectively silenced for the best part of a hundred years.

It was during this period that Roman Northumberland achieved a peace and prosperity not to be repeated for a millennium. The area's mineral wealth (largely in lead) was developed, and as the civilian settlements sprang up outside the forts the comforts of urban life – of baths, sanitation, heating, temples and inns – came to mirror those existing in the rest of the Roman world, if on a rudimentary scale. Not till the last years of the third century did the barbarian attacks begin again in any strength, requiring a rebuilding of parts of the Wall; but these died down, and for almost another century the *Pax* still held, so that a visitor from Hadrian's time would have recognised the world he knew.

Then in 367 a combination of invaders – Picts and the Lowland tribes by land, Saxon pirates by sea – broke in on an island already drained of many of its defenders. Count Theodosius managed to defeat them and for the last time the forts were rebuilt. But soon the regular troops were required for other urgent duties along the threatened frontiers of the Empire, from the Rhine and Danube to the Alps, till the day came in 410 when one of the last of the Emperors of the West could offer no more to the Britons than the sage advice to defend themselves.

What followed can be read in the ruins of Roman rule which the barbarians overthrew but which centuries of ploughing and stone-robbing have not succeeded in effacing: the mounds marking the sites of still unexcavated forts; cross-sections of Ditch and *Vallum* furrowing the countryside; courses of Roman stone in the fields; the abutments of bridges; the still wonderfully impressive traces of the Wall itself striding along the crests of the Whin Sill.

How best to advise the visitor on his tour of the Wall is a problem, for there are any number of possible permutations; indeed, even without leaving industrial Tyneside and its commuter belt it is possible to see impressive evidence of Roman military works at Heddon on the Wall. Nevertheless, the most important Roman sites lie further west, at *Corstopitum* (Corbridge), *Vercovicium* (Housesteads), *Cilurnum* (Chesters), and *Vindolanda* (Chesterholm), all within a radius of a dozen miles from Hexham, which has a service of special buses during the summer months.

If a base in a town is preferred, **Hexham** has good hotels and, with its superb abbey, is a tourist attraction in its own right. Much the same goes for the smaller Corbridge, and there is also the *Manor Hotel* at Haltwhistle, very conveniently placed for the central section of the Wall, and for Allendale Town. Alternatively, in the country, there is the *Twice Brewed*, on the B6318, a haunt of walkers, and the *George Hotel* at Chollerford, with its terrace and lawns overlooking the river, and four miles to the north *The Battlesteads* at Wark on Tyne. From Chollerford Bridge it is less than half a mile to the camp at Chesters, eight to Housesteads; and since trying to absorb too many Roman sites in a day can be extremely tiring my personal advice would be to stop at the *George* or the *Hadrian* at Wall for lunch, see Housesteads, Vindolanda and the Mithraeum at Carrawburgh in the afternoon, return to the hotel for the night (booking in either case is essential in high season) and visit Chesters next morning as a prelude to Hexham, leaving *Corstopitum* till later. If desired, *Vindolanda* can be fitted in with a tour of the South Tyne (see page 311).

Start then from Chollerford at the bridge over the Tyne along the B6318, known locally as 'The Military'. This is not a reference to Roman but to Hanoverian army engineers who built it in 1752/3, after Bonnie Prince Charlie's invasion west of the Pennines had shown there was no lateral road from Newcastle to Carlisle along which defending troops could march. In Roman times the Stanegate would have served the purpose excellently. The 'Military' leads westwards past the Chesters, once the home of John Clayton, the associate of Dobson and Grainger and also an amateur archaeologist who carried out excavations at *Cilurnum*. His mansion is hidden among the trees, but the stable block by Norman Shaw shows up well to one's right just before the beginning of the hill. Hereabouts the tarmac of the modern road overlies the flagstones of the one the Romans built, and on the high ground on the hill-crest stands a splendid section of the old frontier line, with the Wall and Ditch to the right, and the *Vallum* to the left.

Four miles west of Chollerford an 'ancient monument' sign points to the **Mithraic Temple** at *Brocolitia* (Carrawburgh). It has a small car park, is always open, and no charge is made. The worship of Mithras came to Rome from the East, one of the mystery cults involving the sacrifice of a bull, through whose ritual slaying and blood the worshippers found regeneration. Towards the end of the Empire in the West it rivalled Christianity in popularity. Some years ago the ruins of a mithraic temple were found under the London clay, but here at Carrawburgh is the largest and best preserved of the god's shrines to be seen in Britain, though shorn now of its altars and inscriptions which are housed in the Museum of Antiquities in Newcastle along with a full-scale reconstruction of the temple itself.

Near by stood a sanctuary to the Celtic deity Coventina – for the Romans hedged their bets in matters of religion and never neglected the worship of even the most unlikely gods. The spring, bubbling to the surface at this point, was treated by Coventina's worshippers like one of the fountains in modern Rome, and the coins cast there came to light many centuries later in 1876. No fewer than twenty-three thousand were found. The temple's altars are now in the museum at Chesters. These two sites, with their evidence of the varied religious life existing on the frontiers in the third and fourth centuries of the Christian era, provide a good introduction to the fort of *Vercovicium* at **Housesteads** a couple of miles further west.

Housesteads is the most dramatic and scenically the most exciting of the Roman forts, standing high on the Whin Sill, with superb views over the South Tyne valley and northward into what was the half-tamed country beyond the Wall. It is blissful in fine weather, bracing in the wind, and at its best under a powdering of snow, with the crests of the fells pencil-sharp against the sky, a true frontier fort. During the third and fourth centuries it was garrisoned by the First Cohort of Tungrians, originally a unit drawn from Germanic tribes settled in Gaul, but by the time of Severus it was probably mainly recruited from Britain itself. The site, which is maintained by the Department of the Environment, has a large car park at the bottom of the hill, and in August and September it is certainly needed, for this is one of the most popular of all tourist attractions in Britain.

The climb to the fort is by a well-worn grass track. Tickets are bought at the Museum to the west of the excavations, where models of the fort in its heyday and of a typical house in the civilian *vicus* set the scene.

It is an open site where people can wander at will. The visitor should enter by the South Gate. Once inside, turn right for the latrines, which Housesteads proudly boasts are the best relics of their kind in the country. A dozen men at a time could be accommodated – it will certainly bring back memories to ex-servicemen. A connecting stone channel runs from the tank at the south-east angle tower which collected water from the roof. There are no natural springs on Housesteads hill and there had to be a reserve supply to supplement the one pumped up from the burn on the eastern slope.

Higher up the camp is the East Gate, the main entrance to the fort, with the headquarters building facing it. The deep ruts caused by carts and chariot wheels in the stone are four feet eight and a half inches wide, and since this is precisely the gauge chosen by George Stephenson for his railways it has sometimes been believed that he got his measurements from here. To spoil a good tale, one has to add that the East Gate at Housesteads was still unexcavated at the time; but before dismissing it altogether we should remember that in deciding on his gauge Stephenson took an average from the wheel-span of country carts, which may well have been derived over the centuries from Roman measurements.

To see one of the most famous of Northumbrian views, go to the north-east angle of the fort and look out over the rising stretch of the Wall towards King's Crag and Sewingshields. In the foreground is the valley of the Knag Burn (the weak link in the natural defences of the hill), and in this dip in the ground is one of the few gateways through the Wall itself, as opposed to one leading into a camp. It was built very late in the Roman occupation, in the fourth century, and suggests that by then the military uses of Housesteads had been modified to suit the needs of a society trading freely with the tribes outside. The near-by north gateway of the camp itself is an impressive one, but few except the very young and nimble care to scramble down the slope across the Ditch to see it as it must have appeared to the traders from the fells.

Downhill again on the south slope is the central block containing the granaries, not as fine as at *Corstopitum*. Beyond them are the headquarters buildings. Roman camps throughout the Empire were built to a basic plan: with a secretariat, strongroom, armoury and regimental chapel at the heart of them, and next door the station commander's house, which would normally be served by a retinue of servants and slaves. A gold ring was found in this one in the drain of the private loo.

The Housesteads fort and its civilian *vicus* to the south have not even to this day been fully excavated, though work on one of the most interesting buildings, the hospital, is currently exciting archaeologists. The barracks between the central compound and the West Gate still lie below the grass. The West Gate is interesting, with its pivot holes for doorways which, from the size of the blocks, were probably five inches thick. In fairness one must admit that Housesteads is disappointing in what it has to show of itself above ground, lacking the splendidly preserved bath-houses to be seen at Chesters. The low courses of stone in the *vicus* tell us little about their one-time inhabitants, even though one is enticingly labelled 'Murder House' on the strength of a skeleton with a knife blade embedded in it found buried beneath its floor. Yet probably as many as two thousand civilians lived in this suburb on a bleak hillside. To all Roman sites, in fact, the visitor must bring a great deal of imagination – that is why the museums should always be seen first. The models they contain, the inscribed stone altars, the statues, the show-cases filled with coins and artefacts of many kinds, help enormously to give life and meaning to what might otherwise seem no more than a ground plan of stone walls standing not more than a couple of feet above the well trimmed grass. Fortunately at Housesteads there is also the Wall itself stretching out to east and west on the crest of the hill, and here is the real enchantment of the place. Even the shortest stroll along it reveals what a stupendous engineering feat it was in its prime, remembering always that we are seeing no more than the stump of it, with milecastles and signal towers nearly all gone and the fort itself in ruins.

Starting from the north-east corner the walk to Sewingshields Crag and back takes under two hours. It is scenically as beautiful as it is romantic, a journey back into time. The Wall leads through a wood, is lost for a while, and then returns on the summit of a crag with views in every direction. Somewhere below one in a cave King Arthur and his Knights are sleeping as soundly as the Cout of Kielder's henchmen at Hermitage Castle and Hotspur and his hounds in a lost gully below The Cheviot. Northumberland yields to no one in the legends industry. On the lower ground are the ruins of Sewing-shields Castle, and to the north-west the line of an old earthwork, the Black Dyke, can be picked out. It may have been a boundary line between Saxon and British communities during the Dark Ages.

The walk westwards towards the Steel Rigg and the *Twice Brewed Inn* is every bit as fine, with views over the South Tyne valley and the Brampton Fells, and it has this advantage, that for much of the way the track runs along the top of the Wall itself, so that the twentieth-century walker is following in the steps of Hadrian's sentries. The only problem is the weather. As the Cumbrian saying has it, when you can see Cross Fell it's going to rain; when you can't see it it's already raining – a sound enough guide to Wall weather. But there are abundant compensations. Standing high on the crest of the Whin Sill, with Greenlee and Broomlee loughs lying below and mile upon mile of unspoilt country stretching to the horizon on all sides, one is really in the Britain of fifteen centuries ago. There is talk of putting pylons across this land; but the Roman lobby in these parts is both alert and powerful, and I think it unlikely that such vandalism will be permitted. Such is the scale of the scenery that in any event it could absorb the worst anyone can do, as it has already absorbed the rocket-testing towers just over the Cumbrian border on Spadeadam Waste.

The journey to Milecastle 37 in this direction will only test the stamina of the very old. It was built by men of the Second Legion under Platorius Nepos, who proudly recorded their achievement. This part of the Wall is very popular with rock climbers, who have some testing crags perched dizzily above the leaden waters of the lakes below to test their nerve and skills – they make splendid publicity pictures for the Tourist Board. Enthusiastic fell walkers can join the Pennine Way at Rapishaw Gap, going northwards through Wark Forest or southwards on the bleak sector that traverses Cross Fell. The moderately adventurous who want to keep to the Wall itself can prolong their walk westwards to Whinshields Crag, where the Wall climbs to its highest point (1230 ft above sea level), to the stretch between Thorny Doors and Cawfield milecastle where it comes closest to its original shape and size, being thirteen courses high, or to the still unexcavated camp at *Aesica* (Greatchesters), half way between the Tyne mouth and the Solway. Still further ahead lie the romantically named Nine Nicks of Thirlwall* and a signal station (Turret 45 on a modern map) which pre-dated the Wall. Hereabouts chives and herbs have been found growing wild, which some botanists conclude are the still-living remnants of Roman occupation. The excursion can be rounded off near the Walltown quarry where the track joins the B6318 above Greenhead. Agreeably placed near the end of it are the *Milecastle Inn* and the residential *Twice Brewed Hotel*.

On the other side of the Military Road from Housesteads is **Vindolanda**.

This is not a Wall fort but part of an earlier defence system guarding the east–west lateral road through the Tyne gap, the Stanegate, holding the low ground. The first fort on the site seems to have been connected with Agricola and was made of turf with timber buildings. Another very large pre-Hadrianic fort replaced it but fell into disuse when early in the second century the camp at Housesteads was built a couple of miles to the north. This neglect of Vindolanda was short-lived, however, for in the time of the Emperor Severus a stone fort was built on the eastern escarpment of the site (*circa* 208), differently aligned and facing south, which makes it look as though the tribal Brigantes in what is now Yorkshire were the enemy to be feared. This was superseded by a Diocletianic fort facing north, and substantially these are the remains we now see. There was a further reconstruction under Theodosius towards the end of the Roman

*Quarrying has left only five.

271

occupation. The garrison during most of the third and fourth centuries was the Fourth Cohort of Gauls, a mixed body of cavalry and infantry some five hundred strong whose emblem was the stork.

The military camp lies on the east of the site, approached along a remarkable stretch of the original Roman road. There is a fine Roman milestone, the only one in Britain still standing in its original position to full height, and further to the west is the stump of another. The fort's headquarters block (*principia*) has been excavated by Professor Eric Birley to show the usual pattern of low courses of wall set tidily among the grass. It is one of the best preserved examples of its kind and the only fort in Britain which has stone screens standing in front of its chapel.

To the west of the military camp the civilian *vicus* that grew up around it during the third century is being excavated under the auspices of the Vindolanda Trust, founded in 1970 by Mrs Brian Archibald. The excavations are under the direction of Mr Robin Birley, whose booklet gives an up-to-date account of the site and the work in progress.

Every Roman camp had such a *vicus* clustering around it: part residential suburb for the wives and families of serving men and for veterans living on their pensions in an environment where they had spent their working lives, and part workshop for the craftsmen providing services for the garrison. Coal, lead and iron were probably all worked in the vicinity, to judge from the extensive traces of mining along the Chinely and Brackies burns and in the country between the camp and Housesteads. Such a settlement would often be much larger than the military camp alongside it (at Vindolanda three times as large) and in such places if anywhere the spade should reveal the missing part of the story of these indigenous ancestors of ours who lived through the Roman occupation and perhaps continued to find shelter in the ruined buildings long after the troops had gone.

Here is the real fascination of Vindolanda: history in the act of rediscovery. Much that has already come to light is of the utmost interest – the opulent bath-house used by both soldiers and civilians, its wall still standing to a height of seven feet and with some of the original plaster adhering: the *mansio* or inn built around an open courtyard, the only example in Britain of such a building and proof if any were needed of the constant coming and going of officials, couriers and merchants along the road into country reclaimed from the wilderness. A growing number of finds speak of the busy and thriving life once lived here – a bronze military standard; a betrothal

Above. Blanchland – Northumberland's most beautiful village.
Below left. The 'Bagpiper', Prior Leschman's Chantry Chapel (1491),
Hexham Abbey. *Below right.* The famous Roman 'Corbridge Lion'
(third century) from Corstopitum

Overleaf. Thomas Bewick's engraving *Chillingham Bull* (1789),
regarded as his masterpiece

medallion made of jet showing a couple embracing, with a motif of clasped hands on the reverse; a Medusa ring; stone altars with inscriptions to gods and goddesses; combs and hairpins; tombstones; and nine gold coins from a purse lost down a lavatory some fifteen hundred years ago. Many of these finds or reproductions of them can now be seen in the recently opened **Museum** next door at Chesterholm, a charming *cottage orné* built by the antiquary Anthony Hedley, who carried out the first excavations.

The most remarkable discoveries at Vindolanda are still being assessed: they include the largest collection of writing tablets on wood so far found in Western Europe. They had been preserved in the detritus of what was probably a tannery. One of them, dated from internal evidence at AD 103, appears to be the draft of part of a letter written by a private soldier at Vindolanda to an influential friend appealing for his help to secure preferment. They are particularly interesting, for they seem to have been joined together in concertina form, and may be the earliest known paged book in the West. For a full evaluation consult the booklet *The Vindolanda Writing Tablets* by A. K. Bowman and J. D. Thomas, and published by Frank Graham, Newcastle upon Tyne. Such discoveries seem likely to ensure that Vindolanda becomes one of the most important of all our Roman sites. With its mock-up of a section of the Wall, both stone and turf, and of a tower gate, it does a visual service to the visitor by giving him some conception of the one-time strength of the fortifications. Perhaps it tries a little too hard to inform and astonish. In fact at present, like Northumberland itself, Vindolanda is being a little over-sold. The narrow valley and approach roads make for serious congestion at the height of the summer season, though a new car park has eased the worst of it: it used to be nothing short of chaotic. However, it is certainly a place that everyone interested in Roman Britain should visit.

Chapter 18

From Chollerford to Hexham

❧

From *The George* it is less than half a mile along the Carlisle road to
the Roman fort of *Cilurnum* at **Chesters**.

In Roman as in more recent times cavalry was the aristocratic
arm. The commander of an *ala* was a *praefectus equitum* and outranked the mere prefects and tribunes who commanded infantry
battalions, cohorts and the fortifications that housed them; he
usually came from the Roman nobility; his camp was much larger
than an infantry camp; and his personal accommodation was of a
size and grandeur to match.

Cilurnum was a cavalry camp: the home, for an unrecorded span
of its history, of the Second Asturian Horse. Even in ruins most
Roman forts retain a sharp, Spartan edge to them – Housesteads
was obviously not built for sybarites. Cilurnum, however, lies in a
hollow, and though its present park-like atmosphere owes a great
deal to early nineteenth-century landscaping by rich squires, it must
even in classical times have been a luxury site, tucked in on a river
bank with an encircling rim of hills to keep off the worst of the
Northumbrian winds.

The camp itself followed the usual 'playing card' pattern of a gated
quadrilateral divided into three blocks, with barracks and granaries
at either end, and the centre taken up by the administrative headquarters (*principia*) and the Commandant's house.

The *principia* at Cilurnum is said by Professor Eric Birley to be
the most impressive example of its kind to be seen in any Roman
work north of the Alps. It measures a hundred and thirty feet by
ninety. Here at the nerve centre of the fort was the *tribunal* where the
Commandant presided on ceremonial occasions, the regimental
chapel where stood a statue of the reigning Emperor flanked by the
ala's standards and flags, also the offices of the adjutant and his
clerks and of the standard-bearers (*signiferi*) who kept the troop
records, besides acting as paymasters and savings bank accountants.
The efficiency and detail of Roman book-keeping is proved by this
camp alone, where the famous Chesters Diploma came to light. It is

now in the British Museum, but an electrotype copy is on view. This extraordinary document, which even in its fragmentary and damaged state matches anything in modern bureaucracy, was engraved in AD 146 on two bronze plates, attesting the grant of Roman citizenship to a veteran whose name and unit have alas! been lost, though other details have survived, including the name of the governor of Britain at the time the gift was made – Papirius Aelianus. The strongroom which lay below the standard-bearers' office can still be seen, with its flagged floor and third-century roof intact. When first examined in the 1830s even its original oak door, sheathed in iron and riveted with square iron nails, had survived the wear and tear of the centuries, if in 'sadly decayed' condition; however, it did not long survive the attentions of the half-skilled excavators, and is now lost to us.

So is most of the fort, apart from the ground plan of its buildings. Only at the main gates, at the *principia*, the Commandant's house and part of the north-east barrack block are there walls standing above ground to edify the modern visitor. Indeed, the most striking building at Cilurnum is not inside the military compound at all but stands some distance apart on the banks of the Tyne – the **Regimental Bath-house.**

Here are the ruins of a sophisticated all-purpose building, a combination of Naafi and Turkish Bath with a trace of Sauna thrown in – one could take one's choice of steam or dry heat. Our islands had to wait fifteen hundred years before such comforts could be enjoyed again. A macabre and still unexplained circumstance surrounds this particular bath-house, for the first excavators in the 1880s found no fewer than thirty-three human skeletons inside it. Had it been converted into a cemetery after the departure of the Army? Or one day, when its garrison was peacefully at dice in the changing room, did the barbarians break in?

Before leaving Chesters no one should fail to spend some time in the **Clayton Memorial Museum** at the entrance to the site. Some of the most important relics from Roman Britain are to be found here – by no means all of them from Cilurnum itself, for John Clayton (1792–1890), who lived in the adjoining mansion in the park, was a keen collector and accumulated trophies from many other forts on the Wall. A rich selection of Roman altars, inscriptions, statuary, pottery, glass and other artefacts are on view, clearly labelled and displayed. Note in particular the building inscription of the Second Asturian Horse, the statue of a river god reclining at a banquet, and the headless statue of a goddess standing on the back of a (regrettably headless) cow: Juno Regina, consort of the Syrian Jupiter – in spite of its mutilated state a superb work of art.

Quite apart from its size, Cilurnum was one of the key forts on the Wall, for it stood where the fortification crossed the North Tyne – the reclining god in the museum is probably one of the guardians of this beautiful stream. Since Roman times it has slightly changed its course, and only at low water can the abutments of the bridge on the Chesters side be seen. In its final development in Roman times the structure was one hundred and ninety feet long and twenty feet wide, carrying a parapet and sentry walk to the north; there were four bays and three piers with cutwaters upstream, and it also incorporated a mill race and a water mill, traces of whose stone can be seen in the museum. The remains of the bridge, however, should not be viewed from Chesters. Return to *The George*, cross the river and follow the footpath southwards downstream to the **Eastern Abutment** of the third-century bridge, which stands high and dry with its massive blocks of dressed stone still in place and fastened with iron clamps. A phallus cut on the southward face of the pier protected the works against the evil eye – there is another to be seen carved in relief in the fort's *principia*.

From *The George* take the B6318 eastward and almost immediately turn right at Brunton crossroads on to the A6079 towards Hexham. After another couple of hundred yards the most conveniently accessible of all Roman sites can be seen on one's left: **Brunton Turret**, where a conserved stretch of the Wall can be seen plunging down the hill. Another half mile brings one to the village of **Wall**, which has a pleasant small hotel, *The Hadrian*. The village itself is by-passed by the road: it has some charming cottages grouped around a green. Another mile and a half to the top of Signing Bank brings the panoramic view of Hexham, its abbey and two medieval towers enclosed in a ring of hills.

Standing near the confluence of the North and South Tyne which with their tributaries of the Rede, the East and West Allen and the Rowley Burn drain nearly half the county, **Hexham** has for centuries been a town of some importance. 'The Heart of All England', King James I and VI called it on his way south to pick up a crown in London in 1603, a name still commemorated in a steeplechase run in April on the racecourse. This was just his blarney. But certainly Hexham is the heart of West Northumberland. Today its role as a centre of communications is obvious to anyone who glances at a road or rail map. Yet to the dismay of local historians Hexham was almost certainly not a Roman site, though it stands close to a whole phalanx of Roman forts: it enters recorded history in the seventh century with the appearance of Aethelfryth, an East-Anglian princess, more popularly remembered as Etheldreda.

In life this remarkable lady clung to her virginity almost to a fault. Married to a king of Northumbria, she refused all reasonable requests and ended her days as an abbess at Ely. Her lands in what is now 'Hexhamshire' must have come to her through a marriage settlement. At all events, in 674 she gave them to her energetic friend Wilfred, Bishop of York, the man whose eloquence at the Synod of Whitby brought Northumbria under the discipline of Rome and who was later canonised, the first of seven saintly or at least sainted bishops whose idealised features can be seen on the altar screen which stands on the site of his Saxon church which has recently celebrated its thirteen hundredth centenary with a visit from the Queen.

From this act of Aethelfryth's a strange territorial dominion took shape, the 'Regality of Hexham'. Even the archbishops of York who inherited it were never able to set an absolute date to it or to produce deeds of gift, though for centuries they continued to enjoy its fruits. It amounted in fact like Durham to an ecclesiastical kingdom within a kingdom – the archbishops built their own castle, held their own courts, appointed their own Justices of the Peace, and generally acted as sovereigns in a palatinate they seldom visited.

Historians may lament the fact that the Regality is no more; it survives only in some of its buildings and in the 'shire', the tract of land to the south which formed part of Queen Aethelfryth's gift and somehow remains to this day a place apart – you can easily lose yourself in it within four miles of the town, in the hills and along the burn, the Devil's Water, which gave Anya Seton the title for one of her best-selling novels.

For thirteen centuries the focus of the shire has been its priory **Church** standing in the heart of the town on a plateau above the Tyne and overlooked on three sides by the hills that enclose the valley. Signing Bank, from which one approaches it from the north, is supposedly so called because it was from this hill-crest that medieval travellers first saw its squat tower and crossed themselves in gratitude for a safe deliverance from Scots and reivers. Two miles further down one gets the same view foreshortened from the handsome bridge over the Tyne (constructed in 1785/8 by Robert Mylne). This was once one of the best town views in England, but in the '30s

277

it was ruthlessly polluted by the raw red backside of a cinema looming enormous on the bluff above the river, and it is kinder to avert one's eyes. The cinema is now closed but the building remains.

From the big Wentworth car park just south of the bridge it is only a short walk up the hill to the market-place and the first close sight of the Abbey. I am afraid a disappointment is in store in John Dobson's mid-nineteenth-century extension of the choir and presbytery. Thrusting into the town, this graceless and dull east front reminds us how much is lost by the absence of a close. Yet one has only to walk on to the **Seal,** the open grassland that laps the Abbey and its outbuildings on two sides – three if one includes the municipal gardens and bowling green – to see this beautiful church in the setting of earlier centuries when its access to the market place was shielded by buildings long since pulled down.

'Seal' may be a corruption of *Champs du Ciel,* a term used of monastic lands and meadows. Stand off it to the south-west and look eastward along the length of Beaumont Street, with its frenchi-fied Queen's Hall, a toy chateau now given over to Bingo, down the line of Hencotes on the Carlisle road and its row of unpretentious but charming houses, taking in on the way in the foreground the elegant bandstand, and turning always clockwise the classical facade of Hexham House and the Prior's Gate by the old graveyard, now severely tidied up and returfed. This of course is not of the quality of Salisbury or Durham's Palace Green, but it is beautiful in an unfussy and natural way. In fact few English town churches provide so intimate and unharassed a view of themselves as Hexham provides for admirers who care to cross the Seal or sit on the benches in the walled garden of Hexham House, within sound of the click of woods on the bowling green, to look back at the Abbey and what is left of the conventual buildings. Seen from that spot, Temple Moore's decorated twentieth-century nave is not the least attractive part of one of the most remarkable churches in the North.

I cannot too highly recommend that you should already have armed yourself by reading *Saint Wilfrid at Hexham,* edited by D. P. Kirby (Oriel Press, 1974), a collection of scholarly essays on the founder, the monastery that he created, and the political and religious setting in which he worked. It throws what was certainly to me a wholly new light on early Christianity in England.

For a tour of the Abbey, start from the westward side with the outbuildings which serve as a reminder that this was a monastic house, a priory of Augustinian or Austin canons founded on the ruins of a much older church in 1113. One of the buildings known as the Abbey House carries the arms of the Carnabys who purloined it at the Dissolution. Rumour long had it that the Prior resisted and was hanged at his own gate or alternatively at Tyburn, but the truth is that though there were disturbances and Hexham played some part in the northern rebellion of the Pilgrimage of Grace, there seem to have been no executions of the dispossessed. Many of the canons were treated with generosity by the Government, and three years after the legendary hanging the last Prior of Hexham was in fact buying himself a prebend's stall at York.

Remains of the monastic buildings cluster around the Abbey on every side except the east, mixed up with a jumble of eighteenth- and nineteenth-century additions. At the centre the site of the cloister is still clearly distinguishable, its western side lined with traces of the medieval *Lavatorium*, a fine group of seven gabled blank arches, elaborately decorated with tracery, trefoiled lights and shafts with elegant capitals. Opposite them to the east-corbel stones mark the line of the cloister roof, and there is the twelfth-century stonework of the cloister garth and to the north a carrell, a recess in the wall close against the body of the church where the canons had their reading desks.

The chapter house stood to the south of the present entrance to the Abbey, overlooking the market-place though cut off from it by houses pulled down in the middle of the last century. But for a few traces of arcading and vaulting it has wholly disappeared. However, its **Vestibule**, dating from the twelfth and thirteenth centuries, has survived as a chapel of rest open to everyone, and one can still see the beams, formed of solid tree-trunks, under the modern roof. In monastic times the canons' dormitory occupied its upper floor. Most of the area around it is still in use: the Hexham magistrates' court, a clinic and other bodies are housed in this ancient complex of buildings which is bounded to the north by the arch of the **Prior's Gate** – the clinic is particularly in keeping, for in monastic times the canons' infirmary provided a similar service near by, with a covered way for coffins leading into the church itself.

The entrance nowadays is directly from the market-place into the **Slype** – a unique one, for it is treated as a gallery enclosed within the church, and the triforium and clerestory of the south transept are carried above it to the window at the head of the celebrated **Night Stairs**. We are entering a church which in Saxon times was described (admittedly by its founder's biographer) as one without rival north of the Alps, 'of marvellous length and height', famous for its polished stone, fine arches and the richness of its vestments, plate and relics;

but let me confess at once that of that Saxon church hardly anything remains above ground. The Danes sacked it in 875 with savage thoroughness; the townspeople of Hexham borrowed much of its stone; and what one sees today are Early English transepts and choir, an east front from the mid-nineteenth century, and a still more modern Decorated nave. Some one hundred and twenty thousand pounds, most of it raised locally, has been spent on restoring the ancient fabric, and another twenty thousand pounds is still needed.

From the slype you emerge into the south transept, with Queen Aethelfryth's (Etheldreda's) chapel immediately to the right, containing a piscina and outsize aumbry, and, close by, the Saxon cross of Bishop Acca, Wilfrid's successor in the see, along with part of another cross that stood by Acca's tomb and two very ancient grave covers that have been brought here from the old apse that now lies below the choir. The view of the **Transepts** from the crossing is very fine. At the upper levels they are of equal size and larger in proportion to the rest of the fabric than any others in the country. Their nearest echo is said to be Plusgardyn near Elgin; and in fact the whole church, excepting the recent additions, is in spirit more Scottish than English, its choir recalling the nave at Jedburgh. Turn eastwards towards the choir and there is its **Rood Screen** – or more accurately its *pulpitum*, since no cross surmounts it. It was built in the last decade of the fifteenth century by Prior Thomas Smithson, whose name is recorded on it no less than three times. Just under the arch, to left and right on entering the choir and easily missed if the panel lights are not on, are two charming paintings in the Flemish style, an Annunciation and a Visitation. The red and green of the rood screen, particularly when viewed from inside the choir, is extremely effective. At some stage, perhaps early in the Reformation, the whole work was covered with whitewash, traces of which can still be seen. From the crossing, the harmony and indeed meaning of this beautiful work is marred by an organ which must be making poor Prior Smithson turn in his grave.

Once in the **Choir** itself one can mark the variations the builders imposed. The arches on the north side have plain mouldings, those on the south are dentelle. All the capitals on the south side are plain: their opposites to the north show wide variations. Even the triforium arches are dissimilar, for on the north side all are dog-toothed, while on the south all but one and a half bays are plain and the circular *motifs* at their centres show varying patterns on both sides. The string courses between triforium and clerestory mark the line of the original roof, the clerestory itself being very high, exceeding in scale anything in an English church below cathedral status. The misericord seats in the rear rows of the stalls deserve more than a passing glance: they would have been finer still if they had not lost their canopies, demolished to provide gallery seats for the quality in 1725, and if the original back rests had not been sold for firewood in the market-place in 1858. Some of these backs have recently been discovered in the triforium, where they had been used to keep out draughts.

Half way between the high altar and the rood screen is the most ancient piece of furniture surviving from St Wilfrid's church: the **Bishop's Throne**, or Frith Stool, which dates from 681. In those days it stood some feet below its present site in the apse of the Saxon church; since when it has been moved from place to place, so clumsily that one can see the crack in the stone caused when the removal men dropped it in 1860. Close to it, under a rug (an infallible sign anywhere of something the church authorities want to keep to themselves) is a modern trap-door, below which a miniature ladder leads down into the old **Apse**. Permission from the verger is required before one can make the descent. This cramped and tiny space encloses the graveyard of the seventh-century building, with its Roman stones, the probable resting place of Bishop Acca, who died in 740, and the tomb of a child at the southern end. The lids of these two coffins are now in the aisle of the South Transept near Acca's cross.

This by no means exhausts the interest of Hexham choir, for one emerges once more up the ladder into the light to be faced with the fifteenth-century **Screen** to the north of the high altar, with its paintings of the seven canonised bishops of Hexham, including St Wilfrid and the hermit St John of Beverley (third and fourth from the left), and then, close behind it, the **Leschman Chantry**. Roland Leschman died in 1491, the last but two of a long line of priors before the Dissolution of 1536. This was his private chapel, and here he lies in effigy with his cowl drawn down over his eyes, a superb and strangely modern evocation of a man. The **Screen** behind the chantry's altar features a rising from the Sepulchre and instruments from the Cruci-fixion, showing a ladder, spears, dice and tongs. Carpenters from York were largely responsible for the work, but other and cruder hands may have made the stone altar, the aumbry and the figure of a traveller, almost elemental in shape.

At this point you should spare a moment or two for the **Outer Wall** of the chantry to the east. You will find it rewarding, if only for the local interpretations of the Scriptures, a Piers Plowman in stone.

The whole work – perhaps a comment by toiling, underpaid masons – rests on the back of a kneeling figure, no Atlas, only a suffering artisan. Near by is St George, but not rescuing any maiden from the dragon; he is mounted like his Saviour on an ass. Figures of gluttony, piety, penance and scholarship confront one; also a fox in clerical dress busily preaching, a man playing the bagpipes (Scottish ones, since the Northumbrian pipes only made their appearance in 1680), and a Border reiver carrying off a sheep.

Here in this mixture of the colloquial and the grand is one of the charms of Hexham Abbey. Moving along the north aisle of the choir past the knight with his crusading lion – Thomas of Devilstone (Dilston) – and the altar tomb near the crossing with its thirteenth-century arcading and canopy and its 'tree of life' motif, perhaps brought back from the East, one comes to the superb **North Transept** and its Early English windows. The glass is Victorian but it does not intrude. The timbered roof is fourteenth-century. Beyond the lady chapel is a column with an alarming, almost Tower of Pisan list to it; however, for all its interest and beauty, the north transept is best of all a setting for the view as one turns and sees beyond the crossing the **South Transept** and the **Night Stairs** down which the canons came from their dormitory for compline. Down them still, at evensong, in a foam of white surplices and scarlet robes, lighted candles in hand, comes the Abbey choir. No other church in England provides such a processional way. Below them as they descend is one of the treasures of the church, the **Tombstone of a Roman Soldier,** who is seen riding plumed and armed over the fallen body of some barbarian foe. It came to light in 1881 during excavations in the slype, and its inscription can still be read:

DIS – MANIBVS FLAVINUS
EQ – ALAE – PETR – SIGNIFER
TVR – CANDIDI – AN XXV
STIP – VII – H S.

This Flavinus, then, was a young standard-bearer of the crack cavalry regiment called the *Ala Petriana*, the largest mounted unit kept by the Romans in Britain, one thousand strong, stationed for a while at *Corstopitum*, from whose ruins this memorial stone must have been filched by medieval masons in search of building material to repair the abbey church.

After choir and transepts, Temple Moore's worthy but rather frigid **Nave** need not long detain one; but pause a moment, for in the south-east corner some of the original Saxon floor is still exposed, and part of the stonework of the south wall may also date from this time. Beneath it, reached by a staircase in the central aisle, lies the **Crypt** of St Wilfred's church. One must see the verger before visiting it. The descent takes us back in an instant a whole millennium and more. For according to the Saint's biographer, Eddi, the crypt dates from 674. It is virtually intact. The plaster on the walls is original and concrete-hard. Much of the stone is Roman from *Corstopitum* and still bears the broached tooling of the Roman masons' marks. For centuries this unique treasure lay hidden from the world: it was only rediscovered in 1725 when a workman on the site of the ruined nave accidentally fell into it. Traces of the old spiral staircase leading up to the church are still visible. Along the walls are niches that held the oil lamps, the cressets with their chimney above to draw off the fumes. And all around us are the living traces of Rome. The arch-head in the north passage is an altar stone to the god Maponus, dedicated by a centurion of the Sixth Legion; and a roofing slab carries a building inscription commemorating the restoration of a granary at *Corstopitum* between AD 205 and 208. Two emperors' names are on it, Severus and Caracalla; the name of Caracalla's brother and joint Emperor, Gaeta, was erased by order of the tyrant in 212, and one can still see the marks on the stone where it was chipped out.

An abbey of such size and grandeur to serve a town of modest size would seem to be enough, but medieval Hexham had two other churches. Even the site of one of them, St Peter's, is conjectural, but in a ginnel directly to the south of the market-place a bricked-up arch still remains of the old parish church of St Mary's, other traces of which were discovered in the rather secular surroundings of what is now *The Grapes*, a pub of character whose finely decorated glass in the windows looking out on the lane still called St Mary's Chare is most enticing.

The adjoining market-place, spoilt though it now is by the destruction of the old houses that screened the priory from the town and by much insensitive rebuilding, still retains some of its attractions: the Shambles, an open loggia with Tuscan columns dating from 1766, and the Temperley Memorial Fountain which looks much more venerable than its date of 1901. Here on Tuesdays is held the weekly street market to coincide with the cattle and sheep sales off Battle Hill. It is overlooked by a medieval building, a mere stripling when compared with St Wilfrid's crypt, but frowning today on the citizens as it has done for five and a half centuries – the gateway called the **Moot Hall,** which was the courtroom and *garderobe* of the bishops of York when they held the Liberty and Regality of Hexham.

It is an interesting though not particularly attractive building, in appearance reminiscent of the much earlier Black Gate in Newcastle. The ground floor has a semi-circular barrel vault in one span and a newel stair leading up into what was once a chapel. It now houses a library and art gallery – the opening hours are eccentric but are set out on a green plaque just off the market-place. In prints of the town the gateway looks very well in its setting of the market-place before the old houses in Fore Street were pulled down, but nowadays it has an incongruous appearance in company with modern shop fronts and the one-time cinema. In the time of the Prince Bishops it was part of a fortress commanding the hill above the Tyne and forming a position of considerable strength. What was once the bailey of the castle is now taken over by a road, a club and the modern offices of the Tynedale District Council, but its ancient prison – Hexham's second tower, known as the **Manor Office** – still stands, and we know its date with accuracy from the records. It was built between 1330 and 1332, entirely of dressed Roman stone, almost certainly from *Corstopitum*, since a cart-load of similar material was found in modern times where it had overturned in transit when fording the Tyne. In appearance this is a more sympathetic building than the Moot Hall, and though probably older by more than half a century, looks much younger and trimmer because of the superior quality of the stone and the recent cleaning it has received. Even in its prime as a dungeon it was not devoid of heart, for in a report of the first Queen Elizabeth's time we learn that 'Everey man may come to ye dore . . . and talk with ye prisoners at all times' – a typically relaxed Northumbrian attitude to the law. It has now received a new lease of life as a regional information centre.

Beyond it, nearer the slope that overlooks the car park and completing an uncommonly handsome group of buildings, is the one-time **Grammar School** (now in private ownership), a Tudor-looking building of whitewashed stone which actually dates from 1684. Built at a cost of one hundred and fifty pounds, it provided for the teaching of seventy pupils in seven classes. A master and an usher formed the staff, with twelve 'honest and discreet parishioners' as governors. By statute the master had not only to be honest and discreet himself but also earnest, over the age of twenty-six, and well furnished with Greek and Latin. Schooling was free for the sons of parishioners, but outsiders had to pay twelvepence a quarter to the master and sixpence to the usher. Classes began at 6 a.m. and continued till 5 p.m., with a break at noon. Scholars were particularly enjoined not to carry swords or daggers. Such traces of a vanished age add immeasurably to Hexham's charms, like the splendidly Victorian chemist's shop of W. G. Gibson and the decorated front of Portnell's, the solicitors in Fore Street, the fine old houses in St Mary's Chare, in Market Street and Gilesgate (all within a stone's throw of the market-place), the old post office, a handsome Georgian building facing the Prior's Gate, and the still finer Hexham House with its gardens behind the Abbey. Pevsner has a special word of praise for the *Midland Bank* (1896 by George Dale Oliver) at the south end of Fore Street – he does not mention one of its charms: that from one angle it has a distinct resemblance to the Temple of the Winds in Athens.

As a tourist centre Hexham has much to recommend it. It has three residential hotels, one of them, the *Beaumont*, overlooking the Seal, with a fine view of the Abbey from its cocktail bar. The racing man has a choice of National Hunt meetings in March, April, May, September, October and December (details from The Secretary, Hexham Race Club, 4 Gilesgate Bank). There is excellent golf at The Spittal, just off the Carlisle Road, and a nine-holer on Tyne Green, tennis on the Seal and at the Tynedale Club on Prior's flats, boating and canoeing at Tyne Green on the south bank just west of the bridge, excellent trout fishing in the Tyne, and two night clubs. Even the salmon are returning now that industrial pollution downriver is being controlled. A music festival is held in the Abbey every October. The town's popularity is steadily increasing. The next tours which cover south-west Northumberland are grouped around this agreeable and relaxed place.

Chapter 19

From Hexham to Corbridge, Bywell and Ovingham

❦

From Hexham take the A69 eastwards. On the right after two miles, in the woods and hardly visible from the road, are the ruins of **Dilston**, the 'pleasant Dilston Hall' of the poem, from which the ill-fated James, third Earl of Derwentwater, rode out in the Jacobite rising of the 'Fifteen which led him to the block on Tower Green. There is nothing for the modern tourist to see, apart from a pedestrian Elizabethan tower house and a chapel supposedly built with funds subscribed for the Gunpowder Plot. The large barrack-like country house which was being built for the third earl was not completed when the rising broke out and was demolished by other owners half a century later. Yet the Derwentwater legend survives. 'He was a man,' wrote the chaplain to the rebel army, 'formed by nature to be generally beloved; for he was of so universal a beneficence that he seemed to live for others.' He certainly died for them, for a cause he knew in his heart was lost, in payment of a childhood debt of loyalty to his exiled king, in whose company he had been brought up at St Germain. He was only twenty-six, a grandson of Charles II on the wrong side of the blanket through a liaison with a certain Mrs Davis.

The Dilston legend involved others of his family. His brother Charles, already implicated in the 'Fifteen, 'came out' again in the 'Forty-Five and in his turn was taken and executed. The family estates were confiscated by the crown and were granted in 1737 to the Commissioners of Greenwich Hospital. A century later in mid-Victorian times a spurious 'Countess', calling herself 'Amelia Radcliffe' and claiming to be a direct descendant of the third earl's son, arrived in Dilston and captured what was left of the ruins in a masterly *coup de main*. It was another Tichborne Case, and caused a huge furore in the neighbourhood before the squatter was finally evicted by the bailiffs – to the outrage of the local population, which retained its devotion to the Derwentwater memory. Indeed, as late as 1909 the third earl's remains were being treated as semi-holy relics, lodged in the Catholic college of Ushaw in Durham.

Another mile and a half brings one to **Corbridge,** a small town on the edge of the Tyneside commuter belt. In Roman times it was a place of the greatest strategic importance where a bridge over the river carried the main north–south road at right-angles to the Stanegate running westward towards Carlisle. From AD 80 to 395 the camp half a mile west of the present town was first a combat headquarters and then the main supply base for the Wall and for forces using Dere Street into Scotland. Nor did Corbridge's role as a communications centre end with the departure of the Legions, for even in ruins the imperial road system continued to dictate the movement of armies for many centuries in an otherwise roadless land – as late as the Wars of the Roses it was along the Roman spur towards Alston that the Lancastrians marched to their defeat at the Battle of Hexham. Corbridge's situation on the Tyne crossing ensured that it should continue to receive every attention from invaders and other adventurers. In 918 it was the scene of a great Danish victory. In 1138 it was occupied by the Scots, who for many years were intent on detaching what is now Cumbria and Northumberland from England. King John visited it on no fewer than three occasions, in 1202, 1208 and 1212, in his obsessional search for treasure rumoured to be buried in the vicinity. He found nothing but to his credit gave the town a charter all the same. And oddly enough his information was good, for there *was* treasure buried near Corbridge – two hoards of gold coins which later and more fortunate seekers unearthed and which are now in the British Museum, not to mention the Corbridge Lanx, a rectangular silver salver which a nine-year-old girl found in the gravel by the river. These caches had also escaped the Scots, who pillaged and burnt the place under William Wallace in 1296, under Robert the Bruce in 1312, and again in 1346, under David II. Phoenix-like, the town rose from the ashes to become in medieval times the largest of Northumbrian boroughs after Newcastle.

Much of this stirring history the modern citizens of Corbridge have inscribed on a tasteful blue plaque with gold lettering which stands in the market-place. There used to be another at the entrance to the **Bridge,** which itself may claim to be one of the handsomest buildings on view: a seven-arched span with impressive cutwaters, it was built in 1673, and is the only Tyne bridge to have survived the great flood of 1771. Now, alas! it is visually almost ruined by the erection alongside it of a 'temporary' satellite structure to ease the

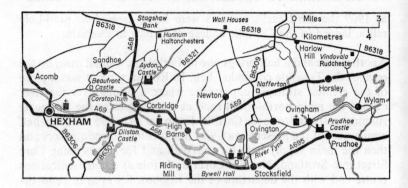

traffic chaos of the summer months. The bridge is seen to best advantage from the Roman station at *Corstopitum*, where its unreconstructed western face appears as good as ever.

The town behind it on the north bank is compact and easy to explore: a grid of three parallel streets leading eastward from the market-place, one of them (Hill Street) running up and down a slope past eighteenth- and nineteenth-century houses against the backdrop of a saucy late Victorian town hall; and beyond it the wide eastern entrance to the town overlooked by the seventeenth-century (restored) *Angel Inn*, a welcoming stopping place for the motorist, particularly in summer when the umbrellas are set out at the tables on the pavement. In the market-place itself is a fine wrought-iron **Cross** erected in the year of Waterloo. Next to it is a stone drinking trough and pyramid of the same date, until recently surmounted by a blue and white pointer, sternly directing one to the Toilets. It was once topped by a ball and cross which have been rediscovered in the long grass outside the north transept of the church. Plans are afoot to restore them to their plinth.

For those with time to spare on a sunny day there is a riverside walk along a footpath that follows the north bank of the Tyne westwards and is reached by turning left from the market-place just before the *Centurion* antique shop. This was the medieval Carelgate which joined the Stanegate. It was in use as a highway till the eighteenth century. It takes one close to the foundations of the Roman bridge, which can be clearly seen when the water is low. If time is running short, however, one should make straight for the **Parish Church**, whose Saxon tower dominates the town.

It is certainly Saxon in its lower stages, and very early Saxon, probably within half a century of St Wilfred's crypt at Hexham. The

The fifteenth-century tomb of Sir Ralph Gray and his wife Elizabeth, St Peter's Church, Chillingham

A female effigy on a wooden table tomb, St Mary's Church, Staindrop

Hexham Abbey

Above. The Night Stairs and
the Saxon Crypt, *below*

Belfry stage, however, was an afterthought, and externally Corbridge cannot compare with two other Tyne churches at Ovingham and Bywell St Andrew. Internally it is another matter; indeed Corbridge contains a number of features which make it one of the most interesting in the country.

The entrance is through a modern porch and then a Norman doorway with zigzag decoration. One of the two excellent guides to the building recommends the visitor at this point to sit down in one of the pews at the back of the nave. I would advise him, on the contrary, to make for the crossing, from which vantage point the church reveals its finest treasures at a glance.

Behind one to the west, between nave and tower, rises a massive and complete **Roman Arch**, lifted by our Saxon ancestors from *Corstopitum*. The original Saxon nave has vanished but traces of its window heads can be seen high up on the north wall of its thirteenth-century successor. Most of the rest of the church is of this period, though the east wall and the lancet windows are replacements, far more appropriate ones than the modern clerestory windows of the nave which give light but are otherwise regrettable. The thirteenth-century **Chancel Arch** is particularly fine, as is the south wall of the **Chancel** with its lancets and its priest's door, now screened by curtains. Such other restoration as has been permitted in the church is unobtrusive, except for the truly appalling window in the west wall of the tower replacing the ancient entrance door. Those who are familiar with Ovingham will notice a resemblance, though here the nave is of three bays, not two, and the chancel is longer, indeed longer than the nave itself. As in so many of these early Northumbrian churches there is not a great deal to be seen in the way of monuments. Behind the vicar's seat is a gravestone used as a window head in the manner that is repeated at neighbouring Blanchland and Bywell. But recessed into the wall at the end of the north transept is a much finer gravestone that tells us something of the man it commemorates – '*Hic Jacet in Terris Aslini Filius Hugo*' – for it is known from other sources that this Hugh, son of Aslin, was a wealthy citizen of Corbridge in 1296, the year of the first devastation of the town by the Scots. On the wall of the south aisle of the nave two carved stone heads of uncertain origin gaze down on the visitor. Masks of Tragedy and Comedy? One of them certainly has a markedly lugubrious air. They are reminiscent of another pair of heads on the gatehouse of nearby Prudhoe Castle. Near them hang a halberd and staff, the insignia of the manor court used at the proclamations of Stagshaw Fair, held from 1204 on the common two miles north of the town.* The photograph on the wall beside them shows these symbols in actual use, but the Fair itself was suppressed by Home Office order in 1927. Also of interest in Corbridge church is the pewter and some ancient books displayed at the entrance to the chancel.

In the churchyard is the one-time **Vicarage**, eloquent of the troubled history of the Border. It takes the form of a thirteenth-century fortified tower house built of Roman stone. It is now restored to house a museum and lecture room, and has a Tourist Information Centre on the ground floor. In fact, Corbridge has two peles, for another dating from the sixteenth century stands at the eastern exit from the town on the Newcastle road, next door to the Jacobean Low Hall.

From the market-place it is only a short distance to Corbridge's other prime attraction, the Roman station of **Corstopitum**. Take the A68 northwards and after one hundred and fifty yards turn left where the 'Ancient Monument' sign points the way, and left again after a quarter of a mile on to the site, which has a car park.

The place is believed to have been chosen by Agricola during his campaign in North Britain in AD 78/84. A forward base was needed on the lines of communication to the north (later called 'Dere Street') along the route of the present A68. Agricola's engineers also built a lateral road running eastward towards Carlisle – the Stanegate – and later a branch spur towards Alston was added to the complex. All these roads met at or near Corbridge, where the ground was favourable for a bridge over the Tyne. *Corstopitum* itself was not part of the Wall, which was built some seventy years later to the north of it in Hadrian's time; but first as a military headquarters, then as a supply base, and finally as depot and centre of Roman influence, the camp survived through many vicissitudes until early in the fifth century the Legions were withdrawn and the whole area lapsed into barbarism. Forts and buildings remained. Perhaps for a while they continued to house a native Romanised population, and later still they provided Hexham and Corbridge with quantities of good dressed stone. Above all the roads remained, ensuring the continued importance of the district for many centuries.

What is left of *Corstopitum* today lacks the scenic grandeur of wild moorland to be found at Housesteads or the cosiness of Chesters in its woods. Nor at first sight does it look very large. One must re-

*Rudyard Kipling stayed at Stagshaw on the line of the Roman Wall when writing *Puck of Pook's Hill*. A BBC radio mast, a landmark for miles around, was built on Stagshaw Hill in 1937.

member that one is seeing only the core of a camp which in Roman times had its fringe of civilian settlements spreading out in cruciform around it. In fact the ruins are much more extensive than they seem – the storehouse alone covers an acre. From the plan in the guide-book one may deduce (though it is not set out in black and white) that the Stanegate bisected the camp: Dere Street to the North crossed it slightly to the east of the present excavations. North of the Stanegate are the **Storehouse**, the largest Roman work in Britain, and the **Granaries**, whose massive shape is eloquent of the scope and efficiency of Roman public works. Experts believe that during the reign of the Emperor Septimius Severus (who was in Britain from 208 until his death in 211) plans may have been made to create a legionary fortress here to replace York; but nothing came of it and the military importance of the site declined with the retrenchment of Roman power in the second half of the third century. South of the Stanegate are the remains of two military compounds and some temples. Most of the rest of the camp seems to have consisted of shops and houses in which lived the blacksmiths, armourers, potters and others who supplied the needs of the garrison.

The modest **Museum** on the site is run by the Trustees of the Corbridge Excavations Committee in alliance with the Department of the Environment and Durham University. The two hoards of gold coins which escaped King John have been moved elsewhere (though you can see replicas in the showcases). But there is still enough on view to fascinate the visitor: the famous **Corbridge Lion** devouring a stag (from one of the Roman mansions which stood on Dere Street), several fine building inscriptions and altars, models of the camp and of the Roman bridge, and movingly the works of the craftsmen who once lived here and left behind them artefacts to lie alongside the goods imported from all over the Roman world – jars, cooking pots, urns, lamps, horse harness, brooches, keys, hair-pins, armour, gardening tools, unspillable inkpots, cow bells, surgical instruments, and fragments of glass of a quality not to be matched in Britain for many a long year.

For a glimpse of the society that slowly and painfully evolved out of the Dark Ages into the Middle Ages in this same countryside along the line of the ruined Wall, take the A68 northward out of Corbridge and after a mile up the hill turn right on the minor road signposted to Halton and Aydon. Follow it for a mile and a half to a T-junction, with a pleasant view to your left of **Halton Tower**, an old North-umbrian pele now restored and in private ownership. However, the adjacent chapel, which stands on a site where a church has existed since the eighth century, is open to the public – the key can be obtained from the cottage close by. For **Aydon** turn right at the junction. There is no signpost, but a further mile brings one to a notice board, 'Bridle Path Only', with the battlements of the **Castle** looming ahead. It is not at the moment of writing open to the public, but restoration is in progress by the Department and Aydon will shortly take its place as one of Northumberland's attractions, a building of outstanding architectural importance – an early fortified manor house with an outer and inner bailey but no keep, situated in a position of great natural beauty above the densely wooded Cor Burn. Its main feature is its Hall on the first floor, reached by an outside staircase. This paramilitary creation, warmed by a huge fireplace on the ground floor, tells us more about the uncertain and vulnerable progress of civilisation in the North than can be learnt from a dozen books and museums. A little further afield is the pretty village of **Matfen**. A stream runs through the centre of the village, and there is an eight-foot-high prehistoric pillar in front of Standing Stone Farm.

From Aydon return to Corbridge and take the A69 towards Newcastle. After two miles turn right on to the minor road towards Stocksfield, turning right just before the bridge over the Tyne into the cul-de-sac to **Bywell**. (One can also go by the A68 and A695 south of the river, turning left just before Stocksfield Station.)

It would be hard to find another such eighteenth-century print of rural England, marred only by the thought that all this beauty was brought about by 'enclosure' and the destruction of a living community. For Bywell was once a place of consequence. A king of England – Henry VI fleeing from Hexham field in May 1464 after the Lancastrian defeat – found shelter in its castle, whose tower house still stands: the royal helmet, sword, horse-trappings and indeed crown were later found within its walls when the fortress surrendered to the Yorkist commander, Lord Montagu. A report of 1570 describes the village as inhabited by 'handy craftsmen' whose trade was in 'yron worke for the horsemen and borderers of that countrey'. In 1580, at the mustering of the Middle March, one hundred and one men from the lordship of Bywell presented themselves before the commissioners. Drawings of 1745 show a still sizeable community strung out along the banks of the Tyne, and as late as 1825 it contained some twenty houses and an inn. Of that village nothing remains but a number of patrician houses and *two* churches.

Standing in retreat, no more than a stone's throw apart in this all but deserted spot, they take some explaining. One local legend (unfortunately without foundation) has it that they were built by two sisters vying in rivalry with one another – perhaps a romanticised folk memory of the fact that they were built in what came to be different baronies, St Peter's in the barony of Baliol, St Andrew's in that of Bolbec. As recently as the beginning of this century they were popularly known in the district as the 'black' and 'white' churches, St Peter's having belonged to the black-robed Dominicans of Durham, St Andrew's to the White Canons whom we shall meet later at Blanchland: an exact reversal of the impression they give the visitor inside their doors, for 'white' St Andrew's is as dark and gloomy as 'black' St Peter's is filled with light and grace. They are still in different parishes. St Peter's is Stocksfield's church, separated from its parishioners by a river and a good mile and a half's walk. St Andrew's has, for all practical purposes, apart from the occasional wedding or funeral, no parishioners at all; its work has been usurped by the church at Riding Mill and it has officially been declared redundant, though fortunately it is to be maintained out of the Church Commissioners' special fund. There can be few odder parochial arrangements than those that are found here in these two fine buildings which have outlived their purpose.

Architecturally **St Andrew's** is the more exciting: its slim un-buttressed **Saxon Tower** is reckoned to be the finest of its kind in Northumberland, an area rich in such work. Its lowest stage, distinguished from the rest by the colour and coarseness of the stone, is of the early tenth century; the other three stages of this elegant campanile with its fine belfry lights date from about a century later, but they too are probably pre-Conquest. The rest of the church (apart from the nineteenth-century additions in the north transept and chancel) is late thirteenth-century, when rebuilding took place following a disastrous fire in 1285 which severely damaged St Peter's also. Some wedding celebrations that got out of hand seem to have been the cause. The outside wall of the north transept is notable for the number of gravestones built into it: these were uncovered during the nineteenth-century restoration and put to another use – a typically thrifty Northumbrian habit which one encounters time and again in these churches. The head of the window at the south end of the south transept is formed of a couple of such stones, and the doorway head at the south entrance to the nave is a similar cover from a woman's tomb, marked with the traditional shears and a Latin cross.

Apart from this the interior of St Andrew's fails to live up to the promise of its tower, being dark and cramped, with a nave only two bays long, a chancel of about the same length, and having its north transept entirely given over to an organ. Though immaculately kept, its spiritual isolation from people is all too evident and gives it a forlorn and rejected air. Yet one of the most cheerful of creative talents was baptised here: Robert Smith Surtees, who introduced Mr Jorrocks to the world. The circular graveyard is supposed to have been so designed to keep out evil spirits.

St Peter's, a hundred yards away, stands on the place where Egbert was consecrated Bishop of Lindisfarne in 802. It has less architectural fame than its sister but to my mind is far more sumptuous and beautiful. Its chief glory is the thirteenth-century chancel with three lancets at the east end, the centre lancet taller than the others, giving a subtle splayed effect which may well be an optical illusion. This was an addition to a much older church: a south aisle of the nave was added at about the same time. After the fire of 1285 the almost ruined nave was shortened and the west end of the church was built, with a strong battlemented tower above it which the parishioners must often have used as a refuge for themselves and their cattle from the Tynedale 'theaves', whose depredations in Bywell as late as the middle of the first Queen Elizabeth's reign caused such concern that all livestock had to be driven into the village street and kept there under guard 'during the night season'. The chantry chapel to the north between the nave and the chancel was added in the fourteenth century: a very elegant and spacious extension of a church which is among the most restful and satisfying in Northumberland. On the outside of the south wall is an ancient scratch-dial clock (a kind of sun-dial) for telling the time of services. The church has seen stirring times, in particular the great flood of 1771 when after days of torrential rain the Tyne burst its banks, swept away all but one of the bridges along its course, and submerged Bywell under several feet of water. Inside Bywell Hall it stood eight feet deep, and there was a rush to save the horses. They were led into St Peter's, where the sagacious beasts managed to save themselves by clinging to the backs of the high pews then installed in the church – one mare is said to have jumped on to the Communion table. A child called Mary Leighton was swept away in her cradle but was recovered at the mouth of the Tyne, apparently none the worse for her adventure.

The road westward from here is, as I have said, a cul-de-sac. One must retrace one's steps, severely hemmed in by 'Private: No Admittance' notices on all sides. The tower house where Henry VI took refuge is similarly forbidden ground. But no one can prevent the public from standing on the road looking east from St Andrew's to enjoy the view of the castle and of the patrician nineteenth-century bridge that takes the road across the river to Stocksfield.

This village is an outrider in the Newcastle commuter belt. A short run east from it along the south bank of the Tyne brings us to the small industrial town of **Prudhoe**, until recently one of the bases of ICI. Its ancient **Castle** on the road signposted to Low Prudhoe, between the river and the main road, is at the time of writing closed to the public, except for the lawns and outworks of Peel Yard, but when the Department of the Environment has finished its current excavations a most rewarding experience will await the visitor at this one-time stronghold of the d'Umfravilles and of the Percy earls who inherited it through a failure in the Umfraville male line about the time of the accession of Richard II. (The tomb of the most famous of the d'Umfravilles, Gilbert II, is in Hexham Abbey with his effigy on it. The lady beside him was probably not his wife; she seems to have been transferred there by mistake. Gilbert was one of Edward I's commanders and died in the same year as his master, 1307.) The keep is earlier, from Henry II's reign: a small but solid structure, originally with a first-floor chamber above a vaulted undercroft, and later given a second-floor chamber. The curtain wall of the outer bailey is in good repair, as is the thirteenth-century semi-circular tower at its north-west corner. But it is the **Gatehouse** of the outer bailey that really takes the eye. The lowest stage is pierced by a gateway with round-headed Norman arches; its ceiling is barrel vaulted; and the massive transverse ribs spring from corbels beneath which are two carved human heads. Reached by an open stairway is the thirteenth-century chapel, with an oriel window in the sanctuary which may be the first of its kind ever built in England. For good measure, alongside the gatehouse is a fourteenth-century **Barbican**, regarded by many experts as of the finest in the North.

This castle, once regarded as impregnable, and indeed strong enough to hold out against a Scottish army on two occasions, had become semi-ruinous by 1586 and two centuries later a mere shell. It was partially restored by the second Duke of Northumberland between 1808 and 1818, when a dwelling house was erected alongside the keep. But something of its strength and romantic history can still be glimpsed by the visitor who crosses the Tyne bridge and looks back at the ruins on the steep bank above the river. Some of modern Prudhoe is hidden from this angle and the castle looks much as it appears in eighteenth-century prints.

*

That rural Northumberland can also be seen looking north to **Ovingham**, a still more ancient site, the tower of whose church was certainly standing when the first d'Umfravilles came here in the Conqueror's time. Seen from the bridge, church, vicarage and village form a harmonious group, with hardly a hint of the suburban development that lies behind the ancient roof-line. There is an old packhorse bridge over the Whittle Burn. The Vicarage is a restored seventeenth-century house with vestiges of a much earlier occupation from the time when it provided lodgings for three canons from Hexham Priory. The **Church**'s unbuttressed **Tower** of coursed rag stone is Saxon work, probably from the last two decades before the Conquest, and reminiscent of Bywell St Andrew, even down to the details of the bell openings of two lights with a pierced circle in the spandrel. Seen at close quarters the workmanship is not as fine and the colour of the stone lacks the glow one finds at Bywell, but it stands better, where far more people can admire it from the bridge or from the pay trains shuttling between Newcastle and Carlisle on the south side of the river.

Entrance is by a fourteenth-century porch enclosing an Early English doorway – a very striking introduction which can be compared with its Norman equivalent at Corbridge. The resemblances and divergences between a whole group of nearly-related churches in the Tyne valley form a fascinating study. Internally, as externally in the tower, Ovingham is an echo of Bywell St Andrew. Repeated is the short two-bay nave, the proportionately large transepts, the aisleless chancel. But here the effect is much more spacious – two further bays carry the arcades of the nave past the entrance to the transepts and lead the eye into the chancel with its superb group of Early English **Lancets** behind the altar. Notice the massive strength of the walls and the great height of the arches of nave and transepts, all subservient to the still higher chancel arch. The old chancel was pulled down in 1195, and what we see in its place must date from the early thirteenth century. Much of the interior of the church is of this period: the transepts with their Early English lancets, also the nave, though its north aisle and windows were restored in the year of Queen Victoria's accession.

The church has a further distinction apart from its architecture: its graveyard is the resting place of Thomas Bewick, who, in the words of the inscription in the chancel, 'restored the art of engraving on wood'. This is no more than the truth, for here is no provincial reputation. From his workshop in St Nicholas's churchyard in

Newcastle between 1790 and 1804 three important books, *The History of Quadrupeds*, *The History of British Land Birds* and *The History of British Water Birds*, raised Bewick to European renown and wood-engraving to a status it had not enjoyed for centuries. He was born on the other bank of the Tyne at Cherryburn. He went to school in the vicarage at Ovingham; he married an Ovingham girl; and at the height of his fame it was Ovingham and its countryside that he remembered and reproduced in many of the enchanting tail-pieces in his books. 'I would rather,' he wrote, 'be herding sheep on Mickley Bank top than remain in London, although for so doing I was to be made Premier of England.'

His creative activity seems to have come about more by accident than anything else, for Bewick was no trained naturalist. Apprenticed at the age of fourteen to Ralph Beilby – of the family responsible for that Beilby engraved glass which now commands such fabulous prices in the sale-room – he seems to have been directed into wood-engraving, the cheap end of the trade, because Ralph was more interested in the prestigious work in silver. Long after he had become his own master, the artist of *Land Birds* spent only a fraction of his time at this kind of task – his living had to be made from copper-plate engravings for bill heads, cheques, invitation cards and so on. Humble artisan though he might seem to be, however, he did not altogether elude the tributes of famous contemporaries. Ruskin, speaking of the 'precision of his unerring hand – his inevitable eye – his rightly judging heart', called him 'the Burns of painting', and Wordsworth (in rather regrettable verse) acclaimed the skill and genius of a man whose observation of nature was the equal of his own. 'The greatest nature teacher and illustrator of his age' is the verdict of Lyall Wilkes in his recent book *Tyneside Portraits* – a timely reminder, for Bewick was in some danger of being forgotten. The high spiked railings which once enclosed his grave have been removed, and even the lettering on the funeral slab is hard to read. The inscribed stone that stood behind it, just outside the west wall of the tower, has been moved also and is now inside the porch, immediately to your right as you enter. I wonder how many glance at it. Near by is the grave of Mabel Stephenson, who should surely be honoured as the grandmother of railways. Her famous son George was born at **Wylam**, the next station to Prudhoe up the line, where their cottage has been preserved. It was from Wylam Colliery that the first of all locomotive engines, *Puffing Billy*, built by William Hedley, pulled coal wagons to Lemington in 1813. Hedley is buried not far off on the other side of the Tyne at Newburn, whose parish registers record George Stephenson's two marriages of 1802 and 1819.

At Nafferton, on the hills behind Ovingham to the north, is supposed to have lived a famous robber and desperado known as Long Lonkin. The neighbouring Lord of Welton had occasion one day to ride far from home:

> The Lord said to his ladie
> As he mounted his horse,
> 'Beware of Long Lonkin
> That lies in the moss.'

> The Lord said to his ladie
> As he rode away,
> 'Beware of Long Lonkin
> That lies in the clay.'

> 'What care I for Lonkin
> Or any of his gang?
> My doors are all shut
> And my windows penned in.'

But alas!

> There are six little windows,
> And they were all shut;
> But one little window,
> And that was forgot.

The ballad is a small masterpiece of menace. Through the open window Long Lonkin crept in to slaughter both mother and child. Welton pele still stands, though incorporated into a farmhouse, a conversion very common in Northumberland. The ruins of Nafferton Tower are shown on some maps as Lonkin's Hall. The murderer's ghost was long supposed to haunt the Whittle Dene near the present reservoirs under Harlow Hill, where tradition has it that he hanged himself on an oak tree or tumbled into the burn and was drowned. The Boggle Burn which runs into the dene may have been named for him, for 'boggle' is Northumbrian for 'ghost'. In her delightful book *Northumbrian Heritage*, Nancy Ridley, who lives near by at Wylam, tells us that as late as the 1890s mothers were still scaring their children with Long Lonkin's ghost if they stayed out after dark.

To return to modern times. From Ovingham a road north of the river passed through workaday **Ovington**, where *The Highlander Inn* is a good place for an evening meal. From here one can rejoin the A69 or take the minor road closer to the river, emerging in either case at Corbridge, from where one can continue on the north bank under the hill on which stands Beaufront Castle (1837/41) to end the round trip at Hexham. Alternatively, from Ovingham the motorist can cross back to the south bank of the Tyne through Stocksfield to **Riding Mill,** whose pleasant *Duke of Wellington Hotel* was once a famous meeting place for witches from all over the county. Four of them were tried at Newcastle in 1673, and there was the usual evidence of dancing with the Devil, transformation into cats and hares, aerial riding, not for a change on broomsticks but on dishes and eggshells, and the local peculiarity of swinging on a rope for rewards of food and wine. The sensible Northumbrian jury acquitted them all.

Chapter 20

From Hexham to Blanchland
and Weardale

Leave Hexham by the road which leads south off the town's main artery of Battle Hill, opposite the entrance to Fore Street and the Midland Bank. Just above the War Memorial Hospital take the left fork on the Slaley road which goes steeply up the slope, and if one looks back from the hill-crest there is a remarkable bird's-eye view of the Abbey almost directly below. Another mile and a half brings one to **Linnels Bridge**. Near it, by the banks of the Devil's Water, the Battle of Hexham was fought in 1464. The name 'Devil's Water' has nothing to do with the carnage of that forgotten field, or with the Devil either, for that matter – the ancient name of the burn was Dyvels, of which Dilston is a corruption – but the fight, though small by the scale of Towton, was of importance, being the last fling of the Lancastrian cause in the North. From the battle-field the poor weak-witted Henry VI fled for sanctuary into Bywell Castle; his army commander, Somerset, was captured and had his head chopped off in Hexham market-place. Confusingly, there were *two* battles of Hexham within a mile of one another, for a year earlier, in 1463, Henry's Queen – the fiery Margaret – had also been defeated along this same burn, to wander forlornly in the woods with her young son (later to be killed by the Yorkists at Tewkesbury) till rescued, tradition says, by a bandit who sheltered and fed them in a cave. (The bandit of the story may have been a certain Robert who was hanged in Hexham market-place after the Lancastrian defeat of the following year.) The place was often shown to hardy and credulous Victorian travellers but can hardly be reckoned a tourist attraction today. However, Linnels Bridge is a delight. It carries a stone inscription duplicated on both the inner and outer sides of the north parapet. Only a few letters can now be made out, but at the beginning of this century the inscription was quite legible and was recorded in the archives:

GOD PRESAR
VE
WMFOIRA ERENGTON
BELLDETE THIS BREGE OF
LYME AND STONE
1581

Slightly rearranged, one sees it is verse:

God preserve Humphrey Errington
(Who) built this bridge of lime and stone
(In) Fifteen hundred and eighty-one.

Sadly, Humphrey Errington's bridge along with its founder has vanished from mortal sight, only this stone remaining. In 1698 the joint owners of the adjoining land found themselves presented by the grand jury at Hexham Quarter Sessions for allowing it to fall into ruin, and it is from this year that probably dates the span we now see leaping the Devil's Water in one graceful arc.

This tract of country, now heavily afforested, is a strangely remote and secretive place. The land drains steeply into the Tyne by the Devil's Water and the Rowley Burn, and its peacefulness attracts wild life. A naturalist friend who lives there tells me that seventy-five species of bird breed in the 'shire'; and that the dipper and heron and pied-flycatcher are often seen along its streams. Three miles to the south of the Linnels Bridge this countryside merges into the moorland which with hardly a break stretches down through County Durham to the Pennines separating Yorkshire from Lancashire. One could hardly find a bleaker place. Then the road rounds the shoulder of a hill and below lies a village which is without doubt one of the most beautiful and idyllic in England – **Blanchland**, named for the Premonstratensian monks, the 'white canons', who built a monastery on this site on the banks of the Derwent towards the middle of the twelfth century.

To see the village in perspective leave the car in the car park outside the north gate, cross the square to the bridge, and then look back from the rising ground beyond it. What one sees is an L-shaped Italianate piazza enclosed by a gatehouse to the north, with a turret adjoining to the east, and the tower, choir and transept of a church set back some distance to the north-east. It is a monastic site, but one that was developed about 1750 with a fine disregard for medievalism by the trustees of a Hanoverian bishop in the altogether more secular time of the Age of Reason. Even Pevsner is uncertain how

301

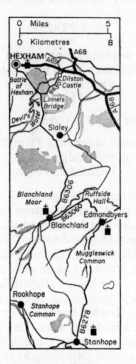

far these self-confident improvers followed the ancient ground-plan in making their model village. But whatever the answer the results are marvellous. There is not an ugly or even an injudicious building to be seen within the square: all is harmony and light. And look beyond it to the houses on the hill: their terracing adds to the general sense of order and serenity.

The *Lord Crewe Arms* stands on the site of what was once the Abbot's lodging and the guest house. Edward III probably stayed there during his visit to the priory in July 1327 on campaign against the Scots. Apart from two gargantuan chimneys and a barrel-vaulted bar it is solidly Georgian. The eighteenth-century spirit has almost wholly absorbed that of the twelfth – the great name in Blanchland is not a Plantagenet king, or Saint Norbert, who founded the Premonstratensian order, but Dorothy Forster the younger, whose part in the rising of the 'Fifteen formed the subject of Sir Walter Besant's romantic novel of that name published in 1884.

Dorothy was the niece of Lady Crewe, who before her marriage to the Bishop of Durham and lord of Blanchland had been also born

302

Dorothy Forster – a very provoking complication to a story which Sir Walter made still more distracting by involving his young heroine, on no historical evidence whatsoever, in an ill-starred passion for James, third Earl of Derwentwater, whose trail we have already crossed at Dilston. But Dorothy's ride in disguise to London and her rescue of her Jacobite brother from the Tower are facts as romantic as any fiction, and the local guide is right in recommending the opening chapters of this stirring book to visitors to the house in which she lived. Portraits of both these ladies, niece and aunt, hang in the hotel – Dorothy the younger in the first-floor room named after her which may have been the parlour of the manor house of her time built on the site of the Abbot's lodging; Lady Crewe on the stairs outside. From reception hall to Georgian dining room and bar, the whole hotel breathes an air of solid comfort. It is a great venue for fell walkers and fishermen. In summer its garden is one of the most peaceful places that I know. All around him the visitor will find traces of the past: stonework of a lost nave jutting out from a wall; an arch of a recess where the canons carried out their ablutions; foundations of a hospital half hidden in the grass.

The **Church**, whose walls one sees from the cloister garden, shows this same quiet, unpretentious character. By comparison with Corbridge or Bywell it is a little disappointing: a truncated, L-shaped building, mirroring in this the pattern of the piazza outside. The tower is set not at the west but at the end of the north transept: a normal arrangement with Premonstratensian abbeys but seldom found elsewhere. No nave is in existence. At some unrecorded stage it either fell down or was destroyed by the Scots, who are known to have been ravaging the countryside around Blanchland in October 1346, two days before their defeat outside Durham at Neville's Cross. On another occasion the canons are said to have been in the act of ringing their bells in thanksgiving for their escape from a Scottish raid, when the raiders, lost in a mist on the fells, heard the glad tidings and turned back to sack the place. The same tale is told of Hexham and Brinkburn Priory. Even naveless, however, and lacking a south transept, Blanchland's church is still a building of charm and piety.

Most of the best of it is close around you as you enter under the tower. The massive round pillar in the transept's east aisle is believed to be part of the original building put up when the white canons first came to the valley in 1165. Nothing else survives from that time, except perhaps the font which seems to be Norman. The tower with its splendid tower arch dates from the fourteenth century; the transept as far as the entrance to the choir is somewhat earlier, and the lancet windows to the right on entering are in Perpendicular style. Opposite them, to the left, several gravestones are let into the floor. Two of those who lie there were abbots, as can be seen from their pastoral staffs; two were abbey huntsmen, with their swords, bows, arrows and hunting horns; one was a woman, Cecilia Herbun, marked by the symbolic scissors or shears cut in the stone.

The rest of the church need not long detain us – it takes the form of an unexciting Hanoverian choir with a Victorian east wall, window, ceiling and reredos. As you stand below the altar, the north wall to your left with its two lancets is thirteenth-century work; so is part of the south wall with one lancet and a circular shaft and capital in the otherwise modern sedilia behind the choir stalls. The glass is modern, except for three interesting thirteenth-century fragments – two of them high on the left above the altar, one in the south window above the sedilia, showing white canons at prayer and a symbolic representation of the Passion. In the churchyard John Wesley preached to the local lead miners in 1747; he was very active in the district about this time, performing the same office, though no doubt to much larger crowds, in Hexham market-place. The thirteenth-century stone cross on the right, half way down the path, may be a memorial to the canons killed in Scottish raids, but this is conjectural. From the village there is a pleasant walk along the banks of the **Derwent Reservoir**, which has a sailing club.

Blanchland lies right on the Durham border, and from Hexham acts as a stage on one of the routes into **Weardale**.

Out of the village the road rises steeply over the bleak moorland that forms the watershed, often impassable in winter. Away to the left is **Edmundbyers**, whose church (heavily restored in 1858) dates from Norman times. It is a real jackdaw of a church that has accumulated furnishings from far and wide. The vestry door in the chancel is from old St Nicholas's in Durham, the pew ends and panelling from Auckland Palace and Durham Castle, the wood of the vestry at the west end from the organ cases at Durham Cathedral and St Mary Radcliffe in Bristol, and its carved doorway from Riding Mill Hall, just over the county border in Northumberland. However, it has managed to retain its own pre-Reformation altar slab. The view from the graveyard looking out from the screen of trees to the moors has a distinct flavour of *Wuthering Heights*. From the high ground on Muggleswick Common there is a grandstand view of the vast ironworks at **Consett**, a spectacular fiery furnace by night when they are

eaton Delaval Hall

bove. The North Front and
e Great Hall, *below*

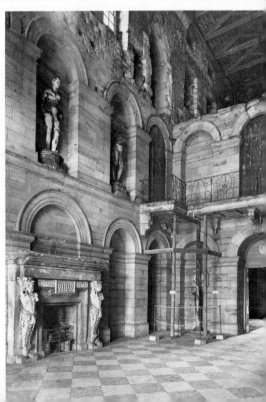

Wallington Hall

Above. The Stables. *Below*. The 'Heads' – eighteenth-century griffins, formerly at Bishopsgate, London

tipping. Consett's railway viaduct at Hounsgill by Sir Thomas Bouch is a fine piece of Victorian engineering (1856).

The roads over the hills going south from Blanchland and Edmund-byers meet a few miles before the descent into Weardale and the ancient village of **Stanhope**, ten miles downstream from the source of the river. Upper Weardale is splendid walking country, abounding in burns and small waterfalls, called 'linns' here as in North-umberland. Both the Harthope and Killhope burns are fascinating places to explore, particularly for the rock formations at Burtreeford Dyke and the old crushing mill at Killhope with its huge waterwheel, one of the great relics of the lead mining which once brought prosperity to these hills (see page 315). In medieval times this countryside formed part of the Forest of Weardale, which had been enclosed as early as 1327 and was the chief 'chase' of the bishops of Durham, well stocked with game, including the wild boar, hunted here for centuries, as we know from tusks found among a cache of Bronze Age tools (now in the British Museum) unearthed in 1850 in Heathery Burn Cave, and from a Roman altar (found on Bollihope Common and preserved in the vestry of Stanhope parish church) dedicated to the god Silvanus by a huntsman in thanksgiving for killing one. The finds in Heathery Burn Cave were of major importance, proving the very early use of wheeled vehicles and domestication of the horse in these islands; and that these settlers who worked the lead mines of the moor were people of substance is shown by the richness and sophistication of the objects they left behind them: a bronze bucket and spearhead and gold ornaments.

The Weardale mines continued to enrich the speculators for centuries – witness Newcastle's own Dick Whittington, Roger Thornton, who in the 1400s made himself a fortune out of them. This wealth was reflected in the growth of the small town of Stanhope down on the river, where the rectorial tithes were of enormous value for the size of the place, reaching upwards of seven thousand pounds a year in Victorian times at the height of the lead-mining boom. Was it this wealth that attracted to Stanhope a succession of out-standing men? At all events the rectory became through the years a breeding ground for bishops – no fewer than eight of them, including Cuthbert Tunstall, later Bishop of London, and in the mid nine-teenth century the celebrated Bishop Butler, who wrote here his *Analogy*, one of the most influential books of his time. The long rectorial list also includes a Frenchman, Isaac Basire, chaplain to Charles I, who went into exile out of loyalty to his master and was later rewarded at the Restoration with this fat living. It was almost certainly Isaac who brought to Stanhope the two oval wooden carvings, *Adam and Eve* and *Peter and the Fishes*, which hang in the chancel, and the painting of Christ carrying the Cross beside them. The rectory he lived in still stands, though now divided into small houses. Its successor is a handsome seventeenth-century building with a stone commemorating the Peace of Ryswick signed by William III and Louis XIV in 1697. The church itself, though attractively placed on rising ground and displaying an impressive tower of *circa* 1210, is disappointing inside. Most of the fabric is of the thirteenth century. The arcades of the north aisle seem to have been re-used and show two distinct colours, the darker stone being Frosterley marble, quarried only a few miles away on the moor. The 'marble' is actually crystallised limestone packed with an infinity of small fossilised marine creatures. As a material for fonts and other church decoration it is frequently found in County Durham and its fame spread to many countries in the western world. In a gap in the churchyard wall facing the main street is Stanhope's most peculiar exhibit: the lower part of the trunk of a fossilised tree that was growing near Edmundbyers two hundred and fifty million years ago. It tends to put things in perspective.

Seven miles downriver from the town is **Wolsingham**, home of England's oldest Agricultural Show.

There are two ways out of Stanhope on the road over Bollihope Common to Middleton. In a dry summer a car can cross the Wear by the ford: a great attraction for children if bad for the brakes. In normal conditions the bridge is better. The route passes Stanhope Hall, a very ancient building now predominantly Tudor in appearance.

For Teesdale and Barnard Castle, see page 315.

Chapter 21

To the South Tyne and Allendale

❦

The South Tyne rises across the Cumbrian border on Bellbeaver Rigg, an outrider of Cross Fell, less than a mile from the infant stream of the Tees. For the first part of its course it runs slightly west of north as though anxious to flow into the Solway rather than the North Sea, but at Haltwhistle makes a sharp U-turn to the east to join its equally wayward sister the North Tyne at Warden rocks, a couple of miles above Hexham. On the way it receives the waters of the united East and West Allen near Bardon Mill, providing some of the best river and dale scenery in Northumberland. Behind the thickly wooded valleys it is lapped by moorland on every side – Alston Moor, Allendale Common, Plenmeller Common, the fells near Brampton and Shepherdshield Moor on the far side of the Roman Wall – but somehow it feels far less remote from the world than North Tynedale, and its villages have the dour appearance of the small mining towns of County Durham. Indeed, the whole area belongs more to Durham than to Northumberland, and this goes for the local accent which is devoid of the long rolled 'r' of the Northumbrian burr. Even its history has been a shade less bloody and devoted to raiding and 'shifting', the way of life along the North Tyne and the Rede. It was fortunate in that the Scots were just that bit further away. And in the eighteenth century it was one of the areas where John Wesley preached and sowed the seeds still to be seen in a multiplicity of Methodist chapels. Another advantage for the modern visitor is that distances between centres are smaller than elsewhere in Northumberland, so that the whole district can easily be covered in a day from Hexham, Allendale or from the *Lord Crewe Arms* in Blanchland.

Leave Hexham by the Carlisle road, the A69. After one and a half miles turn right, cross the bridge, turn right again at the charming *Boat Inn*, and after a furlong right again for **Warden**.

The hamlet stands at the meeting of the North and South Tynes in a wooded setting overlooked by a hill crowned with earthworks

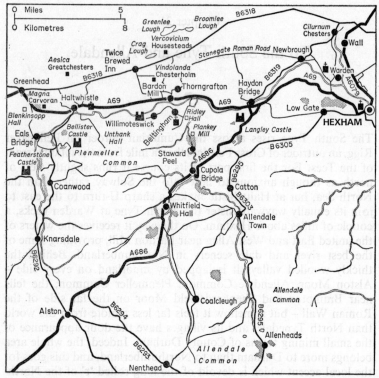

which were probably in existence before the Legions built the Wall and by the Saxon tower and seventh-century parish cross of **St Michael's.** The tower's top stage is a more recent addition; there are no elegant belfry lights as at Bywell St Andrew's, only slits; but the rest of the church is better, with a pleasing view on entering along the line of the plain barrel nave of 1765 to the windows and glass of the chancel rebuilt in 1889 on the old foundations, a perfect and impressive reflection of high Victorian taste, even down to the details of the decorated ceiling and the woodwork of the altar and choir stalls. The transepts, which are very long for so modest a church, are much earlier, of the thirteenth century, though the walls have undergone some restoration and the glass is again late Victorian.

The village has one of the oldest surviving paper mills in England, the buildings of which date from 1763. In the neighbourhood, in the direction of Chesters, is the quaintly named **Homer's Lane**, the scene of a famous unsolved murder a century and a half ago – the killing of Joe the Quilter, whose workmanship can still be seen in many a Northumbrian home and whose ghost, hopping on one leg in search of a clog lost during his last frantic dash for safety across the Tyne, was for long reputed to haunt the road near his house, now disappeared. He was last reported about 1900 by a housemaid returning to the Chesters from a dance – it was either Joe or one of the black and white cattle introduced to the valley about that time.

From Warden return to the *Boat Inn* and the main A69 Hexham to Carlisle road for **Haydon Bridge,** a small unpretentious town at a crossing of the South Tyne. In a cottage overlooking the river at East Land Ends Farm was born one of the most striking of English artists, John Martin (1789-1854), whose apocalyptic visions, transferred into paint, astonished fashionable London and caused Sir Thomas Lawrence to call him the 'most popular painter of the day'. When shown in the capital in 1821 his *Belshazzar's Feast* had to be railed off to protect it from the crowds that milled around it. He was never elected an Academician, but a John Martin Street and a Martin's Close in his native town stand as reminders of a painter, long neglected, who is now enjoying a great and deserved revival. He had a still more notorious brother, Jonathan, who felt it his mission to burn down York Minster and nearly achieved it. A third member of the brotherhood was William Martin, self-proclaimed 'Philosophical Conqueror of All Nations': poet, artist, pamphleteer, butt of public ridicule, and inventor of a thoroughly practical miner's safety lamp, whose bizarre career has recently been the subject of an exhibition at Wallsend, his home for a great part of his life, organised by Keith Armstrong and other Tyneside poets.

From Haydon Bridge the A686 runs south-west in the direction of Alston. A mile and a half along it is **Langley Castle,** a very grand fourteenth-century tower house restored in the 1890s standing impressively in wooded country above the road. It is now in the medieval banqueting business and was featured a while ago in the *Sunday Times* colour supplement, complete with resident monarch, court jester and wenches. Northumbria as a whole now has a whole clutch of these establishments, and this is certainly among the most jokey. Booking ahead is essential – business is booming and it makes a lively night out. There is a bar open to all. I am told by an expert that Langley's medieval loos were of superb and ingenious quality, arranged in three tiers, each having a straight drop into a specially diverted stream below the walls. In a sense therefore the architect of Langley anticipated Sir John Harrington's invention of the water closet in the reign of the first Elizabeth.

A couple of miles further along the road and visible from the steep hairpin bends of the descent into the valley is the meeting of the waters of the East and West Allen at Cupola Bridge. In the woods high above the united river at its junction with the Harsingdale Burn stand the romantic ruins of Staward Pele. Before reaching this point, not far after Langley, a fork to the right leads two and a half miles to **Plankey Mill** where the river flows through a steep wooded glen under a charming if perilous-looking footbridge. It is a great picnicking spot in summer: highly recommended, but not at weekends in August. From here a footpath on National Trust property follows the river past the grounds of Ridley Hall to the Allen's junction with the South Tyne opposite the village of Bardon Mill: one of the county's most idyllic walks, at its best in spring and autumn. Plankey Mill and Allen Banks can be reached another way, by following the A69 on the north bank of the South Tyne and crossing it to Ridley Hall, a mile or so on the Haydon Bridge side of Bardon Mill. A left turn immediately after the bridge leads to the tactful **Allen Banks** car park among the woods. Another bridge crosses the Allen here, and the walk to Plankey Mill can be made upstream.

A right turn after the Tyne bridge at this point leads to **Beltingham**, lost and dreaming in an eighteenth-century countryside within sound of the traffic on the other bank of the river pounding along between Hexham and Carlisle. The small and airy church is dedicated to St Cuthbert, which raises the presumption that his coffin was brought here in its wanderings. Pevsner complains that the building was over-zealously restored in the 1880s, but it still has great charm, standing high above the river haughs on a site that would have been suitable for a castle. In the churchyard are two Roman altars, that at the east end over the grave of the antiquary Anthony Hedley who built Chesterholm which is now *Vindolanda*'s museum. On the north side is a yew tree said to be nine hundred years old, and with its two clamps of ironwork around it and its very dark trunk and foliage it certainly looks it. However, it still flourishes mightily and looks capable of surviving almost as long again. The beautiful Georgian house next door to the church belongs to the Bowes-Lyon family. Hardly a village, Beltingham is with Alnham under the Cheviots the most beautiful hamlet in Northumberland.

A mile beyond it the road comes over a crest and straight ahead on the high ground stands the old fortified manor house of the Ridleys, **Willimoteswick**, looking more Spanish than English against the bare skyline. Glance back over your shoulder and the illusion vanishes, for across the river is workaday Bardon Mill. Willimoteswick, let me add, also works for its living as a thriving farm. Some say it was the birthplace of the most famous of the Ridleys, the Protestant bishop who was burnt for his faith along with Latimer at Oxford in 1555 in the days of Mary Tudor, but near-by Unthank Hall was more probably the site. The Ridleys are still a considerable power in Northumbrian life – Lord Ridley of Blagdon is at the time of writing Chairman of Northumberland County Council; the well-known writer on northern lore, Nancy Ridley, is another of the clan; and recently the late Arthur Ridley of Park End in the North Tyne valley gathered together members of the family from many parts of the world to hold a memorial service for their martyred kinsman.

At Willimoteswick the road ends in a farmyard under a massive fourteenth-century gatehouse, and one has to retrace one's steps to the bridge to rejoin the A69 for Bardon Mill. Just to the north of it lies **Vindolanda** (see page 271), which can easily be included at this point in a tour of the South Tyne, as can **Housesteads** also, for that matter.

Four miles further along the Carlisle road is **Haltwhistle** – a small industrial town which Pevsner chivalrously defends as not being as bad as it is usually painted in the guide-books.

The name often intrigues people, who imagine that perhaps it had something to do with the town's situation as a rail junction on the Newcastle–Carlisle and the Alston branch line. However, the proper derivation seems to be a combination of the French *haut* and Scandinavian *wiscle*: a high crescent of water, perhaps a reference to the sharp bend the river makes above the town. The Alston line incidentally was once British Rail's best scenic value for money south of the Scottish border. It has now been closed down and will soon, like the old North Tyne line from Hexham to Riccarton, be no more than a series of grass-grown embankments under the moor.

On the merits of Haltwhistle Pevsner is probably right. It has quite an attractive town centre, with an ancient pele forming part of the *Red Lion Hotel*, and tucked modestly away behind the high street is a splendidly preserved thirteenth-century parish **Church**, named not for a saint but for the Holy Cross. From the outside it is disappointing. There is no tower, only a bell-cote. Inside, however, Holy Cross is immensely spick and span; it gleams like some Puginesque temple. The screen, the glass (including the very charming work in the three lancets behind the altar), the painted roof of the chancel and the restored lancets in the aisles and clerestory of the nave are certainly

Victorian. But the core of the church, both in nave and chancel, is
Early English, and very fine it is with its battery of lancet windows in
the chancel to north, south and east, the well-proportioned arches
and piers of the four-bay nave, and the sense of spaciousness one
gets looking back into it from the altar – something that could never
be guessed at from the rather mean exterior. The stone font is a
rarity, being decorated with carvings that might from the look of
them have been made by Ancient Britons in Hadrian's time but in
reality date from the reign of Charles II. The effigy of a knight on
the floor to the north of the altar is almost equally primitive. On the
south wall of the chancel is a **Gravestone** set upright and inscribed
with rather touching verse:

> John Ridley, that sometime did be
> The Lord of Walltown,
> Gone is he out of this vale of misery:
> His bones lie under this stone.
> We must believe by God's mercy,
> Into this world gave his Son,
> Them to redeem all Christians,
> So Christ has his soul won.
> All faithful people may be glad,
> When death comes that none can flee,
> The body which the soul kept in pain
> Through Christ is set at liberty,
> Among blessed company to remain.
> To sleep in Christ now is he gone,
> Yet still believes to have again
> Through Christ a joyful resurrection.
> All friends may be glad to hear
> When his soul from pain did go,
> Out of this world, as doth appear,
> In the year of our Lord 1562.

North of the town along the Haltwhistle Burn is a Roman fort
on the Stanegate and a little further north-west on the line of
Hadrian's Wall itself the big camp of *Aesica* at **Greatchesters**. Those
interested should consult Collingwood Bruce's *Handbook to the
Roman Wall*, page 152. A splendid hoard of jewellery was found on
the site. Returning to Haltwhistle, just upstream from the church, a
road turns left off the A69, crosses the South Tyne and follows it
westward on the right bank past Bellister Castle to **Eals Bridge**
(1775/80), a handsome embellishment of the scenery hereabouts

which strikingly resembles the banks of the North Tyne between Greystead and Falstone. On a terrace above the haughs stands **Featherstone Castle**, a grand mixture of the medieval and nineteenth-century Byronic. The road climbs the hill steeply above it, so that you can look right down into its courtyards. In 1530 its owner, Sir Albany de Featherstonehaugh, High Sheriff of the county, was killed in a feud by his neighbours, Nicholas Ridley of Unthank, Hugh Ridley of Hawden, and others. The eighteenth-century historian of Durham, Robert Surtees, wrote some verse about the incident and persuaded his friend Sir Walter Scott into accepting it as a traditional ballad: it was duly introduced into *Marmion*, and very splendid it sounds:

> Hoot awa' lads, hoot awa'.
> Hae ye heard how the Ridleys and Thirlwalls and a'
> Ha' set upon Albany Featherstonehaugh
> And taken his life at the Deadmanshaw?
> There was Willimoteswick,
> And Hardriding Dick,
> And Hughie o' Hawden and Will o' the Wa',
> I canna tell a', I canna tell a',
> And money a mair that the Deil may knaw . . .

The road continues across the high ground on to **Plenmeller Common** where it is joined by another coming up from Haltwhistle past Unthank Hall, from whose crest at the one-thousand-foot-contour line is one of the most all-embracing views over the Roman Wall country that can be got from a motor car. Beyond the watershed is the steepish descent to the hamlet of **Whitfield,** which like Bywell boasts two churches, the 'Old' and the 'New', the latter a striking piece of Victorian Early English with a spire rising splendidly among the trees.

At the junction with the A686 a left turn into the thickly wooded valley leads to the meeting of the East and West Allen at Cupola Bridge. Before reaching it, turn right on a minor road for **Allendale Town,** which claims to be exactly in the middle of Britain and has a sun-dial to prove it. On New Year's Eve people flock here from all over Northumberland and Durham to see the celebrated 'Guysers' prance around a bonfire with huge lighted tar barrels on their heads. No one knows the exact origin of the custom – probably high jinks at the winter solstice – but certainly it is a great encouragement to the local innkeepers and turns Allendale on the night into the liveliest and booziest small town in Britain. The custom was kept up even during Hitler's war by using an enclosed fire in a bucket shielded by a lid from the sky so that the Luftwaffe couldn't get at it. The Guysers are undoubtedly one of the sights of the North, though people of a delicate or retiring nature may be well advised to give them a miss: at most other times of the year, apart from week-ends in August, they will find Allendale a quiet, pleasant spot with a picturesque open square and a spa-like style. Golfers should try the nine-hole golf course on the fells above the town, with grand views over a countryside which was once a great lead-mining area and still sports a number of ruined mine-shafts, giving to the hills a decidedly romantic air, like the scenery around St Just in the Land's End peninsula. Players will find greens roped off to protect them from the sheep which diligently crop the rough: these form moving hazards to add to the enjoyment of a course which is very short and does marvels for the golfing ego.

Allendale makes a convenient stopping place for the night – the *Ashleigh Hotel* half a mile from the village is particularly to be recommended. Beyond it on the route south into County Durham is the village of **Allenheads**, where the eighteenth-century home of Sir Thomas Wentworth is now a hotel, recently modernised and exceptionally lively at week-ends. In winter this is the ski centre of Northumberland. Four clubs operate on the near-by slopes and there are ski-tows – nothing like St Moritz or even Aviemore, but at least Allenheads is trying.

One last word for the East Allen mines, which once produced a seventh of all the lead in the kingdom. Pack-horses took it to Newcastle, and from a later time there are traces on the fells of the old wagon-ways. Armstrong's guns were first tested here in 1856. Recently a fluorspar mine has been opened in the village which will employ two hundred men.

Chapter 22

To Upper Weardale, Teesdale and Barnard Castle

❧

From Allenheads the B6295 descends Burntree Fell to join the B6293, the Alston to Stanhope road, at Capthill in Durham's central heartland of the Wear. This is the alternative southward route to the Blanchland–Stanhope road (see page 305).

The village names of Westgate and Eastgate on the map still mark the limits of the hunting park of the medieval bishops of Durham. But Eastgate now houses Portland Cement's modern factory with its towering chimney, nearly three hundred feet high, and traces of an earlier industrialisation crop up all over the valley in hillsides quarried for their limestone, the ruins of old lead mines and their railway tracks adventuring crazily high among the fells, and in the string of working villages along the river. The motorist who wants to visit a most striking relic of this industrial past has only to turn along the B6293 a distance of three miles towards Alston to find to the left, below one, on the far side of the burn, the old **Park Level Mill** at **Killhope**, with its forty-foot-high wheel which powered the crushing machinery, the washing bays, the traces of the rail system that moved the ore, and some of the living quarters of the miners who worked here in the 1860s when the mill was built – rather late in the day, for Weardale lead mining was nearing its end. It was a hard life, preserved for us in an old mining song of the times:

> The ore's awaitin' in the tubs, the snow's upon the fell,
> Canny folks are sleepin' yet but lead is reet to sell.
> Come my little washer lad, come let's away,
> We're bound down to slavery for fourpence a day.
>
> It's early in the morning, we rise at five o'clock,
> And the little slaves come to the door to knock, knock, knock.
> Come my little washer lad, come let's away,
> It's very hard to work for fourpence a day.

Except on a fine summer's day it is a bleak spot, and something of the bitterness of a past exploitation still seems to live on in the bare

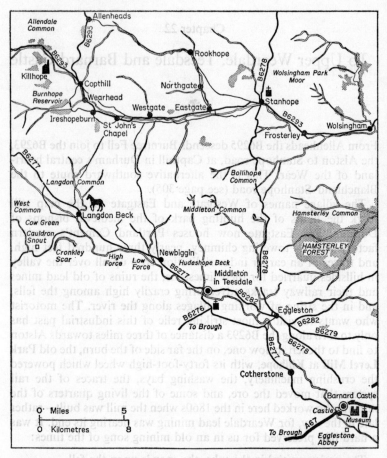

treeless countryside and its dour little towns. I think only a Weardale man would claim that the upper reaches of his river are as fine as the Tees across the watershed to the south. There are many charming small waterfalls along it and its tributary burns, but none to be mentioned in the same breath as Teesdale's High Force or Cauldron Snout. The valley road has some ribbon development and the landscape lacks the wild grandeur of the North Tyne and Coquet and the elegance of Till and Tweed. But for all that the Wear is a handsome river. And towering above it are the fells, a line of heights that on the southern flank are seldom lower than 2000 feet, from Flinty Fell near Nenthead to Westerhope Moor above Westgate, crowned by

316

Burnhope Seat (2452), only a little lower than The Cheviot. On the north bank the hills are lower, though running up close to the 2000-ft contour on Wolfcleugh Common and reaching 2207 ft on Killhope Moor. Most of it is grand country for ramblers. The only disadvantage is that there is a serious lack of accommodation along Weardale itself. Stanhope (see page 305) is a charming, small town but hardly meets the need. Nor can Teesdale easily cope with the overspill of tourism at the height of the summer season where the cars descend in their thousands on these two playgrounds.

The watershed between the valleys is crossed by a road which leaves the Wear at St John's Chapel and at Chapel Fell reaches 2056 ft, the highest classified road in England, before coming down to join the B6277 just above the *Langdon Beck Hotel*. There is a Youth Hostel a little further down the valley road. Unlike the Wear, the Tees is not exclusively a Durham river, for it rises in the peat bogs of Cross Fell in what is now Cumbria, and for most of its length forms the boundary with Yorkshire. It is one of the most beautiful of English streams: at its dramatic best in the ladder of waterfalls from Cauldron Snout to Low Force.

Cauldron Snout is not a single waterfall but a two-hundred-yard-long cascade, a superb sight when the river is in spate. It lies just below the dam of the new **Cow Green Reservoir** and is reached by a track over Widdybank Fell starting from the car parks some two and a half miles along the metalled road that leads off the B6277 at the *Langdon Beck Hotel*. Conservationists may lament this new intrusion, but in fairness it has to be admitted that visually the reservoir has a certain grandeur, and nothing can spoil Cauldron Snout itself. The walk to it passes through the Teesdale Nature Reserve. The Durham countryside brochure remarks proudly on the rare arctic and alpine plants to be found here, but does not happen to mention that the botanical paradise of Cow Green itself now lies beneath the waters.

At Cauldron Snout, near the meeting place of three counties – Yorkshire, Durham and Cumbria – we again cross the **Pennine Way** which follows the river downstream to Middleton in Teesdale, past Falcon Cliffs and the dramatic black screes of Cronkley Scar, till below Low Force it sheds its character of an upland burn and flows through woods and meadows alive in spring and summer with wild flowers and, if Mr Wainwright in his *Pennine Companion* is to be believed, with botanists in full plumage lying prone on the grass.

This is an expedition for the fit and vigorous, but the motorist on the valley road is almost equally well catered for. He will pass

numbers of green signposts leading to the Pennine Way and giving
him the opportunity for a stroll. And three miles down from Langdon
Beck, exactly opposite a hotel, a footpath (tolls in summer) leads a
comfortable stretch to **High Force**, England's biggest (though I am
told not her highest) waterfall – a seventy-foot plunge between
Cyclopean rocks into the cauldron lying under the banks of a
thickly wooded dell. In normal weather, till the very last turn in the
track is reached, there is only a murmur to be heard. Then the
orchestra opens up and the milk-white filament of the falls appears
between the curtain of the trees. At close quarters, particularly in a
wet season, it is an awesome sight. But go backstage in summer above
the sound and the fury, and there is the parent river of the Tees,
little more than a burn bumbling along over the rocks. It makes a
remarkable contrast: two widely differing worlds.

A mile and a half downstream, between Bowlees and the Winch
Bridge, is **Low Force**, in more open country. By the time **Middleton
in Teesdale** is reached the river is widening, after receiving the waters
of the sizeable Gudeshope Beck. Middleton, a good centre for
Ramblers, is a small and attractive town with a church possessing
the only detached belfry in the county. A number of roads converge
on it from either side of the Tees, and this pattern is repeated three
miles further downstream on the north bank at **Eggleston** and its
seventeenth-century bridge. From here a public footpath follows
the well wooded river bank to Barnard Castle as an alternative to the
B6278 main road. For river scenery the section from Langdon Beck
southwards is the finest and most varied in Northumbria, and the
whole area, though close to large centres of population, is – if we
except the drowning of Cow Green – still remarkably unspoilt.
Durham County Council, essentially an urban body, may have its
faults, but it has been at great pains both to preserve its countryside
and to display it to the visitor – a little preachily at times, as in some
of its handbooks and nature trails, but with a true understanding of
its beauty and of the dangers to the environment that go with it.

Barnard Castle, 'Barney' to its inhabitants and the surrounding
countryside, is named for one Bernard, son of Guy Baliol who had
been a friend of William the Conqueror. Bernard built a fortification here on land granted to his family by William Rufus in 1093.
The castle later came into the hands of the powerful Nevilles of
Raby, and through Anne Neville to the crown in the person of her
redoubtable husband, Richard III. In 1626 it was bought by Sir
Harry Vane, who purloined its name when he was granted a barony;

and in his family it remained till presented by Lord Barnard in 1952 to the Ministry of Works – one of the bonniest sets of ruins in the kingdom.

Entering from any direction but the west the visitor sees no sign of any castle but only an agreeable market town full of unpretentious eighteenth- and early-nineteenth-century housing – at its hub the fine octagonal **Town Hall** or market cross of 1747. Opposite it is the **Parish Church**, whose tower of 1874 is placed at the west end of the north aisle, replacing an earlier one in this somewhat curious position. The Victorian restoration was very thorough and the church has lost most of its Norman and Transitional flavour. It still has a delightful Perpendicular chancel arch with fleurons on the outer moulding, also a thirteenth-century south aisle with an original east window in the south transept. In the north transept is a dark pre-Reformation font.

From the market cross, a street called 'The Bank', lined with ancient houses, plunges downhill toward the river. Notice in particular, on the left, the remarkable Tudor **Blagroves House** with its projecting square bay windows and figures of musicians on the facade. Barney believes, *asserts*, that Oliver Cromwell stayed here in 1648. Further down the hill are the Georgian **Thorngate House** and an interesting row of weavers' cottages. This brings one to the Tees, which is crossed a little upstream by a fine Elizabethan **Bridge** (1569) under the lea of the **Castle** which now appears on its eighty-foot-high bluff, a splendid *château fort* dominating the valley. Opposite the bridge a footpath winds up the side of the mound on which it stands, and it is a climb worth making. Below flows the river, an ebullient stream, and on the opposite bank stands a derelict mill (1760–1932) of considerable charm, for which it is to be hoped some modern use can be found before it collapses into the water. Above one rises the castle's Northam Tower, once five storeys high, and beyond it the mullioned oriel window of the Great Chamber, probably put in by Richard Crookback, whose emblem of the boar is carved on one of the cover stones inside. Whatever the truth of the crimes associated with his name, Richard was always popular in the North, where support for his cause lingered on long after his death at Bosworth, and indeed he still has his defenders. The castle's most imposing feature is the **Round** or **Baliol Tower**, probably built towards the end of the thirteenth century on Norman foundations, but little excavation has been attempted on this site and most of its early history is obscure. The bailey is approached through the fourteenth-century North Gate and the Department of the Environment's ticket office. Apart from the emblem of the Boar and the Ladies' Chamber on the second floor of the Baliol Tower there is not a great deal to see, but the Ministry's trim lawns make this a pleasant place in which to linger on a summer's day, and there is a fine view over the river hurrying by far below.

From the North Gate it is only a short stroll back to the town centre. Many of the older houses between the bailey and the Market Cross were built of stone quarried from the castle, the trend being set by Sir Harry Vane, who had no sooner bought the place than he began stripping the lead from its roof. A building with interesting literary connections is the **King's Head**, where Dickens stayed when he was in search of material for the Dotheboys Hall episodes in *Nicholas Nickleby*; his model was the near-by Bowes Academy, which seems to have been a far more respectable establishment than the immortal one presided over by Mr Wackford Squeers. Nor was this Dickens's only debt to Barnard Castle, for he owes it also the title of one of his works. 'Ah, Master Humphrey's Clock!' he is said to have exclaimed on being told by the local clockmaker, Thomas Humphrey, that the timepiece he had admired in the shop window had been made by the craftsman's son – and *Master Humphrey's Clock* duly took its place in the gallery of Dickensiana, a series of adventure tales which attempted to restore Mr Pickwick and the Wellers to the world's affections, along with Tony Weller the younger, Mr Slithers, a barber, Joe Toddyhigh, John Podgers, and Belinda, 'a distressed damsel'. This miscellany, which was issued in weekly numbers at threepence a copy and was illustrated among others by George Cattermole, 'Phiz' (H. A. Browne) and George Cruikshank, was launched on 4 April 1840 and follows immediately after *Nicholas Nickleby* in the canon. It ran to eighty-eight numbers and is among the most easily forgettable of the master's works.

Barnard Castle nowadays is indeed a charming if somewhat remote place. The last thing one would expect to find there is a huge French château housing the largest collection of French and Spanish painting in Britain – yet that is precisely what is to be found at the **Bowes Museum** half a mile from the Market Cross.

For the unwary traveller who sees it from the road for the first time the effect can be one of incredulity. What is a building modelled on the old palace of the Tuileries doing in County Durham? And indeed its founders had originally intended to erect it at Calais. The French connection is by no means accidental, for John Bowes, the only son of the tenth Earl of Strathmore (legitimised at the eleventh

hour by his father's marriage to his mother on the day before the old Earl's death) married a French actress and spent most of his youth in Paris and Louveciennes. Political unrest in France put an end to the dream of a great cultural centre on the Channel coast, and instead the enormously rich but childless couple returned to the Bowes estates in Teesdale, where a purpose-built mansion was created for them by the French architect Jules Pellechet. The work began in 1869, but neither of the founders lived to see the final emergence of their brainchild in 1892.

The 'Bowes', which may certainly claim to be among the most remarkable museums in Europe, has something for everyone. Recent acquisitions have provided a rich haul of interior décor from great houses from Tudor to Victorian times; there are displays of the pre-history of the area, of tapestry, costume, embroidery, furniture, and for the children a special room of their own in addition to the grand attraction in the entrance hall of the Silver Swan in its glass case, which at stated times, surrounded by a heavy breathing and enraptured audience, goes through a ritual of waving its beak in the air – rather a provoking bird, if the truth were told, and nothing like as ingenious as the clockwork golden mouse and the distinctly creepy mechanical spider in Room 13. All these, however, are really subordinate to the brilliant collection of pottery and china, pre-Revolutionary and First Empire furniture, and the French, Spanish and Italian paintings which form our most important collection of this kind outside of London.

John Bowes and his wife were spiritual exiles in the North. Their tastes were Continental, and so were most of their treasures which one can see displayed in the setting they devised. The furniture and *objets d'art* from their houses in France are on the first floor in Rooms 11 to 17: particularly noteworthy the Chantilly and St Cloud porcelain and French *faïence* in Room 13, a writing table made for Marie Antoinette's *Petit Trianon* (11) and the beautiful Psyche tapestries (12), probably woven at Beauvais during the reign of Louis XIV. Room 14 features the Empire style that came in with Bonaparte, inspired by models reaching France after his Egyptian campaign and by revolutionary ardour for the supposed austerity of classical Rome. In Rooms 15 and 16 one can see the cultural backlash against this style and the return to pre-Revolutionary forms which by the 1840s were everywhere triumphant in French cultural circles. Room 17 contains purchases made at the Paris Exhibition of 1867. The main displays of pottery and porcelain are in Rooms 38 and 39 on the second floor, but for a sight of the founders' splendid collection of oriental china one must go to the Gulbenkian Museum in Durham where it is on long loan.

Paintings are everywhere, many of them hanging in corridors where it is easy to overlook them. Perhaps it would have been better if the larger-than-life poodle in Room 37 had been consigned to a very dark corner indeed -- only the stool made of a stone embedded with shells and with a tiger-skin seat can compare with it for horror. Such rare lapses from good taste help to highlight the beauty of the exhibits in the three galleries on the second floor (35, 36, 37) where the bulk of the European painting is concentrated. The French collection is so large that only a fraction of it can be put on show -- the best of it is in Room 37 along with some of the Italian canvases, where Francois Boucher's superb *Landscape with a Water Mill* is shown alongside Tiepolo's *Harnessing of the Horses of the Sun*. At the entrance to this gallery hang two large Canalettos of Venetian scenes recently acquired on long loan. The Spanish collection in Room 36 is of particular importance, for it includes two remarkable Goyas: the well-known portrait of Melendez Valdes and a moving study of the interior of a prison, with manacled prisoners held in the shadows of an arch against the light of the outside world beyond. Room 35 features sixteenth- and seventeenth-century European painting (excepting Spain): outstanding among them the *Rape of Helen* by Francisco Primaticcio (1504-70), the only painting in Britain by this artist. In Room 19, the Gothic Room, is a triptych by the Delft painter known as the Master of the *Virgo inter Virgines*, and the *Miracle of the Holy Sacrament* by Stefano de Giovanni, known as *Il Sasseta*.

Excellent guide-books to the paintings as well as general guides to the Museum are on sale at the reception desk. There is a Rest Room (40) on the second floor and a restaurant beyond the Founders' Room. There is also a café, entered from outside in the grounds to the right of the main doors. Car parking is free.

From Barnard Castle the quickest way to Scotch Corner on the road south is across the town bridge into Yorkshire and then along the B6277, turning left at the big crossroads on to the A66 for Greta Bridge. Perhaps it would be unkind to try to hug the visitor too closely to one's bosom on this final lap of a long tour, but there is still some agreeable country left on the Durham bank of the Tees, along the minor road that leads to the pretty village of **Whorlton**, opposite Yorkshire's Wycliffe (the birthplace of the great fifteenth-century religious reformer), and, further back, nearer to Barnard

Castle, the elegant bridge that crosses the Tees to the ruins of **Egglestone Abbey,** not to be confused with Eggleston, on the way to Middleton. From Whorlton it is possible for the motorist with a good navigator in the passenger seat to set a course for the A66 and Scotch Corner, but the more sensible plan is to turn north for a mile on to the A67 for **Winston,** which has a thirteenth-century church and a remarkably daring bridge of 1764, an engineering masterpiece of its kind and date. The next village along the road is Gainford, the next Piercebridge, and then the circuit of Northumbria is complete.

Appendix 1

Opening Times of Castles, Museums and Places of Interest

❧

The opening hours vary greatly according to ownership except in the case of those buildings in the care of the Department of the Environment, which have standard hours as follows:

March, April, October	Weekdays	9.30 a.m. – 5.30 p.m.
	Sunday	2.00 p.m. – 5.30 p.m.
May – September	Weekdays	9.30 a.m. – 7.00 p.m.
	Sunday	2.00 p.m. – 7.00 p.m.
November – February	Weekdays	9.30 a.m. – 4.30 p.m.
	Sunday	2.00 p.m. – 4.30 p.m.

One variation found sometimes is that the Sunday opening commences at 9.30 a.m. instead of 2.00 p.m.

Free admission is noted, but not entrance fees.

CHAPTER 1

Raby Castle and Gardens, Staindrop, Co. Durham: Easter – 31 May, Sun only 2.00 p.m. – 5.00 p.m.; June, July, Sept, Wed, Sat, Sun, 2.00 p.m. – 5.00 p.m.; August, daily exc. Fri, 2.00 p.m. – 5.00 p.m.

Timothy Hackworth House and Museum, Shildon, Co. Durham: April – Sept, Wed to Sun, 10.00 a.m. – 5.00 p.m.

CHAPTER 2

Durham Cathedral, Durham City: April – Sept, Mon to Sat 7.15 a.m. – 8.45 p.m., Sun, 7.15 a.m. – 7.45 p.m.; Oct – Mar, Mon to Sat, 7.15 a.m. – 5.30 p.m., Sun, 7.15 a.m. – 7.45 p.m.

Monks Dormitory: Mon to Sat, 10.00 a.m. – 4.00 p.m.; Sun, 1.00 p.m. – 4.00 p.m.

Durham Castle, Durham City: April and 1 July – 30 Sept, Mon to Sat, 10.00 a.m. – 12.00 noon and 2.00 p.m. – 4.30 p.m.; at other times, Mon, Wed, Sat, 2.00 p.m. – 4.00 p.m.

Durham Light Infantry Museum, Durham City: Tues to Sat, 10.00 a.m. – 5.00 p.m., Sun, 2.00 p.m. – 5.00 p.m.; open on Bank Holidays

Gulbenkian Museum of Oriental Art, Durham City: Mon to Fri, 9.30 a.m. – 1.00 p.m. and 2.15 p.m. – 5.00 p.m.; Sat, 9.30 a.m. – 12.00 noon and 2.15 p.m. – 5.00 p.m.; Sun, 2.15 p.m. – 5.00 p.m.; between Christmas and Easter there is no weekend opening

Finchale Priory, near Durham City: Department of Environment standard hours exc. Sun, open 9.30 a.m.

Ushaw College, near Durham City: Open at most times, but it is advisable to write or telephone the Rev. Procurator beforehand (Tel Langley Park 254)

CHAPTER 3

The Church of St Cuthbert (the Parish Church), Darlington, Co. Durham: Closed on Tues

Darlington Museum and Art Gallery, Tubwell Row: Daily exc. Sun; Mon, Tues, Wed, Fri, 10.00 a.m. – 1.00 p.m. and 2.00 p.m. – 6.00 p.m., Thurs, 10.00 a.m. – 1.00 p.m., Sat, 10.00 a.m. – 1.00 p.m. and 2.00 p.m. – 5.30 p.m.; free

Darlington North Road Station Railway Museum: Mon to Fri, 10.00 a.m. – 4.30 p.m.

Preston Hall Museum and Park, Eaglescliffe, Stockton: April – Sept, Mon to Sat, 10.00 a.m. – 6.00 p.m., Sun, 2.00 p.m. – 6.00 p.m.; Oct – March, weekdays only, 10.00 a.m. – 6.00 p.m.; free

Stockton Ticket Office Museum, 41 Bridge Street: Tues to Sat, 10.00 a.m. – 6.00 p.m.; free

CHAPTER 4

Lambton Pleasure Park (incorporating the Lambton Lion Park), *Chester le Street, Co. Durham:* 1 Mar – 31 Oct, 10.00 a.m. – 5.00 p.m. (the last admission is 5.00 p.m., but visitors may stay until dusk)

Washington Old Hall, Tyne & Wear: Daily (exc. Friday), 10.00 a.m. – 1.00 p.m. and 2.00 p.m. – 6.00 p.m.

Gibside Chapel, near Rowland's Gill, Tyne & Wear: April – Sept, daily exc. Tues; Oct and March, Wed, Sat, Sun, 2.00 p.m. – 6.00 p.m.; Nov and Feb, Sun only; free

Beamish North of England Open Air Museum, near Stanley, Co. Durham (off. A693): Easter – Sept, exc. Mon, 10.00 a.m. – 6.00 p.m.; Oct – Easter, Fri. Sat, Sun, 10.00 a.m. – 5.00 p.m.; open on Bank Holidays

CHAPTER 5

Ryhope Engines Museum, Sunderland (Ryhope Pumping Station): Easter – Sept daily, 11.00 a.m. – 6.00 p.m. exc. Sun, 2.00 p.m. – 6.00 p.m.; last admission 5.15 p.m. For visits at other times Tel Sunderland 210235

Monkwearmouth Station Museum, Sunderland: Mon to Fri 9.30 a.m. – 5.30 p.m. Sat, 9.30 a.m. – 4.00 p.m.; free

St Peter's Chapter House Museum, Monkwearmouth, Sunderland: Daily, 10.00 a.m. – 5.00 p.m.

National Music Hall Museum, Sunderland: Daily 10.00 a.m. – 7.00 p.m.; free

CHAPTER 6

South Shields (Arbeia) Roman Museum, Co. Durham: Mon to Sat, 10.00 a.m. – 6.00 p.m., Sun, 2.00 p.m. – 6.00 p.m.

Jarrow Hall Museum, Co. Durham: April – Sept, Tues to Sat, 10.00 a.m. – 5.30 p.m.; Oct – Mar, Tues to Sat, 11.00 a.m. – 4.30 p.m., Sun 2.30 p.m. – 5.30 p.m.

Tynemouth Castle and Priory (Northumberland): Department of Environment standard hours.

CHAPTER 7

Seaton Delaval Hall, Whitley Bay, Tyne & Wear: May – Sept, Wed, Sun and Bank Holidays, 2.00 p.m. – 6.00 p.m.

Museum of Antiquities, the University, Newcastle upon Tyne: Weekdays, 10.00 a.m. – 5.00 p.m.; free

Balmbra's Music Hall, Cloth Market, Newcastle upon Tyne: During licensing hours

Blackgate National Bagpipe Museum, Newcastle upon Tyne: April – 30 Sept, Mon, 2.00 p.m. – 5.00 p.m., Tues to Sat, 10.00 a.m. – 5.00 p.m.; Winter closing time 4.00 p.m. *The Keep:* same times as for museum

Guildhall, Newcastle upon Tyne: closed to the public. Special permission must be sought from Newcastle upon Tyne City Council, Civic Centre (Tel Newcastle 815129)

Hancock Museum, Barras Bridge, Newcastle upon Tyne: Mon to Sat, 10.00 a.m. – 5.00 p.m., Sun (April – Sept only), 2.00 p.m. – 5.00 p.m.

John George Joicey Museum (in the former Holy Jesus Hospital, City Road, Newcastle upon Tyne): Weekdays, 10.00 a.m. – 6.00 p.m.; free

Keelman's Hospital, City Road, Newcastle upon Tyne: Now Newcastle upon Tyne Polytechhic student accommodation. For permission to view, contact the Polytechnic, Tel Newcastle 26002

The Keep, Newcastle upon Tyne: Summer, Mon, 2.00 p.m. – 5.00 p.m., Tues to Sat, 10.00 a.m. – 5.00 p.m.; Winter closing time 4.00 p.m.

Laing Art Gallery, Higham Place, Newcastle upon Tyne: Mon to Sat, 10.00 a.m – 6.00 p.m., Sun, 2.00 p.m. – 5.00 p.m.; free

Old Assembly Rooms, Westgate Road, Newcastle upon Tyne: Open during evening licensing hours with restaurant and bar

Museum of Science and Engineering, Exhibition Park, Newcastle upon Tyne: Mon to Sat, 10.00 a.m. – 6.00 p.m., Sun, 2.00 p.m – 5.00 p.m.; free

Trinity House, Broad Chare, Newcastle upon Tyne: Courtyard, Mon to Fri, 8.00 a.m. – 6.00 p.m. Only exceptionally is permission given to view inside

CHAPTER 8

Wallington Hall, near Cambo, 12m. W. of Morpeth, Northumberland: House, 27 Mar – 30 Sept, daily exc. Tues and Fri, 2.00 p.m. – 6.00 p.m.; open on Good Friday; Oct, Sat and Sun, 2.00 p.m. – 5.00 p.m. *Gardens,* 27 Mar – 30 Sept, weekdays, 10.00 a.m. – 6.00 p.m.; weekends and Bank Holidays, 10.00 a.m. – 7.00 p.m.; Oct, daily, 10.00 a.m. – 5.00 p.m.

CHAPTER 9

Woodhorn Church, near Ashington, Northumberland. (Changing exhibitions with particular emphasis on Christianity in Northumbria): Daily exc. Sun and Mon, 10.00 a.m. – 12.00 noon and 1.00 p.m. – 4.00 p.m.; free

Warkworth Castle and Hermitage, Northumberland: Department of Environment standard hours exc. Sun, open 9.30 a.m.

Alnwick Castle, Northumberland: 9 May – 30 Sept, daily exc. Fri, 1.00 p.m. – 5.00 p.m.; no admittance after 4.30 p.m.

Hulne Park and Priory (tickets at Alnwick Castle): Same dates and times, but only on Wed and Sun

CHAPTER 10

Howick Hall Gardens, Northumberland: Easter – 30 Sept, 2.00 p.m. – 7.00 p.m.

Dunstanburgh Castle, Northumberland: Department of Environment standard hours

Bamburgh Castle, Northumberland: 3 April – 10 Oct, daily; April, May, June, Sept, 2.00 p.m. – 5.00 p.m.; July, 2.00 p.m. – 6.00 p.m.; August, 2.00 p.m. – 7.00 p.m.; Oct, 2.00 p.m. – 4.30 p.m.

Grace Darling Museum, Bamburgh: 1 April – 2 Oct, doily, 11.00 a.m. – 7.00 p.m.

NORTHUMBRIA

CHAPTER 11

Lindisfarne Castle, Holy Island, Northumberland: 1 April – 2 June and 24 June – 30 Sept, daily exc. Tues, 1.00 p.m. – 5.00 p.m.; 3 June – 23 June, Wed only, 1.00 p.m. – 5.00 p.m.
Lindisfarne Priory: Department of the Environment standard hours exc. Sun, open 9.30 a.m.

CHAPTER 12

Ford Village School, Ford, Nothumberland: Daily, 10.00 a.m. – 6.00 p.m.
Heatherslaw Mill, Nr Ford, Nothumberland: Daily, 11.00 a.m. – 6.00 p.m.
Museum of the King's Own Scottish Borderers, Berwick, Northumberland: Daily exc. Sun, Mon to Fri, 9.00 a.m. – 12.00 noon and 1.00 p.m. – 4.30 p.m., Sat, 9.00 a.m. – 12.00 noon
Town Hall Gaol, Berwick: Only by special permission from Berwick-on-Tweed Borough Council, Tel Berwick 6332

CHAPTER 13

Norham Castle, Northumberland: Department of the Environment standard hours

CHAPTER 14

Chillingham Cattle at Chillingham Castle, Northumberland: Weekdays exc. Tues; 10.00 a.m. – 12.00 noon and 2.00 p.m. – 5.00 p.m., Sun, 2.00 p.m. – 5.00 p.m., contact the Warden, Chillingham Castle, Tel. Chatton 250
Glanton Bird Research Station, Glanton, Northumberland: June – Oct, 2.00 p.m. – 6.00 p.m.
Callaly Castle, Whittingham, Northumberland: Whit Sunday – 31 Oct, Sat and Sun, 2.15 p.m. – 6.00 p.m.
Cragside, Rothbury, Northumberland: Gardens – Thurs before Easter – 30 Sept, 10.00 a.m. – 7.30 p.m.
Brinkburn Priory, Nr Rothbury, Northumberland: Department of the Environment standard hours, exc. Sun (April – Sept), when it is open from 9.30 a.m.

CHAPTER 15

Otterburn Mill, Northumberland: Daily exc. Sun; *Mill processes,* Mon to Thurs, 9.00 a.m. – 12.30 p.m. and 1.30 p.m. – 5.00 p.m.; Fri, 9.00 a.m. – 12.30 p.m. and 1.30 p.m. – 3.00 p.m. *Showroom,* Mon to Fri, 9.00 a.m. – 5.00 p.m., Sat, 9.00 a.m. – 12.30 p.m. and 1.30 p.m. – 5.00 p.m.; free

CHAPTER 16

Border Forest Museum, Kielder Castle, Northumberland: Mon to Fri, 8.00 a.m. – 12.00 noon and 1.00 p.m. – 4.00 p.m., Sat and Sun, 12.00 noon – 6.00 p.m.; free. In view of the building of Kielder Reservoir over the next five years, it is advisable to check times. Tel Kielder 50209

CHAPTER 17 – ROMAN SITES

Housesteads Roman Fort (Vercovicium), Hadrian's Wall: Department of the Environment standard hours
Vindolanda Fort & Vicus (Chesterholm), 2m W.SW of Housesteads: Site, daily, July, 9.30 a.m. – 7.30 p.m.; May, June, Sept, 9.30 a.m. – 6.30 p.m.; April, Oct, 9.30 a.m. – 5.30 p.m.; Mar, 9.30 a.m. – 5.00 p.m. *Museum,* times as for site exc. Nov – March, when it is open only at weekends.

NORTHUMBRIA

CHAPTER 18

Chesters Roman Fort (Cilurnum), Chollerford, Northumberland: daily, May –
Sept, weekdays, 9.00 a.m. – 5.30 p.m., Sun, 2.00 p.m. – 5.00 p.m.; Oct – Feb,
weekdays, 9.30 a.m. – 4.30 p.m. Sun, 2.00 p.m. – 4.00 p.m.; March – April,
weekdays, 9.00 a.m. – 5.00 p.m., Sun, 2.00 p.m. – 4.30 p.m.

CHAPTER 19

Corstopitum Roman Station (Corbridge): Department of the Environment
standard hours, exc. Sun when it is open from 9.30 a.m.

CHAPTER 20

Barnard Castle, Co. Durham: Department of Environment standard hours exc.
Sun opening 9.30 a.m., April – Sept
The Bowes Museum, Barnard Castle: May – Sept, weekdays, 10.00 a.m. – 5.30 p.m.;
Oct – Mar, April, weekdays, 10.00 a.m. – 5.00 p.m.; Nov – Feb, weekdays,
10.00 a.m. – 4.00 p.m.; Sun, 2.00 p.m. – 5.00 p.m. exc. Nov – Feb, 2.00 p.m. –
4.00 p.m.

Appendix 2

Hotels, Inns and Restaurants

❧

People engaged professionally in the recommendation of hotels and restaurants usually issue an annual assessment. It is easy to see why, for standards can change appreciably and quickly. Here I have simply listed places which I know personally, and in which when last visited I would be happy to have my friends stay, if they were not staying with me. They range from the simple to the luxurious, and many are referred to in the text.

A warning about 'inns'. Some of these, especially the old posting inns, have ample accommodation. Often, however, particularly in country places, they have only a limited number of rooms, so that it is wise to book ahead. Some indeed have none.

Up-to-date prices are given in the excellent booklet *Where to Stay – Northumbria*, published yearly by the English Tourist Board, which also gives details of guest houses, private accommodation, camping and caravan sites. The name of the telephone exchange is only given when it differs from the name of the place under which the hotel is listed.

CHAPTER 1

Piercebridge: The George. Tel 576

CHAPTER 2

Durham City: Royal County, Old Elvet. Tel 66821
  Three Tuns, New Elvet. Tel 64326
  (nr) Ramside Hall, Carrville (3 m N.E. on A690). Tel 65282
  (nr) Bowburn Hall, Bowburn (5 m S.E. on A177). Tel Coxhoe 770311

CHAPTER 3

Darlington: King's Head, Priestgate. Tel 67612
  Europa Lodge, Blackwell Grange. Tel 60111
Sedgefield: (nr) Hardwick Hall. Tel 20253
Stockton-on-Tees: Swallow, High Street. Tel 69621
Croft-on-Tees: Croft Spa Inn. Tel Darlington 720319
Hartlepool: Grand. Tel 66345
Seaton Carew: Staincliffe. Tel Hartlepool 4463

CHAPTER 4

Chester-le-Street: Lumley Castle. Tel 885326
Gateshead: Five Bridges, High West Street. Tel 771105
Lamesley (nr Gateshead): Ravensworth Arms. Tel Low Fell 876023
Whickham (nr Gateshead): Woodman's Arms, Fellside. Tel 887656
Lanchester: Burnopside Hall. Tel 520222

330

CHAPTER 6

Tynemouth: Royal Sovereign. Tel N. Shields 70577
Whitley Bay: Croglin, South Parade. Tel 523317

CHAPTER 7

Seaton Delaval: Seaton Delaval Hall (banquets). Tel 481759
Newcastle upon Tyne: Gosforth Park, High Gosforth. Tel Wideopen 4111
   Royal Station. Tel 20781
   Royal Turks Head, Grey Street. Tel 26111
   Swallow, Newgate Street. Tel 25025
   Three Mile Inn, Great North Road, Gosforth. Tel Gosforth 856817

RESTAURANTS

CENTRAL: Empress I, The Side. Tel 21219
   Golden Bengal, 39 Groat Market. Tel 20471
   Koh-i-noor, 26 Cloth Market. Tel 25379
   Rajah, 18 Cloth Market. Tel 611040
   Roma, 22 Collingwood Street. Tel 20612
QUAYSIDE: Cooperage, The Close. Tel 28286
   Moulin Rouge, 27 Sandhill. Tel 20377

CHAPTER 8

Wallington Hall: The Clock Tower (Rest.). Tel Scots Gap 274
Whalton: The Beresford Arms. Tel 225
Morpeth: Queen's Head, Bridge Street. Tel 2083

CHAPTER 9

Warkworth: Warkworth House, Bridge Street. Tel 276
Alnmouth: Schooner, Front Street. Tel 216
Alnwick: Hotspur, Bondgate Without. Tel 2924
   White Swan, Bongate Within. Tel 2109

CHAPTER 10

Bamburgh: Lord Crewe Arms. Tel 243
Belford: Blue Bell. Tel 203
North Sunderland: White Swan. Tel Seahouses 211

CHAPTER 12

Etal: Black Bull Inn. Tel Crookham 200
Berwick on Tweed: King's Arms, Hide Hill. Tel 7454
   Turret House, Etal Road. Tel 7344.

CHAPTER 13

Cornhill-on-Tweed: Collingwood Arms. Tel Coldstream 2424
   Tillmouth Park. Tel Coldstream 2255

CHAPTER 14

Wooler: Tankerville Arms, Cottage Road. Tel 581
Holystone: The Salmon Inn. Tel Harbottle 285
Alwinton: The Rose and Thistle Inn. Tel Harbottle 226

NORTHUMBRIA

CHAPTER 15

Otterburn: Otterburn Hall Holiday Hotel. Tel 663
   Otterburn Tower. Tel 673
   Percy Arms. Tel 261
Rochester: Redesdale Arms. Tel Otterburn 668
Byrness: Byrness. Tel Otterburn 231

CHAPTER 16

West Woodburn: Bay Horse Inn. Tel 60218
Tarset: Reivers of Tarset, The Comb, Tarset, Hexham. Tel Greenhaugh 40245
Wark: The Battlesteads. Tel 30209
Barrasford: Barrasford Arms. Tel Humshaugh 237

CHAPTERS 17 & 18

Chollerford: The George. Tel Humshaugh 205
Wall: The Hadrian. Tel Humshaugh 232
Haltwhistle: Manor House. Tel 210
Hexham: Beaumont, Beaumont Street. Tel 2331
   County, Priestpopple. Tel 2030
   Royal, Priestpopple. Tel 2270
   Heart of All England Tavern, Market Street. Tel 3375
Whitley Chapel (Hexham): Fox and Hounds Inn (The Click 'Em In). Tel
   Slaley 238

CHAPTER 19

Corbridge: The Angel Inn, Main Street. Tel 2119
Ovington: The Highlander Inn. Tel Prudhoe 32016
Riding Mill: The Wellington. Tel 531

CHAPTER 20

Blanchland: Lord Crewe Arms. Tel 251

CHAPTER 21

Warden: The Boatside Inn. Tel Hexham 2233
Haydon Bridge: Langley Castle (banquets). Tel 481
Allendale Town: Ashleigh, Thornley Gate (nr the Golf Course). Tel 351
Allenheads: Allenheads Inn. Tel 200

CHAPTER 22

Barnard Castle: King's Head, Market Place. Tel 3356
   Morritt Arms at near-by Greta Bridge. Tel Whorlton 232

Appendix 3

The Railways of Northumbria

❧

Northumbria has many connections with the earliest days of railways, and there are numerous lines still in operation for passenger and freight traffic. I have listed various interesting relics, as well as operating lines that are of special interest to visitors.

DARLINGTON NORTH ROAD STATION RAILWAY MUSEUM

North Road, Darlington
This station is situated on the branch line from Darlington Bank Top Station to Bishop Auckland. Dating from 1841, the main section of the station has been converted to a railway museum covering the area. Several full-size locomotives are on show, many of them from the National Railway Museum collection, including Stephenson's original *Locomotion*. Open daily, except Sundays, throughout the year.

TIMOTHY HACKWORTH MUSEUM

Soho Cottages, Hackworth Close, Shildon, Co. Durham
Hackworth lived in this house after the opening of the Stockton & Darlington Railway. In conjunction with the sesquicentenary celebrations in 1975, Sedgefield District Council restored the building and converted it to a museum. It mainly depicts the railways of the immediate area. Open weekdays throughout the year, and on Sundays from April to September.

STEPHENSON'S COTTAGE, KILLINGWORTH

Two miles off the A188 or A189, six miles north-east of Newcastle
Where George Stephenson lived from 1805 to 1823. House *not* open to visitors.

WHORLTON LIDO RAILWAY

Near Greta Bridge, Barnard Castle, Co. Durham (one mile off the A66)
A fifteen-inch gauge line that operates at weekends from Easter until September.

NORTH YORK MOORS HISTORICAL RAILWAY TRUST

Pickering Station, North Yorkshire
The Trust operates a preserved railway running for some seventeen miles from Pickering north to Grosmont on the Esk Valley line of British Railways. Train services are operated from Easter until October, with steam traction and diesel railcars. The locomotive shed is at Grosmont and can be reached by walking through the original tunnel for horse-drawn trains built by Stephenson in 1836.

BRITISH RAILWAYS ESK VALLEY LINE

British Railways operate a regular service from Middlesbrough via Battersby and Grosmont to Whitby. The diesel railcars used on this route enable passengers to enjoy the scenery, and special literature and maps are available at booking offices.

NORTH EASTERN RAILWAY, HASWELL

Haswell Lodge, Haswell, Co. Durham (Near Junior School in Haswell Village)
A fifteen-inch gauge line operates at weekends and on bank holidays from Easter until September.

NEWCASTLE MUSEUM OF SCIENCE ENGINEERING

Exhibition Park, Great North Road, Newcastle upon Tyne
The collection includes Stephenson's Killingworth Colliery locomotive *Billy*, built in 1826. The museum is open daily throughout the year.

NATIONAL COAL BOARD RAILWAYS

There are many National Coal Board railways in the area, but these are not usually accessible to the public. Some of the operations on the Hesledon rope-worked inclines can be seen from public roads at Dawdon and Seaham Harbour. Part of the Bowes Railway in the Springwell area (Gateshead) may be preserved and opened to the public.

STEPHENSON'S COTTAGE, WYLAM

Two miles off the A69, eight miles west of Newcastle
George Stephenson's birthplace, with the former Wylam wagonway in front, later to become part of British Railways but now lifted. House *not* open to visitors.

STOCKTON AND DARLINGTON RAIL TRAILS

Shildon – Witton Park
For the 150th Anniversary of the Stockton & Darlington Railway a five-mile rail trail was inaugurated, enabling visitors to see many of the old relics still *in situ* along the original track of the railway. There is access by road to several locations on the trail, and it is well sign-posted. Details can be obtained from the Hackworth Museum.

STOCKTON & DARLINGTON TICKET OFFICE

Bridge Street, Stockton-on-Tees, Cleveland
The Stockton & Darlington Railway terminated on the quayside at Stockton. A building nearby at St John's Crossing is known colloquially as 'The First Railway Booking Office', and was converted to a small railway museum, now run by the Stockton District Council. Open by prior arrangement with Preston Park (see below).

PRESTON PARK AND MUSEUM

Yarm Road, Eaglescliffe, Stockton-on-Tees, Cleveland
A vertical-boilered 0–4–0 industrial locomotive is preserved in the grounds. Open throughout the year.

TANFIELD RAILWAY LTD

Marley Hill Engine Shed, Sunniside, Gateshead, Tyne & Wear. Registered office: 3 Farndale Close, Winlaton, Tyne & Wear (one mile out of South Shields along the A6076)

The non-profit-making company has an engine shed which houses twelve industrial locomotives. The shed is open to visitors every Sunday throughout the year, and the company hopes to have a locomotive in steam on these occasions between Whitsun and the end of September. Plans are also under way to relay part of the Tanfield Wagonway and operate a passenger service over it.

NORTH OF ENGLAND OPEN AIR MUSEUM

Beamish, Stanley, Co. Durham (off the A693, just east of Stanley)
An open-air museum which recreates a picture of life in the north-east as it was. There are various items of railway interest including the reconstructed Rowley Station, Stephenson's Hetton Colliery locomotive of 1821, a working electric tramway, and, at weekends in the summer, the replica of *Locomotion* in steam.
Open (summer) Tuesdays to Sundays; (winter) Fridays to Sundays. For up-to-date details telephone Stanley (02073) 3586/3580

SHORT LIST OF RAILWAY BOOKS COVERING NORTHUMBRIA

The North Eastern Railway. Its Rise & Development, W. W. Tomlinson (David & Charles)
Regional History of Railways of Great Britain, Vol. 4 The North East, K. Hoole (David & Charles)
Rail 150: The Stockton & Darlington and What followed, Ed. J. Simmons (Eyre & Methuen)
The Stockton & Darlington Railway 1825-1975, P. J. Holmes (First Avenue)
Exploring the Stockton & Darlington Railway, P. W. B. Semmens (Frank Graham)
Stockton & Darlington: 150 Years of British Railways P. W. B. Semmens (New English Library)
Railway History in Pictures: North East England, K. Hoole (David & Charles)
North Eastern Album, K. Hoole (Ian Allan)
Newcastle & Carlisle Railway, J. S. Maclean (Robinson, Newcastle)
Railway History in Pictures: Stockton & Darlington Railway, K. Hoole (David & Charles)
North Eastern Railway Historical Maps, K. Hoole, R. A. Cook (Railway Canal and Historical Society)
Rural Branch Lines of Northumberland, C. R. Warm (Frank Graham)
The Bedlington Engine and Iron Works, E. Martin (Frank Graham)
The First Locomotive Engineers – Their Work in the N.E. of England, L. Charlton (Frank Graham)
Wylam and Its Railway Pioneers, P. R. B. Brooks (Wylam Parish Council)

Appendix 4

Bibliography

❧

From the time of Bede Northumberland and Durham have been fortunate in their historians. The Saxon churches, the great Norman cathedral, the border castles and the extensive remains of an earlier civilisation in the Roman Wall and forts caught the imagination of scholars. From the eighteenth century research began in earnest and led to the formation of learned societies whose publications are indispensable for reference. Most of these are listed below:

Archaeologia Aelina: Proceedings of the Society of Antiquaries of Newcastle-upon-Tyne
Transactions of the Architectural and Archaeological Society of Durham and Northumberland
The Berwickshire Naturalists Club Journal
The Durham University Journal
Transactions of the Surtees Society
Transactions of the Natural History Society of Northumberland, Durham and Newcastle-upon-Tyne
Northumberland County History Committee: A History of Northumberland, 15 vols, 1893-1940
The Victoria County History of Durham, 3 vols, 1905-28 and *The Calendar of Border Papers*, 2 vols must be added. The classic histories are *John Hodgson: History of Northumberland*, 7 vols 1820-58. *Robert Surtees: History and Antiquities of the County Palatine of Durham 1816-23*

There is a vast choice of books and pamphlets. No complete bibliography is yet available, though the Local History Society of Northumberland plans one and has produced two volumes (Vol 1 - General, Vol 2 - Topography) which can be obtained from the Record Office, Melton Park, Gosforth, Northumberland. Durham County Library have recently (1973) published their third edition of *Books of Local Interest*. I have therefore made a selection of books helpful and illuminating to me.

W. W. TOMLINSON, *Comprehensive Guide to the County of Northumberland* 1888 (reprinted 1974)
J. R. BOYLE, *Comprehensive Guide to the County of Durham* 1892. Both as comprehensive as their titles indicate, and still useful.
SIR C. HEADLAM, *The Three Northern Counties of England* 1939
A. E. SMAILES, *North England* 1960
E. EKWALL, *Oxford Dictionary of English Place-names* 1960
J. TALBOT WHITE, *The Scottish Border and Northumberland* 1973
SIR TIMOTHY EDEN, *Durham*, 2 vols 1953. Beautifully urbane introduction to the county.

336

D. D. DIXON, *Whittingham Vale* 1895. *Upper Coquetdale* 1903. Nostalgic memories and amusing tales of these valleys.

A. G. BRADLEY, *The Romance of Northumberland* 1908

P. A. GRAHAM and H. THOMPSON, *Highways and Byways in Northumbria* 1920. Both have charming illustrations.

U. POPE HENNESSY, *Durham Company* 1941. A distinguished company, among them the Byrons and Wordsworth and Coleridge courting the Hutchinson sisters in the idyllic Sockburn peninsular.

N. RIDLEY, *Northumbria Heritage* 1969

W. ILEY, *Corbridge – Border Village* 1975

J. R. ATKINSON (ed), *The Durham Book*, Durham County Council Planning Committee, 1973

H.M.S.O. *National Forest Park Guide. The Border* 1962

J. PHILIPSON, *Northumberland National Park Guide no 7*, 1969

D. A. ROBSON, *Geology of Northumberland and the Borders* in transactions of the Nat. Hist. Soc. of Northumberland and Durham 1965.

R. NEWTON, *The Northumberland Landscape* 1972

NORTHUMBERLAND & DURHAM NATURALISTS TRUST, *The Natural History of Upper Teesdale* 1972

H. PEGLER, *The Natural History of Northumberland and Durham 1972*

H. TEGNER, *Beasts of the North Country* 1961

G. K. WHITEHEAD, *The Ancient White Cattle of Britain and their descendants* 1953

G. HICKLING, *Grey Seals and the Farne Islands* 1962

T. BEWICK, *History of British Birds vol 1 Land Birds* 1797. *Vol 2 Water Birds* 1804.

P. H. BLAIR, *The Origins of Northumbria* 1948

G. JOBEY, *A Field Guide to Prehistoric Northumberland Part 2* 1974. Invaluable information about Iron Age Camps.

J. COLLINGWOOD BRUCE, *Handbook to the Roman Wall* 1863, *12th edition*. Edited by I. A. Richmond, 1965 – the classic book.

E. BIRLEY, *Research on Hadrian's Wall* 1961

R. BIRLEY, *Report on the Excavations at Vindolanda* (annually)

I. A. RICHMOND, *Roman Britain* 1963

ROGER J. A. WILSON, *A Guide to Roman Remains in Britain* 1975 deals very fully and clearly with remains in Durham as well as Northumberland.

T. H. ROWLAND, *Dere Street, The Roman Road North* 1974

BOWMAN & THOMAS, *The Vindolanda Writing Tablets* 1974

BERGSTROM & BOYLE, *The Roman Wall* 1975. Photographed throughout its length.

F. H. MARES (ed), *Memoirs of Robert Carey* 1972 in the series Studies in Tudor, Stuart literature. Fascinating experiences, and knife-edge relationship with his cousin, Queen Elizabeth.

G. M. TREVELYAN, *The Middle Marches in Clio, a Muse* 1931

H. PEASE *Lord Wardens of the Marches of England and Scotland* 1913

J. LOGAN MACK, *The Border Line* 1924

W. SITWELL, *The Border – from a soldier's point of view* 1927

G. M. FRASER, *The Steel Bonnets* 1971. Border families and their feuds.

T. SHARP, *Anatomy of the Village* 1946

J. G. LOCKHART, *Memoirs of the Life of Sir Walter Scott 1837-8* 7 vols (an abridged edition published in Everyman in 1906)

F. J. CHILD *English and Scottish Ballads* 1905. The most complete collection.

W. BEATTIE, *Border Ballads* 1952 – A good selection.

Wilson's Tales of the Border: A selection (The Moray Press) 1934

M. A. RICHARDSON, *The Local Historian's Table Book 1841-6.* 5 vols historical, 3 vols legendary

W. SCOTT, *Minstrelsey of the Scottish Border* 3 vols 1803.

The Monthly Chronicle 1887-91. A mine of fascinating information about both counties, their towns, castles, churches, outstanding personalities, legends, flora and fauna, birds – everything, in fact. Wonderful bedtime books

N. PEVSNER, *The Buildings of England, County Durham* 1953, *Northumberland* 1957. Invaluable for a detailed exposition of all buildings of note.

H. M. and J. TAYLOR, *Anglo-Saxon Architecture 2 vols* 1965

W. GREENWELL, *Durham Cathedral from 1879-1932* various editions

R. HUGILL, *Borderland Castles and Peles* 1970.

RAM, MCDOUGALL, and MERCER, *Sheilings and Bastles* (H.M.S.O.) 1971.

D. STROUD, *Capability Brown (1716-83)* 1950

WILKES and DODDS, *Tyneside Classical* 1964. Excellent introduction to the planned city centre of Newcastle upon Tyne

L. WILKES, *Tyneside Portraits* 1971

C. E. HARDY, *John Bowes and the Bowes Musem* 1970

B. ALLSOP, *Historic Architecture of Newcastle upon Tyne* 1967

ALLSOP and CLARK, *Historic Architecture of Northumberland* 1969

WHITTAKER and CLARK, *Historic Architecture of Co. Durham* 1971. All three books photograph buildings from earliest time to the present day.

THE VENERABLE BEDE, *A History of the English Church and People* (Penguin) 1970

A. HAMILTON THOMPSON, *Bede, his Life, Times and Writings* 1935

Jarrow Lectures from 1958. Annual lecture given by a specialist, obtainable from the Rector, St Paul's Rectory, Borough Road, Jarrow upon Tyne

H. COLGRAVE, *St Cuthbert of Durham* 1955

C. F. BATTISCOMBE, *The Relics of St Cuthbert* 1956

D. P. KING (ed), *St Wilfred at Hexham* 1974. Scholarly essays as an introduction to Hexham Abbey.

D. MILBURN, *A History of Ilshard College* 1964

E. HUGHES, *North Country Life in the eighteenth century* 1952

J. RUSH, *Beilby Glass* 1944

J. W. HOUSE, *The North-East* 1969

S. and B. WEBB, *The Story of the Durham Miners 1662-1921*, 1921

L. T. C. ROLT, *George and Robert Stephenson*, 1960

D. DOUGAN, *The History of North East Shipbuilding* 1968

D. THOMAS, *Strike a Light (John Walker 1781-1859)*, Teeside Museums Service. Life of the Stockton chemist who invented the match.

Ramblers Cheviot and Ramblers Tynedale (Harold Hill, Newcastle upon Tyne).

A. WAINWRIGHT, *A Penine Way Companion* (Westmorland Gazette Ltd, Kendal, Cumbria) 1968

J. SEYMOUR, *The Companion Guide to the Coast of North East England* 1974. For all those interested in boats, coasts, and harbours.

A. A. H. DOUGLAS, *The Bruce* – an epic poem by John Barbour, Archdeacon of Aberdeen c. 1375 translated into modern English by the editor. (William Maclellan, 104 Hill Street Glasgow G.3.) 1964

W. SCOTT, *Marmion*

R. SMITH SURTEES (JORROCKS), *Handley Cross* 1843

R. KIPLING, *Puck of Pook's Hill* 1906

DUKE OF NORTHUMBERLAND, *The Shadow on the Moor* 1930. A gripping ghost story in Cheviot Country, published in *Strange Tales from Blackwood* 1950

J. B. PRIESTLEY, *English Journey* 1934

A. SETON, *Devil's Water* 1962

E. GRIERSON, *The Massingham Affair* 1962

A. J. CRONIN, *The Stars Look Down* 1935

Index

❧

Numbers in italics signify main reference

341